FOREIGN AID: NEW PERSPECTIVES

RECENT ECONOMIC THOUGHT SERIES

Editors:

Warren J. Samuels
Michigan State University
East Lansing, Michigan, USA

William Darity, Jr.
University of North Carolina
Chapel Hill, North Carolina, USA

Other books in the series:

Davis, John B.: THE STATE OF THE INTERPRETATION OF KEYNES
Wells, Paul: POST-KEYNESIAN ECONOMIC THEORY
Hoover, Kevin D.: MACROECONOMETRICS: DEVELOPMENTS, TENSIONS AND PROSPECTS
Kendrick, John W.: THE NEW SYSTEMS OF NATURAL ACCOUNTS
Groenewegen, John: TRANSACTION COST ECONOMICS AND BEYOND
King, J.E.: AN ALTERNATIVE MACROECONOMIC THEORY
Schofield, Norman: COLLECTIVE DECISION-MAKING: SOCIAL CHOICE AND POLITICAL ECONOMY
Menchik, Paul L.: HOUSEHOLD AND FAMILY ECONOMICS
Gupta, Kanhaya L.: EXPERIENCES WITH FINANCIAL LIBERALIZATION
Cohen, Avi J., Hagemann, Harald, and Smithin, John: MONEY FINANCIAL INSTITUTIONS AND MACROECONOMICS
Mason, P.L. and Williams, R.M.: RACE, MARKETS, AND SOCIAL OUTCOMES
Gupta, Satya Dev: THE POLITICAL ECONOMY OF GLOBALIZATION
Fisher, R.C.: INTERGOVERNMENTAL FISCAL RELATIONS
Mariussen, Å. and Wheelock, J.: HOUSEHOLDS, WORK AND ECONOMIC CHANGE: A COMPARATIVE INSTITUTIONAL PERSPECTIVE
Gupta, Satya Dev: GLOBALIZATION, GROWTH AND SUSTAINABILITY
Gupta, Satya Dev: DYNAMICS OF GLOBALIZATION AND DEVELOPMENT
Medema, Steven G.: COASEAN ECONOMICS: LAW AND ECONOMICS AND THE NEW INSTITUTIONAL ECONOMICS
Peoples, James: REGULATORY REFORM AND LABOR MARKETS
Dennis, Ken: RATIONALITY IN ECONOMICS: ALTERNATIVE PERSPECTIVES
Ahiakpor, James C.W.: KEYNES AND THE CLASSICS RECONSIDERED
Wolfson, Murray: THE POLITICAL ECONOMY OF WAR AND PEACE
Jain, A.K.: ECONOMICS OF CORRUPTION
Wheelock, J. and Vail, J.: WORK AND IDLENESS: THE POLITICAL ECONOMY OF FULL EMPLOYMENT

FOREIGN AID: NEW PERSPECTIVES

Edited by

Kanhaya L. Gupta
University of Alberta

KLUWER ACADEMIC PUBLISHERS
BOSTON / DORDRECHT / LONDON

Distributors for North, Central and South America:
Kluwer Academic Publishers
101 Philip Drive
Assinippi Park
Norwell, Massachusetts 02061 USA
Telephone (781) 871-6600
Fax (781) 871-6528
E-Mail <kluwer@wkap.com>

Distributors for all other countries:
Kluwer Academic Publishers Group
Distribution Centre
Post Office Box 322
3300 AH Dordrecht, THE NETHERLANDS
Telephone 31 78 6392 392
Fax 31 78 6546 474
E-Mail <orderdept@wkap.nl>

Electronic Services <http://www.wkap.nl>

Library of Congress Cataloging-in-Publication Data

Foreign aid : new perspectives / edited by Kanhaya L. Gupta; [contributing authors Ebenezer Asem ... et al.].
p. cm. — (Recent economic thought series ; 68)
Includes bibliographical references (p.) and index.
ISBN 0-7923-8404-0 (alk. paper)
1. Economic assistance—Developing countries. 2. Economic assistance—Developing countries—Case studies. 3. Developing countries—Economic policy. I. Gupta, Kanhaya L. (Kanhaya Lal), 1935- II. Asem, Ebenezer. III. Series.
HC60.F59154 1999
338.91'09172'4—dc21 98-49109
CIP

Printed on acid-free paper.

Printed in the United States of America.

For Jonathan and Karuna

CONTENTS

CONTRIBUTING AUTHORS

Ebenezer Asem has a Ph.D. in Economics from the University of Alberta and is currently a Ph.D. student in Finance at the same university.

Christian Friis Bach is Assistant Professor of Development Economics at the Institute of Economics at the University of Copenhagen. He holds an M.Sc. in Agronomy and a Ph.D. in International Economics from the Royal Veterinary and Agricultural University. He has work experience from the World Bank's International Trade Division and has published on international trade and development issues, including in particular the negotiations in the Uruguay Round, Chinese trade and agriculture, and general equilibrium modelling. Christian Bach is currently also Chairman of the Danish Association for International Co-operation (MS-Denmark), a leading Danish Non-governmental Organisation (NGO).

Søren Baunsgaard is a graduate student and Research Assistant at the Institute of Economics at the University of Copenhagen, attached to the Development Economics Research Group (DERG), coordinated by Finn Tarp. Mr. Baunsgaard has work experience both as a Teaching Assistant at the University of Copenhagen and from field work in Indonesia.

Arne Bigsten is Professor of development economics at Gothenburg University. His research has focussed on African economic development. He has published extensively on growth, income distribution, rural development , industrial economics, development policy and aid.

Taeke Cnossen has an MA in the Department of Economics at the University of Nottingham and is currently an ODI Fellow with the Central Bank of Solomon Islands. He has also worked as a research assistant in the Centre for Research on Economic Development and International Trade at the University of Nottingham and a researcher at the National Institute for Economics and Social Research in London.

Kanhaya L. Gupta is Professor of Economics at the University of Alberta. His research interests include macro and monetary economics and development economics. He has published extensively in these fields. His latest publications include *Financial Liberalization and Development* (with Robert Lensink, 1996) and *Experiences with Financial Liberalization* (Editor, 1997).

Kiyoun Han has a Ph.D. in Economics from Duke University and is currently a consultant in Seoul, South Korea.

Henrik Hansen is Associate Professor of Empirical Macro Economics at the Unit of Economics at the Danish Royal Veterinary and Agricultural University. He holds M.Sc. and Ph.D. degrees in Economics from the University of Copenhagen. He has previously published on time series econometrics, including in particular cointegrated time series.

Panos Hatzipanayotou teaches at the Aristotelian University of Thessalonikin and IMOP.

Anisul M. Islam is an Associate Professor of Economics in the College of Business, the University of Houston-Downtown, Houston, Texas, U.S.A. Previously, he served as a faculty member at the Dhaka University and a number of other universities in Canada and the U.S. before joining the UH-Downtown. Dr. Islam has a Ph.D. degree in Economics from the University of Alberta, an M.S. degree in Economics from the University of Waterloo, and an M.A. and a B.A. (Honours) degree from the University of Dhaka. He has coauthored a book *Foreign Capital, Savings and Growth: an International Cross-section Study* (Publisher: D. Riedel Publishing Co., 1983) and has published a number of articles in peer reviewed professional journals. In recent years, his articles have appeared in *Applied Economics, Journal of Economics, Journal of Economics and Finance*, and *Journal of Real Estate Appraisal and Economics*, among others.

Catrinus J. Jepma (1953) is Professor of International (Environmental) Economics at the University of Groningen (acting), University of Amsterdam, and Open University, the Netherlands. He has (co)authored more than thirty books and monographs, and published more than a hundred articles and papers, mainly in the field of North-South economic relations and international environmental issues. Dr. Jepma has served as an advisor to a.o. the Netherlands government, the Organization for Economic Co-operation and Development, and the Secretariat of the UN Framework Convention on Climate Change, and is actively involved in the assessment process of the Intergovernmental Panel on Climate Change.

Sajal Lahiri is Professor of Economics at the University of Essex, UK. Received PhD from the Indian Statistical Institute in 1976. Main area of research is International Trade and Development Economics. Has spent extended periods researching in India, Japan, U.S.A., and Australia. Personal home page http://privatewww.essex.ac.uk/~lahiri/

Alan Matthews is an Associate Professor of Economics at Trinity College, Dublin. His research interests include agricultural policy and international trade. He has acted as a consultant to the Food and Agricultural Organization on issues to do with international agricultural policy reform.

Mark McGillivray is Associate Professor of International Development at RMIT University in Melbourne, Australia. He is also an External Fellow of the centre for Research on Economic Development and International Trade in the Department of Economics at the University of Nottingham in England.

Michael S. Michael teaches at the University of Cyprus.

Oliver Morrissey is Senior Lecturer in Economics and Co-Director of the Centre for Research on Economic Development and International Trade in the Department of Economics at the University of Nottingham in England.

Pascalis Raimondos-Møller is an Associate Professor at the Institute of Economics, Copenhagen Business School, and Deputy Director at the Economic Policy Research Unit, University of Copenhagen. He holds a B.A. from the University of Athens and a M.Sc. and Ph.D. from the University of Essex. His research is mainly concentrated in issues related to Trade Theory and Public Finance. He has published articles in journals such as *Journal of International Economics, Journal of Development Economics, Journal of Public Economics,* and *Canadian Journal of Economics.*

Jørn Rattsø is Professor of Economics at the Norwegian University of Science and Technology in Trondheim. His research interests include development macroeconomics, political economy and fiscal federalism. He has published in journals like the *Journal of Development Economics, World Development* and the *Cambridge Journal of Economics.*

Fikret Senses is Professor Economics at the Middle East Technical University in Ankara-Turkey. He holds degrees from University of Warwick (B.A), University of Lancaster (M.A), and the London School of Economics (Ph.D.). He was the editor of *METU Studies in Development* during 1983–87. He is the editor of *Recent Industrialization Experience of Turkey* published by Greenwood Press in 1994 and is the author of papers published in Turkey and abroad, in edited volumes as well as various journals.

Finn Tarp is Associate Professor of Development Economics at the Institute of Economics at the University of Copenhagen from where he holds M.Sc. and Ph.D. degrees in Economics. Formerly with the Food and Agricultural Organisation of the United Nations (FAO), he worked as an economist in Southern Africa from 1978 to 1988. He ha previously published on agricultural price policy, agrarian transformation, income distribution and growth, project planning and analysis, as well as international debt issues, stabilisation and structural adjustment and Danish foreign aid. Finn Tarp is currently also coordinating the Development Economics Research Group (DERG), a joint initiative by three Copenhagen based research institutions.

Ragnar Torvik is Associate Professor of Economics at the Norwegian University of Science and Technology. His main publications are in development economics, international economics and macroeconomics in general in journals such as the *Cambridge Journal of Economics* and the *Journal of African Economics.*

Edward Tower is Professor of Economics at Duke University. He has consulted on economic development problems for the Harvard Institute for International Development, the World Bank and USAID, and in a number of countries.

Howard White has worked in a number of countries in Africa and Asia for a wide range of agencies. This work, and his academic research, relate to aid effectiveness at all levels, on which he has published in a wide range of journals. He is a Research Fellow at the Institute of Development Studies, University of Sussex, UK.

Leonard S. Wilson earned a B.Sc in mathematics (1965), a B.Ed in secondary mathematics (1970), and an MA in economics (1971), all from the University of Alberta, and a Ph.D. in economics (1974) from the University of Essex. He returned to the Department of Economics at the University of Alberta in 1979. Professor Wilson worked as a secondary school teacher (1966–67) and as a systems analyst in the Provincial Auditor's Department of the Government of Alberta (1967–69) before beginning the study of economics. Since becoming an economist he has been an assistant professor at Queen's University, (1974–79), a visiting fellow at the University of Essex (1988–89) and Visiting Scholar at Queen's University (1995–96). For the periods 1985–87 and 1990–93 he was seconded to the Ministry of Planning and National Development of the Government of Kenya as a Senior Economic Advisor. Since 1994 he has been Senior Canadian Advisor to the Malaysian Institute for Economic Research. Professor Wilson's teaching and research interests lie in the areas of public economics and the economics of developing countries. He has published articles in the *Canadian Journal of Economics*, the *Journal of Public Economics*, *Public Administration and Development*, and *Canadian Public Policy* among others. He has also published a number of reports, book reviews, and chapters in edited volumes.

ACKNOWLEDGEMENT

My thanks to Constance E. Smith, L.S. Wilson and Yingfeng Xu for acting as referees and to Charlene Hill for her excellent help with typing.

PREFACE

This volume is yet another one in the series "Recent Economic Thought" published by Kluwer Academic Publishers under the general editorship of Professors William J. Darity, Jr. of the University of North Carolina at Chapel Hill and Warren J. Samuels of Michigan State University, East Lansing.

Foreign aid has been an area of active scholarly investigation since the end of the Second World War, but particularly since the early 1950s when a large number of the erstwhile colonies became independent. Few areas of public policies, involving the developed and the developing countries, have aroused more passion and ideological debate than foreign aid. It is not the intention of this volume to survey that terrain, because there is by now voluminous literature on that (see, for example, Riddell, 1987 and White, 1992, among others). But what is surprising to note is that in spite of the massive amount of work in the field, even after nearly half a century, there is still not enough work in two areas. The first is the mechanisms through which aid influences economies of the donor and the recipient countries and the second, country-specific assessments of the effectiveness of foreign aid, this in spite of the fact that we now have long enough time series data to carry out such studies. This volume is aimed at making a contribution in these two areas.

The importance of contributions in these two areas can hardly be overemphasized. Given that the people and the governments of the developed countries are suffering from aid "fatigue", and therefore the general trend towards more conservative policies which frowns upon aid in any form, except perhaps for purely humanitarian purposes, it is a good time to have a serious look at the issues involved from the analytical as well as the policy point of view. It may well be that if we understood the workings of aid better or if the experiences of the donor and the recipient countries demonstrates "productive" outcomes about the uses of aid, we may be less cynical about the continuation of aid and instead devote ourselves to designing more effective aid giving and aid utilization policies. Hopefully, this volume will add to our understanding of the workings and the effectiveness of aid.

Given the broad purposes of the volume as outlined above, the contents are divided into four parts. Part I deals with some theoretical aspects of aid, while the second part analyses some general policy aspects. Part III turns to the donor experience and includes one paper on the Danish experience. The last part considers the recipient experience and consists of five case studies. A brief outline of the chapters now follows.

Section I includes three chapters. Chapter 1 by Panos Hatzipanayotou and Michael S. Michael examines conditions under which aid may increase world welfare, that is, the welfare of both the donor and the recipient countries. This is done by specifying a two-country general equilibrium model which allows for the fact that developed countries use income taxes to generate tax revenues and transfer a portion of these revenues as aid to developing countries. Under certain plausible conditions, they show that if the portion of taxes transferred as aid is increased, this will simultaneously raise welfare in both sets of countries.

Chapter 2 by Sajal Lahiri and Pascalis Raimondos-Møller examines the rationality of donor behavior in giving aid when, in the absence of any distortion, such behavior reduces the welfare of the donor country. They do this by modelling altruism on the part of the consumers of the donor country. They consider three scenarios: (i) absence of any distortions; (ii) presence of tariffs; and (iii) presence of import quota. They derive and compare the optimal value of foreign aid under the three scenarios.

Chapter 3 by Ebenezer Asem and Kanhaya L. Gupta turns to yet another aspect of foreign aid and this one deals with the implications of foreign aid for the welfare cost of inflation. Using an intertemporal model of a representative agent, it evaluates the welfare cost of inflation with and without foreign aid. It shows that for a given deficit, an inflow of aid will reduce the deficit financing needs of the government and hence reduce inflationary finance and inflation, ceteris paribus. This will thus improve welfare. However, to properly compare the welfare cost of inflation we would have to increase inflation to the level prior to the inflow of aid which will adversely affect welfare. These welfare effects are assessed as is the sensitivity of the effectiveness of aid (in terms of its influence on welfare) to the level of inflation.

Section II deals with some general policy implications of aid. The chapters in this section are not directed to any specific country. There are five chapters in this section.

Chapter 4 by Catrinus Jepma deals with a relatively new area. This has to do with the role that foreign aid may play in the pursuit of global environmental policies. To what extent can aid be used to persuade developing countries to accept policies which otherwise do not seem to be in their best interest as first best policies?

Chapter 5 by Alan Matthews deals with an aspect of aid which, despite its obvious importance, does not get treated in the main stream of the literature on aid. This has to do with the role that aid may play in ensuring food security for developing countries. Matthews examines, in some detail, the history of this issue and the current status of the debate. This chapter examines the changing nature and extent of external assistance to agricultural development and food security focussing, in particular, on three main areas: (i) the changing role of food aid; (ii) aid flows to agricultural and rural development; and (iii) policy conditionality focussed on agricultural policy reforms attached to structural adjustment programmes.

Chapter 6 by Mark McGillivray and Oliver Morrissey examines a somewhat neglected area in the literature. This has to do with the relationship between aid and trade. Drawing on the literature on the impact of aid on the public sector, they specify and estimate a number of reduced form equations which suggest a relationship between aid and trade. One of the more interesting implications of their model is that a link between aid and trade can exist quite independently of the commercialization of aid. The results are suggestive though the authors readily admit that a more formal modelling of the links between aid and trade is required.

Chapter 7 by Howard White deals with a relatively new area in the literature on aid. This has to do with the role aid "recipients" might play in aid donor policies. This is a radical departure from the usual thinking in which aid recipients were treated as passive players. This chapter reviews evidence from the assessments carried out for three aid donors: the Netherlands, the United Kingdom and the World Bank. White deals with both the methodology of the studies as well as their implications for aid policies.

In Chapter 8 Leonard S. Wilson tackles an aspect of aid which again does not receive adequate attention in the literature. This has to do with the problem of "indigenization" of foreign aid projects involving technical assistance. He examines in some detail why technical assistance by donor countries often fails in its ultimate objective of developing local expertise and what can the donor countries do to rectify the situation. Particular attention is paid to the existence of market failures in the recipient countries and the role which the donors can play in rectifying them. The policy implications of the arguments for project design are then drawn.

Section III includes one chapter that is by Finn Tarp, Bach, Hansen and Baunsgaard. This is a case study from the donor point of view. They review Danish aid policy as it has evolved since the 1960s. In order to understand the rationale for Danish aid, they specify and estimate a two-step model. The first step is meant to explain whether to select a country, while the second deals with the amount of aid to give. Their estimates seem to support the model. They do not find a "small" country bias but do report an Eastern and South Africa bias.

The final section deals with the recipient experience. The distinguishing characteristic of this section is that it is country specific, except for Chapter 10, but even this one is region specific. This section, thus, sharply deviates from the standard practice of cross-country studies. There are five chapters in this section. Each chapter highlights the role of aid from a different perspective as will become clear from the chapter descriptions which follow.

Chapter 10 by Arne Bigsten examines the role of foreign aid on growth in Africa. The chapter is both a review of the relevant literature as well as an examination of how to make aid more effective. For this purpose considerable emphasis is put on the role of good governance in stimulating growth. Bigsten then examines how aid might be used to induce the recipient countries in Africa to adopt policies conducive to good governance, thus making aid more effective.

Chapter 11 by Kiyoun Han and Edward Tower is a case study of Sudan. Sudan provides a particularly interesting case study because of it being a highly distorted economy. They construct a four sector linearized general equilibrium model to carry out a cost-benefit analysis of aid for the Sudanese economy. They report that the benefits and costs depend strongly on how the economy adjusts to foreign aid and the reforms required.

Chapter 12 by Anisul Islam is a case study of Bangladesh. Bangladesh is one of the poorest countries in the world, but over the years it has also received a large amount of foreign aid which has financed a very high proportion of its development budgets. It is thus an interesting case study about the effectiveness of aid. The chapter examines the sources and the nature of aid flows, types of aid flows, the issue of aid dependence and the effectiveness of different types of aid flows in promoting development.

Chapter 13 by Fikret Senses is a case study of Turkey's experience with foreign aid. He reviews Turkey's experience from Marshal Aid to Cold War and to Structural Adjustment Loans in the 1980s. Special attention is paid to aid from the United States. An interesting feature of this chapter is its attempt to examine the extent to which aid is used as an instrument for influencing recipient country preferences in economic policy making and the extent to which non-economic factors (in particular, strategic factors) influence the size and type of aid. These latter issues are examined particularly with respect to the events since the 1980s.

Chapter 14 by Jørn Rattsø and Ragnar Torvik is a case study of Zimbabwe. This chapter argues that the effectiveness of aid depends on how the foreign exchange constraint is handled. They identify two policy regimes for Zimbabwe during the 1990s, that is first import rationing and then trade liberalization. They specify and estimate a CGE model with closures representing the two alternate policy regimes. Their results show that the economy is more responsive to aid under import rationing. Their results imply a reconsideration of the "Dutch disease" since real exchange rate depreciation can go hand in hand with more aid.

REFERENCES

Riddell, R. *Foreign Aid Reconsidered*, The Johns Hopkins University Press, 1987.

White, H. "The macroeconomic impact of development aid: a critical survey", *The Journal of Development Studies*, 1992.

I

Some Theoretical Aspects of Foreign Aid

CHAPTER 1

FOREIGN AID AND EMPLOYMENT POLICIES IN LDCS

Panos Hatzipanayotou
and
Michael S. Michael

INTRODUCTION

Conventional wisdom among international trade and development economists is that an effective redistribution of resources from rich developed to poor developing countries is required, among other things, in order to bridge the gap between them. To this end, foreign aid has been a principal source of international transfers from the former to the latter countries. In the international economics literature, the long standing interest in the welfare implications of foreign aid (*i.e.*, unilateral transfers) dates back to a 1929 debate between Keynes and Ohlin, regarding the reparation payments of Germany after the end of World War I. Since then, a voluminous literature has established that, within the neoclassical trade theory, in a two-country competitive, Walras-stable and distortion free world, exogenous (*i.e.*, financed through non-distortionary means, and independently chosen of other policy instruments) transfers benefit the recipient country and hurt the donor. Within this neoclassical trade paradigm, however, despite the exogeneity of transfers and the existence of Walrasian stability, it has been shown that in several cases, mainly due to transfer induced changes in the terms of trade, welfare paradoxes (*i.e.*, donor country enrichment and recipient country impoverishment) can be induced by international transfers. Among others, these are cases of *(i)* many-countries *(i.e.*, at least three*)* *(e.g.*, Bhagwati *et al.* 1983, Turunen-Red and Woodland 1988*)*, *(ii)* endogenous or exogenous distortions *(e.g.*, Bhagwati *et al.* 1985), *(iii)* wholly or partially tied aid *(e.g.*, Kemp and Kojima 1985a, 1985b*)*, *(iv)* production of public goods *(*Hatzipanayotou and Michael 1995*)*, *(v)* tied aid in the presence of quantitative restrictions (Lahiri and Raimondos 1995), tied aid to trade policy reforms by the recipient country when the amount of the income transfer and trade taxes are endogenously selected (Lahiri *et al.* 1997), *(vi)* aid tied to final goods in a model with increasing returns and monopolistic competition (Brakman and van Marrewijk 1995*)*, and *(vii)* aid tied either to intersectorally mobile or sector specific capital when the recipient country may or may not suffer from unemployment (Michael and van Marrewijk 1998).

Systematic empiricism, however, has shown that, more than often, aid is not exogenously financed but rather internally determined by the budgetary process in donor countries or by the level of development of recipient countries. Thus, aid from rich donor to poor recipient countries more than often relates to the overall economic policy agenda in these countries. For example, aid can be tied to their respective levels of expenditure and/or GNP, or can be used by recipient countries to remedy structural weaknesses of their economies (e.g., overcoming unemployment).[1]

The economies of most aid receiving developing countries are described well by the Harris-Todaro (henceforth HT) model. The international trade and development economics literature has extensively used this HT framework to analyze the impact of various economic policies on the economies of the developing countries. Within this framework, in attaining full employment and maximizing welfare, a uniform wage subsidy to both (urban and rural) sectors has been recommended as the first-best policy choice, while a wage (or production) subsidy to either sector has been shown to serve as a second-best choice. The financial and administrative costs of a uniform wage subsidy, however, is considerably very high and for practical point of view has been ruled out. Thus, the second-best wage subsidy to the urban sector would constitute the practically feasible alternative. Even so, a core question remains unsatisfactorily answered in the relevant literature. How can a resource limited developing economy finance such an urban wage (or production) subsidy? Although in the relevant literature, the issue and its subsequent consequences are noted early enough (e.g., Bhagwati and Srinivasan 1974, Basu 1980), most studies take a rather simplistic and quite non-practical approach to this question. That is, wage or production subsidies are financed through non-distortionary lump-sum taxation. To the best of our knowledge, two noted exceptions to this convention are McCool (1982) and Gupta (1995) who consider more practical ways to finance such wage subsidies. The former study considers alternative schemes (i.e., taxation of rural-urban profits, taxation of only urban profits, and import tariffs) to finance a subsidy in either sector or across sectors. Gupta (1995), in a (HT) model with sector specific and internationally mobile capital considers the case where the urban wage subsidy is financed through taxes on the, otherwise repatriated, earnings of foreign capital. The purpose of this paper is, among other things, to consider another way, the use of foreign aid, of financing the urban wage subsidy. That is, foreign aid is tied to the urban wage subsidy in the recipient country. The importance of this alternative is that probably it constitutes, from the recipient developing country's point of view, the only possible non-distortionary means of financing such a wage subsidy.

We construct a two-country general equilibrium trade model whereby the developed donor country endogenously finances the amount of foreign aid either by a fraction of its income tax revenue, or, as noted in footnote 1, by a fraction of its GNP.[2,3] On the other hand, in the developing recipient country characterized by a dual HT structure, aid is either lump-sum distributed to domestic households, or it is tied to the provision of an urban wage subsidy to reduce unemployment in the modern sector. The chapter examines the terms of trade and welfare effects of the two types of aid and derives sufficient conditions according to which, among other things, aid can raise welfare in the donor country, can impoverish welfare in the recipient country, and can improve world welfare. In the latter case there is a possibility of welfare enrichment for both the donor and the recipient countries.

The rest of the chapter is organized as follows. The next section develops the two-country model of foreign aid and unemployment. Section 3 describes the equilibrium of the world economy. Assuming that the recipient country lump-sum distributes the aid to domestic households or ties it to financing the provision of an urban wage subsidy, sections 4 and 5 examine the terms of trade, and welfare effects of foreign aid, financed by a certain fraction of income tax revenue in the donor country. The last section offers some concluding remarks.

THE TWO-COUNTRY MODEL OF FOREIGN AID AND UNEMPLOYMENT

In this section we develop a two-country general equilibrium trade model of foreign aid. Aid by the developed donor country is financed through income taxes, and it is dispensed either in the form of lump-sum transfers to consumers, or through financing an urban employment subsidy in the developing recipient country characterized by (HT) unemployment. Each country produces two traded goods; a manufacturing (M) exported by the donor country and imported by the recipient, and an agricultural for which the pattern of trade is the reverse. The latter commodity is chosen as the *numeraire* good. Constant returns to scale characterize the production technologies of both goods. All commodity and factor markets are assumed perfectly competitive, and international trade in both goods is assumed free.

Next, we briefly describe the structure of the recipient (HT) economy characterized by urban unemployment. The workings of the full employment donor country follow from that model.

The Harris-Todaro Recipient Country

Consider a two-sector — an urban and a rural — general equilibrium trade model of an open economy with unemployment. The urban sector produces an import competing manufacturing good (M) and the rural sector an exported agricultural good (A). Labor (L) is the intersectorally mobile factor, capital (K) is sector-specific in the production of the manufacturing output and land (N) is sector-specific in the production of the agricultural one. All three factors are assumed to be internationally immobile.

Production technologies exhibit constant returns to scale with positive and diminishing marginal products of factors, and positive cross-partials. The production functions for the two outputs are given by:

$$M = M(L^M, \overline{K}), \text{ and} \tag{1.1}$$

$$A = A(L^A, \overline{N}), \tag{1.2}$$

where L^i, i=M, A, denotes, respectively, the amounts of labor employed in the two sectors, $\overline{K}$ and $\overline{N}$, respectively, are the fixed endowments of the sector-specific capital and land.

According to the (HT) paradigm, we assume that the rural wage (w^A) is competitively determined ensuring full employment of labor in that sector. In the urban sector, the existence of an institutionally fixed minimum wage ($\overline{w}$) above the market clearing level results in sectoral unemployment.[4] Rural-urban labor migration, or vice versa, is the connecting element between the two sectors. This internal migration emerges when the competitive rural wage (w^A) differs from the expected wage in the urban sector (w^e), and it ceases when the two rates are equalized. The urban expected wage is defined as the minimum wage ($\overline{w}$) multiplied by the probability of finding employment in the urban sector. Thus, the labor market equilibrium condition is:

$$w^A = w^e = [\, L^M /(L^M + L^u)] \; \overline{w} \;, \tag{1.3}$$

where L^u is the number of urban unemployed workers, and $[\, L^M /(L^M + L^u)]$ is the probability of finding employment in that sector. Defining $\lambda(=L^u / L^M)$ to be the unemployment ratio in the urban sector, the labor market equilibrium condition can be rewritten as:

$$\overline{w} = (1+\lambda)\, w^A \tag{1.4}$$

Fixed labor endowment ($\overline{L}$) must equal the sum of employment of labor in manufacturing and agriculture plus the number of urban unemployed. Using the definition of λ, the economy's labor endowment constraint can be written as:

$$(1+\lambda)\, L^M + L^A = \overline{L} \,. \tag{1.5}$$

Under perfect competition in product and factor markets, labor is paid the value of its marginal product in each sector. That is:

$$\overline{w} - s = pM_L\,(L^M,\ \overline{K}\,)\text{, and} \tag{1.6}$$

$$w^A = A_L\,(L^A,\ \overline{N}\,)\,, \tag{1.7}$$

where s denotes a wage (employment) subsidy to the urban sector, p is the domestic and world relative price of the manufacturing good. Finally, $M_L(=\partial M / \partial L)$ and $A_L(=\partial A / \partial L)$, respectively, denote the sectoral marginal product of labor. For the rest of the analysis all subscripts denote partial derivatives.

To conclude the specification of the production side of this (HT) open economy, we define $R^*(p, \lambda, \overline{K}, \overline{N}\,)$ to be the gross national product (GNP) function. It represents the maximum attainable revenue from production given the producer relative price p, the unemployment ratio λ, and the fixed endowments of the sector specific capital ($\overline{K}$) and land ($\overline{N}$). Later on, the fixed endowments of the two specific factors are omitted from the GNP function since they do not affect the analysis. By the envelop theorem, the partial derivative of the GNP function with respect to p (*i.e.*, $R^*_p(p, \lambda)$) is the supply function of the manufacturing good. Lastly, λ enters as an argument into the GNP function in order to capture the loss to the economy due to unemployment, measured by the shadow wage of labor. Since $\lambda = (L^u / L^M)$, the loss to the economy due to a one-unit increase in λ is $R^*_\lambda = -w^A L^M$ (*e.g.*, see Beladi and Chao, 1993). Since λ is a function of p, s (see the Appendix for derivations), for the rest of the analysis we use the notation $\widetilde{R}_p^*(p,s)$ to indicate the supply function of the manufacturing good. The function $\widetilde{R}_p^*(p,s)$ is assumed to be strictly convex in *p* (*i.e.*, $\widetilde{R}_{pp}^* > 0$).

We assume identical consumers whose utility depends positively on the consumption of the two goods, which are normal. Let $E^*(p, u^*)$ be the minimum expenditure required to achieve utility u^* at prices *p*. Its derivative with respect to *p* (*i.e.*, E_p^*) is the compensated demand function for the imported good. The expenditure function is assumed strictly concave in *p* (*i.e.*, $E_{pp}^* < 0$).

EQUILIBRIUM IN THE WORLD ECONOMY

Consider a world of two countries, the donor and the recipient, where an income transfer occurs from the former to the latter country. The donor country gives as aid to the recipient country a certain fraction of its income tax revenue. In turn, the recipient country either distributes this aid in the form of lump-sum transfers to domestic consumers, or uses it to finance the wage subsidy to the manufacturing sector. Equilibrium in the world economy is characterized by the following conditions:

$$E(p, u) = R(p) - \alpha\,\tau\, R(p), \tag{1.8}$$

$$E^*(p, u^*) = R^*(p, \lambda) + \delta\,\alpha\,\tau\, R(p) - T^*, \tag{1.9}$$

$$Z_p(p, u) + Z_p^*(p, s, u^*) = 0, \tag{1.10}$$

$$(1-\delta)\alpha\tau R(p) + T^* - sL^M = B^* = 0, \tag{1.11}$$

where τ (>0) is the income tax rate in the donor country, α is the fraction of income tax revenue transferred as aid, Z_p $(=E_p - R_p) < 0$ denotes the donor country's export supply of the manufacturing good, and $Z_p^*(=E_p^* - \widetilde{R}_p^*) > 0$ is the recipient country's import demand function for the manufacturing good.[5] Asterisks denote the variables for the recipient country.

Equation (1.8) is the donor country's budget constraint, indicating that expenditure in that country equals revenue from production of traded goods minus the amount of income taxes used to finance the transfer (*i.e.*, $\alpha\tau R$). For simplicity, full employment of all factors is assumed for the donor country. Equation (1.9), the recipient country's budget constraint, indicates that expenditure (*i.e.*, $E^*(p, u^*)$) equals revenue from production of traded goods (*i.e.*, $R^*(p, \lambda)$) plus a fraction δ, $0 \le \delta \le 1$ of the income transfer (i.e., $\delta\alpha\tau R(p)$) that is lump-sum distributed to domestic consumers minus T^* lump-sum taxes. We assume that when $\delta=1$, all aid is lump-sum distributed, then the amount T^* of lump-sum taxes is used to finance the urban employment subsidy.[6] With only two goods, Walras's Law implies that world goods markets equilibrium is characterized by equation (1.10). That is, the world excess demand for the manufacturing good must equal zero. Lastly, equation (1.11) is the recipient country's government budget constraint (B^*) indicating that the cost of subsidy is financed partly through the foreign aid and partly through locally raised lump-sum taxes *(i.e.,* T^**)*. We assume that the government maintains a balanced budget constraint.

Equations (1.8) to (1.11) contain four endogenous (*i.e., u,* u^*, *p* and *s)* and three exogenous *(i.e.,* α, τ, and T^**)* variables. For the purposes of our analysis we only consider changes in α. Totally differentiating equations (1.8) to (1.11), keeping τ and T^* constant, and using the properties of the expenditure and revenue functions, yields the following equations:

$$du + (Z_p + \alpha\tau R_p)dp = -\tau R d\alpha, \tag{1.12}$$

$$du^* + (Z_p^* - \delta\alpha\tau R_p - R_\lambda^*\lambda_p)dp - R_\lambda^*\lambda_s ds = \delta\tau R d\alpha\,, \tag{1.13}$$

$$Z_{pu}du + Z_{pu^*}du^* + \widetilde{S}_{pp}dp + Z_{ps}^* ds = 0\,, \tag{1.14}$$

$$[(1-\delta)\alpha\tau R_p - s\,L_p^M\,]dp - (sL_s^M + L^M)ds = -(1-\delta)\tau R d\alpha\,, \tag{1.15}$$

where by choice of units $E_u = E_u^* = 1$, $L_p^M > 0$ and $L_s^M > 0$ (see the Appendix), $Z_{ps}^* = -\widetilde{R}_{ps}^* = -M_L L_s^M < 0$, and $\widetilde{S}_{pp} (= Z_{pp} + Z_{pp}^*)$ is the change in the world excess demand for the donor's exported (manufacturing) good due to a change in its world price.

Equation (1.12) indicates that, other things equal, a higher fraction of income tax revenue transferred to the recipient country in the form of aid lowers the donor country's welfare (*i.e.,* $(\partial u/\partial\alpha) = -\tau R < 0$). An improvement in the terms of trade (i.e., $dp > 0$) affects the donor country's welfare positively through a higher value of exports (*i.e.,* $-Z_p > 0$) and negatively through an increase in income tax revenue transferred as aid to the recipient country (*i.e.,* $-\alpha\tau R_p < 0$). It is reasonable to assume that $-Z_p > \alpha\tau R_p$, that is, an increase in *p* increases the value of exports more than the value of aid, and thus $(\partial u/\partial p) = -(Z_p + \alpha\tau R_p) > 0$. Equation (1.13) indicates that, for given *p*, an increase in the rate of the wage subsidy, or in the fraction of income taxes transferred from the donor affects positively the recipient country's welfare. A higher *p*, entailing a deterioration in the recipient country's terms of trade, affects its welfare negatively through more expensive imports, but positively through increased income due to the income transfer (*i.e.,* $-\delta\alpha\tau R_p$) and reduced unemployment ratio (i.e., $R_\lambda^*\lambda_p$).[7] Equation (1.15) captures, for given T^*, the effects of changes in *p*, *s*, and α on the recipient country's budget constraint. Thus, B^* declines with a higher wage subsidy, and it increases with a higher fraction of income taxes transferred from the donor country. When $\delta=1$, *i.e.*, aid is lump-sum distributed, an increase in *p*, *i.e.*, a deterioration in the recipient's terms of trade, reduces the government's net revenue (*i.e.,* $(\partial B^*/\partial p) = -sL_p^M < 0$).[8] When $\delta=0$, *i.e.*, aid is used entirely to finance the wage subsidy, $(\partial B^*/\partial p) = \alpha\tau R_p - sL_p^M$. Finally, note that for the government to maintain a balanced budget, i.e., $B^*=0$, when $\delta=1$, $(ds/dp) = -(sL_s^M + L^M)/sL_p^M < 0$, That is, a higher *p*, which raises employment in the urban sector (i.e., $L_p^M > 0$), increases the total cost of the wage subsidy. For B^*=0, the wage subsidy per urban worker must fall. To have B^*=0, when δ=0, $(ds/dp)=(sL_s^M+L^M)/(\alpha\tau R_p-sL_p^M)$.

Equations (1.12)–(1.15) produce the following matrix system:

$$\begin{bmatrix} 1 & 0 & Z_p+\alpha\tau R_p & 0 \\ 0 & 1 & Z_p^*-\delta\alpha\tau R_p-R_\lambda^*\lambda_p & -R_\lambda^*\lambda_s \\ Z_{pu} & Z_{pu}^* & \tilde{S}_{pp} & Z_{ps}^* \\ 0 & 0 & (1-\delta)\alpha\tau R_p-sL_p^M & -(sL_s^M+L^M) \end{bmatrix}\begin{bmatrix} du \\ du^* \\ dp \\ ds \end{bmatrix}=\begin{bmatrix} -\tau R \\ \delta\tau R \\ 0 \\ -(1-\delta)\tau R \end{bmatrix}d\alpha, \quad (1.16)$$

where $\Delta=-\beta[\tilde{S}_{pp}+Z_{pu}^*(\partial u^*/\partial p)+Z_{pu}(\partial u/\partial p)]-(\partial B^*/\partial p)(Z_{ps}^*+Z_{pu}^*R_\lambda^*\lambda_s)$, is the determinant of the left-hand-side coefficients matrix of the system of equations (1.16), $\beta=-(\partial B^*/\partial s)=(L^M+sL_s^M)>0$. The determinant must be positive if the world goods markets are Walras stable.

In the following sections, we examine the effects of an increase in the fraction of income taxes financing the transfer *(i.e., dα > 0)* on the terms of trade, on the national levels of welfare, and on the world (i.e., the two countries jointly) level of welfare, when aid to the recipient country is (i) lump-sum distributed to domestic households, and (ii) tied to finance the urban employment subsidy.

TERMS OF TRADE EFFECT OF THE TRANSFER

In the theory of international transfers it is well established that in a two-country, Walras-stable and distortion-free world, (untied) foreign aid worsens the donor country's terms of trade if the country's own marginal propensity to consume its exported good exceeds the marginal propensity of consuming that good in the recipient country.[9]

This section considers the terms of trade effect of an increase in the fraction of income taxes transferred as aid in two cases. First, when aid in the recipient country is lump-sum distributed to households (*i.e.,* δ=1), and any wage subsidy to enhance urban employment is financed through local lump-sum taxes (T^*), second when aid is tied to financing the wage subsidy to the urban sector (*i.e.,* δ=0). Solving the system of equations (1.16) with respect to (*dp/dα*) yields:

$$(\tau R)^{-1}\Delta(dp/d\alpha)=\beta(\delta Z_{pu}^*-Z_{pu})+(1-\delta)(Z_{ps}^*+Z_{pu}^*R_\lambda^*\lambda_s). \quad (1.17)$$

When δ=1, aid is lump-sum distributed, the right-hand-side of equation (1.17) reduces to $\beta(Z_{pu}^*-Z_{pu})$. Thus, a higher α, which raises foreign aid, deteriorates the donor country's terms of trade if the country's marginal propensity to consume its own exported good exceeds the recipient country's marginal propensity of consuming the same commodity. Otherwise the donor's terms of trade improve. Moreover, in the present context of (HT) unemployment, this traditional result holds regardless of whether the recipient country can raise locally enough lump-sum tax revenue (T^*) to finance the urban wage subsidy, i.e., regardless of whether $s\geq 0$.

When δ=0, the right-hand-side of equation (1.17) reduces to $-\beta Z_{pu}+(Z^*_{ps}+Z^*_{pu}R^*_{\lambda}\lambda_s)$. The term $-\beta Z_{pu}$ captures a negative effect of a higher α, to finance foreign aid and, thus, a higher wage subsidy in the recipient country, on the donor country's terms of trade through the reduction in its demand for the importable.[10] The term $(Z^*_{ps}+Z^*_{pu}R^*_{\lambda}\lambda_s)$ shows the effect of a higher α on the donor's terms of trade, through a higher wage subsidy, due to changes in the excess demand for the importable in the recipient country. Due to increased aid, the higher wage subsidy raises employment and manufacturing output which, in turn, entails a negative effect on the donor's terms of trade (*i.e.*, $Z^*_{ps}=M_L L^M_s<0$). But, it also reduces the unemployment ratio, thus it increases income (*i.e.*, $R^*_{\lambda}\lambda_s>0$) and consumption of the manufacturing affecting positively the donor's terms of trade (*i.e.*, $Z^*_{pu}R^*_{\lambda}\lambda_s>0$). Note however, that $|Z^*_{ps}|>Z^*_{pu}R^*_{\lambda}\lambda_s$, thus, overall the term $(Z^*_{ps}+Z^*_{pu}R^*_{\lambda}\lambda_s)$ entails a negative effect on the donor's terms of trade. The intuition of this result is as follows. The higher wage subsidy, which raises manufacturing output, also reduces the output of the agricultural good. Thus, because of the higher wage subsidy, the increase in income (*i.e.*, $R^*_{\lambda}\lambda_s$), that is the increase in the value of total production, is smaller than the increase in the value of manufacturing output. Since also $0\le Z^*_{pu}\le 1$, then $|Z^*_{ps}|>Z^*_{pu}R^*_{\lambda}\lambda_s$.

Therefore, in the present context, when foreign aid is used by the recipient country to finance the wage subsidy, a higher α unambiguously worsens the donor country's terms of trade.

> ***Proposition 1:*** *Assume that foreign aid by the donor country is financed through income taxes, and that the recipient country is characterized by (HT) unemployment. Then, the traditional effects of international transfers on the terms of trade emerge, when aid is lump-sum distributed. When aid is used to finance an employment subsidy in the manufacturing sector, then international transfers unambiguously worsen the donor country's terms of trade.*

WELFARE EFFECTS OF THE TRANSFER

In a two-country, Walras stable and distortions free world, international transfers do not create paradoxical welfare effects, *i.e.*, donor enrichment and recipient impoverishment. Such paradoxical welfare effects have been shown, as reviewed in the introductory section, to emerge in a variety of contexts. By and large in these works, it is assumed that aid is financed through lump-sum taxation in the donor country, regardless of the way of its disbursement in the recipient.

In this section, we assume that aid by the donor is financed through income taxation, and that the country increases the fraction of this revenue income that finances the foreign aid. We examine the welfare effects of such an international transfer on national and world welfare, when the recipient country suffers from (HT) unemployment, and aid is either lump-sum distributed to domestic households or it is tied to the urban wage subsidy to enhance domestic employment.

The Welfare Effect in the Donor Country

Solving equations (1.16) with respect to *(du/dα)*, assuming that in the recipient country aid is lump-sum distributed (*i.e.*, δ=1) and that the urban wage subsidy is financed through local lump-sum taxes (*i.e.*, *s* >0), after some manipulations we obtain:

$$A^{-1}\Delta_1(du/d\alpha) = 1 + \widetilde{S}_{pp}^{-1} Z^*_{pu} R^*_{\lambda}\lambda_p + \widetilde{S}_{pp}^{-1}(Z^*_{ps} + Z^*_{pu} R^*_{\lambda}\lambda_s)(ds/dp), \qquad (1.18)$$

where $A(=\tau R(L^M + sL^M_s)\widetilde{S}_{pp}) < 0$, Δ_1 (>0) is the value of the determinant Δ_1 when δ=1 and *s*>0. Also, since δ=1, use was made of equation (1.15) to write $-sL^M_p = (L_M + sL^M_s)(ds/dp) < 0$. Recall that R^*_{λ}, Z^*_{ps}, λ_p, λ_s are all negative.

Equation (1.18) shows that a higher fraction of income tax revenue transferred as aid to the recipient country affects the donor's welfare in three ways. The first right-hand-side term (*i.e.*, $A\Delta_1^{-1} < 0$) captures the direct negative effect of such an income transfer on the donor's welfare. The other two right-hand-side terms are the effect of the higher α on the donor's welfare through induced changes in the country's terms of trade. Both these terms indicate an improvement in the country's terms of trade that affects positively its level of welfare.

The second right-hand-side term (*i.e.*, $A\Delta_1^{-1}\widetilde{S}_{pp}^{-1} Z^*_{pu} R^*_{\lambda}\lambda_p$ >0) captures a positive effect on the donor country's terms of trade and welfare through higher income and consumption in the recipient country. Intuitively, since δ=1, a higher α increases income, consumption and imports by the recipient country. This raises p, the donor's terms of trade, which in turn reduces the unemployment ratio and further increases income consumption and imports by the recipient country (*i.e.*, $Z^*_{pu} R^*_{\lambda}\lambda_p$). As a result, a positive effect emerges on the donor's terms of trade and welfare. The last right-hand-side term of equation (1.18), i.e., $A\Delta_1^{-1}\widetilde{S}_{pp}^{-1}(Z^*_{ps} + Z^*_{pu} R^*_{\lambda}\lambda_s)(ds/dp) > 0$, captures the effect on the donor's welfare due to aid induced changes in the recipient country's subsidy payments required to maintain a balanced budget (*i.e.*, B^*=0).[11] That, is an increase in *p*, the donor country's terms of trade, other things equal raises the total cost of the subsidy. In the recipient country, for the government to maintain a balanced budget, the rate of the subsidy per worker must fall.[12] The induced reduction in the wage subsidy rate, through this term, affects the donor country's welfare through a supply effect (*i.e.*, $A\Delta_1^{-1}\widetilde{S}_{pp}^{-1} Z^*_{ps}(ds/dp) > 0$), and a demand effect (i.e., $A\Delta_1^{-1}\widetilde{S}_{pp}^{-1} Z^*_{pu} R^*_{\lambda}\lambda_s(ds/dp) < 0$). The supply effect implies a reduction in urban employment and manufacturing output, thus, positively affecting the country's imports, and the donor's terms of trade and welfare. The demand effect implies that the lower wage subsidy raises the unemployment ration, and reduces income, consumption and imports by the recipient country. As a result, the donor country's terms of trade and welfare are affected negatively. Since, as previously discussed $(Z^*_{ps}+Z^*_{pu}R^*_\lambda\lambda_s)<0$, the supply effect dominates the demand effect. Thus, through this term, the higher α increases the recipient's demand for imports, affecting positively the donor's terms of trade and welfare.

A special case of the above results is to consider the situation where δ=1 and s=0.[13] That is, when aid is lump-sum distributed, and the recipient country has no alternative sources of financing the wage subsidy. In this case, equation (1.18) reduces to:

$$A_1^{-1}\Delta_{11}(du/d\alpha)=1+\widetilde{S}_{pp}^{-1}Z^*_{pu}R^*_\lambda\lambda_p, \tag{1.19}$$

where $A_1(=\tau RL^M\widetilde{S}_{pp})<0$, and Δ_{11} (>0) is the value of the determinant Δ when δ=1 and s=0. Following the previous discussion, a higher rate of α worsens (improves) the donor country's welfare if the direct effect dominates (is smaller than) the induced indirect effect due to changes in the country's terms of trade.

Concluding the discussion of equations (1.18) and (1.19) we note the following. When in the recipient country aid is lump-sum distributed, and a higher α, to finance foreign aid, improves the donor's terms of trade, a "welfare paradox" (i.e., donor's enrichment) emerges as long as the positive terms of trade effect dominates the negative direct effect of the income transfer. Otherwise, the standard result emerges, i.e., donor's welfare impoverishment.

Next, consider the effects of a higher α on the donor country's welfare when aid is wholly used to finance the urban wage subsidy in the recipient country(*i.e.,* δ=0). In this case, from equations (1.16), we have:

$$A^{-1}\Delta'(du/d\alpha)=1-(\beta\widetilde{S}_{pp})^{-1}(Z_p+sL^M_p)(Z^*_{ps}+Z^*_{pu}R^*_\lambda\lambda_s)]-$$
$$\widetilde{S}_{pp}^{-1}Z^*_{pu}(Z^*_p-R^*_\lambda\lambda_p), \tag{1.20}$$

where Δ′ (>0) is the value of the determinant Δ when δ=0, β=$(L^M+sL^M_p)$, and recall that $Z_p(=-Z^*_p)<0$.

In equation (1.20) the first right-hand-side term (*i.e.,* $A(1/\Delta')<0$) is the direct negative effect of the income transfer on the donor's welfare. The second right-hand-side term (*i.e.,* $-\tau R(Z_p+sL^M_p)(Z^*_{ps}+Z^*_{pu}R^*_\lambda\lambda_s)/\Delta'$) is the effect of the higher α through the reduction in the country's terms of trade (see discussion of equation (1.17)) on the recipient country's government net tax revenue, thus, production of the manufacturing, income and consumption. The term $-(Z_p+sL^M_p)$ can be interpreted as the change in B^* due to a change in p, holding the income level of the donor country constant (*i.e.,* $u=\bar{u}$).[14] Intuitively, if the smaller price for the manufacturing good reduces, other things equal, government net tax revenue (*i.e.,* $(\partial B^*/\partial p)_{\bar{u}}>0$) the wage subsidy must fall for the government to maintain a balanced budget. The decrease in wage subsidy rate affects the donor's welfare via, first, a production effect (*i.e.*, $-\tau R(Z_p + sL_p^M)Z_{ps}^* / \Delta' > 0$), because of reduced urban employment and manufacturing output, and increased imports and p, the donor's terms of trade. Second, a demand effect (*i.e.*, $-\tau R(Z_p + sL_p^M)Z_{pu}^* R_\lambda^* \lambda_s / \Delta' < 0$), due to increased unemployment ratio, reduced income, consumption and imports, in the recipient country, affecting negatively the donor's terms of trade.[15] Because $(Z_{ps}^* + Z_{pu}^* R_\lambda^* \lambda_s) < 0$, through this term the higher α affects positively the donor's welfare. Per the discussion of equation (1.13), when δ=0, then $(Z_p^* - R_\lambda^* \lambda_p) = -(\partial u^* / \partial p) > (<) 0$. Consequently, the last right-hand-side term of equation (1.20) captures the effect of a higher α on the donor country's welfare due to the reduction in its terms of trade, via changes in the recipient country's income. Intuitively, if $(Z_p^* - R_\lambda^* \lambda_p)$ is positive the lower p reduces income in the recipient country, demand for imports falls, adversely affecting the donor country's terms of trade and welfare.

Equation (1.20) and the previous analysis show that when δ=0 it is possible for the donor country's welfare to improve. This result, however, cannot occur. Equation (1.12) indicates that changes in the donor country's welfare, other things equal, emerge through changes in its terms of trade. The latter unambiguously deteriorate when δ=0, and thus its welfare must also decrease.

The Welfare Effect in the Recipient Country

Solving equations (1.16) with respect to ($du/d\alpha$), assuming that in the recipient country aid is lump-sum distributed (i.e., δ=1) and that the urban wage subsidy is financed through local lump-sum taxes (i.e., s>0), after some manipulations we obtain:

$$A^{-1}\Delta_1 (du^* / d\alpha) = -1 - R_\lambda^* \lambda_p \widetilde{S}_{pp}^{-1} Z_{pu} - (Z_{ps}^* + R_\lambda^* \lambda_s Z_{pu})(ds / dp) \widetilde{S}_{pp}^{-1} . \qquad (1.21)$$

Equation (1.21) shows that a higher α to finance foreign aid, exerts on the recipient country's welfare, first, a positive effect due to the international transfer as such (*i.e.*, $-A\Delta_1^{-1} > 0$). Second, a negative effect (*i.e.*, $-A\Delta_1^{-1} R_\lambda^* \lambda_p \widetilde{S}_{pp}^{-1} Z_{pu} < 0$) through changes in the donor country's income inducing changes in the recipient country's terms of trade and welfare. Intuitively, an increase in α increases the overall cost of the wage subsidy (*i.e.*, A) which, however, burdens the donor country. Income and consumption in the latter country fall, thus, raising its exports of manufacturing and lowering its terms of trade. This decrease in p increases the urban unemployment ratio and reduces income in the recipient country, thus, affecting negatively its welfare. Third, through the last right-hand-side term $-A\Delta_1^{-1} (Z_{ps}^* + R_\lambda^* \lambda_s Z_{pu}) (ds / dp) \widetilde{S}_{pp}^{-1}$, a negative effect due to terms of trade induced changes in the country's subsidy payments required to maintain a balanced budget (*i.e.*, B^*=0). The intuition of this result is again as follows. When δ=1 and s >0, then an increase in p, which raises the total cost of the subsidy payments, requires a reduction in s (i.e., ds/dp <0) for the recipient country's government to maintain a balanced budget. This decrease in the subsidy rate entails a negative supply effect (*i.e.*, $-A\Delta_1^{-1}\tilde{S}_{pp}^{-1}Z_{ps}^*(ds/dp)<0$) by which production of manufacturing falls and imports increase, and a positive demand effect (*i.e.*, $-A\Delta_1^{-1}R_\lambda^*\lambda_s(ds/dp)\tilde{S}_{pp}^{-1}Z_{pu}>0$) by which the increase in p reduces the unemployment ratio and raises income and imports. Since, however, $(Z_{ps}^*+R_\lambda^*\lambda_s Z_{pu})<0$, the negative production effect dominates. That is, the increase in p and subsequent decrease in s to keep B^*=0, increases the country's demand for imports, thus affecting negatively its terms of trade (1/p) and welfare.

A special case of the above results is to consider the situation where δ=1 and s=0. That is, when aid is lump-sum distributed the recipient country has no alternative sources of financing the subsidy. In this case, equation (1.21) reduces to:

$$A^{-1}\Delta_{11}(du^*/d\alpha)=-1-R_\lambda^*\lambda_p\tilde{S}_{pp}^{-1}Z_{pu}\,. \tag{1.22}$$

Equation (1.22) indicates that when aid is lump-sum distributed in the recipient country and no wage subsidy is provided for urban employment, aid improves (worsens) its welfare if the direct effect (*i.e.*, $-A^{-1}\Delta_{11}>0$) dominates (is smaller than) the induced indirect effect through the impact of foreign income and terms of trade changes on the recipient's urban unemployment ratio and income (*i.e.* $-A^{-1}\Delta_{11}R_\lambda^*\lambda_p\tilde{S}_{pp}^{-1}Z_{pu}<0$).

Concluding the discussion of equations (1.21) and (1.22) we note that when aid is lump-sum distributed and s is either positive or zero, it is possible for the recipient's welfare to decrease as a result of aid

Next, consider the effects of a higher α on the recipient country's welfare when aid is wholly used to finance the urban wage subsidy (*i.e.*, δ=0). In this case, from equations (1.16), and recalling that $(\partial B^*/\partial p)=-(Z_p+sL_p^M)$, we have:

$$(\tau R\tilde{S}_{pp})^{-1}\Delta'(du^*/d\alpha)=$$
$$-R_\lambda^*\lambda_s[1+\tilde{S}_{pp}^{-1}(\partial B^*/\partial p)_{\bar{u}}Z_{pu}]-(\partial u^*/\partial p)\tilde{S}_{pp}^{-1}(Z_{ps}^*-\beta Z_{pu})\,. \tag{1.23}$$

The term $-\tau R\tilde{S}_{pp}R_\lambda^*\lambda_s/\Delta'(>0)$ is the direct positive effect of foreign aid on the recipient country's unemployment ratio, income and welfare. The term $-\tau RR_\lambda^*\lambda_s\,(\partial B^*/\partial p)_{\bar{u}}Z_{pu}/\Delta'$ is the effect of the higher α on the recipient country's welfare through changes in government net tax revenue, induced by changes in the donor's income and terms of trade. Intuitively, a higher α, to finance the foreign aid, reduces the donor country's income, consumption of the manufacturing good, and the country's terms of trade. In the recipient country, if $(\partial B^*/\partial p)=-(Z_p+sL_p^M)>0$ the wage subsidy must fall for the government to maintain a balanced budget. As a result, the unemployment ratio rises, affecting negatively income and welfare in the country. The last right-hand-side term of equation (1.24), (*i.e.*, $\tau R(\partial u^*/\partial p)(Z_{ps}^*-\beta Z_{pu})/\Delta'$) captures the effect of the higher α on the recipient country's welfare through terms of trade induced changes in the country's income due to a local production effect (*i.e.*, $\tau R(\partial u^* / \partial p)Z^*_{ps} / \Delta'$) and due to a demand (income) effect in the donor country (*i.e.*, $-\beta\ \tau R(\partial u^* / \partial p)Z_{pu} / \Delta')$). The higher α, to finance foreign aid, raises the subsidy rate in the recipient country, resulting in higher urban employment and manufacturing output, lower imports and improved terms of trade (*i.e.*, lower p) for the recipient country. If this improvement in the recipient's terms of trade affects positively its income (*i.e.*, $(\partial u^* / \partial p) < 0$), then there is also a positive effect on its welfare. At the same time, the higher α raises the cost of the subsidy to the donor country (*i.e.*, β), affecting negatively its income and consumption, raising its exports and lowering the country's terms of trade. If $(\partial u^* / \partial p) < 0$, then there is again a positive effect on the recipient country's income and welfare. Overall, the higher α, resulting in more aid financing the urban wage subsidy in the recipient country, (*i*) entails a direct positive effect on the recipient's welfare due to the reduction in the unemployment ratio and increase in income, and (*ii*) improves its terms of trade. This improvement in its terms of trade, however, while it makes its imports cheaper, it also increases the unemployment ratio. Thus, the overall effect on its welfare is ambiguous. The results of equations (1.18)-(1.23) are summarized in the following proposition.

Proposition 2: *Assume that there is an increase in the fraction α of income tax revenue transferred as aid to the recipient country characterized by HT unemployment. If, in the recipient country, aid is lump-sum distributed, then welfare in that country improves and in the donor falls, if the direct effect of the income transfer dominates the indirect, terms of trade, effect. Otherwise, welfare paradoxes may emerge due to such an income transfer. When aid is tied to an urban wage subsidy in the recipient country, a higher α reduces the donor's welfare, while its effect on the recipient country's welfare is, in general, ambiguous.*

The Effect on World Welfare

We turn now to evaluate the effect of such an international transfer on world (the donor and recipient countries combined) welfare, when aid to the recipient country is either lump-sum distributed (*i.e.*, δ=1) or used entirely to finance the provision of the urban wage subsidy.

When in the recipient country aid is lump-sum distributed and s >0, through local lump-sum taxation, equations (1.18) and (1.21), using equation (1.15), yield:

$$A^{-1}\Delta_1[(du/d\alpha)+(du^*/d\alpha)] = \tilde{S}_{pp}^{-1}(Z^*_{pu} - Z_{pu})\ R^*_\lambda[\lambda_p + \lambda_s(ds/dp)]. \quad (1.24)$$

Equation (1.24) indicates that when δ=1 and s >0, the effect of a higher α on world welfare depends, first, on the intercountry differences in the marginal propensities of consuming the manufacturing good, and second, on changes in the recipient's income due to terms of trade induced changes in the country's unemployment ratio, direct (*i.e.*, $R^*_\lambda \lambda_p$) and an indirect (*i.e.*, $R^*_\lambda \lambda_s(ds/dp)$), through the government's balanced budget. Consider the case where a higher α improves the donor country's terms of trade (*i.e.*, $(dp/d\alpha) > 0$). By equation (1.14), when $\delta = 1$ then $(dp/d\alpha) > 0$ if $Z^*_{pu} > Z_{pu}$, that is, the recipient's marginal propensity to consume the manufacturing exceeds that of the donor's. In the recipient country, such an increase in p, on the one hand, lowers the unemployment ratio and raises income (i.e., $R^*_\lambda \lambda_p > 0$), and it exerts a positive effect on world welfare. On the other, a higher p requires a reduction in the subsidy rate (*i.e.*, $(ds/dp) < 0$), for the government to maintain a balanced budget. Such a lower subsidy increases the unemployment ratio and reduces income in the recipient (*i.e.*, $R^*_\lambda \lambda_s (ds/dp) < 0$). The latter term exerts a negative effect on world welfare. Consequently, a higher α in the donor country to finance the lump-sum distributed foreign aid, raises world welfare if (*i*) improves the donor country's terms of trade, and (*ii*) the direct effect of such a terms of trade improvement on the recipient's unemployment ratio dominates its indirect effect. In this case, there is a possibility that aid can improve welfare of both countries. World welfare can also improve when $Z^*_{pu} > Z_{pu}$, and the indirect effect of p on λ, through changes in B^* and s, dominates the direct effect.[16] If none of these two cases holds, then aid reduces world welfare, and there is a possibility for the welfare in each country to decrease. In the case where $\delta=1$ and $s=0$, then aid unambiguously improves world welfare with an improvement in the donor country's terms of trade (*i.e.*, $A_1^{-1}\Delta_{11}[(du/d\alpha)+(du^*/d\alpha)] = \tilde{S}_{pp}^{-1}(Z^*_{pu} - Z_{pu})\, R^*_\lambda \lambda_p > 0$).[17]

We now examine the effects of a higher α on world welfare, when in the recipient country aid is used entirely to finance the wage subsidy. Equations (1.21) and (1.24), after some manipulations yield:

$$A^{-1}\Delta'[(du/d\alpha)+(du^*/d\alpha)] = (1-\beta^{-1}R^*_\lambda \lambda_s) + (\beta\tilde{S}_{pp})^{-1} Z^*_{ps}(R^*_\lambda \lambda_p - sL^M_p)$$
$$-(\beta\tilde{S}_{pp})^{-1}(Z_{pu} - Z^*_{pu})[\beta(\partial u^*/\partial p) + R^*_\lambda \lambda_s (Z_p + sL^M_p)]. \qquad (1.25)$$

The first right-hand-side term of equation (1.25), *i.e.*, $A(1/\Delta')(1-\beta R^*_\lambda \lambda_s)$, is the direct effect of the higher α on world welfare. Since aid is used to finance the wage subsidy in the recipient country, this term indicates that the higher α affects positively world welfare if the direct benefit of aid to the recipient country (*i.e.*, $-A(1/\Delta')\beta R^*_\lambda \lambda_s > 0$) exceeds the cost to the donor (*i.e.*, $A(1/\Delta') < 0$). Otherwise, the direct effect of aid on world welfare is negative. The second right-hand-side term (*i.e.*, $\tau R Z^*_{ps}(R^*_\lambda \lambda_p - sL^M_p)$) is the effect of the higher α on world welfare through a terms of trade induced negative income effect (*i.e.* $\tau R Z^*_{ps} R^*_\lambda \lambda_p < 0$), and a positive production effect (*i.e.*, $-\tau R Z^*_{ps} s L^M_p > 0$) in the recipient country. The higher α raises the wage subsidy, thus, urban employment and manufacturing output in the recipient country. Its imports decrease, thus reducing p, the world price of the manufacturing good. This reduction in p, through the former effect, raises the unemployment ratio, lowers income in the recipient country, and affects negatively world welfare. On the other hand, it reduces the total cost of the subsidy, and affects world welfare positively. The last right-hand-side term is the effect of the higher α on world welfare due to terms of trade induced changes in the recipient's income, directly (*i.e.*, $-\beta(\partial u^* / \partial p)$) and indirectly (*i.e.*, $R^*_\lambda \lambda_s (Z_p + sL^M_p)$) through changes in the government net tax revenue at constant foreign income.[18]

A Transfer Between Two Small Open Economies

A special case of the above general results is to assume a world of many countries where both the developed donor country and the developing recipient are small open economies unable to affect world commodity prices through changes in their demands for goods. As a result, equation (1.10) of the original general equilibrium system falls out, and $dp=0$. In this case, simple algebraic calculations demonstrate that a higher α, to finance foreign aid, either for purposes for lump-sum distribution or subsidy financing in the recipient country, do not yield welfare paradoxes for the individual countries. Moreover, using equation (1.25), the effect of the higher α on world welfare is shown to be:

$$[\tau R(1-\delta)]^{-1}[(du / d\alpha) + (du^* / d\alpha)] = -1 + R^*_\lambda \lambda_s . \tag{1.26}$$

When $\delta=1$, the higher α leaves world welfare unaffected, while when $\delta=0$ world welfare increases (decreases) if the induced income benefits due to lower unemployment ratio in the recipient country exceed (are smaller than) the direct cost of aid to the donor.

> ***Proposition 3:*** *Assume that there is an increase in the fraction α of income tax revenue transferred as aid from the donor to the recipient country characterized by HT unemployment. When aid is lump-sum distributed and $s>0$ sufficient conditions for the higher α to raise world welfare are that (i) the donor terms of trade improve, and (ii) the recipient's unemployment ratio falls. When aid is lump-sum distributed and $s=0$, condition (i) suffices to ensure an improvement in world welfare due to the higher α. When aid is tied to the urban wage subsidy in the recipient country, the effect of the higher α on world welfare is, in general, ambiguous.*

CONCLUDING REMARKS

The analytical motivation of this paper is to combine and challenge some of the conventional wisdom on two popular, and mostly separately treated, issues of the international trade and economic development literature. Those of foreign aid, and of wage subsidies as a suitable policy intervention in the case where an open developing economy suffers from unemployment. Specifically, the literature on international transfers has assumed, by and large, that donor countries finance foreign aid through non-distortionary lump-sum taxation, and that such aid is unrelated to other policy instruments in these countries. On the other hand, in overcoming unemployment and maximizing welfare in a (HT) developing economy, a uniform wage subsidy has been recommended as the first-best policy option, and an urban wage subsidy as the suitable second-best alternative. By and large, such subsidies are assumed to be financed through lump-sum taxation, a rather infeasible policy option. In the relevant literature it is only a couple of studies which acknowledging this constraint examine feasible ways of financing wage subsidies (e.g., taxes on profits, trade, and internationally mobile capital).

The purpose of this paper is, among other things, to consider another way, the use of foreign aid, of financing the urban wage subsidy. That is, foreign aid is tied to the urban wage subsidy in the recipient country. The importance of this alternative is that it probably constitutes the only possible non-distortionary mean through which a recipient developing country can finance such a wage subsidy.

To address these issues jointly, we develop a two-country perfectly competitive trading world general equilibrium model, where foreign aid is financed through a fraction of the donor country's income tax revenue, and is either lump-sum distributed or tied to finance the provision of an urban wage subsidy in a recipient, dual (HT), economy. Within this context, we examine the effects of raising the fraction of income taxes transferred as aid on the terms of trade, and on national and world welfare. Rather than repeating the results of the paper, summarized in the various propositions, we conclude by conjecturing on whether, in the present framework, untied (lump-sum distributed) or tied aid to the wage subsidy is preferred by each country, and the world as a whole. We also discuss some analytical extensions of the present framework.

In the present context, and regardless of how foreign aid is used, the income transfer affects welfare in the two countries directly, and indirectly due to terms of trade induced changes in the countries income, and in the recipient country's unemployment ratio directly and indirectly through maintaining a balanced government budget. As expected, the direct effect is negative for the donor and positive for the recipient country, while the indirect effect depends, to a large extent, on the impact of foreign aid on the terms of trade.[19] The donor's terms of trade unambiguously deteriorate when aid is tied to the wage subsidy. When aid is lump-sum distributed, its effect on the donor's terms of trade is ambiguous depending on the intercountry difference in marginal propensities to consume. Without loss of generality, it is reasonable to assume that the marginal propensity to consume the donor's exported manufacturing good is higher in the richer developed donor rather than in the poorer developing recipient country. If so, aid reduces the donor country's terms of trade. Under this, plausible assumption, this particular form of aid reduces the donor country's terms of trade, and increases those of the recipient. Thus in both regimes, the donor's terms of trade deteriorate with aid. When aid is untied, however, this deterioration in the donor's terms of trade is smaller compared to when aid is tied to the wage subsidy. The reason for this result is that in both regimes the donor country's excess demand for the manufacturing good falls by the same amount. In the recipient country, however, excess demand for the manufacturing increases when aid is untied, and falls when aid is tied to the urban wage subsidy.

Under these qualifications of our results, the donor country is expected to favor untied rather tied aid to the urban wage subsidy, since the incurred deterioration in its terms of trade in the former case is smaller than in the latter. Regarding the recipient country, despite the improvement in its terms of trade, the welfare effect of foreign aid is ambiguous in both regimes. In either case, the direct positive effect of aid may be outweighed by the indirect negative effect of the improvement in its terms of trade on the unemployment ratio. As a result, it is unclear which of the two regimes prefers the recipient country. Finally, world welfare may increase with aid tied to the wage subsidy, or with untied aid.

It can be shown that the results of the paper are qualitatively similar when the donor country finances aid through lump-sum taxes, as it is conventionally assumed in the literature. Instead of following this standard practice, the analysis exploits a more practical way of financing foreign aid in the donor country. Moreover, the present framework can be extended to accommodate other related analytical features for the donor or for the recipient country. In particular, the effects of the income transfer could be studied for the case where the donor finances aid through the imposition of indirect (*e.g.*, consumption) taxes, or where capital in the recipient country, presently treated as sector specific, is intersectorally mobile.

NOTES

[1] The Inter-Governmental Group on Indonesia, a group of donor countries assisting that country's development has agreed on lowering, in real terms, their assistance due to its recently flourishing economy (see, *e.g.*, Brakman and Marrewijk 1990). Moreover, United Nations resolutions (*e.g.*, no. 2626, the Pearson Committee Report) stipulate that about 1 percent of the rich countries GNP should be used for aid to less developed countries (LDCs).

[2] The two financing schemes generate similar results as long as the donor country taxes incomes. To the best of our knowledge, Brakman and Marrewijk (1990) is the only study which ties aid to the donor and recipient countries GDP. The objective of their analysis, however, is to demonstrate that transfer paradoxes occur in the endogenous case only when they occur in the exogenous case. The present analysis considers a different framework of how governments in donor countries generate revenue and finance foreign aid, and of how they use aid in recipient countries.

[3] In a different context, endogenous aid could be determined by the outcome of political process or of negotiations among countries. This, however, is not a concern of the present paper (*e.g.*, see Lahiri *et al.* 1997).

[4] Alternatively, the urban wage can be indexed in terms of consumer prices. The essence of the results, however, remains the same.

[5] Assuming that the donor country transfers as aid a fraction of its GNP, the amount of this international assistance to the recipient country is $\alpha R(p)$.

[6] Note that when $\delta=1$, utility of the recipient country is a direct and indirect function of α, *i.e.*, $u^*=u^*[\alpha, p(\alpha), \lambda(p(\alpha), s(\alpha))]$. When $\delta=0$, u^* is only an indirect function of α, *i.e.*, $u^*[p(\alpha), \lambda(p(\alpha), s(\alpha))]$.

[7] Note that under full employment (*e.g.*, $\lambda_p=0$) and $\delta=0$, a deterioration in the recipient country's terms of trade (*i.e.*, $dp>0$), other things equal, has a negative effect on the recipient country's welfare (*i.e.*, $(\partial u^* / \partial p) < 0$).

[8] This reasoning holds provided that when aid is lump-sum distributed, the government is able to finance the subsidy (*i.e.*, $s > 0$) through local lump-sum taxes. Otherwise, when $\delta = 1$, $(\partial B^* / \partial p) = 0$.

[9] This is known as the "orthodox" view. When foreign aid leads to the opposite result, we have the so called "anti-orthodox" view. If no presumptions can be made about the direction of movements in the terms of trade due to foreign aid we have the so called "neutral" view (*e.g.*, see Hatzipanayotou and Michael 1995 for a brief survey on the subject).

[10] Note that $\beta(= \partial(sL^M)/\partial s)$ is the change in the cost of subsidy, and it is paid by the donor country. Thus, the donor's demand for the manufacturing falls by βZ_{pu}.

[11] Recall from the discussion of equation (1.15) that when $\delta = 1$ and $s > 0$, $(ds/dp) < 0$ for $B^* = 0$.

[12] An increase in p, raises urban employment in the recipient country ($L_p^M > 0$, in the Appendix), and subsequently the overall cost of the wage subsidy. Using equation (1.15) when $\delta = 1$, $sL_p^M = -(L_M + sL_s^M)(ds/dp) > 0$.

[13] A case also examined by Michael and van Marrewijk (1998).

[14] Using equations (1.12) and (1.15), when $\delta = 0$, $(\partial u / \partial p) = -(Z_p + \alpha\tau R_p)$, and $(\partial B^* / \partial p) = (\alpha\tau R_p - sL_p^M)$. The two results yield, $(\partial B^* / \partial p) = -(\partial u / \partial p) - (Z_p + sL_p^M)$. Thus, given $u = \bar{u}$, $(\partial B^* / \partial p)_{\bar{u}} = -(Z_p + sL_p^M)$ which is positive or negative depending on whether $-Z_p > (<) sL_p^M$.

[15] The reasoning for the two effects is similar to that following the discussion of equation (1.18).

[16] In this case, the improvement in world welfare emerges while there is deterioration in the donor's terms of trade, and unambiguous decrease in the donor country's welfare.

[17] If $\delta = 1$ and regardless of whether $s \geq 0$, then $[(du/d\alpha) + (du^*/d\alpha)] = 0$ in the extreme case where $Z_{pu}^* = Z_{pu}$.

[18] See footnote (10) for $(\partial B^* / \partial p)_{\bar{u}} = -(Z_p + sL_p^M)$.

[19] Recall that when aid is tied to the wage subsidy, its direct effect on the recipient's welfare emerges "indirectly" through a reduction in the urban unemployment ratio and an increase in domestic income.

REFERENCES

Beladi H., and C.-C. Chao, 1993, Non-traded goods, urban unemployment and welfare in LDCs, *European Journal of Political Economy* 9, 281–292.

Bhagwati, J., R. Brecher, and T. Hatta, 1983, The generalized theory of transfers and welfare: Bilateral transfers in a multilateral world, *American Economic Review* 73, 606–618.

_____, 1985, The generalized theory of transfers and welfare: Exogenous (policy-induced) and endogenous (transfer-induced) distortions, *Quarterly Journal of Economics* 100, 697–714.

Basu,, K., 1980, Optimal policies in dual economies, *Quarterly Journal of Economics* 95, 187–196

Brakman, S. and C. van Marrewijk, 1990, A note on endogenous transfers, *Journal of Economics* 54, 171–178.

______, 1995, Transfers, returns to scale, tied aid and monopolistic competition, *Journal of Development Economics* 47, 333–354.

Dixit, A. and V. Norman, 1980, *Theory of international trade*, Cambridge University Press: Cambridge.

Gupta, M. R., 1995, Tax on foreign capital income and wage subsidy to the urban sector in the Harris-Todaro model, *Journal of Development Economics* 47, 469–79.

Hatzipanayotou, P. and M. S. Michael, 1995, Foreign aid and public goods, *Journal of Development Economics*, 47, 455–467.

Kemp, M. and S. Kojima, 1985a, Tied aid and the paradoxes of donor-enrichment and recipient-impoverishment, *International Economic Review* 26, 721–729.

_____, 1985b, The welfare economics of foreign aid, in G. Feiwel, ed., *Issues in contemporary microeconomics and welfare*, Macmillan: London.

Keynes, M., 1929, The German transfer problem, *Economic Journal* 39, 1–7.

Lahiri, S. and P. Raimondos, 1995, Welfare effects of aid under quantitative trade restrictions, *Journal of International Economics* 39, 297–317.

Lahiri, S., P. Raimondos-Moller, K.-Y. Wong and A. D. Woodland, 1977, Optimal income transfers and tariffs, *EPRU working paper* 97/06, Copenhagen Business School.

McCool, T., 1982, Wage subsidies and distortionary taxes in a mobile capital Harris-Todaro model, *Economica* 49, 69–79.

Michael, M. S. and C. van Marrewijk, 1998, Tied to capital, or untied foreign aid? *Review of Development Economics* 2, 61–75.

Ohlin, B., 1929, The reparation problem: A discussion, *Economic Journal* 39, 172–178.

Turunen-Red, A. and A. Woodland, 1988, On the multilateral transfer problem, *Journal of International Economics* 25, 249–269.

APPENDIX

Totally differentiating equations (1.5), (1.6), and (1.7), using equation (1.4) yields:

$$\begin{bmatrix} pM_{LL} & 0 & 0 \\ 0 & A_{LL} & w^A(1+\lambda)^{-1} \\ (1+\lambda) & 1 & L^M \end{bmatrix} \begin{bmatrix} dL^M \\ dL^A \\ d\lambda \end{bmatrix} = \begin{bmatrix} -M_L \\ 0 \\ 0 \end{bmatrix} dp + \begin{bmatrix} -1 \\ 0 \\ 0 \end{bmatrix} ds$$

The determinant of the matrix of coefficients given by $D = pM_{LL}\ [L^M A_{LL} - w^A(1+\lambda)^{-1}]$ is positive assuming diminishing marginal product of labor in the two sectors, i.e., $M_{LL} < 0$ and $A_{LL} < 0$. Using Cramer's rule we can solve for the effects of a change in (i) the terms of trade (e.g., $dp > 0$), and (ii) the wage subsidy to manufacturing (e.g., $ds > 0$), on sectoral employment (dL^M, dL^A) and on the rate of unemployment ($d\lambda$).

(I) Terms of Trade

$(dL^M/dp) = -(pM_{LL})^{-1}\ M_L > 0$
$D(dL^A/dp) = -w^A M^L < 0$
$D(d\lambda/dp) = (1+\lambda)\ M_L A_{LL} < 0$

(II) Urban wage subsidy

$(dL^M/ds) = -(pM_{LL})^{-1} > 0$
$D(dL^A/ds) = -w^A < 0$
$D(d\lambda/ds) = (1+\lambda)\ A_{LL} < 0$

CHAPTER 2

ALTRUISM, TRADE POLICY, AND THE OPTIMALITY OF FOREIGN AID

Sajal Lahiri
and
Pascalis Raimondos-Møller

INTRODUCTION

There are many studies in the literature that deal with the welfare effects of income transfers between nations in a general equilibrium setting. An important impetus for this extensive literature was the demonstration of the transfer paradox; that the donor country could actually gain from a transfer of income to another, and that the recipient could lose as a result of the gift. The reason for this paradoxical result is that the transfer gives rise to a terms-of-trade effect that may be especially beneficial to the donor and detrimental to the recipient. Subsequently, many papers have established conditions under which this paradox will or will not occur. Early work by Samuelson (1954) was followed by demonstrations of paradoxes by Gale (1974), Ohyama (1974), Brecher and Bhagwati (1982) and Bhagwati, Brecher and Hatta (1983, 1985), and Dixit (1983) among others.[1] More recently, many studies have examined whether or not foreign aid — tied and untied — can be welfare improving for both the donor and the recipient (see, for example, Turunen-Red and Woodland (1988), Kemp and Wong (1993), Schweinberger (1990), Hatzipanayotou and Michael (1995), Lahiri and Raimondos-Møller (1995, 1997), Djajić, Lahiri and Raimondos-Møller (1996a, 1996b), and Lahiri, Raimondos-Møller, Wong and Woodland (1997)).[2]

The present chapter distinguishes itself from the existing literature in two important ways. First, with the exception of Lahiri *et al* (1997), none of the studies consider the question of optimality of foreign aid: the amount of transfer is exogenous.[3] In contrast, the amount of aid is treated endogenously in this paper, decided optimally by the donor. The second and related point is that the motive of giving aid is not modeled explicitly in any of the papers. There is strong evidence to suggest that the motive of giving aid is often self-interest on the part of the donors.[4] It is commonly believed that often the donors give aid with the understanding that the recipients in return would import more from the donor countries. However, this cannot be the sole motive. It is in fact inconceivable that aid is provided purely for selfish reasons. There are many citizens in most donor countries whose welfare, for one reason or other, depends on the well being of nationals of the recipient countries.

Some people genuinely want to improve the economic conditions of the poor in another country without expecting anything in return. Simple altruism could be one reason for such interdependence of welfare. This being so, in a meaningful political economic model of foreign aid, one has to take this interdependence of utilities into account in the welfare analysis of foreign aid.

Although hard-headed self-interest motives in the decision making by individuals form the backbone of 'modern' economics, the issue of ethical considerations in decision making in general, and altruism in particular, is not new in economics, and dates back at least to the work of Aristotle.[5] The existence of informal social security arrangements in most developing countries exist not only for reasons of collective survival in a very risky environment devoid of formal market mechanisms, but also for sincere concern for the welfare of the deprived members of the society.[6] Intra-family altruism has also been the subject of extensive studies in recent years. For example, Stark (1995) has examined how the preferences of one member of a family is influenced by, and impinges upon, those of another member of the same family.

In the literature of international trade, self-interest (not necessarily at the expense of others) in the form of 'beggar thy neighbour,' 'gains from trade,' 'multilateral co-ordinations' etc. is the predominant paradigm in which altruism has no role. In recent years, the concept of 'ethical trade' has begun to surface. It is said that imports from the developing countries of commodities which are produced under 'unethical' conditions should be restricted. The idea is that such restrictions would improve the working conditions or well being of poor people in the developing countries, and therefore they are altruistic in nature. Although some people honestly believe this to be the case, there exists considerable skepticisms among many that these restrictions are being promoted by powerful protectionist lobbies in the developed countries under the guise of ethical trade, anxious to replace trade liberalisations agreed in the last GATT negotiations, such as removal of the multi-fibre agreement and agricultural subsidies, by new non-tariff barriers. In short, altruism has on the whole been ignored in the analysis of issues related to international trade.

Apart from ethical considerations, there are other non-economic factors that determine how and why aid is given. Political variables have been found to be important in this decision making process (see, for example, McKinlay and Little (1977) and Trumbull and Wall (1994)). However, this does not mean that economic factors are unimportant. In identifying economic motives one has to distinguish between the role of tied and untied aid. Economic motives of the donor can directly manifest itself in tied aid, for example, aid tied to more imports from the donor. However, untied aid can also have beneficial effects on the donor via increased income of the recipient. As Maizels and Nissanke write, 'The *trade interest* of a donor country would be in promoting growth ... in developing countries which are its major trading partners ...' (Maizels and Nissanke (1984, p. 884)). Even though it is difficult to estimate the magnitude of such beneficial effects of untied aid, Hopkin (1970), Maizels and Nissanke (1984) and Khilji and Zampelli (1994) have found such income effects to be significant. The income effects of aid have also been the cornerstone of the trade theoretic analysis of foreign aid, mentioned at the beginning of this paper. These income effects affect welfare via changes in the international terms of trade. In the analysis to follow, these terms-of-trade effects would form an important part along with altruism.

In the following section a trade theoretic model of foreign aid is developed in which the nationals of the donor county are altruistic and trade is distorted by tariffs or quotas. Section 3 of the chapter characterises the optimal amount of aid and analyses its properties when the recipient country has tariff restrictions on its imports. Section 4 carries out similar exercises when the trade barrier is quota on imports, rather than tariffs. Finally, some concluding remarks are made in section 5.

THE MODEL WITH TARIFFS AND QUOTAS

There are two countries labeled donor (α) and recipient (β), and three tradable goods, 1, 2 and 3. All product and factor markets are assumed to be perfectly competitive. Both countries have convex technologies and preferences, but their technologies, preferences, and factor endowments may be different. Without loss of generality, good 1 is chosen as the numeraire, and p_j denotes the international price of good *j* relative to good 1.

The specific trade tax imposed by the recipient country β on good 2 is denoted by t. Trade in good 3 is subject to import quota imposed once again by the recipient country β. Country α, the donor, gives an aid of T to country β, the recipient, in terms of the numeraire good. We denote the revenue or GDP functions of country α and β by $r^{a}(1, p_2, p_3)$ and $r^{\beta}(1, p_2+t, p_3^{\beta})$, where p_3^{β} is the domestic price of the quota restricted good 3.[7] A revenue function, which summarises all aspects of the production side of the economy, is defined as the maximum possible value of total output that can be produced given producer prices, endowments of primary factors of production, and technology. In a perfectly competitive economy, the market mechanism ensures the attainment of this maximum possible GDP. It is well known that the partial derivative of a revenue function with respect a producer price gives the output supply function of that good, and that with respect to an endowment of a primary factor of production gives the price of that factor.[8]

The expenditure function of the recipient country is given by $e^{\beta}(1, p_2+t, p_3^{\beta}, u^{\beta})$ where u^{β} is the utility level of the representative consumer in the recipient country. As for the representative consumer in the donor country, we assume that she is altruistic and her utility level, u^{α}, is given by $u^{\alpha} = \overline{u}^{a} + \lambda u^{\beta}$; where $\overline{u}^{\alpha}$ is the direct utility derived from consumption and λ is the altruism parameter. This simple specification of altruism where the utility is additive in direct self utility and the utility of the foreign consumer is made for analytical simplicity, and most of our results will go through under the more general specification $u^{\alpha} = f(\overline{u}^{a}, u^{\beta})$ where the function *f* is an increasing function of both its arguments. The expenditure function in the donor country is thus written as $e^{\alpha}(1, p_2, p_3, u^{\alpha} - \lambda u^{\beta})$. Like, as mentioned above, a revenue function captures all aspects of the production side of an economy, an expenditure function summarises the consumer side of the economy. It is defined as the minimum consumption expenditure that a consumer has to make in order to attain a certain level of utility for given consumer prices and the preference ordering of the consumer. It is well known that the partial derivative of an expenditure function with respect to a price gives the compensated demand function of that good, and that with respect to the utility gives the reciprocal of the marginal utility of income.[9]

The trade expenditure function of country α and β can be defined respectively as the difference between the expenditure function and the revenue function, i.e.

$$E^{\alpha}(1, p_2, p_3, u^{\alpha} - \lambda u^{\beta}) \equiv e^{\alpha}(1, p_2, p_3, u^{\alpha} - \lambda u^{\beta}) - r^{\alpha}(1, p_2, p_3)$$

and

$$E^{\beta}(1, p_2 + t, p_3^{\beta}, u^{\beta}) \equiv e^{\beta}(1, p_2 + t, p_3^{\beta}, u^{\beta}) - r^{\beta}(1, p_2 + t, p_3^{\beta});$$

and represents the excess of expenditure over income.

The (compensated) import demand function for good j in country i is equal to $m_j^i = E_{p_j}^i(\cdot)$, which is the partial derivative of E^i with respect to the domestic price $p_j (i = \alpha, \beta; j = 2,3)$. Throughout the paper we shall assume that the recipient country is an importer of goods 2 and 3 so that $m_2^{\beta} > 0$ and $m_3^{\beta} > 0$.

Assuming that the entire trade tax revenue and the foreign aid is distributed to the consumers in a lump-sum fashion, we can write the national budget constraints as:

$$E^{a}(1, p_2, p_3, u^{\alpha} - \lambda u^{\beta}) = -T,$$

$$E^{\beta}(1, p_2 + t, p_3^{\beta}, u^{\beta}) = T + tE_{p_2}^{\beta} + (p_3^{\beta} - p_3)E_{p_3}^{\beta}$$

where $tE_{p_2}^{\beta}$ and $(p_3^{\beta} - p_3)E_{p_3}^{\beta}$ are the tariff revenues and the quota rents respectively. Implicitly, it is assumed that licences for the imports of the quota restricted good are auctioned off by the government competitively, so that the price of a license to import one unit of the good is equal to $p_3^{\beta} - p_3$. Note that aid T is provided in terms of the numeraire good for simplicity and without any loss of generality. Given that our model is not a monetary model, all transactions have to take place in terms of a commodity and here it is assumed that the commodity used is the numeraire.[10]

The equilibrium conditions for the world market of the non-numeraire goods, viz. the exports of the one country need to be equal to the imports of the other, are given by:[11]

$$E_{p_2}^{\alpha} + E_{p_2}^{\beta} = 0,$$

$$E_{p_3}^{\alpha} + E_{p_3}^{\beta} = 0.$$

Finally, imports of good 3 in the recipient country are determined by the quota imposed:

$$E_{p_3}^{\beta} = \overline{m}_3^{\beta},$$

where $\overline{m}_3^\beta$ is the exogenously specified quota on the imports of commodity 3 in country β.

The last five equations described above determine the model's five endogenous variables u^α, u^β, p_2, p_3^α and p_3^β. Having specified the general framework, we consider two simple cases: (i) a model with only tariff distortions, and (ii) a model with only quota distortions.

TARIFFS AND OPTIMAL AID

In this section we assume away the existence of sector 3 and concentrate on the following simplified model:[12]

$$E^\alpha(1, p, u^\alpha - \lambda u^\beta) = -T\,, \tag{2.1}$$

$$E^\beta(1, p+t, u^\beta) = T + tE_p^\beta\,, \tag{2.2}$$

$$E_p^\alpha + E_p^\beta = 0\,. \tag{2.3}$$

To facilitate the analysis of the optimal amount of foreign aid, we totally differentiate equations (2.1)–(2.3) and express the endogenous variables in terms of changes of the policy instruments T and t and the altruism parameter λ:

$$ZE_u^\beta\, du^\beta = A\, dT + B\, dt\,, \tag{2.4}$$

$$ZE_u^\alpha\, du^\alpha = D\, dT + G\, dt + F\, d\lambda\,, \tag{2.5}$$

$$Z\, dp = -\frac{E_{pp}^\beta}{1-tc_y^\beta}\, dt + \left(c_y^\alpha - \frac{c_y^\beta}{1-tc_y^\beta}\right) dT\,, \tag{2.6}$$

where

$$Z = E_{pp}^\alpha - m^\alpha c_y^\alpha + \frac{E_{pp}^\beta - m^\beta c_y^\beta}{1-tc_y^\beta}\,,$$

$$A = E_{pp}^\beta\left(1 + c_y^\alpha t\right) + E_{pp}^\alpha\,,$$

$$B = \left[\left(E_{pp}^\alpha - m^\alpha c_y^\alpha\right)t + m^\beta\right]E_{pp}^\beta\,,$$

$$D = -\frac{E_{pp}^\alpha\left[1 - c_y^\beta t\right] + E_{pp}^\beta}{1-tc_y^\beta} + \lambda\cdot\frac{E_u^\alpha}{E_u^\beta}\cdot\frac{A}{1-tc_y^\beta}$$

$$G = m^\alpha E_{pp}^\beta + \lambda\cdot\frac{E_u^\alpha}{E_u^\beta}\cdot\frac{B}{1-tc_y^\beta}\,,$$

$F = ZE_u^{\alpha} u^{\beta}$.

Note that Z represents the slope of the uncompensated world excess demand function and thus is negative under Walrasian stability, i.e. $Z < 0$. Furthermore, $c_y^i = E_{pu}^i / E_u^i$ so that $(p+t^i)c_y^i$ represents the marginal propensity to consume the non-numeraire good in country i, and thus, assuming normality,[13] is always positive.

We start with some general remarks followed by some specific ones. First, a transfer has direct as well as indirect effects. The direct effect is a straightforward loss of income to the donor and a gain to the recipient. However, this initial change in the international distribution of income would have asymmetric effect on the world demand for the goods to the extent that the marginal propensities of consumption are different in the two countries, which in turn would have an effect on the international price of the good. This effect is given by the second term on the right hand side of (2.6). If this secondary effect is such that the price of the good that the donor exports increases, clearly the donor will enjoy a 'secondary blessing' (the so-called terms of trade improvement) and the recipient a 'secondary curse'. The sum of these two effects are captured in the coefficients A/Z and D/Z. If it so happens that the secondary effect dominates the primary effect so that the donor benefits from the transfer and the recipient loses, one would have the so-called transfer paradox mentioned at the outset of this paper. It is now well known that this paradox can happen only under the existence of some distortions in the economy (see, for example, Bhagwati, Brecher and Hatta (1985)).

Having made some general remarks, we now turn to a number of specific remarks on the above equations. First, it is to be noted that the altruistic parameter λ has no direct influence on the terms-of-trade and the utility of the recipient country. Second, from (2.4) it is easy to see that $A < 0$. That is, the effect of a transfer is always positive for the recipient country $(du^{\beta} / dT > 0)$. Therefore, any amount of aid offered by the donor will always be accepted by the recipient. The sign of B depends on whether the recipient country applies an optimal trade tax or not, i.e. $B \gtreqless 0 \Leftrightarrow t \gtreqless t^*$, t^* being the level of optimal tariff. In other words, B represents the shadow premium of the trade tax.

In equation (2.5) the coefficient F is negative implying that higher altruism on the part of the consumers in the donor country, *ceteris paribus*, is beneficial to them. Furthermore, the coefficient D is positive in the absence of altruism, i.e. when $\lambda = 0$. This implies that, in the absence of altruism, aid is always welfare reducing for the donor country. This is the standard result in the literature: aid is recipient enriching and donor immiserising in a two country framework with tariff distortions and with no inferior goods (see Bhagwati *et al* (1985)). However, the coefficient D would be negative for large enough values of the altruism parameter λ, and therefore aid can be welfare enhancing for the donor. These results can be stated formally as:

Proposition 1: *If the donor country is sufficiently altruistic, a transfer of income is strictly Pareto improving.*

Turning to the question of optimal level of aid, we can obtain it setting

$$\frac{\partial u^{\alpha}}{\partial T} = \frac{D}{E_u^{\alpha} Z} = 0, \tag{2.7}$$

giving rise to the optimality condition:

$$\lambda = \frac{E_{pp}^{\alpha}\left(1 - c_y^{\beta} t\right) + E_{pp}^{\beta}}{E_{pp}^{\beta}\left[1 + c_y^{\alpha} t\right] + E_{pp}^{\alpha}} \cdot \frac{E_u^{\beta}}{E_u^{\alpha}}. \tag{2.8}$$

In the absence of any tariff, i.e. $t = 0$, the above formula reduces to:

$$\lambda = \frac{E_u^{\beta}}{E_u^{\alpha}}. \tag{2.9}$$

That is, it is optimal for the donor to provide aid until the point where the marginal loss from providing an extra unit of aid — measured by the marginal utility of income $1/E_u^{\alpha}$ is equal to the marginal benefit from it. The latter is expressed by the direct positive effect that aid has on the recipient's welfare — measured by the marginal utility of income in the recipient country, $1/E_u^{\beta}$, multiplied by the weight that this benefit has on donor's utility, i.e. the altruistic parameter λ. In the presence of tariff, the optimality rule given by (2.8) can be similarly interpreted, although here there are additional costs and benefits. These additional costs and benefits arise because the transfer-induced income effects affect the demand for the non-numeraire good in both countries (going up in the recipient and going down in the donor country) and therefore the international price of the good. If, for example, $c_y^{\alpha} > c_y^{\beta}/\left(1 - tc_y^{\beta}\right)$, the international price of the non-numeraire good goes down (see (2.6)) and therefore the imports of it in the recipient country go up. This way the donor country is able to affect, with the help of the aid instrument, the basic distortion in the model which is 'too little' imports of the non-numeraire good by the recipient country. Because of this extra target for the donor to aim at with the instrument of aid, the expression in (2.8) is more complicated than that in (2.9).

Having obtained the optimality rule, we shall, first of all, examine how a change in the altruism parameter affects the optimal level of aid. Denoting the optimal level of aid by T^*, from (2.7) we obtain:

$$\frac{dT^*}{d\lambda} = -\frac{\left.\dfrac{\partial D}{\partial \lambda}\right|_{T = T^*}}{\left.\dfrac{\partial D}{\partial T}\right|_{T = T^*}}, \tag{2.10}$$

where $\left.\partial D/\partial T\right|_{T=T^*} > 0$ because of the second order condition for the optimality of T.

It follows from (10) that $dT^*/d\lambda > 0$ if and only if $\partial D/\partial \lambda < 0$. From (2.4)–(2.6), assuming all the third order partial derivatives to be insignificant, we get:

$$\frac{E_u^\beta\left(1-tc_y^\beta\right)}{A}\cdot\frac{\partial D}{\partial\lambda}=E_u^\alpha+\lambda E_{uu}^\alpha u^\beta . \tag{2.11}$$

We assume the preferences of the consumers to exhibit diminishing marginal utility of income, so that:[14]

$$E_{uu}^i>0\,,\ i=\alpha\,,\beta\,. \tag{2.12}$$

Because of (2.12) and the fact that $A<0$ and $1-tc_y^\beta>0$, we obtain from (2.11) that $\partial D/\partial\lambda$ is always negative. Therefore, we can state the following proposition.

Proposition 2: *Even in the presence of tariff distortions, an increase in altruism on the part of the donor would increase the optimal amount of aid.*

The final exercise we carry out in this section is to see how the optimal level of aid reacts to changes in import tariffs in the recipient country. For this, similar to (2.10), we write:

$$\frac{dT^*}{dt}=-\frac{\left.\dfrac{\partial D}{\partial\lambda}\right|_{T=T^*}}{\left.\dfrac{\partial D}{\partial T}\right|_{T=T^*}} \tag{2.13}$$

For reasons of tractability, we shall only consider an increase in the tariff rate t when its initial level is zero. It follows from (2.13) that $dT^*/dt<0$ if and only $\partial D/\partial t>0$. From (2.4)–(2.6), once again assuming all the third order partial derivatives to be insignificant, we get:

$$\frac{Z}{m^\beta E_{pp}^\beta}\cdot\left.\frac{\partial D}{\partial t}\right|_{t=0,\,T=T^*}=-\frac{E_{uu}^\beta\left(E_{pp}^\beta+E_{pp}^\alpha\right)}{\left(E_u^\beta\right)^2}-\frac{E_{uu}^\alpha\left(E_{pp}^\beta+E_{pp}^\alpha\right)}{E_u^\beta E_u^\alpha}+\left(c_y^\beta-c_y^\alpha\right)^2 . \tag{2.14}$$

It at once follows from (2.13) and (2.14) that dT^*/dt is negative when the initial value for t is zero. Formally:

Proposition 3: *An increase in the tariff on imports (from an initial no tariff situation) by the recipient country results in a reduction in the amount of aid it receives.*

The intuition behind the above result is straightforward. From (2.8) it is clear that a change in tariff (t) affects the optimal level of aid (T^*) basically via changes in the marginal utilities of income in the two countries. An increase in t affects the marginal utility of income in the donor country, $1/E_u^\alpha$, via changes in the international price p and the utility levels in the donor country and the recipient country, u^α and u^β, the latter because of the existence of altruism. An increase in t reduces p and u^α and increases u^β (see (2.4)–(2.6)), implying an unambiguous increase in the marginal utility of income in the donor country. Similarly, an increase in t increases the domestic price in the recipient country ($p + t$) and the utility level u^β, resulting in an unambiguous reduction the level of marginal utility of income in the recipient country. However, the optimality rule (2.8) says that the ratios of marginal utilities should be kept at a constant level. This can only be done by a reduction in the level of aid, which reduces marginal utility of income in the donor country and raises that in the recipient country.

From the above proposition it follows that an increase in tariffs from the initial zero level by the recipient country has two opposing affects on its welfare. First, it has a positive terms of trade effect which is given by the second term on the right hand side of (2.4). But, this increase in tariffs also has a negative effect on the recipient's welfare, given by the first term on the right hand side of (2.4), because of the resultant reduction in the level of aid. Interestingly, it is to be noted that

$$\left.\frac{du^\alpha}{dt}\right|_{t=0} = 0,$$

that is, an increase in tariffs by the recipient country from an initial no tariff situation, has no effect on the welfare level of the donor country. An increase in t has two opposing effects on u^α. First, it results in a deterioration of the donor's terms of trade resulting in a loss of welfare. Second, a deterioration in the donor's terms of trade is an improvement in the recipient's terms of trade. Since the donor also cares about the recipient's welfare because of altruism on the part of the former, this latter effect affects the donor's welfare positively. It so happens that these two opposing effects cancel each other out when aid is chosen optimally. It is to be noted that, because of the envelope theorem, the indirect effect on u^α via changes in the level of aid is absent here.

QUOTAS AND OPTIMAL AID

In this section we shall consider the existence of import quota and assume away that of tariffs. That is, in terms of the model described in section 2, we omit sector 2 from the model. The simplified model is the following:

$$E^\alpha\left(1, p, u^\alpha - \lambda u^\beta\right) = -T, \tag{2.15}$$

$$E^\beta\left(1, p^\beta, u^\beta\right) = T + \left(p^\beta - p\right)E_p^\beta, \tag{2.16}$$

$$E_p^\alpha + E_p^\beta = 0, \tag{2.17}$$

$$E_p^\beta = \overline{m}, \tag{2.18}$$

where $\overline{m}$ is the import quota on the non-numeraire good and p^{β} is the domestic price of that good in country β so that $\left(p^{\beta}-p\right)\overline{m}$ is the quota rent accruing to the consumers in country β.

Totally differentiating (2.15)–(2.18) we get:

$$E_u^{\beta}\, du^{\beta} \;=\; \frac{E_{pp}^{\alpha}}{z}\, dT + \left[p^{\beta} - p + \frac{\overline{m}}{z}\right] d\overline{m}\,, \tag{2.19}$$

$$\begin{aligned} E_u^{\alpha}\, du^{\alpha} \;=\; & -\frac{E_{pp}^{\alpha}}{z}\left(1-\lambda\frac{E_u^{\alpha}}{E_u^{\beta}}\right) dt + E_u^{\alpha} u^{\beta}\, d\lambda \\ & + \left[\frac{\lambda E_u^{\alpha}\left(p^{\beta}-p\right)}{E_u^{\beta}} - \frac{\overline{m}}{z}\left(1-\lambda\frac{E_u^{\alpha}}{E_u^{\beta}}\right)\right] d\overline{m} \end{aligned} \tag{2.20}$$

$$z\, dp \;=\; c_y^{\alpha}\, dT - d\overline{m}\,, \tag{2.21}$$

$$zE_{pp}^{\beta}\, dp^{\beta} \;=\; -c_y^{\beta} E_{pp}^{\alpha}\, dT + \left[z\left\{1-\left(p^{\beta}-p\right)c_y^{\beta}\right\} - c_y^{\beta}\overline{m}\right] d\overline{m}\,, \tag{2.22}$$

where $z = E_{pp}^{\alpha} - m^{\alpha} c_y^{\alpha}$, and the Walrasian stability condition implies that $z < 0$.

We notice that the donor's terms of trade change is negatively, and the recipient's terms of trade positively, related to a small increase in aid $\left(dp/dT < 0,\, dp^{\beta}/dT > 0\right)$. An increase in aid reduces income in the donor country, and the reduced income in turn lowers the demand for, and therefore the international price of, the non-numeraire good. Similarly, increased income in the recipient country raises the demand for, and therefore the domestic price of, the same good. As for welfare, aid unambiguously raises welfare in the recipient country, like in the case of tariffs $\left(du^{\beta}/dT > 0\right)$. However, in contrast to the case of tariffs, the formula for optimal aid in this case is exactly the same as in the case of no distortions.[15] That is, the optimality condition is given by

$$\frac{\partial u^{\alpha}}{\partial T} \equiv H = \frac{E_{pp}^{\alpha}}{E_u^{\alpha} z}\left(1-\frac{\lambda E_u^{\alpha}}{E_u^{\beta}}\right) = 0 \quad \Leftrightarrow \quad \lambda = \frac{E_u^{\beta}}{E_u^{\alpha}} \tag{2.23}$$

which has the same form as (2.9).

To explain the reason for the difference between the optimality condition under tariff and under quota, we refer to the paragraph after (2.9). There we mentioned that, in the presence of tariffs, the aid instrument can affect the basic distortion in the model, viz. too little imports by the recipient, and therefore the optimality rule reflects this additional role for the instrument. However, under quota, the instrument of aid cannot affect the level of imports as it is fixed, and therefore aid does not have any role in correcting the trade distortion.

Like in the preceding section, we shall carry out two exercises here, viz., we shall attempt to obtain the signs of $dT^*/d\lambda$ and $dT^*/d\overline{m}$. Concerning the former, we obtain:

$$\frac{dT^*}{d\lambda} = -\frac{\left.\dfrac{\partial H}{\partial \lambda}\right|_{T=T^*}}{\left.\dfrac{\partial H}{\partial T}\right|_{T=T^*}} \tag{2.24}$$

where H is defined in (2.23) and the denominator on the right hand side of (2.24) is positive because of the second order condition for optimality of T^*.

Clearly, $dT^*/d\lambda > 0$ if and only if $\partial H/\partial\lambda < 0$ at $T = T^*$. From the expression of H in (2.23), we obtain:

$$E_u^{\beta} \left.\frac{\partial H}{\partial \lambda}\right|_{T=T^*} = -E_u^{\alpha} - \lambda u^{\beta} E_{uu}^{\alpha}. \tag{2.25}$$

Since $E_{uu}^{\alpha} > 0$ (see (2.12)), we can say from (2.24) and (2.25) that an increase in λ raises T^*. Formally,

Proposition 4: *Even in the presence of import quota, an increase in altruism on the part of the donor raises the amount of aid given.*

Turning to the last exercise, i.e. obtaining the sign of $dT^*/d\overline{m}$, we shall once again, for the sake of tractability, consider a reduction in $\overline{m}$ from the free trade level of imports characterised by $p^{\beta} = p$. From the expression of H in (2.23) we get:

$$\frac{dT^*}{d\overline{m}} = -\frac{\left.\dfrac{\partial H}{\partial \overline{m}}\right|_{T=T^*}}{\left.\dfrac{\partial H}{\partial T}\right|_{T=T^*}} \tag{2.26}$$

and

$$z \left.\frac{\partial H}{\partial \overline{m}}\right|_{T=T^*, p^{\beta}=p} = c_y^{\alpha} + \frac{z - c_y^{\beta}\overline{m}}{E_{pp}^{\beta}} + \frac{E_{uu}^{\beta}\overline{m}}{\left(E_u^{\beta}\right)^2} + \frac{E_{uu}^{\alpha}\overline{m}}{E_{uu}^{\beta}E_u^{\alpha}}. \tag{2.27}$$

From (2.26) and (2.27) it follows that

$$\left.\frac{dT^*}{d\overline{m}}\right|_{p^{\beta}=p} > 0.$$

That is, if the recipient country reduces the level of import quota (from the free trade level), the amount of aid receives will go down as a result. Formally:

***Proposition 5:** A decrease in import quota (from an initial free trade level) by the recipient country results in a reduction in the amount of aid it receives.*

The intuition behind this result is similar to the one for the case of tariffs (see the paragraph after proposition 3). We conclude this section by noting that, as in the case of tariffs, a decrease in the level of quota (from the initial free trade level) has no effect on the welfare level of the donor country when the amount of aid is optimally set. The reason for this result is the same as in the case of tariffs.

CONCLUSION

Why does a country give aid? Why do countries receive aid? How does a donor country decide how much aid to give? The first two questions have been discussed extensively in the literature of both development economics and international trade theory. The motives for giving aid on the part of the donor and that for receiving aid on the part of the recipient, have been shown to be numerous. However, the third question is a relatively neglected one. The bulk of the trade theoretic models cannot themselves justify why countries give untied aid. In some of the cases where aid improves the welfare of both the recipient and the donor countries and therefore where its existence can be justified, there is no reason why the amount of aid given should be limited.

This chapter develops a model which can answer the three questions raised at the outset of this section. The model is built on the assumption that the consumers in the donor country are altruistic in the sense that they care about the welfare of their counterparts in the recipient country. This assumption of altruism is a major point of departure from the existing literature which assumes self interest on the part of the donors. This is not to say that we do not believe self-interest is never a motive of the donors. In fact, there is strong empirical evidence to suggest that selfish motives are indeed important determinants of aid. However, selfish motives cannot be the only reasons why we observe aid, and we strongly believe that simple and old-fashioned altruism is a very important determinant of aid as well. Having set up the model and shown the existence of an optimal amount of aid which is neither zero nor infinity, we examined how the amount of aid given reacts to trade policy changes in the recipient country. We considered two alternative forms of trade policy, viz. tariff and quota. We find that tightening of trade restrictions in the recipient country is likely to lead to a fall in the amount of aid it receives, no matter what form the trade restriction takes. This happens because an increased restriction on trade by the recipient country reduces the domestic price and the utility level in the donor country, and increases them in the recipient country, implying unambiguous increase in the level of marginal utility of income in the donor country and an unambiguous decrease in the marginal utility of income in the recipient country. This divergence in the marginal utilities in the two countries due to an increase in the level of protection in the recipient country can be counteracted only by an reduction in the level of transfer. Thus, any attempt by the recipient country to intervene in trade in a way that brings its trade policy closer to what is non-cooperative optimal, and therefore damaging to the donor country, will be met by retaliation by the donor in the form of reduced aid. In other words, one of the policy implications of our paper is that, even though the donor country gives aid to the recipient country because of simple altruism on the part of the former, there is a role of trade policies in determining the exact quantity of aid that is given. The recipient country can increase the amount of aid it receives by liberalising its trade policy.

To summarise, in this paper we have attempted to explain the existence of foreign aid in terms of a simple of model of international trade in which the trade relationship between the two countries and the interdependence of preferences between the consumers of the two countries have implications for the amount of aid that is actually transferred.

NOTES

[1] Some of the early literature is reviewed by Bhagwati, Brecher and Hatta (1983); a more recent survey is provided by Kemp (1992).

[2] Most studies work within a static framework; the exceptions are Galor and Polemarchakis (1987) and Djajić, Lahiri and Raimondos-Møller (1996a, 1996b).

[3] Lahiri and Raimondos-Møller (1997) consider the question of allocation of foreign aid between alternative recipients. In their analysis, the total amount of aid is exogenous, but the allocation between the two recipients is endogenous.

[4] See, for example, Maizel and Nissanke (1984).

[5] See Sen (1987) for an excellent discussion of the issues.

[6] See Ahmad et al (1991) for in depth analysis of the social security arrangements in developing countries.

[7] Since factor endowments do not change in our analysis, they are left out of the revenue functions.

[8] See Dixit and Norman (1980) for the properties of a revenue function.

[9] See Dixit and Norman (1980) for properties of an expenditure function.

[10] For a discussion of these issues see Kemp and Kojima (1985).

[11] The world market clearing equation for the numeraire commodity has been omitted due to Walras's law.

[12] Note that, by considering only one non-numeraire sector, we drop the subscripts 2 and 3 that refer to the sectors.

[13] From the normality assumption it also follows that $1-tc_y^\beta>0$ irrespective of the sign of t.

[14] See Dixit and Norman (1980, pp. 60–61).

[15] This is not to say that the optimal level of aid is the same as in the case of no distortions.

REFERENCES

Ahmad, E., J. Dréze, J. Hills and A. Sen (eds.), 1991, *Social security in developing countries* (Oxford: Clarendon Press).

Bhagwati, J. N., R. Brecher and T. Hatta, 1983, The generalized theory of transfers and welfare: bilateral transfers in a multilateral world, *American Economic Review* 73, 4, 57–76.

Bhagwati, J. N., R. Brecher and T. Hatta, 1985, The generalized theory of transfer and welfare: exogenous (policy-imposed) and endogenous (transfer-induced) distortions, *Quarterly Journal of Economics*, 100, 697–714.

Brecher, R. A. and J. N. Bhagwati, 1982, Immiserising transfers from abroad, *Journal of International Economics*, 13, 353–64.

Dixit, A. and V. Norman, 1980, *Theory of international trade*, (Cambridge University Press, Cambridge).

Dixit, A., 1983, The multi-country transfer problem, *Economics Letters* , 13, 49–54.

Djajić, S., S. Lahiri and P. Raimondos-Møller, 1996a, Foreign aid, domestic investment and welfare, Discussion Paper No.463 , Department of Economics, University of Essex.

Djajić, S., S. Lahiri and P. Raimondos-Møller, 1996b, Logic of aid in an intertemporal setting, EPRU Working Paper 96-21, Copenhagen Business School.

Gale, D., 1974, Exchange equilibrium and coalitions: an example, *Journal of Mathematical Economics*, 1, 63–66.

Galor, O., and H. Polemarchakis, Intertemporal equilibrium and the transfer paradox, *Review of Economic Studies*, 54, 147–156.

Hatzipanayotou, P. and M.S. Michael, 1995, Foreign aid and public goods, *Journal of Development Economics*, 47, 455–467.

Hopkin, B., 1970, Aid and the balance of payments, *Economic Journal* 80, 1–23.

Kemp, M. C., 1992, The static welfare economics of foreign aid: A consolidation, chapter 13 in D. Savoie and I. Brecher (eds.), *Equity and efficiency in economic development: essays in honor of Benjamin Higgins*, McGill-Queens University Press, Montreal, 289–314.

Kemp, M.C. and S. Kojima, 1985, More on the effects of foreign aid, *Journal of Japanese and International Economics* 1, 97–109.

Kemp, M. C. and K.-Y. Wong, 1993, Paradoxes associated with the administration of foreign aid, *Journal of Development Economics*, 42, 197–204.

Khilji, N.M. and E.M. Zampelli, 1994, The fungibility of U.S. military and non-military assistance and the impacts on major aid recipients, *Journal of Development Economics* 43, 345–362.

Lahiri, S. and P. Raimondos-Møller, 1995, Welfare effects of aid under quantitative trade restrictions, *Journal of International Economics* 39, 297–315.

Lahiri, S., P. Raimondos-Møller, 1997, On the tying of aid to tariff reform, *Journal of Development Economics*, 54, 479–491.

Lahiri, S. and P. Raimondos-Møller, 1997, Competition for aid and trade policy, *Journal of International Economics* 43, 369–385.

Lahiri, S., P. Raimondos-Møller, K-y. Wong and A. Woodland, 1997, Optimal income transfers and tariffs, EPRU Working Paper 97-06, Copenhagen Business School.

Maizel, A., and M.K. Nissanke, 1984, Motivation for aid to developing countries, *World Development*, 12, 879–900.

McKinlay, R.D. and R. Little, 1977, A foreign policy model of US bilateral aid allocation, *World Politics* 30, 58–86.

Ohyama, M., 1974, Tariffs and transfer problem, *Keio Economic Studies*, 11, 29–45.

Schweinberger, A.G., 1990, On the welfare effects of tied aid, *International Economic Review* 31, 2, 457–462.

Samuelson, P. A., 1954, The transfer problem and transport costs II: analysis of effects of trade impediments, *Economic Journal* 64, 278–304.

Sen, A., 1987, *On ethics and economics* (Oxford: Basil Blackwell)

Stark, O., 1995, *Altruism and beyond* (Cambridge: Cambridge University Press).

Trumbull, W.N. and H.J. Wall, 1994, Estimating aid allocation criteria with panel data, *Economic Journal* 104, 876–882.

Turunen-Red, A. H. and A. D. Woodland, 1988, On the multilateral transfer problem: existence of Pareto improving international transfers, *Journal of International Economics*, 22, 57–64.

CHAPTER 3

FOREIGN AID AND THE WELFARE COST OF INFLATION

Ebenezer Asem
and
Kanhaya L. Gupta

INTRODUCTION

Foreign aid has been of interest to many economists and over the years large empirical and theoretical discussions on foreign aid have emerged. The debate has focused on the effects of foreign aid on national saving, investment, and growth [see, Obstfeld (1995) for an overview of the empirical and theoretical debates]. The issue of whether foreign aid has any effect on the welfare cost of inflation, however, has not been addressed presumably because of the less obvious relationship between foreign aid and the welfare cost of inflation. In this paper, we investigate whether an inflow of foreign aid has any effect on the welfare cost of inflation, and if so, how the welfare cost is affected. This will throw more light on the effects of foreign aid. Official development assistance has been an important source of external financing for many developing countries accounting for about 99.7% of net foreign resource inflow to the least-developed countries, about 55.6% to the low-income developing countries, and about 9.9% to high-income developing countries in the period 1992–1995[1]. The least-developed countries for which foreign aid constitutes quite substantial proportion of their net external financial receipts are likely to be the countries that rely heavily on inflation tax[2] to finance their public expenditures and this emphasizes the importance of studying the effect of foreign aid on the welfare cost of inflation. If foreign aid increases the welfare cost of inflation as the study suggests, the potential benefits of foreign aid will be reduced.

As far back as the 1920s, Keynes and Ohlin attempted to address the question of whether international transfers raise the recipient country's saving more or less than its investment, and if so by what amount. This started the debate on the effects of foreign aid on national savings, investment, and growth in recipient countries. The framework that is usually used to study the effects of foreign aid is a modified version of the Harrod-Domar growth model [see, for example, Papanek (1972), and Grinols and Bhagwati (1975)]. The traditional argument following from the accounting relationship that equates investment with the sum of domestic and foreign savings from these models suggests that the two forms of savings are additive. That is foreign aid would add to domestic saving and this would increase investment and growth.

These models thus predict that foreign aid would increase savings and investment which would enable the economy to grow faster. This positive view of the effect of foreign aid is also support by Barro (1990), who argues that foreign aid would allow the benevolent dictator (social planner) to reduce distortionary taxes and this would lead to faster growth and investment.

Not all economists agree that foreign aid would increase savings, investment and growth. Indeed, there are both theoretical and empirical reasons to doubt the predictions of the Harrod-Domar based models. A theoretical shortcoming of these models is that the behavioral relationships are not based on any welfare objective. Any plausible intertemporal utility function would lead optimizing agents to marginally allocate any increase in available resource partly to current and future consumption, and partly to current and future investment. In fact, Friedman (1958) and Bauer (1971) for example, argue that recipient countries would consume foreign aid since lack of domestic savings reflects lack of investment opportunities. They blame political regimes for introducing distortionary policies that benefit the political elites and perpetrate poverty in developing countries. Thus they contend that foreign aid can actually cause poverty if it strengthens 'harmful' political regimes. Boone (1996) models politics and the effectiveness of foreign aid and finds that the impact of foreign aid is not sensitive to the type of political regime. He argues that foreign aid benefits the wealthy political elites whether the regime is liberal and democratic or highly repressive.

In this chapter, we try to capture an entirely different potential influence of foreign aid, that is its effect on the welfare cost of inflation. An increase in foreign aid can increase consumption directly [Friedman (1958) and Bauer (1971)] or indirectly through investment and growth [Papanek (1972), and Grinols and Bhagwati (1975)]. The increase in consumption will decrease the marginal utility of consumption and this, in equilibrium, will lead to an increase in leisure for any plausible utility function[3] that has consumption and leisure as its arguments. The question of interest is how these endogenous changes induced by foreign aid influence the cost of leisure relative to consumption, as leisure increases when there is inflation[4]. The study shows that the cost of leisure decreases as foreign aid increases. This means that for a given inflation, economic agents will reduce labor supply more when the country is receiving foreign aid. Thus, the distortion caused by inflation is "deepened" by foreign aid and this results in a larger welfare cost.

THE MODEL

The Economic Environment

Economic agents are assumed to be identical and live infinitely with preferences defined over consumption and leisure. The representative economic agent consequently maximizes the expected value of a discounted stream of utilities given by equation (3.1);

$$\max_{C_t, I_t} E_0 \sum_{t=0}^{\infty} \beta^t U(C_t, L_t), \quad 0 < \beta < 1, \tag{3.1}$$

where C_t and L_t are consumption and leisure, respectively at time t, and β is the rate of time discount. E_0 is the expectation conditional on information at time t=0. The utility function is assumed to be well behaved, being concave and increasing in both consumption and leisure.

Factor inputs are supplied by the representative household who rents out the household's capital stock, K_t, at real interest rate r_t, and also supplies N_t units of labor at real wage rate w_t in any period t to the firms. Thus, at the end of period t, the household receives $r_t K_{p,t}$ as payment for hiring out its capital, $w_t N_t$ as wage earning, and V_t as lump sum transfer payment from the government. These, in addition to the household's undepreciated capital and it's unspent money balances constitute the funds available to the households in any period t. The household's resources are used to finance consumption, as well as capital and money balances that are carried to period t+1. Thus, the typical household's budget constraint can be described by equation (3.2);

$$C_t + K_{t+1} + \frac{M_{t+1}}{P_t} \le r_t K_t + w_t N_t + (1 - \delta_K) K_t + \frac{M_t + V_t}{P_t}. \tag{3.2}$$

Labor supply is also subject to a time constraint which is normalized to one and is described by equation (3.3), and consumption is subject to a CIA constraint (3.4).

$$1 \ge L_t + N_t \tag{3.3}$$

$$P_t C_t \le M_t + V_t \tag{3.4}$$

The government's role in the economy is to print fiat money and receive foreign aid which it transfers to economic agents. In any period t, therefore, the government's budget constraint can be described by equation (3.5);

$$\frac{M_{t+1} - M_t}{P_t} + FA_t = \frac{V_t}{P_t}\,^{5}, \tag{3.5}$$

where M_t is per capita nominal money balance in period t, FA_t[6] is per capita real foreign aid in period t, and V_t is lump-sum per capita transfer payment in period t. It is assumed that the government is credible in its announcement of money growth rates at the beginning of each period, and hence the model abstracts from any unanticipated money growth or unexpected inflation effect.

The representative firm hires K_t units of capital and n_t units of labor to produce output Y_t. Output can be consumed or invested; that is $Y_t = C_t + I_t$, where I_t is gross per capita investment in period t, and Y_t is per capita output. The production function is assumed to be described by equation (3.6);

$$Y_t = F(K_t, n_t; z_t), \tag{3.6}$$

where z_t is the productivity shock, and K_t is per capita private capital in period t. The evolution of capital is described by equation (3.7);

$$K_{t+1} = (1-\delta_K)K_t + I_t, \tag{3.7}$$

where δ_K is the rate of depreciation assumed to be the same for both private and public capital.

Equilibrium Conditions

The representative household's problem is to choose consumption, labor supply, stock of capital, and money balances such that equation (3.1) is maximized subject to the constraints in (3.2), (3.3), and (3.4). The solution to the household's problem can be obtained by solving the following Bellman's equation;

$$V(K_t, M_t; S_t) = \max_{C_t, l_t, K_{t+1}, M_{t+1}} [U(C_t, L_t) + \beta E_t V(K_{t+1}, M_{t+1}; S_{t+1})], \tag{3.8}$$

where $S_t=(K_t, M_t; z_t)$ is the state of the economy in period t.

The firm's optimization problem involves choosing K_t and n_t to maximize profits. That is, firms solve equation (3.9);

$$\max_{K_t, n_t}[F(K_t, n_t; z_t) - r_t K_t - w_t n_t]. \tag{3.9}$$

Competitive equilibrium allocation rules for the households and the firms are defined by the market clearing conditions in (3.10)–(3.12), CIA constraint (3.13), and efficiency equations (3.14) and (3.15);

$$C_t + K_{t+1} = F(K_t, n_t; z_t) + (1-\delta_K)K_t + FA_t, \tag{3.10}$$

$$N_t = n_t, \tag{3.11}$$

$$M_{t+1} + P_t FA_t = M_t + V_t, \tag{3.12}$$

$$P_t C_t = M_t + V_t, \tag{3.13}$$

$$U_2(C_t, L_t) = \beta E_t\left[\frac{U_1(C_{t+1}, L_{t+1})}{P_{t+1}/P_t}\right] F_2(K_t, n_t; z_t), \tag{3.14}$$

$$\frac{U_2(C_t, L_t)}{F_2(K_t, n_t; z_t)} = \beta E_t\left[\frac{U_2(C_{t+1}, L_{t+1})}{F_2(K_{t+1}, n_{t+1}; z_{t+1})}\right][F_1(K_{,t+1}, n_{t+1}; z_{t+1}) + 1 - \delta_K], \tag{3.15}$$

where U_i and F_i are the differentials of the respective function with respect to the i–th argument and E_t is the expectation operator at time t.

Equation (3.14) guides the consumer's labor supply decision. From this equation, the consumer's equilibrium is characterized by equating the marginal cost of reducing leisure to the marginal benefit of labor supply in terms of utility. The LHS of (3.14) can be interpreted as measuring the cost of reducing leisure, and the RHS as measuring the benefit from the last unit of labor supply. The benefit from the last unit of labor supply is equal to the time t expected discounted marginal benefit of the real returns from labor. The presence of inflation in the allocation rule is due to the cash-in-advance constraint which ensures that income earned in any period can only be spent the next period. Thus, perfectly anticipated inflation distorts labor supply and hence influences the real variables in the economy. This, potentially, affects the economy in two ways. Firstly, in multiple goods environment with credit goods, this can lead to a deviation of the marginal rate of substitution between cash and credit goods from their marginal rate of transformation (e.g. Braun, 1994). Secondly, the reduction in labor supply will reduce overall output. These effects of inflation underpin most of the welfare cost of inflation studied within the CIA models (see e.g. Cooley and Hansen, 1989, 1991)[7]. Since only the second inflationary distortion is captured in the setup here, the model abstracts from a more general economic environment where inflation causes additional distortions (e.g. Dotsey and Ireland, 1996) and rather focuses on the effect of foreign aid on the welfare cost of inflation.

Equation (3.15) governs the household's capital demand. The equation indicates that the consumer will equate the cost of acquiring capital to its benefits in equilibrium. The cost of acquiring the marginal unit of capital is given by the LHS of equation (3.15). The benefit is the return earned by holding the marginal unit of capital for one period which is given by the next period's marginal product of capital plus undepreciated capital valued in that period's utility and discounted to period t.

MODEL PARAMETERIZATION AND CALIBRATION

In order to solve for the competitive equilibrium, specific forms of the utility and the production functions are assumed and values assigned to the various parameters in the model. The paper focuses on steady states since the cyclical characteristics of the model, like most other models of the welfare cost of inflation, are unaffected by the average growth rate of money (see Cooley and Hansen, 1989). For steady state to be feasible, permanent technical change must be expressible in labor augmenting form (Swan, 1963, and Phelps, 1966). Consistent with this and adopting a Cobb-Douglas production function, the following technical production constraint is used:

$$Y_t = K_t^{\theta_1}(z_t n_t)^{\theta_2}, \ \theta_1+\theta_2=1, \tag{3.16}$$

where z_t is permanent productivity shock. Temporary productivity shocks are ignored here and attention is focused on steady state welfare. The production function, as specified by (3.16), implies that the steady state growth rate of output, capital, and consumption per capita are all equal to the growth rate of the labor augmenting technical progress, and the growth rate of labor is zero.

The feasible steady state growth rate would be compatible with an optimal competitive equilibrium if restrictions are imposed on the utility function (see King et al., 1988, for these conditions). The conditions imply the following class of utility functions;

$$U(C,L) = \frac{C^{1-\sigma}}{1-\sigma}V(L), \tag{3.17}$$

where $1/\sigma$ is the constant intertemporal elasticity of substitution in consumption for these functions[8]. To fully parameterize the utility function, the following constant relative risk aversion functional form is adopted;

$$U(C_t, L_t) = \frac{[C_t^{\omega}, L_t^{1-\omega}]^{1-\gamma}}{1-\gamma}, \qquad 0 < \gamma < 1 < \gamma, \tag{3.18}$$

where γ is the coefficient of relative risk aversion and ω determines the relative importance of consumption and leisure.

To analyze the model with steady state growth, the economy is transformed into a stationary one where the dynamics facilitate computation. This balanced growth transformation involves dividing all real variables in the model by the growth component, z_t, so that $c_t=C_t/z_t$, $y_t=Y_t/z_t$, $k_t=K_t/z_t$, and $p_t=P_tz_t/M_t$ are stationary.

Given the homogeneity properties of the utility and the production functions and the transformations, the efficiency equations (3.14) and (3.15), and the market clearing conditions (3.10)–(3.12) can be transformed to give the following equations which facilitate computation of equilibrium;

$$c_t + \left(\frac{z_{t+1}}{z_t}\right) k_t = F(k_t, n_t) + (1-\delta_K) k_t, \tag{3.19}$$

$$\mu U_2(c_t, L_t) = \beta \left(\frac{z_{t+1}}{z_t}\right)^{1-\sigma} E_t\left[\frac{U_1(c_{t+1}, L_{t+1})}{p_{t+1}/p_t}\right] F_2(k_t, n_t), \tag{3.20}$$

$$\frac{U_2(c_t, L_t)}{F_2(k_t, n_t)} = \beta \left(\frac{z_{t+1}}{z_t}\right)^{-\sigma} E_t\left[\frac{U_2(c_{t+1}, L_{t+1})}{F_2(k_{t+1}, n_{t+1})}\right] [F_1(k_{t+1}, n_{t+1}) + 1 - \delta_K], \tag{3.21}$$

$$m_{t+1} = m, \tag{3.22}$$

$$p_t c_t = m \tag{3.23}$$

The model is calibrated to represent a typical developing country. The procedure used here is to infer the values of the various parameters from their US counterparts. Capital's share of income in the US is about 34%[9]. Since the contribution of capital to output in the US is higher than in a typical developing country, we calibrated with 20%. Depreciation rate of 0.025 per quarter is used for capital[10] as in most US business cycle models (see Kyland and Prescott, 1982, Cooley and Hansen, 1989, and King et al., 1988). Following evidence from the study by Mehra and Prescott (1985), that the coefficient of relative risk aversion lies between 1 and 2, we set this to 1.5[11]. Evidence also indicates that the per capita time spent on work by US working population is about 24% (see, for example, Gomme, 1993). We calibrated using .3[12]. The parameter ω, which governs the importance of consumption relative to leisure is set such that, on average, this proportion of time is spent on work in the benchmark economy. The value of ω together with the value of σ implies that γ is equal to 2.27167. The time discount factor, β, is chosen such that the real return on capital of 5% per annum is obtained. This yielded a value of 0.999 by equation (3.15).

WELFARE ANALYSIS

This section deals with the welfare measures of different monetary and fiscal policies for the economic framework described earlier. This enables us to compute the welfare losses that result from inflation for different levels of foreign aid. To do this, let the sum of discounted utilities of the representative agent be V^{a1}, then V^{a1} will be given by equation (3.24);

$$V^{a1}(m_0,k_0;s,\lambda)=E_0\sum_{t=0}^{\infty}\beta^t U(c_t^{a1}+\lambda y_t^{a1},L_t^{a1}), \tag{3.24}$$

where the superscripts "a" and "1" denote equilibrium values of the relevant variable for monetary policy "a" and foreign aid level "1", respectively[13], and λy_t is a lump-sum equivalent variation payment made to households to attain a certain utility level. Using these definitions, the welfare cost of operating monetary policy "a" under foreign aid level "1" rather than monetary policy "b" and foreign aid level "2" is measured by the value of λ satisfying equation (3.25);

$$V^{a1}(m_0,k_0;s,\lambda)=V^{b2}(k_0,m_0;s,\lambda=0). \tag{3.25}$$

The value function in (25) can be rewritten as;

$$V^{a1}(m_0,k_0;s,\lambda)=z_0^{1-\sigma}E_0\sum_{t=0}^{\infty}\beta^t U(c_t^{a1}+\lambda y_t^{a1},L_t^{a1})\left[\prod_{\tau=0}^{t}\frac{z_{\tau+1}^{a1}}{z_\tau^{a1}}\right]^{\sigma}, \tag{3.26}$$

and in steady state equation (3.26) can be written as

$$V^{a1}(m_0,k_0;s,\lambda)=\frac{z_0^{1-\sigma}U(c^{a1}+\lambda y^{a1},L^{a1})}{1-\beta\left[\left(\frac{z_{t+1}}{z_t}\right)^{a1}\right]^{1-\sigma}}. \tag{3.27}$$

Thus, if zero inflation policy is denoted by an asterisks superscript, then the cost of operating monetary policy "a" relative to a zero inflation policy, given foreign aid level "Ω", will be given by (3.28);

$$U(c^{*\Omega},L^{*\Omega})=U(c^{a\Omega}+\lambda y^{a\Omega},L^{a\Omega}),\qquad \text{for } \Omega=1,2,... \tag{3.28}$$

The steady state results obtained from experiments with various monetary policies under different foreign aid levels are reported in Table 3.1. Experiments were conducted for zero, 10%, 20%, and 100% inflation for a fixed exogenous gross growth rate of 1.00766 per quarter, the average quarterly per capita growth rate for low income developing countries between 1960 and 1990 (see Gillis et al., 1992). The effect of inflation is considered when there is no foreign aid and when foreign aid is 10%, 20%, and 30% of recipient nation's income[14].

From the tables, the welfare cost of 10% inflation when there is no foreign aid is .8415% of income. The corresponding figures when foreign aid is 10%, 20%, and 30%

Table 3.1. Welfare Cost of Inflation Under levels of Foreign Aid.

NO FOREIGN AID				
	Inflation			
Variable	zero	10%	20%	100%
n	0.306494	0.297295	0.288996	0.243701
k	2.482077	2.407582	2.340375	1.973563
c	0.384629	0.373085	0.36267	0.305828
y	0.465693	0.451717	0.439107	0.370285
p	2.619825	2.766015	2.908019	3.918266
U	−1.681749	−1.690294	−1.69893	−1.763987
V	−350.048828	−351.827423	−353.624878	−367.166229
wel cost	0	.003801	.007447	.030641
FOREIGN AID IS 10% OF INCOME				
	Inflation			
Variable	zero	10%	20%	100%
n	0.286596	0.277797	0.269898	0.226901
k	2.320942	2.249686	2.185718	1.837509
c	0.403205	0.390826	0.379713	0.319221
y	0.435461	0.422092	0.41009	0.344758
p	2.499126	2.640454	2.777497	3.75388
u	−1.607087	−1.616972	−1.62675	−1.697562
v	−334.508118	−336.565613	−338.600891	−353.340088
wel cost	0	.004823	.009349	.036954

n is labor supply, k is capital, c is consumption, y is income, p is price level, u is one period utility, and v is the value function.

of recipient country's income is 1.1426%, 1.4781%, and 1.7932% of income, respectively. Thus, with foreign aid the welfare cost of inflation increases. The reason is straightforward. The increase in goods and services[15] made possible by foreign aid leads to increases in consumption and leisure. This has the effect of reducing the marginal utilities of both consumption and leisure. Whilst the lower marginal utility of consumption induces the consumer to reduce labor more when there is inflation, the lower marginal utility of leisure induces the agent to reduce labor by less. Thus, whether economic agents will reduce labor supply by more or less when there is foreign aid will depend on the cost of increasing leisure at different levels of income (foreign aid increases income). The results show that the relative cost of leisure de-

Table 3.1 *(continued)*. Welfare Cost of Inflation Under levels of Foreign Aid .

FOREIGN AID IS 20% OF INCOME				
	Inflation			
Variable	zero	10%	20%	100%
n	0.269098	0.2607	0.253201	0.2123
k	2.17924	2.111223	2.050494	1.719272
c	0.419475	0.406383	0.394693	0.330938
y	0.408875	0.396113	0.384719	0.322574
p	2.402191	2.539373	2.67208	3.620975
u	−1.546423	−1.557345	−1.567979	−1.643342
v	-321.881317	-324.154541	-326.368103	-342.054565
welcost		.005855	.011174	.042868
FOREIGN AID IS 30% OF INCOME				
	Inflation			
Variable	zero	10%	20%	100%
n	0.253601	0.245501	0.238301	0.1995
k	2.053733	1.98814	1.929832	1.615612
c	0.43385	0.419993	0.407675	0.341279
y	0.385327	0.37302	0.36208	0.303125
p	2.322602	2.457084	2.58699	3.511068
u	−1.496168	−1.508036	−1.519471	−1.598206
v	-311.420807	-313.891113	-316.271332	-332.659668
welcost		.006689	.012798	.04814

n is labor supply, k is capital, c is consumption, y is income, p is price level, u is one period utility, and v is the value function.

creases when there is an inflows of foreign aid. In particular, with no inflation, the marginal utility of leisure per unit marginal utility of consumption is .855959, .8722712, .8857438, and .897077[16] when foreign aid is zero, 10%, 20%, and 30% of recipient's income, respectively. The less penalty suffered by agents when they reduce labor in the presence of foreign aid leads to a larger reduction in the labor supply and domestic output, which results in a higher welfare cost when there is inflation. With a 10% inflation, for example, the labor supply decreased by 3.01%, 3.07%, 3.12%, and 3.19%, when foreign aid is zero, 10%, 20%, and 30%, respectively. It should be noted, however, that despite the decrease in labor supply and output, the level of consumption and welfare are higher with foreign aid.

It is worth mentioning that the reduction in labor supply due to foreign aid has the effect of increasing the marginal product of labor which tends to increase the welfare cost associated with increasing leisure when there is inflation. This effect, however, is "neutralized" in this model[17] by a reduction in the demand for capital when there is an inflow of foreign aid. The reason for this is that labor and capital are complimentary in production. If they were substitutes, then a reduction in labor supply would lead to an increase in capital which would increase the marginal product of labor further. In this case, the effect of foreign aid on welfare would be ambiguous and the welfare cost of inflation could decrease with an inflow of foreign aid.

From the tables, a 20% inflation costs 1.69594%, 2.27974%, 2.90445%, and 3.53457% of income when foreign aid is zero, 10%, 20%, and 30%, respectively. The corresponding welfare costs when inflation is 100% are 8.27497%, 10.71882%, 13.28935%, and 15.88123%. These results suggest that the welfare cost of inflation increases with increasing levels of foreign aid. The study, therefore, suggests that if recipient countries rely on inflationary finance then the benefits of foreign aid would not be as much as traditional methods which ignore the effect on the cost of inflation would suggest. For example, a developing country with a 10% inflation and no foreign aid would incur an inflationary welfare cost of about .3% of income if it starts receiving 10% of its income in foreign aid. The corresponding figures when it starts receiving 20% and 30% of its income in foreign aid are about .6% and 1% of income, respectively. At 20% inflation, a developing country would incur additional welfare cost of about .6%, 1.2%, and 1.8% if it receives 10%, 20%, and 30% of income in foreign aid, respectively. The additional welfare costs when inflation is 100% are about 2.4%, 5%, and 7.6% of income. Thus, depending on the rate of inflation and the level of foreign aid, the additional inflationary cost can be substantial and this reduces the "effective" aid received. "Effective" aid here is the actual aid minus the associated inflationary cost. For example, if a developing country has 100% inflation and 20% of its income is in foreign aid, the "effective" aid will be 15%.

CONCLUSION

The main lesson from this study is that the welfare cost of inflation is sensitive to the flow of foreign aid. In particular, the study reveals that foreign aid can increase the welfare cost of inflation which reduces any potential benefits associated with an inflow of aid. This is because foreign aid changes the relative importance of leisure and consumption in the utility function and consequently impacts on the welfare cost of inflation. Specifically, the marginal utility of leisure per unit marginal utility of consumption increases with inflows of foreign aid which means that leisure becomes relatively more important. This induces economic agents to substitute more away from labor and into leisure when there is inflation resulting in a higher welfare cost of inflation.

A mitigating factor against this effect is that a reduction in labor supply as a result of an inflow of foreign aid would potentially increase the marginal product of labor which would make substituting away from labor more expensive. However, in the model used here labor and capital are complementary inputs and consequently both labor and capital decrease with an inflow of foreign aid such that the marginal product of labor is preserved. If capital and labor are substitutes or the reduction in capital is not sufficient to "neutralize" the effect of the reduction in labor on its marginal product then the effect of foreign aid on the welfare cost of inflation would be ambiguous.

The study suggests that the welfare cost of inflation is not independent of foreign aid. In particular, foreign aid "deepens" the distortions caused by inflation and consequently leads to a higher inflation cost. This suggests that if foreign aid is combined with inflation reduction policies, the potential benefits of foreign aid would be better realized particularly for high inflation developing countries.

NOTES

[1] Data are compiled from tables in OECD, *Geographical Distribution of Financial Flows to Aid Recipients*, 1991–1995; 25–35.

[2] Calculations from Cukierman et al. (1992) suggest that inflation tax is over 20% for some developing countries between the period 1971–1982.

[3] If utility is linear in both arguments, the importance of leisure relative to consumption will not change. However, if the utility function is concave, as is commonly assumed, the relative importance of the arguments could change at different levels of income.

[4] In CIA models, inflation decreases the effective return on labor and this induces the substitution out of labor to leisure.

[5] Also see Boone, 1996, where foreign aid received by the government can be transferred to economic agents.

[6] To simplify the analysis, it is assumed that foreign aid is fixed at a certain level forever.

[7] In their formulation, inflation causes economic agents to inefficiently substitute out of market activities and into leisure, devote more productive time to economize on the holding of cash, and reduces the growth rate as well and the level of output through allocative effects.

[8] The assumption of concavity of U(C,l) implies that V(l) is increasing and concave for σ less than or equal to 1 and decreasing and convex for σ greater than 1.

[9] Capital's share of income has been relatively stable in the US since the post-war [see Prescott (1986)].

[10] We believe the rate of capital depreciation is the same for the US and developing countries in the absence of evidence to the contrary.

[11] We also calibrated with 2 and there is only a slight different in the effect of foreign aid. With a coefficient of 1.5, the welfare cost of 10% inflation increased by .9517% of income when foreign aid is increased from zero to 30%. The corresponding figure when the coefficient is 2 is .943%. The welfare cost of 100% inflation when foreign aid is increased by the same amount is 7.714% and 7.606% of income when the coefficient is 2 and 1.5, respectively.

[12] The 24% of time endowment spend on market activities for the US works out to a time about 40 hours a week. In a typical developing country, we can assume 6 days of 8 hours a day which works to roughly 30%.

[13] The first superscript describes monetary policy (uses alphabets), and the second denotes the level of foreign aid (uses numbers).

[14] See World Bank Development Report 1990, pp. 216–217, where foreign aid varies from less than .5% to over 30% of recipient nation's for low income developing countries.

[15] It should be noted that foreign aid, by increasing imports, increases consumption in this model although it reduces domestic output via reduction in labor supply.

[16] The importance of leisure relative to consumption can be measured by $\frac{U_l}{U_c} = \frac{(1-\omega)c}{\omega l}$

[17] For example, with zero inflation the marginal product of labor is 1.2155383, 1.2155388, 1.215539, and 1.2155381 when foreign aid is 0%, 10%, 20%, and 30% of income, respectively.

REFERENCES

Bailey, M. J. (1956) "The Welfare Cost of Inflationary Finance." *Journal of Political Economy* 64: 93–110.

Barro, R. J. (1990) "Government Spending in a Simple Model of Endogenous Growth." *Journal of Political Economy* 98(5): S103–S125.

Boone, P. (1996). "Politics and the Effectiveness of Foreign Aid." *European Economic Review* 40: 289–329.

Cooley, T. F. and G. D. Hansen (1989) "The Inflation Tax in a Real Business Cycle Model." *American Economic Review* 79: 733–748.

Cukierman, A., S. Edward, and G. Tabillini (1992). "Seigniorage and Political Instability." *American Economic Review* 82(3): 537–555.

Dotsey, M. and P. Ireland (1996) "The Welfare Cost of Inflation in General Equilibrium." *Journal of Monetary Economics* 37: 29–47.

Economic Report of the President (Various Issues), United States Government Printing Office, Washington, DC.

Glimmer, M. (1993) "The Welfare Cost of Inflation in a Cash-In-Advance Economy with Costly Credit." *Journal of Monetary Economics* 31: 97–115.

Gillis, M., Perkiness, D. H., Romer, M., and Snodgrass, D.R. (1992) *Economics of Development,* Third Edition; W.W. Norton & Company, New York.

Gomme, P. (1993) "Money and Growth Revisited." *Journal of Monetary Economics* 32: 52–77.

Grinos, E., and J. Bhagwati (1976) "Foreign Capital, Savings and Dependence." *Review of Economics and Statistics* 58: 416–424.

King, G. R., C. I. Plosser and S. T. Rebelo (1988) "Production, Growth, and Business Cycles." *Journal of Monetary Economics* 21: 195–232.

Kimborough, K.P. (1986). "Foreign Aid and Optimal Fiscal Policy." *Canadian Journal of Economics* 86(1): 35–61.

Obstfeld, M. (1995). "Effects of Foreign Resource Inflows on Saving: A methodological Overview". Manuscript (University of California, Berkeley).

Prescott, E. (1986) "Theory Ahead of Measurement." *Federal Reserve Bank of Minneapolis Quarterly Review*, Fall: 9–22.

II

Foreign Aid, Some General Policy Aspects

CHAPTER 4

FOREIGN AID AND GLOBAL ENVIRONMENTAL POLICIES

Catrinus J. Jepma

INTRODUCTION

A range of motives has always inspired development assistance. Economic self interest of the donor country, geopolitical considerations (gradually becoming less important since the end of the Cold War), genuine concern about poverty and starvation, the wish to interfere with the political system and human rights' situation in the recipient country, and preservation of former colonial links are enumerated as such. As far as the economic self interest of the donor country is concerned, it may be realised both through export potential (via tying of aid and procurement back in the donor country through other mechanisms) and through the preparation of the ground for or enhancing Foreign Direct Investment (FDI).

Despite the multitude of motives to maintain a flow of official concessional resources from the industrialised world towards LDCs, the actual size of ODA as a percentage of OECD countries' GDP has witnessed a declining trend. Probably, this is due to a combination of factors:

- The end of the Cold War;
- A growing concern about the effectiveness of national aid programmes;
- The shift of attention towards the countries in transition, particularly in Central and Eastern Europe;
- The strong tendency in many OECD-countries to reduce both the overall role of government and the budget deficit both of which factors may have contributed to a proportional shrinking of budget categories including the ODA part of it; and
- The very strong economic growth performance — particularly in the 1980s and 1990s — in various mainly Asian countries which has made many policymakers realise that countries can grow without external support.

One increasingly recognised that aid should be a temporary phenomenon. After all, the ultimate purpose of aid that tries to support economic progress in a recipient country is to make itself redundant.

Another element that has become even clearer, particularly during the last few years, is the strong role of FDI in the sphere of international financial transfers from

North to South, and the importance of a good enabling environment in the recipient without which also aid cannot have much of a significant and lasting macroeconomic impact. The sad thing about aid probably is that if the policy conditions in the recipient are right, FDI and other non-concessional financial flows will become available relatively easily as a source of foreign finance for economic development. If, however, the policy conditions are wrong, aid is most likely less effective.

Finally, even if aid projects and programmes as such are evaluated as being reasonably effective and having sufficiently sustainable impact, quite often it will still be fairly hard to demonstrate their macroeconomic implications with any degree of statistical significance: the so-called micro-macro paradox. This is still a phenomenon under research but probably, among others, due to various crowding out mechanisms. Among these mechanisms one may find: aid crowding out domestic savings and domestic taxes, aid used indirectly for interest payment and amortisation of written-off bad loans, aid being fungible and therefore used for financing low-priority government expenditures, aid encouraging rent-seeking behaviour, corruption and nepotism; aid even sometimes enabling wrong policies (and "wrong" policy regimes) to remain in place, and so on.

All this does not mean that a considerable part of past development is or has been ineffective or inappropriate, but that the overall outcome of the debate is in the direction of a less prominent role for the traditional motives for and patterns of aid flows than in the past. Even insofar as official flows are used to promote particular donor exports or FDI interests (e.g. via mixed credits), there is at least the general recognition that it is wrong if OECD-countries would compete with each other in subsidising these activities. It happens so not only because such competition is generally useless and in conflict with WTO-, OECD- and other international rules to create an international level playing field. The other reason is that such competition eventually easily boils down to a case where the domestic donor country's taxpayer finances a slight subsidy for domestic business and a huge subsidy for the foreign customer. This eventually will keep the use of aid for these purposes under control, although real practice has demonstrated that it requires quite a lot of time and patience to get rid of official flows used for these purposes.

The question therefore arises: whether traditional official concessional flows from the North into the LDCs are going to gradually fade away. Whether they remain limited only to some resources for emergency relief or for direct poverty alleviation in some of the least developed countries, or maybe they achieve some balance of payments support and some NGO-driven support for particular types of appealing projects. In the following, we will argue that this may not be the case. There is a new upcoming motive for official flows that may well become a dominating one during the next few decades or so, which has remained fairly unnoticed in the aid community thus far: the concern about the global environment.

THE ISSUE AT STAKE

There are a number of truly global environmental issues that one has generally become aware of during the last decade, such as:

- Global warming through the increasing concentration of greenhouse gases (GHGs) in the atmosphere;
- The depletion of the ozone layer through the use of CFCs and other gases with the same impact;
- The deforestation process which causes a continuous and dramatic loss of biodiversity;
- The overuse of the oceans;
- The pollution and threat of disappearance of vulnerable ecosystems with global significance, etc.

In the following, however, we will concentrate on the climate change issue. First, because it is a truly global concern. Second, because its policy implications may have a pervasive impact in both North and South, and, finally, because the issue may well have considerable implications for North-South transfers.

With respect to the global climate issue, one has come to know that increasing fossil energy use since the Industrial Revolution has led to the rapid accumulation of GHGs in the atmosphere, well above their naturally occurring or historical levels. This has, for instance, led to the increase of the CO_2-concentration in the atmosphere from pre-industrial (before 1800) levels of some 280 parts per million by volume (ppmv) to the present level of about 360 ppmv. Without policy action concentration levels will further increase, obviously depending on the main assumptions vis-à-vis economic growth, population increase, energy efficiency improvement, the speed of introducing non-fossil fuels, and so on. However, the most recent (but soon to be updated), rather authoritative IPCC scenario approach would indicate that without action, by the year 2100 atmospheric CO_2 concentration levels may well have risen to levels ranging between just below 500 and some 950 ppmv (to rise further thereafter). The increase is associated with projected global temperature rise of 1°C to 4,5°C, and sea level rise of 13 to 94 cm, respectively, to mention just some of the potential physical implications of climate change.

Inspired by this range, most damage assessments concentrate on the assumed global warming impact of a benchmark figure of twice the pre-industrial atmospheric CO_2 equivalent concentrations. A presumed level of 560 ppmv will, under business-as-usual, probably be reached anywhere between 2050 and 2100. Try to assess what might occur assuming the benchmark figure would apply right now (thereby most likely underestimating the flexibility of society to adjust assuming adjustment potential increases with time available). The assessments of future damages associated with global climate change are extremely relevant because they reveal at least part of the benefits of climate policy action (think in this respect also of the various externalities associated with climate policy which should be taken into account as well). On the other hand, however, the various damage assessments have also given rise to considerable methodological debates (how to value ecosystem loss, or a statistical human life, as well as how to determine the appropriate social discount rate?), and many of the underlying assumptions have been topic of considerable discussion.

Table 4.1. Range of Likely Climate Change Scenarios (with and without intervention).

Scenario and Year	Net Anthropogenic Carbon Emissions (Gt/yr)	Carbon Concentration (ppmv)	Cumulative Carbon Emissions from 1990 to 2100 (GtC)	Temp. Rise (°C)	Sea Level Rise (cm)
Actual (in 1900)	<0.5	315	—	0.3–0.6 below 1990	10–25 below 1990
Actual (in 1990)	7	350 (rising)	—	0	0
Mid-range (IS92a) non-intervention (in 2100)	20	680 (rising)	1500	2 (rising)	50 (rising)
	IS92a *Economic Growth (per year)* 2.9%: 1990–2025 2.3%: 1990–2100 *Energy supplies* 12,000 EJ Oil 13,000 EJ natural gas *Population* 11.3 billion in 2100			IS92a profile with increasing aerosol concentrations and moderate climate and ice-melt sensitivities	
Best (IS92c) non-intervention (in 2100)	5	480 (stabilising)	770	0.9 (rising)	13 (rising)
	IS92c *Economic Growth (per year)* 2.0%: 1990–2025 1.2%: 1990–2100 *Energy supplies* 8,000 EJ Oil 7,300 EJ natural gas *Population* 6.4 billion in 2100			IS92c profile with increasing aerosol concentrations and low climate and ice-melt sensitivities	
Worst (IS92e) non-intervention (in 2100)	36	1000 (rising)	2190	4.5 (rising)	94 (rising)
	IS92e *Economic Growth (per year)* 3.5%: 1990–2025 3.0%: 1990–2100 *Energy supplies* 18,400 EJ Oil 13,000 EJ natural gas phaseout nuclear investments by 2075 *Population* 11.3 billion in 2100			IS92e profile with constant 1990 aerosol concentrations and high climate and ice-melt sensitivities	
Mid-range S450/S650 with intervention (in 2100 and 2500)	2.5 to 9 in 2100 1 to 2 in 2500	450–600 in 2100 450–650 in 2500	630–1190	0.8 to 1.3 in 2100 1.1 to 2.2 in 2500	25 to 30 in 2100 85 to 145 in 2500
	S450 to S650 range of profiles			S450 to S650 range of profiles with constant 1990 aerosol concentrations and moderate climate and ice-melt sensitivities	

Table 4.1 *(continued)*. Range of Likely Climate Change Scenarios (with and without intervention).

Scenario and Year	Net Anthropogenic Carbon Emissions (Gt/yr)	Carbon Concentration (ppmv)	Cumulative Carbon Emissions from 1990 to 2100 (GtC)	Temp. Rise (°C)	Sea Level Rise (cm)
Best (S450) with intervention (in 2100 and 2500)	2.5 in 2100 1 in 2500	450 in 2100 450 in 2500	630–650	0.5 in 2100 0.7 in 2500	10 in 2100 10 in 2500
	S450 profile			S450 profile with constant 1990 aerosol concentration and low climate and ice-melt sensitivities	
Worst (S650) with intervention (in 2100 and 2500)	9 in 2100 2 in 2500	550–600 in 2100 650 in 2500	1030–1190	2 in 2100 3.5 in 2500	70 in 2100 325 in 2500
	S650 profile			S650 profile with constant 1990 aerosol concentration and high climate and ice-melt sensitivities	

Source: Jepma and Munasinghe, 1998, pp. 286–7.

Table 4.2. $2xCO_2$ Damage in Physical Units: Different World Regions (2.5°C Warming)

Type of Damage	Damage Indicator	EU	USA	Ex-USSR	China	Non-OECD	OECD	World
Agriculture	Welfare loss (%GNP)	0.21	0.16	0.24	2.10	0.28	0.17	0.23
Forestry	Forest area lost (km^2)	52	282	908	121	334	901	1,235
Fishery	Reduced catch (1,000 t)	558	452	814	464	4,326	2,503	6,829
Energy	Rise in electricity demand (TWh)	54.2	92.0	54.6	17.1	142.7	211.2	353.9
Water	Reduced water availability (km^2)	15.3	32.7	24.7	32.2	168.5	62.2	230.7
Coastal protection	Annual capital costs (m$/yr)	133	176	51	24	514	493	1,007
Dryland loss	Area lost (1,000 km^2)	1.6	10.7	23.9	0	99.5	40.4	139.9
Wetland loss	Area lost (1,000 km^2)	9.9	11.1	9.8	11.9	219.1	33.9	253.0
Ecosystem loss	Number of protected habitats lost, assuming 2% loss	16	8	NA	4	53	53	106
Health/mortality	Number of deaths (1,000)	8.8	6.6	7.7	29.4	114.8	22.9	137.7
Air pollution (Tropical O_3)	Equivalent increase in emissions (1,000t NO_X)	566	1,073	1,584	227	2,602	1,943	4,545
Air pollution (SO_2)	Equivalent increase in emissions (1,000t SO_2)	285	422	1,100	258	1,864	873	2,737
Migration	Additional immigrants (1,000)	229	100	153	583	2,279	455	2,734
Hurricanes								
— Casualties	Number of deaths	0	72	44	779	7,687	313	8,000
— Damage	M$	0	115	1	13	124	506	630

Source: Jepma and Munasinghe (1998), Pearce et al. (1996), after Fankhauser (1995).

Therefore, the next table is only to be considered as an illustration of some guesstimates of what the physical impact of benchmark global warming could be in the various regions of the world.

The table illustrates clearly, however, the mere consensus in the literature, i.e. that a considerable part of damage will actually be concentrated in the non-industrialised, mainly LDC world. This is precisely the area where not only GDP/capita and per capita energy consumption is lowest, but also the historical contribution to the rise of the GHG atmospheric concentration level.

As far as the cost side of the climate policy is concerned, a whole range of studies has now been carried out. The purpose of the studies is to get at least some feeling of what the implications of various policy ambition levels may be for those countries that would be engaged in climate policy action. The major part of the cost studies focus on the US-situation, but the number of studies dealing with other regions is now rapidly growing. Again, it is extremely complex to try to present some clear information on GHG abatement policy costs, because much will depend not only on the policy instruments and the way they are applied, but also on when and where abatement action is taking place. Probably the most interesting information, which has come to the fore, based on different methodologies is that the costs of GHG mitigation action will differ widely, depending on *where* the action is initiated. Therefore, there may be considerable scope for climate policy cost savings if climate policy is taking place at such a regional mix that the marginal costs of abatement in the various regions would become more or less the same world-wide. Assessments of global cost savings by applying this principle instead of the rule that national abatement policies need to be carried out within the own country, would indicate overall savings to depend on the mitigation target level, but for most reasonable policy scenarios to be in the order of 40–80%.[1]

Figure 4.1.

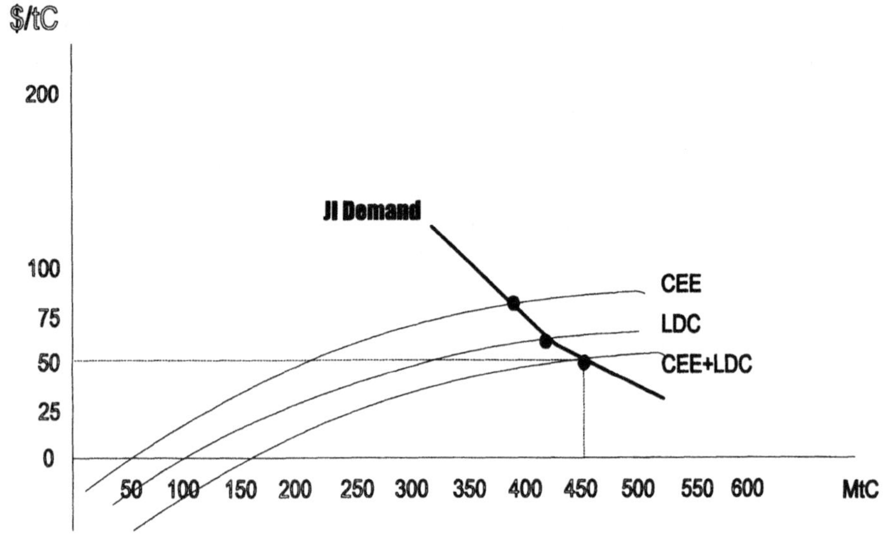

CLIMATE POLICY AND NORTH-SOUTH CO-OPERATION

It is precisely against this background that a whole new area creating scope for North-South transfers has opened. Indeed, the growing conviction that one has to initiate climate policy action and use the optimal regional mix potential, but that the primary responsibility for this should lie with the industrialised world, has initiated a huge debate on how to design a climate policy system. The system would involve the LDCs, but does not let them pay the price for a phenomenon for which they have a relatively limited historical responsibility, or in any case do not feel responsible for in terms of committing themselves to providing resources in order to deal with it. The main outcome of this discussion, which to some extent prevented the 1992 UNCED Conference from producing serious concrete results on this issue, has been the adoption in the legal document dealing with global climate policy — the 1994 Framework Convention Climate Change (FCCC) and its 1998 (Kyoto) Protocol (KP) — of the principles of: "common but differentiated responsibilities", non-additionality, and of the possibility of Joint Implementation (JI).

The first principle of "common but differentiated responsibilities" broadly states that all countries joining UNFCCC (early 1998 about 175) have a responsibility with regard to the global climate, but that the cost of action should be born by the so-called Annex I-group, the industrialised countries (including most of the countries in transition), not by the LDCs (non-Annex I). Consequently in the KP only the Annex I-group countries adopted national Quantified (GHG) Emissions Limitation and Reduction Commitments (QELRCs, Table 4.3) to be assessed for the first time during the first commitment period (2008-2012) as a first step hopefully contributing to eventually stabilise GHG atmospheric concentration level at about a 550 ppmv or less.

The additionality principle argues that insofar as Annex countries' governments would use official flows in order to support climate action via the provision of financial and technological resources in non-Annex countries in the various GHG mitigation (or sequestration-via-sinks) projects, those flows should be additional to future "regular" ODA and GEF flows in order to prevent crowding out. However, since accepted projections of future ODA-flows or GEF-funding do not exist, and since the trend in ODA as a percentage of DAC-countries' GDP is declining anyhow, it is rather hard to see how the additionality principle can be substantiated in the future. Suggestions to individualise the principle by making additionality dependent on individual donor countries' actual ODA contribution — e.g. no additionality in JI-projects if a donor country's ODA is significantly less or declining significantly faster than the corresponding OECD-ODA-average figure — have obviously thus far met with great resistance, particularly from the side of the USA.

The third principle — to accept the possibility of JI — simply states that an investor (=Annex I) and host-country partner (from another Annex I or a non-Annex I) can jointly implement a project. The net GHG abatement impact of the project will be credited, and the credits can then be used to fulfil QELRCs during the first and subsequent commitment periods.

Table 4.3. Annex B to the Kyoto Protocol: Party Quantified emission limitation or reduction commitment.

(Committed percentage of emissions in comparison to emissions in base year period, for the first commitment period 2008-2012; between brackets the relevant percentages for individual countries within the EU "bubble")

Australia	108	Liechtenstein	92
Austria	92 (87)	Lithuania*	92
Belgium	92 (92.5)	Luxembourg	92 (72)
Bulgaria*	92	Monaco	92
Canada	94	Netherlands	92 (94)
Croatia*	95	New Zealand	100
Czech Republic*	92	Norway	101
Denmark	92 (79)	Poland*	94
Estonia*	92	Portugal	92 (127)
European Community	92	Romania*	92
Finland	92 (100)	Russian Federation*	100
France	92 (100)	Slovakia*	92
Germany	92 (79)	Slovenia*	92
Greece	92 (125)	Spain	92 (115)
Hungary*	94	Sweden	92 (104)
Iceland	110	Switzerland	92
Ireland	92 (113)	Ukraine*	100
Italy	92 (93.5)	United Kingdom of Great Britain and Northern Ireland	92 (87.5)
Japan	94		
Latvia*	92	United States of America	93

* Countries that are undergoing the process of transition to a market economy.

Given the legal framework — the UNFCCC also ratified by 140 LDCs (as of January 1998) and its KP, thus far (as of 15 July 1998) signed by 21 LDCs (out of a total of 47 Parties) — and given its main principles relevant for official financing now being accepted, the question arises what the implications of this new policy area can be for the size and pattern of future North-South transfers.

THE SCOPE FOR JI

Obviously, the answer to this question can only be speculative at the present state since much will depend on a host of conditions. The best one can do is just to list some of the key elements to get a flavour of what might evolve, recognising that in order for official flows to be initiated not only the donor countries' intention-to-provide (supply) is relevant, but also the recipient countries' willingness-to-accept (demand). In the end, according to the UNFCCC text, a formal requirement for any JI-project to become officially recognised (a prerequisite for being credited) is the approval of both the investor and host country's government.

JI demand

As far as demand is concerned, the LDC-position, quite often but not always unified by a G77 position, has thus far been rather reserved which brought them commonly on one line with most of the Western environmental NGOs. Indeed, the idea that projects would be set up in LDCs, albeit (mainly) based on some Annex I country's resources, the net GHG abatement result of which would provide credits for the investing country's government in order to meet its UNFCCC-commitments, met with considerable resistance. The main arguments used were

- that Annex I-countries' primary true intentions to do something about GHG emissions would only be taken seriously if at least a considerable part of the action were taken at home, instead of "exporting" the issue in order to remain able to go on with prevailing domestic GHG pollution practices;
- that the investing countries, by exploiting the least cost- or even no-regret-options in LDCs first, would pick the low hanging fruits, depriving LDCs from the future possibility to use the same opportunities for their own purposes; and
- That JI being an Annex I countries' escape valve would reduce Annex countries' incentives to invest in less GHG polluting technology and therefore retard technological progress. In addition, some felt that if sinks-based projects such as forestry would be allowed next to mitigation projects, parts of LDC surfaces might develop into areas with carbon plantations crowding out small-farmers and subsistence population that used or intended to live there.

Despite these reservations, probably at least partly inspired by taking a strong bargaining position during UNFCCC climate negotiations, the growing realisation that JI can also bring considerable benefits to the recipients — technology, information, financial resources, private sector capital, etc. — probably finally led to the decision taken during the first Conference of the Parties (CoP I) in Spring 1995 (Berlin). The participants decided to experiment with the JI-concept until 2000, but not to credit any of the projects' net GHG abatement. Projects during this phase were called Activities Implemented Jointly. Despite the rather artificial character of this pilot phase, at the time of writing (summer 1998) still about 103 AIJ projects have now been *officially* recognised by the governments involved, most of the projects being located in Central/Eastern Europe (CEE) and in Central America (see Table 4.4 for an overview). In addition, 21 countries/groups of countries adopted national official AIJ programmes.

In the KP, however, a full-blown (i.e. inclusive of crediting) JI-mechanism for co-operation with non-Annex I countries is foreseen. It is now called Clean Development Mechanism (CDM), which even allows for the possibility to bank credits produced as from 2000 on in order for the amount accumulated during 2000–2008 to be used during the first commitment period (KP art.12.10). (The odd thing is that thus far a similar JI-mechanism is foreseen within Annex I, particularly relevant for JI-projects set up in CEE, *without*, however, the opportunity to bank early reductions.)

Table 4.4. Planned and ongoing AIJ pilot projects.

Countries with (planned) official AIJ/JI (pilot) programs

Australia, Belgium, Canada, Chile, Costa Rica, the Czech Republic, France, Germany, Guatemala, Japan, Mexico, the Netherlands, the Nordic countries (Denmark, Finland, Iceland, Norway and Sweden), Norway, Poland, South Africa, Sri Lanka, Sweden, USA, and Vietnam.

The projects listed on this page have been accepted, approved and endorsed by the designated national authorities for AIJ of the host and investing countries and have been or will be reported to the FCCC Secretariat. The projects in *italics* have not yet been officially reported to the FCCC Secretariat (as per 17 February 1998; visit also *http://www.unfccc.de/fccc/ccinfo/aijproj.htm* for more information). For descriptions of the projects *1,3,6–13,16,18,19,24,25, 28,29,34,37,38,43 see: http://www.northsea.nl/JIQ*

1	Decin, the Czech Republic	53	Võru district heating, Estonia
2	Rio Bravo conservation and forest management, Belize	54	Haabneme boiler conversion, Estonia
3	CARFIX, Costa Rica	55	Narva Jõesuu boiler conversion, Estonia
4	Plantas Eolicas S.A. Wind Facility, Costa Rica	56	Paldiski boiler conversion, Estonia
5	ECOLAND, Costa Rica	57	Tartu-Aardla boiler conversion, Estonia
6	Solar-based rural electrification project, Honduras	58	Valga boiler conversion, Estonia
7	RUSAFOR-SAP, the Russian Federation	59	Viljandi boiler conversion, Estonia
8	Krkonose/Sumava forest rehabilitation, the Czech Republic	60	Saldus energy efficiency, Latvia
9	Profafor, Ecuador	61	Balvi district heating, Latvia
10	Energy efficiency improvement by municipalities and utilities, Hungary	62	Aluksne district heating, Latvia
11	RABA/IKARUS Compressed Natural Gas Fuel Engine, Hungary	63	Jelgava district heating, Latvia
12	Sanitary landfilling with energy recovering, the Russian Federation	64	Jelgava energy efficiency, Latvia
13	Horticulture Tyumen, the Russian Federation	65	Viesite boiler conversion, Latvia
14	ILUMEX, Mexico	66	Aluksne boiler conversion, Latvia
15	Coal-to-Gas Conversion, Poland	67	Balvi boiler conversion, Latvia
16	Reforestation in Vologda, the Russian Federation	68	Brocenia boiler conversion, Latvia
17	Klinki forestry, Costa Rica	69	Daugavgriva boiler conversion, Latvia
18	El Hoyo-Monte Galan Geothermal, Nicaragua	70	Janmuiza boiler conversion, Latvia
19	Bio-Gen Biomass Power Generation Phase I, Honduras	71	Jekabplis boiler conversion, Latvia
20	Dona Julia Hydroelectric, Costa Rica	72	Jurmala boiler conversion, Latvia
21	Tierras Morenas windfarm, Costa Rica	73	Rauna boiler conversion, Latvia
22	Aeroenergia wind facility, Costa Rica	74	Slampe boiler conversion, Latvia
23	Biodiversifix forest restoration, Costa Rica	75	Valka boiler conversion, Latvia
24	RUSAGAS-Fugitive Gas Capture, the Russian Federation	76	Ugale boiler conversion, Latvia
25	Micro Hydroelectricity, Bhutan	77	Saldus district heating, Latvia

Table 4.4 *(continued)*. Planned and ongoing AIJ pilot projects.

26	Uganda National Park FACE roject, Uganda	78	Coke dry quenching, China
27	Renewable Energy Systems, Indonesia	79	fifteen fossil fuel fired Power Units, Ukraine
28	Ainazi windpower project, Latvia	80	Beet sugar plant, Ukraine
29	Virilla river basin, Costa Rica	81	Glassworks factory, Ukraine
30	Skoda-Mlada Boleslav, the Czech Republic	82	Byczyna district heating, Poland
31	Bel/Maya Biomass Power Generation, Belize	83	Bacstej dairy factory, Hungary
32	Bio-Gen Biomass Power Generation Phase II, Honduras	84	Baisogale boiler conversion, Lithuania
33	Zelenograd district heating improvement, the Russian Federation	85	Birzai boiler conversion, Lithuania
34	Salicornia: Halophyte Cultivation in Sonora, Mexico	86	Kazlu Ruda boiler conversion, Lithuania
35	Noel Kempff M. Climate Action Project, Bolivia	87	Sventupe boiler conversion + energy efficiency, Lithuania
36	Reforestation of Chiriqui Province, Panama	88	Varena boiler conversion, Lithuania
37	Sustainable Energy Management, Burkina Faso	89	Vienybe boiler conversion, Lithuania
38	Renel-SEP, energy efficiency, Romania	90	Ziegzdriai boiler conversion + energy efficiency, Lithuania
39	Bilsa-Reserve forest conservation, Ecuador	91	Staciunai district heating, Lithuania
40	Scolel Té, sustainable land management-carbon sequestration, Chiapas, Mexico	92	Rural Solar Electrification, Bolivia
41	Reduced Impact Logging, Indonesia	93	SELCO-rural electrification, Sri Lanka
42	Territorial and financial consolidation of biological reserves, Costa Rica	94	Drink water supply in Targu Mures, Romania
43	Ushgorod Corridor Wolgotransgas, the Russian Federation	95	Waste water treatment in Targy Mures, Romania
44	Järvakandi district heating, Estonia	96	Waste water treatment at coffee plants, Costa Rica
45	Adavere district heating, Estonia	97	CFL efficient lighting, Honduras
46	Mustamäe tee, Ehitajate tee, Sutiste tee energy efficiency, Estonia	98	APS/CFE Renewable energy, Mexico
47	Mustamäe — Vilde tee energy efficiency, Estonia	99	Community Silviculture, Mexico
48	Võru boiler conversion, Estonia	100	Lytkarino district heating, the Russian Federation
49	Orissare district heating, Estonia	101	Cheliabinsk district heating, the Russian Federation
50	Türi district heating, Estonia	102	Steel heat furnace, Thailand
51	Valga district heating, Estonia	103	Paper mill plant, Indonesia
52	Vändra district heating, Estonia		

Source: Joint Implementation Quarterly, 1998, p.14.

Indeed, the CDM, introduced at the Kyoto Conference, based on a Brazilian proposal in particular, has been formulated in the KP art. 12 containing the aim "to assist Parties not included in Annex I in achieving sustainable development and in contributing to the ultimate objective of the Convention, and to assist Parties included in Annex I achieving compliance with their quantified emission limitation and reduction commitments". This phrase essentially means that JI-projects can get started, but that LDCs would in addition expect some support in coping with their adaptation to climate change.

JI supply

As far as the supply side is concerned, it is clear that Annex-countries will be interested in setting up JI-projects with LDCs as long as this would provide a net cost savings compared to other alternatives to meet QELRCs foreseen in the KP. The main alternative options being (except for the option simply not to comply, which we shall rule out): domestic action, JI within Annex (e.g. in CEE in particular), and Emission Trading (ET). The final option mentioned — ET — has been included in the Protocol (KP Art. 17). Its purpose is to allow for international trade of national "GHG-credits", i.e. expected surpluses of "GHG-credits" insofar as Annex I countries *presume* that during the commitment period 2008–2012 they will actually emit less GHGs than the amount specified via their QELRCs, the so-called assigned amount. The ET option is highly contentious, however, as long as no rules on non-compliance and the associated liability risk of the (early) buyer or seller of these "GHG-credits" have been established, and therefore will here be disregarded as well. Therefore, in our simple framework the scope for JI ultimately depends on the scope for low-cost abatement/carbon sequestration options being "available" outside a country facing a QELRC.

Now let us take a set of rather heroic assumptions, in order to see what can be said about the scope for JI. This is simply because for the time being information is so scarce, scattered and imprecise that this is probably the best one can do. First of all, a considerable amount of marginal cost data per country and per technology have been combined in order to provide a picture of what can broadly be perceived as a typical marginal abatement/sequestration-based cost function (see Figure 4.2), which is representative for:

- the OECD area;
- the CEE area; and
- the LDC area.

The cost curves represent unauthorative guesstimates, and are only qualitatively backed up by the cost-curve information available with the author. Sources of the marginal cost data were: Markal (IEA), Efom-Env (EU DG XII) for the OECD area; OECD[2] and ECN[3] for the CEE area; and Jackson[4], Mills et al[5], and Rubin et al.[6] for the non-Annex I area, respectively.

It is important to note what the precise meaning of the cost functions used is. Essentially, with respect to the three respective areas the assumption has been made that the QELRCs as specified in the KP roughly boil down to (vis-à-vis 1990 emission levels) –5%; 0% and no limitation, respectively. By implication, the marginal cost curve of the Annex I area associated with a –5% abatement target essentially is a reciprocal demand curve. This is to say that we assume that the Annex I country with the highest marginal cost per technological option if all abatement would be carried out domestically[7] will be the first actor in demand for JI on the JI demand curve, to be followed by the country with the next highest marginal abatement cost, etc. By combining the various point estimates of per country/per technology marginal costs given the various national abatement targets, an overall Annex I marginal abatement cost function can be derived which has been represented in a slightly stylised form in Figure 4.2. The supply of JI from both the CEE- and LDC area can be arrived at in a similar manner: by putting in sequential order the most efficient (= actually no-regrets) options first (specified per technology per country), to be followed by the next-best options and so on.

In Figure 4.2, the stylised JI demand curve of the Annex I area is confronted with the stylised aggregate supply curve of JI options of both the CEE and LDC area taken together. The CEE and LDC marginal cost curves have also been represented in order to illustrate what the implications would be if JI would remain restricted to one of the two areas only. We would like to remind the reader of the remark made earlier, namely that banking of early emission reductions as of the year 2000 would only be possible via the CDM, i.e. not via JI with CEE countries.

Now, one can easily infer by combining the assumptions that the scope for JI would be formidable indeed. Assuming all the JI-investment financing would come from OECD, the amounts involved could grow to levels such as generating cost savings world-wide which would be formidable (literally tens of billions of dollars; see the area between the JI demand and CEE+LDC supply curve in Figure 4.2). It is hard to see — except for the institutional noise which will retard the decision-making process, also because of the huge interests involved with the JI mechanism, and possibly except for the still unclear role of ET as a vehicle to satisfy QELRCs — why the above picture would not be the direction into which we are going. Much of the investment involved with the JI-concept will have to be made by the private not by the public sector. Nevertheless, since the topic at stake — the global climate — is a common good, eventually the consumer and taxpayer will be charged for this, so that the distinction between (in) direct abatement subsidies and official transfers would in some respect become blurred. So, even if only a part of these savings would give rise to official transfers — either directly to the JI host country participant or government, or indirectly via tax-relief, subsidies, etc. to the investor, or both – this could mean an enormous shift in the pattern, scope, size and purpose of official North-South flows during the next decades.

Finally, Figure 4.2 would also suggest that potentially the market for JI credits can become enormous indeed, assuming the curves would broadly portray something not too far from reality. Given that the KP requires the Annex I countries to reduce their annual C-emissions by the commitment period with some 700 MtC compared with baseline projections (based on Markal), a full-blown JI regime would imply, according to our data as represented in Figure 4.2, that some 150 MtC emission reduction would be achieved jointly with CEE partners, and, in addition, some 300 MtC with partners in the LDC region. The price of abatement of 1 tC would then tend to a level of about \$50. This would imply an annual production of C-credits in LDCs via JI to an amount of some \$15 bn, which is another illustration of the potential major implications of the KP for North-South co-operation.

NOTES

[1] For some calculations, see for instance Jepma and Lee, 1995; Manne et al., 1993; Richels et al., 1996.

[2] OECD, 1996.

[3] ECN, 1994.

[4] Jackson, 1991.

[5] Mills et al., 1991.

[6] Rubin et al., 1992.

[7] Note that we used the national QELRCs as specified in Table 4.3 inclusive of the EU bubble as a starting point for assessing the national marginal abatement cost functions.

REFERENCES

ECN, 1994. *Strategies for Reducing Emissions and Depositions in Central and Eastern European Countries: the case of Slovakia; idem: the case of Czech Republic,* ECN Policy Studies.

Fankhauser, S., 1995. Valuing climate change: The economics of the greenhouse effect. London: Earthscan.

Jackson, T., 1991. "Least-cost Greenhouse Planning: Supply Curves for Global Warming Abatement," *Energy Policy,* Vol. 19, No. 1, Jan/Feb., pp. 35–46.

Jepma, C.J. and M. Munasinghe, 1998. *Climate Change Policy: Facts, Issues, and Analysis,* Cambridge University Press, UK.

Jepma, C.J. and C.W. Lee, 1995. "Carbon Dioxide Emissions: A Cost-effective Approach." In: C.J. Jepma (ed.), 1995, *The Feasibility of Joint Implementation,* Kluwer Academic Publishers, Dordrecht, pp. 57–68.

Joint Implementation Quarterly, 1998, Vol. 4, No.2, June 1998, Paterswolde, the Netherlands.

Manne, A.S., R. Mendelsohn, and R.G. Richels, 1993. *MERGE: A Model for Evaluating Regional and Global Effects of GHG Reduction Policies,* Electric Power Research Institute, Palo Alto, CA.

Mills, E., D. Wilson, T.B. Johansson, 1991. "Getting Started, No-regrets Strategies for Reducing GHG emissions", *Energy Policy,* July/August, pp. 526–42.

OECD, 1996. *Financing Energy Efficiency in Countries with Economies in Transition (Tranche 1),* Main report 1996, and appendix to Working Paper 6.

Pearce, D.W., et al., 1996. "The social costs of climate change: greenhouse damage and the benefits of control." In: J.P. Bruce, H. Lee, and E.F. Haites (eds.), Climate Change 1995: Economic and social dimensions of climate change. Contribution of Working Group III to the Second Assessment Report of the Intergovernmental Panel on Climate Change. Cambridge University Press, pp. 170–224.

Richels, R., J. Edmonds, H. Gruenspecht, T. Wigley, 1996. *The Berlin Mandate: The Design of Cost-effective Mitigation Strategies,* Sub-group on the Regional Distribution of the Costs and Benefits of Climate Change Policy Proposals, Energy Modelling Forum-14, Stanford University, Stanford, CA.

Rubin, E.S., et al., 1992. "Realistic Mitigation Options for Global Warming", *Science,* Vol. 257, July, pp. 148–9, 261–6, American Association for the Advancement of Science.

CHAPTER 5

INTERNATIONAL DEVELOPMENT ASSISTANCE AND FOOD SECURITY

Alan Matthews

Food security exists when all people, at all times, have physical and economic access to sufficient, safe and nutritious food to meet their dietary needs and food preferences for an active and healthy life. In recent decades there has been a significant improvement in food security. Current food availabilities for the world as a whole were estimated at 2720 calories per person per day in 1990–92, up from 2300 calories in 1961–65 or an increase of 18 per cent (FAO, 1996a). Coupled with some small improvement in the way these global food supplies are distributed, the proportion of undernourished people in developing countries has fallen substantially from 35 per cent in 1969–71 to 21 per cent in 1990–92. This decline has taken place in all regions with the exception of Sub-Saharan Africa. Famines, which were once an almost inevitable occurrence in low-income societies, have been virtually confined in recent decades to conflict situations.

But progress has been uneven, leaving an unacceptably large number of undernourished or food-insecure individuals. FAO estimates that currently more than 800 million people suffer from malnutrition, with millions more at risk from sudden and unforeseen adverse shocks to food production, prices or supplies (*op.cit.*). The role of international assistance in promoting food security has been debated at two major international conferences in the past three decades, the World Food Conference in 1974 and the World Food Summit in 1996. Yet despite the evident need for coordinated international action to tackle the causes of hunger, in recent years there has been a steady falling-off in the international commitment to this goal. International aid to agriculture dropped dramatically during the 1990s. Food aid flows to developing countries peaked in 1993 and have fallen significantly since then. The 1996 World Food Summit attempted to redress these trends and to refocus world attention on the problem of hunger, but the Declaration and Plan of Action adopted at the Summit contained little that was new in firm commitments.[1]

Given the close relationship between poverty and food insecurity, a wide range of international actions indirectly impinge on food security. The overall level and terms of financial flows, the generosity of debt rescheduling and relief, market-opening trade policy measures and international economic co-ordination all vitally affect the economic growth prospects of the most food-insecure countries. To comprehensively cover all of the international actions which impact on food security is beyond the scope of this chapter. Instead, it examines two areas where external support can prove useful to countries implementing food security strategies:

- by providing funds for investment in increasing food production, including agricultural research
- by providing food aid to meet emergencies and to raise the nutritional standards of particularly vulnerable households

The chapter investigates the reasons for the declining commitment of donors to these areas and whether this can be reversed.

FINANCE FOR AGRICULTURE AND RURAL DEVELOPMENT

The bulk of the development finance to agriculture is provided by countries belonging to the Development Assistance Committee (DAC) of the OECD and by the international financing institutions (IFIs) such as the World Bank and the Regional Banks. Official development finance includes both official development assistance (ODA) as well as flows on more commercial terms. Analysis of aid flows to agriculture and rural development ideally should be based on the net flow of resources to these sectors. However, there is no sectoral breakdown of the data on resource flow disbursements, nor is it feasible to net the gross flows to any individual sector such as agriculture. Under the circumstances, the best that can be done is to examine the trends in the *commitments* of external financial assistance to agriculture (Bhattacharjee, 1977). Data on commitments tend to exaggerate the actual flow of resources, in part because repayments of loans are not netted out, and in part because of the time lag between the commitment of assistance and its disbursement. We should also note that data on external assistance to agriculture are classified according to two definitions. The *narrow* definition includes activities directly contributing to the development of agricultural production such as crop and livestock development, fisheries, forestry, irrigation and land development, supply of fertilisers and other inputs, agricultural services and storage. The *broad* definition includes, in addition, agro-industries, rural infrastructure, construction of plants for fertilisers and other inputs and projects for rural, regional and river basin development.

After the food crisis in the early 1970s annual commitments in current terms rose to around US$12 billion. This was maintained through the first half of the 1980s and increased to US$15 billion towards the end of the decade. Thereafter commitments fell back to US$12 billion in 1992 and have continued to decline since, falling to around US$10 billion per year by 1995. The fall during the 1990s appears even more dramatic if adjusted for inflation. In real terms, annual flows averaged just over $17 billion (at 1990 prices) in the early 1980s and were only just below this figure in the years at the end of the 1980s. In the early 1990s they fell to $13 billion and to just $10 billion annually by the mid-1990s (Table 5.1). The fall in the assistance to production agriculture is even more stark as the sectoral statistics increasingly include support for environmental protection and natural resource management which, essential though they are, have less direct and immediate impact on food production.

Table 5.1. Official commitments of external resources to agriculture (broad definition, millions constant 1990 US dollars).

	1980–82	1983–86	1987–89	1990–92	1993–95
Total	17,168	16,433	16,845	13,299	10,038
Bilateral	6,415	6,020	7,510	5,394	4,035
Multilateral	11,283	10,413	9,335	7,905	6,002
Share bilateral %	37%	37%	45%	40%	40%

Sources: 1980–1990 data at constant 1985 prices from Von Braun et al., 1993; 1991–1995 data at 1990 prices from Statistical Analysis Service, FAO; 1985 prices converted to 1990 prices using the Export Manufactures Unit Value index from UNCTAD, *Handbook of International Trade Statistics*, 1993.

The multilateral agencies have always been the most important source of development finance to agriculture and their share has varied between 55 and 65 per cent of the total. Lending to agriculture by the World Bank alone in most years exceeds bilateral aid to agriculture from the DAC countries. World Bank resources are not provided on concessional terms (except to the group of low-income countries eligible for IDA financing), so it may be concluded from these figures that most external finance for agriculture is loan finance which must be repaid. Both multilateral and bilateral donors reduced their assistance to agriculture equally severely in the 1990s, although the share of the multilateral agencies recovered slightly from its relatively low point at the end of the 1980s. Total bilateral commitments from DAC countries have fluctuated around US$4 billion annually during the past five years. Just over half of total bilateral commitments in 1995 came from Japan, which increased its share from one-third in 1991. Germany was the second highest donor in 1995, followed by the Netherlands, the United States and France. The US share of bilateral agricultural aid has steadily decreased from more than 30% in the early 1980s to less than 10% in 1995 (Table 5.2).

Table 5.2. External assistance to agriculture committed by the DAC countries.

Region	1991	1992	1993	1994	1995
	(US$ million)				
EU	1,599	2,127	1,609	1,419	1,512
Japan	1,354	2,101	1,562	1,500	2,218
US	632	442	363	460	378
Other	381	325	248	299	218
Total	3,967	4,995	3,781	3,679	4,327
	(per cent shares)				
EU	40.3%	42.6%	42.5%	38.6%	35.0%
Japan	34.1%	42.1%	41.3%	40.8%	51.3%
US	15.9%	8.8%	9.6%	12.5%	8.7%
Other	9.6%	6.5%	6.6%	8.1%	5.0%
Total	**100.0%**	**100.0%**	**100.0%**	**100.0%**	**100.0%**

Source: FAO Statistical Analysis Service, 1997

The proportion of a donor's total aid budget allocated to the agricultural sector is one measure of its commitment to this sector. The aggregate figures mask very large variations among individual donors in the changing shares of agricultural aid. The big drop in the proportion of total bilateral aid going to agriculture occurred in 1990. In the second half of the 1980s, assistance to agriculture averaged around 12 per cent; throughout the 1990s the figure has remained around 7.5 per cent. The biggest change in commitment to agriculture occurred in the US and among the 'Other' category of donors although the proportion of EU bilateral aid to agriculture and, to a smaller extent, Japanese aid also fell (Table 5.3).

Trends in bilateral aid are mirrored in the lending behaviour of the multilateral development banks. The most important lender, the World Bank, had a strictly agricultural portfolio with a commitment value of about US$25 million in 1996 (17 per cent of the total Bank portfolio). Adding in the non-agricultural rural portfolio of projects classified in other sectors but with rural components, the total rural portfolio had a commitment value of US$35 billion (24 per cent of the Bank total) (World Bank, 1996). However, World Bank new lending to agriculture, as a share of total lending, has fallen from 30 per cent in the mid-1980s to 12 percent in 1996 (Table 5.4). A recent analysis of EU aid (i.e. that portion of European Union aid which is managed by the European Commission) also demonstrated the sharp falling off in the commitment to agriculture by the EU, and particularly for more broadly-based rural development projects (Table 5.5).

INVESTMENT NEEDS AND DEVELOPMENT ASSISTANCE FLOWS

The relative scale of external assistance to agriculture can be illustrated using FAO data. FAO has estimated that net investments in on-farm improvements in developing countries may have been US$26 billion per year in the recent past (US$77 billion gross) and in the post-production sector US$15 billion per year (US$34 billion gross). In addition to these largely private investments, public expenditure on research and extension in LDCs may be estimated at about US$10 billion per year and on rural infrastructure at, very tentatively, US$20 billion annually. Even with external assistance at the low levels in the mid-1990s of around US$10 billion annually, it is

Table 5.3. Percentage of bilateral aid committed to production agriculture, 1985-95

Region	1985–1989 %	1990–1992 %	1993–1995 %
EU	13.2	8.6	8.0
Japan	11.9	11.7	9.1
US	10.2	2.7	5.4
Others	14.8	9.5	7.6
Total DAC	**12.0**	**7.3**	**7.5**

Source: OECD, *Development Co-operation*, various. Figures for the EU and Others are unweighted averages. Spain and Portugal only included in the EU total since

Table 5.4. Sectoral distribution of the lending of the Multilateral Development Banks for the years 1986, 1991 and 1996 (percentages).

	IBRD/IDA			IDB/FSO			AsDB/AsDF			AfDB/AfDF		
Sector	**1986**	**1991**	**1996**	**1986**	**1991**	**1996**	**1986**	**1991**	**1996**	**1986**	**1991**	**1996**
Agriculture	29	16	12	21	11	8	41	21	15	37	24	13
Other productive	45	40	37	48	35	17	41	66	57	53	58	55
Social	11	22	27	21	11	30	14	13	13	10	3	4
Other	16	23	26	10	44	46	5	0	16	0	14	29
Total	**100**	**100**	**100**	**100**	**100**	**100**	**100**	**100**	**100**	**100**	**100**	**100**

Source: OECD 1998, based on data compiled by the North-South Institute of Canada from the multilateral development banks' *Annual Reports*.

Table 5.5. EU multilateral aid by selected purposes, 1986-1995.

Sector	**1986–1989**	**1990–1992**	**1993–1995**
Food aid	18.7	18.9	10.1
Humanitarian aid	2.9	7.4	11.9
Agriculture	9.6	7.9	5.5
Rural development	8.8	2.4	0.9

Source: Cox and Koning, 1997.

clear that it has funded a significant share of public investment in the rural sectors of developing countries. For many of the poorer developing countries, external assistance is almost the only source of public investment in agriculture and to a large extent also of recurrent costs (FAO, 1996b).

As to future investment, FAO estimates that to increase food production in developing countries in line with effective demand until 2010, gross investment of some US$86 billion will be required annually in primary agricultural production (including irrigation), US$43 billion for related post-production facilities and US$37 billion for public support services and infrastructure. Nearly three-quarters of this future investment will consist of private commitments by farmers for land improvements, new equipment, expansion of livestock herds and plantations, and for private investments in the post-production chain. The remaining one-quarter, representing about US$41 billion per year, will consist of complementary public investments to create and maintain the conditions for profitable private sector investment. If external multilateral and bilateral financial support for these public investments were to provide the same share as in the past, i.e. around one-third overall, external commitments would need to rise by some US$5 billion per year, from US$10 to US$15 billion annually, i.e. to the level provided in the late 1980s.

International net private capital flows into developing countries are now much more important than official development finance, having risen from US$49 billion in 1990 to US$234 billion in 1996, compared to total official development finance of about US$66 billion net in that year (OECD 1998). However, little of this private investment went into primary agricultural production. Private finance has a role in funding programmes for plantation crops, large irrigation projects and other activities to do with input supply, processing and marketing which it can usually run more efficiently and more flexibly than government-run institutions. The World Bank has even supported the use of private sector institutions to carry out research and deliver information in ways that are more responsive to farmers' demands (World Bank, 1996). However, the record is that private investment is highly selective, going mainly to China and a handful of other growth centres in Asia and Latin America, and often requires complementary public sector investments to create the right opportunities. It would be naive to assume that agriculture's financing needs can be met from private sources alone, particularly in low-income food-deficit countries (LIFDCs).[2]

REASONS FOR AGRICULTURAL AID FATIGUE

Will donors be willing to meet the challenge of finding additional resources for agricultural development? To answer this question, it is necessary to understand why aid to agriculture has been falling in recent years. Previous work on trends in aid to agriculture undertaken at IFPRI distinguished two major categories of causes: economic and political economy. Economic reasons centre around the hypothesis that agricultural development assistance did not pay off and, therefore, donors turned elsewhere. Political economy reasons revolve around two hypotheses: that the power of political interest groups led to reduced emphasis on agriculture, and that certain bureaucratic distortions in aid agencies undermined a commitment to agriculture (von Braun et al., 1994). The continuing relevance of their arguments are briefly reviewed in this section.

The poor performance of many agricultural projects has not helped the case for additional resources. At the World Bank, a dismal 58 per cent of completed agricultural projects were judged satisfactory or better in the period 1981–89, ten percentage points worse than the Bank average (World Bank, 1996). There are various reasons why aided agricultural projects performed so poorly. In some cases, the original projects may have been poorly designed from a purely technical perspective. Second, even well-designed projects which would yield acceptable rates of return in a favourable macro-policy context can perform poorly if the general macroeconomic environment turns hostile. For example, commodity prices play an important role in the outcome of a project, and declining prices result in decreased returns. Third, in many countries unfavourable price trends may have been exacerbated by domestic policies seeking to promote non-agricultural sources of growth. The growing awareness of the key role of the macroeconomic environment in determining success or failure of agricultural projects led many donors to turn away from direct project lending towards support for structural adjustment and policy-based lending. Opportunities to invest in agricultural projects were ignored on the view that, until appropriate sectoral policies were adopted, specific project investments would fail (von Braun et al., 1994).

While the poor return on agricultural projects helped to 'push' funding away from agriculture, the increased pressures for programme lending to support economic reforms and debt relief, as well as the desire to divert finance to the high-profile environmental protection and social sectors helped to 'pull' funding away from the sector. The rise in the share of social spending and the growth of programme lending in the late 1980s emerges clearly in Table 5.6. Social and environmental spending are undoubtedly important, but should be closely linked to production agriculture. For example, there is an important link between environmental protection and increases in agricultural production. Farmers who increase yields per unit of land have less reason to push into marginal, environmentally sensitive lands to meet food needs. And local resourcing for initiatives in the social sector, such as schools, health services etc. cannot be sustained without an improvement in the underlying economy.

From a political market perspective, the allocation of development assistance is a product of competition among pressure groups in both donor and recipient states. von Braun et al. (1994) argue there were several political market forces at work in the 1980s which acted to reduce the supply of development assistance to agriculture.

As the over-production of farm commodities in developed countries increased and prices fell, domestic farm lobbies increasingly opposed assistance which was perceived as increasing the supply capacity of potential markets. This was especially the case in the United States where the combination of increased production and an appreciating exchange rate put severe pressure on farm incomes in the 1980s. At the same time as farmer support for aid to agriculture was waning, other groups tried to influence the composition of aid in their favour. Financial institutions and banks were

Table 5.6. Distribution of bilateral aid commitments by major purpose, per cent.

	1982–83	1987–88	1989–90	1991–92	1993–94	1994–95
Social and administrative infrastructure	22.1	24.6	23.3	20.2	26.2	29.0
Economic infrastructure	21.3	19.5	17.0	17.5	20.4	22.7
Agriculture	12.1	12.0	8.6	7.2	7.5	7.4
Industry and other production	15.1	7.8	5.8	6.3	3.9	3.1
Food aid	6.9	5.5	3.6	3.3	3.2	1.2
Programme assistance	13.5	16.4	11.9	11.6	7.5	5.8
Other (inc debt relief)	11.0	14.4	29.7	34.2	31.5	30.7
Total	**100**	**100**	**100**	**100**	**100**	**100**

Source: OECD, *Development Co-operation Annual Reports*, Paris. The classification used in the first column may not be exactly similar to that used from 1987-88 onwards.

concerned at the ability of developing countries to service and repay loans and lobbied for adjustment lending to support macro and micro policy reforms. Nor did policy-makers in developing countries push for a higher priority for agriculture. Agriculture was often viewed as a declining sector, and therefore not important for development. Falling real food prices over two decades perhaps led to complacency. Urban interests still dominate in political systems where the rural poor have little voice.

In situations like this, the IFIs might have taken a more independent line in pushing the results of research findings which emphasise the critical role of developing agriculture for overall economic growth and the reduction in poverty, especially in low-income developing countries. However, von Braun et al. note two bureaucratic changes which undermined the willingness and ability of the banks to take a leadership role. First, in a number of donor agencies, including the World Bank, there was a shift away from functional units to regional departments. This meant there was no longer a single budget for agricultural projects for which different countries could compete; instead, agricultural projects in individual countries had to compete with other sector projects in those same countries. With agricultural projects performing poorly relative to other sectors, a declining agricultural share is not surprising. Second, the numbers of technically competent staff in agriculture shrunk, making it even more difficult to design successful projects to claw back some of the share which was lost.

FOOD ASSISTANCE AND THE CONTRIBUTION OF FOOD AID

Assisting food production is the first way in which international assistance can contribute to food security. Helping to overcome chronic malnutrition arising from lack of access to food is a second way. Traditionally, this has been a major rationale for food aid, and the commitment to raise cereal food aid to a minimum 10 million tonnes a year was one of the main achievements of the 1974 World Food Conference. Actual deliveries (including non-cereals food aid of between 1 and 2 million tonnes) peaked at almost 17 million tonnes in 1993, subsequently falling to 7.5 million tonnes in 1996 with forecasts for a similar volume in 1997. In the mid 1980s, gross cereal imports by developing countries amounted to around 100m tonnes, of which around 12 million tonnes were supplied by food aid deliveries. By 1996, gross cereal imports had risen to around 150m tonnes, but only 7.5 million were supplied by food aid. The significance of food aid is even more important for the LIFDCs, although a decline in its relative contribution to gross cereal imports has also occurred for these countries (Table 5.7).

Food aid as a proportion of overall ODA has gradually fallen from a high point of over 10 per cent in the mid-1980s to less than 5 per cent at the present. The US has traditionally been the largest single donor although its share of total food aid has been slipping. In 1996, 44% of global deliveries were financed by the USA, 35% by the European Union and its Commission, 6% by Japan and 15% by other donors. Food aid has generally accounted for around 15% of total US ODA and this proportion has not altered much over time. The other important donor is the EU through its

Table 5.7. Global food aid deliveries, 1988-96.

	1988	1989	1990	1991	1992	1993	1994	1995	1996
Total food aid	14848.3	11733.6	13641.8	13195.9	15219.0	16846.1	12644.8	9845.8	7488.2
Low-income, food deficit countries	12812.2	9455.1	10083.2	11064.7	12148.6	10443.3	9868.3	7571.9	5823.6
Proportion of cereal imports of LIFDCs covered by food aid (%)	15	14	17	16	16	12	11	9	6

Source: WFP (Interfais); FAO, *Food Aid in Figures* and *Food Outlook* last row

Table 5.8. Global food aid deliveries by category for 1988-94.

Years	Total	Programme	Relief	Project
	(*million tonnes*)			
1988-90	13408.0	7340.5	2812.2	3255.3
1991-92	14202.0	7156.3	4265.4	2780.3
1993-94	14880.5	7223.4	4403.3	2753.9
	(*per cent*)			
1988-90	100%	55%	21%	24%
1991-92	100%	50%	30%	20%
1993-94	100%	49%	30%	19%

Source: WFP (Interfais)

'Community action', i.e. food aid disbursed through the EU budget. Food aid has traditionally represented a large proportion of EU aid, amounting to 26 per cent of the total 1986. This proportion has declined to 9–11 per cent of all EU aid between 1993–95 (Cox and Koning, 1997).

Associated with the decline in the overall volume of food aid there has been a shift in its use and distribution. Three categories of food aid can be distinguished: programme, relief and project aid. Programme aid is not targeted on specific groups. Rather it is provided on a bilateral basis to support recipient government's budgets or reduce balance of payments deficits. Relief food aid is aimed at people suffering from natural or personmade disasters, such as drought or civil strife. Project food aid is provided to selected groups to support specific development objectives. The nutritional impact of the three categories of food aid varies. Relief and project aid most directly contributes to food security by providing additional food assistance. The major benefit of programme food aid is that it may substitute for commercial imports and thus release foreign exchange for general development purposes. Another significant difference between the categories is that a high proportion of programme aid is provided on concessional loan terms, whereas virtually all relief and project aid is provided in grant form.

About 50 per cent of global food aid deliveries in 1993–94 was provided as programme aid, 30 per cent as relief assistance, and 20 per cent as support for development projects. Since 1990/91, the use of food aid for emergencies has grown. In the 1980s, the annual amount of food aid for emergencies averaged 2.4 million tonnes, whereas over the last three years (1992–95) it averaged 4 million tonnes. This increase has been at the expense of both project and programme food aid.

During the 1960s, India was the main recipient of global food aid. Asia as a whole received nearly two thirds of all food aid in the form of cereals until the mid 1970s and remained the largest recipient region until 1980. At that point Sub-Saharan Africa became the main recipient region and its share of total food aid has remained fairly steady at around one-third of the total over the past decade. The main change in the geographical distribution of food aid in recent years has been the major reallocation of food aid to Europe and ex-USSR countries. At their peak these countries absorbed over one-third of total food aid, most of which was earmarked for balance of payments support. Their increased share was not at the expense of Sub-Saharan Africa but of Asia and, in particular, North Africa and the Middle East. Similarly, the main gainers from the reduced flows to Europe and the CIS region in 1995–96 have been the Asian countries.

Table 5.9. Total food aid by region.

	1988–1990	1991–92	1993–94	1995–96
	(million tonnes)			
Sub-Saharan Africa	3558.6	5008.1	4560.9	2862.9
N.Africa/M.East	2814.3	2340.5	1011.6	740.6
South/East Asia	3770.4	2895.1	2283.0	2144.0
L. America/Caribbean	2306.2	1929.8	1710.1	838.5
Europe and CIS	958.5	2034.0	5180.0	2081.2
Total	**13407.9**	**14207.5**	**14745.5**	**8667.0**
	(per cent)			
Sub-Saharan Africa	27%	35%	31%	33%
N.Africa/M.East	21%	16%	7%	9%
South/East Asia	28%	20%	15%	25%
L. America/Caribbean	17%	14%	12%	10%
Europe and CIS	7%	14%	35%	24%
Total	**100%**	**100%**	**100%**	**100%**

Source: WFP (Interfais)

ARE HIGHER FOOD AID FLOWS JUSTIFIED?

Because food aid is doubly tied, it is often seen as a less desirable form of aid. Falling food aid flows, from this perspective, may simply reflect a desirable adjustment in donors' portfolios. It is thus worth asking whether falling food aid is a threat to food security and whether additional food aid flows could make a positive contribution to reducing hunger.

Projections of food aid needs are made regularly by agencies such as the US Department of Agriculture and the World Food Programme. Studies of this kind forecast that food aid needs will nearly double by the middle of the next decade, even with optimistic assumptions about recipient countries' ability to produce their own food or to have the financial capacity to import food commercially. For example, a 1995 USDA study projected total food aid needs to maintain consumption and meet emergency needs for refugees at 15 million tonnes in 1996, rising to 27 million tonnes by 2005. More food aid would be required if recipient countries' financial capacity to import food commercially lagged or if the consumption target was to meet minimum nutritional standards (Shapouri, 1995). The increasing incidence of humanitarian crises and political turmoil in recent years is one factor behind the growing demand for food aid. Nonetheless, in the USDA study only 20 per cent of the needs are classified as emergency needs resulting from production variability and political conflict. About 80 per cent of the food aid needs are classified as chronic (prolonged). Given the forecasts for the continued growth in the absolute numbers of people malnourished by 2020, the role for food aid targeted on food insecurity is set to increase.

The debate continues, of course, as to whether these needs would not be better met by increased financial aid rather than food aid. The main defence of food aid is that it is not a substitute for financial aid but additional to it. The rationale for this argument is traced back to the origins of food aid in surplus disposal which effectively lowered the real or opportunity cost to donors of providing food aid. This is buttressed by the further argument that food aid is supported by a coalition of political forces which are attracted to food aid because of its specific characteristics (in providing an outlet for surplus agricultural commodities, or because it facilitates market development) and who would be unlikely to give support for financial aid of equivalent value. Additionality may also arise where food aid is the responsibility of ministries of agriculture and allocated separately from the mechanisms for deciding on financial aid.

A second defence of food aid as a preferred instrument to financial aid is that it is more likely to succeed in reaching the very poor and food-insecure. Food aid is seen as having a comparative advantage in reaching large numbers of the world's most vulnerable people. Particularly project food aid, used as a wage resource that transfers income to poor households through labour-intensive public works programmes, or as an incentive to children and mothers to attend school or health clinics, is of direct benefit to very food-insecure people in food deficit countries.

EXPLANATIONS FOR THE DECLINE IN FOOD AID

Given these arguments in favour of food aid, the puzzle is to understand why food aid commitments have fallen sharply in recent years. Precisely because of its additional nature, the factors influencing the supply of food aid are not necessarily the same as those which explain the decline in external assistance to agriculture. Explanations can draw on two lines of enquiry into the factors which have influenced the supply of food aid. One is a statistical approach which tries to identify the major determinants of donors' propensity to grant food aid; the other is a political economy approach which focuses on the reasons why a country might prefer to provide food aid rather than financial aid or no aid at all.

Statistical analysis highlights the influence of the level of public stocks of agricultural commodities, the price of food aid commodities as well as evidence of need (Saran and Konandreas, 1991). Many donors accumulate public stocks as a result of domestic farm price support policies. These stocks are costly to store and in some cases may physically deteriorate in storage. There is often only a small likelihood that the stocks can be resold on the market at anything close to their purchase price. Giving these stocks away saves the resource costs of storage and avoids their price-depressing effect on world markets. The price of food aid commodities has also been shown to be an important factor affecting the level of food aid shipments. In the short-run food aid flows vary inversely with commodity prices. In many countries food aid budgets are fixed in nominal rather than volume terms; as commodity prices rise, less food can be bought. The analysis also reveals that donors in general have responded positively to the increased needs in recipient countries arising from short-term production shortfalls, although the response is only a partial one and covers only a small fraction of the cereal production shortfalls experienced.

More generally, the multiplicity of objectives of donors' food aid programmes is well documented. Programmes combine diplomatic, commercial, humanitarian, surplus disposal and development objectives to varying degrees. Support for food aid will respond to the shifting balance between different domestic constituencies whose interests it affects. In the US, for example, the general farm organisations have been strong supporters of food aid programmes in the past. As the US has adopted more market-oriented farm policies and the likelihood of surpluses reduces, the farm interest group constituency for food aid has diminished. Increasingly, export enhancement programmes outside of food aid are preferred as a more effective way of disposing of surpluses (Ruttan, 1993)

The link between food aid and surplus disposal has also weakened for other reasons. Food aid is increasingly competitive with financial aid. In the US, for example, the Gramm-Hollings-Rudman Amendment shifted the attributable cost of PL480 to the foreign assistance budget (Clay and Stokke, 1991). In the EU food aid is very deliberately not seen as linked to surplus disposal. In 1988, for example, despite the very limited availabilities and high prices in EU and world markets, the EU maintained the quantity of dairy products in its food aid programme at the level of previous years. For the individual EU member states, bilateral food aid programmes (known as 'national actions' as distinct from 'Community actions') are funded from national aid budgets and are not directly linked to the surpluses generated by the

EU's Common Agricultural Policy in any case (Saran and Konandreas, 1991). The gradual diversification of sources of food aid since the late 1960s to include most industrialised countries has also made the link between food aid and surplus disposal more tenuous.

Paradoxically, de-linking food aid from surplus disposal has not increased its popularity with the other important constituency of voluntary development organisations. Non-emergency food aid is frequently criticised by the development NGOs, in spite of their growing involvement in the delivery of food aid for nutritional objectives. Many of the criticisms of food aid are based on arguments well rehearsed in the academic literature, such as the alleged disincentive effects of food aid in recipient countries, the possibility that it can undermine local food markets and encourage the growth of inappropriate food tastes. As a consequence of such criticisms, official food aid programmes are now more firmly embedded in a food security framework (see, for example, European Council, 1996).

Saran and Konandreas (1991) argue that the opportunity cost of food aid is an important factor behind food aid decisions. Food aid donations tend to raise the commercial price of food aid commodities above what they would be in the absence of food aid and the revenue gain on commercial sales (for exporters) helps to offset the revenue loss from providing some food as aid. The size of this world price effect depends on the relative elasticities of demand in the commercial and food aid markets, as well as on the degree of leakage of food aid commodities from the food aid to the commercial market. For exporting countries over the period 1971 and 1988 the opportunity cost of food aid in wheat was hardly one fourth of its average international price (Saran and Konandreas 1991). This cost is further reduced if account is taken of the fact that much food aid has been provided on concessional or easy credit terms and donors recover part of the cost over time.

For various reasons, however, the opportunity costs of food aid have been increasing and may now be close to the world price of the donated food commodities. For importing food aid donors, the opportunity cost necessarily lies above the world price. Even for exporters, however, the offsetting factors are less important than before. Food aid is now a much smaller part of world trade in the main food aid commodities, so its leverage effect on world prices is also that much smaller. Donors increasingly bear the non-food costs of food aid, such as the costs of procurement, transport and delivery to the final destination, and these have been increasing. Moves to source a higher proportion of food aid deliveries in developing countries through triangular transactions, as favoured by the EU, also raise the opportunity cost. Thus the putative cost advantages of food aid, and which helped to make the case for additionality in the past, are now much less persuasive and attractive to those running foreign aid programmes.

IMPLICATIONS OF URUGUAY ROUND AGREEMENT

The implementation of the Uruguay Round Agreement on Agriculture will impact on future food aid flows. Some commentators have argued that the Agreement could encourage a more favourable attitude to food aid donations, particularly if it fails to prevent the continued generation of food surpluses and high subsidy costs in developed countries. Because subsidisation of exports is disciplined under the Agreement, *bona fide* food aid may be the only outlet for exporting countries (Singer and Shaw 1996). These authors argue that increased food aid flows could assist the liberalisation objectives of the Agreement by removing a substantial overhang of food from commercial markets which would facilitate the adjustments required by developed countries while giving time for commercial markets to grow in developing countries. However, as the emergence of surplus food stocks would be a sign of inadequate adjustment to the disciplines of the Agreement, it is not clear why the food aid option would not simply become a crutch to postpone the necessary reforms rather than facilitating them.

The more likely outcome is that the reform process will reduce the availability of food surpluses in the future. As these have been positively associated with food aid levels in the past, the Agreement will probably lead to reduced food aid volumes. The higher world market prices resulting from the Agreement will also reduce volumes, given fixed food aid budgets. This interpretation is supported by the large downward adjustment from 7.52 to 5.35 million tonnes of cereals which the donor countries made in 1995 to their minimum food aid commitments under the Food Aid Convention and by the decline in actual food aid deliveries documented above.

The Agreement included a Decision on Measures Concerning the Possible Negative Effects of the Reform Programme on Least-Developed and Net Food-Importing Developing Countries. The Decision establishes mechanisms which provide for: (i) review of the level of food aid and the initiation of negotiations in the appropriate forum to establish a level of food aid commitments sufficient to meet the legitimate needs of developing countries during the reform programme; (ii) the adoption of guidelines to ensure that an increasing proportion of food aid is provided to the least developed and nonfood importing developing countries in fully grant or highly concessional forms; (iii) financial and technical assistance under aid programmes to improve agricultural productivity and infrastructure; and (iv) differential treatment in the context of an agreement to be negotiated on agricultural export credits. The Decision also takes into account the question of access to the resources of international financial institutions under existing facilities, or such facilities as may be established, in order to address short-term difficulties in financing normal levels of commercial imports. The follow-up to these commitments is monitored by the WTO Committee on Agriculture.

CONCLUSIONS

Official development assistance to developing countries declined in volume terms throughout the 1990s. The focus of this chapter has been on the declining *share* within this total of external assistance to agricultural development and food aid. The chapter has proposed some explanations for these trends, and it has highlighted their detrimental impact on one of the most basic human rights, to food security. When the world community met in Rome at the World Food Summit in November 1996, it adopted the Rome Declaration on World Food Security which pledged its commitment to achieve food security for all and to an ongoing effort to reducing the number of undernourished people to half their present level no later than 2015. It further committed the donor community to make efforts to mobilise technical and financial resources from all sources, including external debt relief for developing countries, to reinforce national actions to implement sustainable food security policies. As we approach the new millenium, what are the prospects that these words will be translated into a reversal of aid commitments to agricultural development and the improvement of nutrition?

The review of the reasons for the decline in external assistance to agriculture highlighted a number of issues: the poor performance on average of some types of agricultural projects; the complexity and cost of lending to agriculture; the futility of project aid in a hostile policy environment to agricultural development; the influence of farming and environmental lobbies in developed countries; crowding out by lending for structural adjustment and debt relief; the reduction in specialised agricultural staff in external assistance agencies; and falling international agricultural commodity prices.

The review also highlighted the predominant role of the international financial institutions in providing official development finance for agricultural development. Thus it is important that the World Bank Rural Development Action Plan produced in October 1996 recognised that attention to rural development had declined in the World Bank Group. It proposed a series of measures to redress this situation and put forward a series of revised principles intended to guide World Bank lending in this area in the future. The Bank has also tackled the problem of poorly-performing agricultural projects. The proportion of satisfactory or better projects in the agricultural portfolio had increased to 78 per cent in 1995, 10 percentage points above the Bank average for all projects in that year. The Action Plan sets a target of satisfactory ratings for at least 80 per cent of completed projects by the year 2000 and beyond, recognising that improved project performance is essential to increased commitment both inside and outside the World Bank Group.

The Plan recognises that the 80 per cent satisfactory rating target by the year 2000 is its only quantitative target. Crucially, no targets are set for overall lending to agriculture. Indeed, it is recognised that increased lending volume in recipient countries which agree to buy into higher priority for agriculture and rural development will be offset by a complete or nearly complete withdrawal from countries where efforts to build a consensus on giving higher priority to agriculture fail. Nonetheless, the Plan clearly hopes that a renewed commitment by the Bank to agricultural lending will send a signal both to other donors and to developing countries which will lead to an overall increase in the volume of flows.

There is evidence that other donors are beginning to follow suit. For example, the EU states that it 'has made food security a priority in development policy' and that 'the range of development policy instruments, whether in the framework of the Lomé Convention or in the framework of other agreements with different regions, is increasingly centred upon priorities for food security,' (European Commission, 1996). Certainly, favourable policy changes to encourage agricultural development within many developing countries, as well as the steps taken to open agricultural markets in the Uruguay Round, create a more positive environment for new agricultural aid projects compared to the past.

While these create the potential for increased external assistance to agriculture, reversing the declining trend in aid volumes will require active political support in donor countries. The views of development NGOs and agricultural interest groups are particularly important. NGOs are rightly concerned that aid should be directed towards the most vulnerable communities and households. Much agricultural aid in the past, which went to promote export agricultural crops, irrigation projects and large-scale land development, failed to have a clear poverty focus. Not surprisingly, NGO support went instead to increasing aid flows to areas such as environmental protection and the social sector. One of the requirements for rebuilding support for increased agricultural aid will be to re-think the strategy of agricultural development in order to emphasise the links with poverty alleviation. One of the refreshing things about the World Bank Rural Development Action Plan is its explicit recognition of this requirement.

The influence of agricultural interest groups in the formulation of aid policy varies across countries and is more significant in the United States than in Europe. The United States is a major food exporter, and in periods of low world market prices and rising food surpluses, farmers have lobbied hard against extending aid to agricultural projects in developing countries which might provide additional competition. The extensive research on whether foreign aid complements or conflicts with the interests of US producers shows decisively that even farmers in the industrialised countries gain from faster agricultural growth in developing countries (as an example, see Rosegrant et al., 1995). This is a message which needs to be communicated again and again.

Unfortunately, the prospects for a reversal of the decline in food aid are less buoyant.

Food aid programmes will probably continue for the rest of this decade at the lower levels seen in recent years. Despite the evidence that the LIFDCs could absorb double the food aid volumes provided even in the peak year of 1993, the political coalitions which sustained food aid in the past have begun to dissipate and fragment. De-linking of food aid from agricultural policy may improve its quality, but also reduces political support for higher volumes. Food aid is now more competitive with financial aid and donors see few reasons why a higher proportion of shrinking financial aid budgets should be diverted to food aid. The pledge in the Decision attached to the Uruguay Agreement on Agriculture to review the level of food aid established under the Food Aid Convention 'to establish a level of food aid commitments sufficient to meet the legitimate needs of developing countries during the reform programme' will probably mean no further reduction in these commitments over the lifetime of the Agreement. These minimum commitments under the Food Aid Convention set a floor which guarantees the continuation of food aid programmes at more or less the current level, but there seems little reason for donors to exceed these levels in future.

The food security implications of this drop in food aid need to be carefully evaluated. Aid for emergencies will continue to have first call on food aid budgets. More careful targeting of food aid on the most needy countries is essential, but with 80 per cent of deliveries now going to LIFDCs, there is little excess to be squeezed in this area. Project food aid is also likely to be protected because of the institutionalisation of WFP and NGO programmes which make effective use of this kind of aid. The main brunt of the reduction in food aid will fall on programme aid where the food security implications are more indirect and depend on the developmental use of the counterpart funds. Assuming these trends continue, then the nutritional impact of declining food aid budgets will be limited. It implies, however, an even greater responsibility to ensure that adequate financial aid is made available to overcome the barriers to access to food among poor and vulnerable households. The one issue which might alter this prognosis would be a series of food emergencies leading to a massive growth in refugees and displaced persons.

NOTES

[1] A balanced review of what the Summit achieved and failed to achieve is provided in ODI (1997).

[2] LIFDSs include all food-deficit countries with per capita incomes below the level used by the World Bank to determine eligibility for IDA assistance (i.e. US$1305 in 1992).

REFERENCES

Bhattacharjee, J., 1977, External assistance for food and agricultural development in the Third World, *World Development* 5, 5–7, 633–639.

Clay, E. and Stokke, O., 1991, Assessing the performance and economic impact of food aid: the state of the art, in Clay, E. and Stokke, O., eds., *Food Aid Reconsidered: Assessing the Impact on Third World Countries*, London, Cass.

Cox, A. and Koning, A., 1997, *Understanding European Community Aid*, London, Overseas Development Institute.

European Commission, 1996, *EC Food Security and Food Aid Programme, Activity Report 1995/96*, Brussels, European Commission.

European Council, 1996, Regulation on Food Aid Policy and Food Aid Management and Special Operations in Support of Food Security, No 1292/96, Brussels.

FAO, 1996a, Food, agriculture and food security: developments since the World Food Conference and prospects, *Technical Background Document No. 1 for the World Food Summit*, Rome.

FAO, 1996b, Investment in agriculture, *Technical Background Document No. 10 for the World Food Summit*, Rome.

FAO, 1997a, External Assistance to Agriculture, Statistical Analysis Service, Rome, FAO (mimeo).

OECD, 1998, *Development Co-operation 1997*, Paris, OECD.

Overseas Development Institute, 1997, *Global Hunger and Food Security after the World Food Summit*, Briefing Paper 1, February, London, ODI.

Rosegrant, M., Agcaoili-Sombilla, M. and Perez, N., 1994, *Global Food Projections to 2020: Implications for Investment*, Food, Agriculture and the Environment Discussion Paper 5, Washington, D.C., International Food Policy Research Institute.

Ruttan, V., 1993, Does food aid have a future?, in Ruttan, V., ed., *Why Food Aid?*, Baltimore, Johns Hopkins.

Saran, R. and Konandreas, P., 1991, An additional resource? A global perspective on food aid flows in relation to development assistance, in Clay, E. and Stokke, O., eds., *Food Aid Reconsidered: Assessing the Impact on Third World Countries*, London, Cass.

Shaw, D. and Singer, H., 1996, A future food aid regime: implications of the Final Act of the Uruguay Round, *Food Policy,* 21, 4/5, 447–460.

Shapouri, S., 1995, *Food Aid Needs and Availabilities: Projections for 2005*, GFA-6, Washington, D.C., US Department of Agriculture Economic Research Service.

Von Braun, J., Hopkins R., Puetz, D. and Pandya-Lorch, R., 1993, *Aid to Agriculture: Reversing the Decline*, Food Policy Report, Washington, D.C., International Food Policy Research Institute.

Von Braun, J., Hopkins, R., and Pandya-Lorch, R., 1994, The changing political economy forces of aid to agriculture, *Agriculture and Rural Development*, 1,1, 4–7.

World Bank, 1996, *Rural Development: From Vision to Action*, Paper prepared by the rural development staff of the World Bank, Washington, D.C., World Bank.

CHAPTER 6

IS THERE A LINK BETWEEN AID AND TRADE FLOWS?
An Econometric Investigation

Mark McGillivray
Oliver Morrissey
and
Taeke Cnossen

INTRODUCTION

Is there a link between bilateral aid and trade flows? Official aid policy statements and reports on aid appear to answer in the affirmative. Various references are made to the commercial "return" from aid, directly by promoting donor exporters (especially tied aid which subsidises exports) or indirectly by increasing recipient growth and capacity to purchase exports. References are also made to linking the allocation of aid to donor commercial interests, with emphasis being given to important export markets, both current and potential. Taking the official line at face value, one could therefore be forgiven for assuming that there is indeed a causal bi-directional link between aid and trade flows: aid leads to trade and trade leads to aid. This impression is reinforced by reading much of the independent NGO literature on aid and trade (see Randal and German, 1994). It is often simply taken for granted, even by academic commentators, that such a link exists, yet there has been little research which has sought to empirically validate, in any systematic way, whether a link between aid and trade actually exists.

There are many reasons why one might expect to observe a correlation between aid and trade flows from a donor to a particular recipient. An obvious case is tied aid, where the granting of aid is contingent on purchasing goods from the donor. More generally, aid may be given to countries, such as ex-colonies, which have strong trading ties with the donor. Donors being more likely to grant aid to countries which purchase their exports; in this context, trade (with the donor) is often found to be a significant explanatory variable in aid allocation regressions. Alternatively, aid may engender trade dependency, where recipients purchase imports from donors granting them large amounts of aid because the aid is considered contingent on the imports. Yet another suggestion is that aid is trade creating: the aid contributes to economic growth in the recipient which generates an increase in donor exports to the recipient. Such trade creation benefits the donor, and can be a strong factor in maintaining or increasing the value of aid flows.

While there is an empirical literature on aid allocation (reviewed in McGillivray and White, 1993), and thus of the trade leading to aid hypothesis, there has been very little on the hypothesis that aid leads to trade and thus very little on bi-directional causality. At the micro-level, there is considerable anecdotal and some empirical evidence: Morrissey *et al.*, (1992) review the UK literature, including reports by business groups, while Andersson and Hellstrŝm (1994) provide a detailed study for Sweden. These studies, especially business reports, generally refer to tied aid but the evidence that tied aid leads to increased exports (which is by no means conclusive) is rarely generalisable: while it may be true that particular firms benefit from aid-supported exports, this does not mean that a donor country benefits in that it exports more to a particular recipient in the presence of tied aid than it would have were there no tied aid flows between the two. While the micro studies are informative, we confine attention to macro studies based on aggregate aid and trade flows. Clearly, there are problems with aggregate data, but the objective is to assess if such data offer any evidence to support the micro data. Consequently, this chapter provides an econometric investigation of the aid-trade link, testing *inter alia* for bi-directional causality between these flows.

The chapter is structured as follows. In Section II we outline the various theories or explanations of why we may expect to see a relationship between aid and trade flows, and demonstrate that a number of different links are possible. Section III turns to the main objective of the paper: testing whether aid causes trade and trade causes aid. It is concerned specifically with French, German and British aid and trade flows to a sample of African countries. Section IV concludes and considers some possible directions for future research.

LINKAGES BETWEEN AID AND TRADE FLOWS: THEORIES AND APPROACHES

The reasons why one might expect a causal link between aid and trade vary from the simple to the complex. In some cases such as aid tying these links will be direct, in others they will be indirect. The fundamental requirement for a bi-directional link is that each flow must be greater given the presence of the other than would be the case were the other flow absent. That is, the various impacts of aid must culminate in a higher level of donor exports than would be the case without aid, and the various impacts of bilateral trade (in particular donor exports) must result in a higher level of aid than would otherwise be the case. The reasons why this may or may not be the case can be considered under two broad headings, those asserting a causal link from aid to trade and those asserting a causal link from trade to aid.

ARGUMENTS FOR CAUSALITY FROM AID TO TRADE

Aid flows may induce donor exports either because of the general economic effects on the recipient, or because the aid is directly linked to trade, or because it reinforces bilateral economic and political links (or a combination of all three). However, each of these reasons linking aid to trade can operate in reverse, such that aid reduces trade.

Macroeconomic impact of aid

Traditional macroeconomic theories of aid impact posit that aid supplements domestic savings, leading to higher investment which contributes to higher rates of economic growth than would be the case without aid (White, 1992, provides a comprehensive survey). This growth induces a greater capacity of recipient countries to absorb foreign goods and services, including those originating from donors (in line with their global competitiveness). More recently, aid is often linked to the implementation of structural economic reforms, especially the liberalisation of foreign trade regimes (Morrissey, 1995); World Bank adjustment programmes and associated financing are a good example of this type of aid, and bilateral donors have typically tied their aid to the existence of such an agreement with the Bank. This can have an indirect effect on donor exports, in the sense the reductions in trade barriers can increase their access to markets in developing countries and/or the aid financing averts import compression. Thus there are a number of economic mechanisms through which aid can induce donor exports by increasing recipient import capacity, notably through economic growth.

Despite the early optimism associated with aid, there is no consensus regarding its macroeconomic impact. Aid may have a negligible macroeconomic impact due to the practices of recipient governments (Heller, 1975): if aid is treated as income it will finance increases in both savings and consumption, provided the marginal propensity to save in recipient countries is less than unity (the lower it is the less the impact of aid on investment and growth). Even if all aid is saved and invested it may crowd-out public investment and increase the price of investment goods, with the end result of lower growth than would otherwise be the case (Mosley *et al.*, 1987, show that this is an empirical issue for which the evidence is mixed). A similar result can emerge if donors require matching funds. To raise these funds recipients must increase taxes and/or the public sector borrowing requirement, which can increase interest rates and crowd-out private sector investment (White and McGillivray, 1992). Other undesirable macroeconomic consequences include Dutch Disease (van Wijnbergen, 1986). The empirical evidence on the impact of aid is correspondingly inconclusive (Mosley *et al.*, 1987).

Aid tying

The most direct link between aid and trade is *formal tying*, where the provision of aid is dependent upon the recipient purchasing goods from the donor. In practice this usually means that aid is provided in the form of goods and services procured in the donor country, thus the aid itself is trade (donor exports). In addition to the exports directly financed tied aid also increases recipient exposure to donor goods and services which encourages follow-on orders and expands, or at least consolidates, commercial ties; in this way aid is used as an instrument of trade policy (Morrissey, 1993a). A common variant of tied aid is mixed credits, where donors provide an export subsidy to their companies seeking contracts in developing countries, paying for this out of the aid budget; while individual exporters can gain huge commercial benefits, there is a lack of evidence that the donor derives a net economic benefit (Morrissey, 1991). A less direct form of tying is *informal*, where donors direct aid towards projects, goods or countries in which its own industries have a strong competitive advantage (in which case it is likely that tenders would go to firms in these industries even in the absence of tying); in practice it is difficult to distinguish resulting trade from competitive advantage. There is a related argument that aid generates political goodwill, from the recipient towards the donor, such that the recipient may feel more disposed, if not obliged, to purchase goods from the donor (Morrissey, 1993a).

Aid tying can also retard economic growth in recipient countries and as such be counterproductive in promoting donor exports. It has been argued that if aid was untied, so that the recipients could choose how to spend it, they would have the opportunity to determine their own investment projects, to determine the technology appropriate to their own investment projects, to determine the technology appropriate to their own long-term interests and to purchase exports at world prices (Morrissey, 1993a). Empirical studies have shown that exports provided under tied aid are overpriced, compared to prevailing world prices, by between 10 and 40 percent (Jepma, 1991). Moreover, "the goods offered are of low priority to the recipient, are excessively capital-intensive, are highly dependent on Western technologies and are import biased" (Jepma, 1989, p.10). Thus, under tied aid, recipients may experience lower growth than would otherwise be the case (as they are prevented from purchasing the most appropriate goods at the best price). There is also an argument that aid-tying has a detrimental economic impact on donors. Tied aid often supports inefficient industries: such a use of public funds has a high opportunity cost, in that resources used by these industries could be diverted to more efficient uses, and imposes a real economic cost on the donor (Morrissey *et al.*, 1992).

Aid-induced trade dependency

Even in the absence of tied aid there are ways in which aid can induce recipient dependence on donors for the supply of goods and services. For example, aid tends to fund projects that require the import of capital goods, typically produced by donors. This effect is not necessarily isolated to the life of the project; where equipment and machinery are involved, replacement parts are often only available in the original source country. Another example is food aid. It has been argued widely that food aid distorts the allocation of resources in recipient countries away from the production of food, and can exacerbate and prolong the very shortages it is intended to overcome, and can distort domestic consumption patterns (Maxwell and Singer, 1977). An outcome is prolonged dependence on donor countries not only for food aid but for food purchased on commercial terms.

A counter-view is that aid dependency discourages trade with donors. Radical critiques of aid argue that it merely serves to keep poor countries poor, through tying or insofar as aid acts as a barrier to sociopolitical change and therefore preserves the *status quo* in developing countries. In such cases aid can cause a great deal of ill-feeling toward donors, especially when it is perceived within the recipient as being of poor quality, or motivated by donor interest and not recipient need, or if aid is seen (as it often still is) as a form of imperialism. It is worth noting that if aid were given untied and disinterestedly but effectively in promoting recipient growth, the benefits would spread to donors in many ways; donor concerns that they are deriving insufficient benefits lead them to distort aid, so reducing potential benefits to all and often undermining any relationship of partnership between donor and recipient.

ARGUMENTS FOR CAUSALITY FROM TRADE TO AID

The view that trade can lead to aid is generally attributed to effects of aid allocation policies of donors. These policies, in turn, are argued to be the result of the various pressures, exerted by domestic lobby groups, to which policy formulation is subject. Business groups and sections of the donor bureaucracy concerned with trade promotion are particularly active in this regard (Morrissey, *et al.*, 1992). Trade can lead to further aid if donors give preference in the allocation of their aid to countries with which they have the greatest commercial links. With respect to the geographical allocation of aid, one would therefore expect that, *ceteris paribus,* the greater the value of donor exports to a given LDC, the greater the amount of aid it would be allocated by the donor. Should exports to this country increase over time, one would also expect that aid would increase (in line with increases in the donor aid program); if a recipient's share of donor exports increases relative to other recipients one would expect its share of aid to increase. In these events, the donor is rewarding the LDC for purchasing its exports, or seeking to consolidate and/or expand its market in the country through the expectation that aid will have one or more of its trade-inducing effects.

There are scenarios where a negative relationship between aid and donor exports may be observed, especially from cross section data. A donor may well decide to pursue a more aggressive and indeed risky strategy; rather than focusing on established export markets, it could instead use aid to promote export ties in those countries which currently are lesser markets (McGillivray and Oczkowski, 1992). In this case, one would expect the geographical allocation of aid to be inversely related to export flows. This could also result if donors base their aid allocation decisions not on the level of exports to countries, but on the intensity of their trade with recipients, measured by their exports to a particular country as a proportion of world exports to it; the greater the intensity the greater the amount of aid allocated. This could result in a negative relationship between aid and exports if there is a systematic inverse relationship between exports and intensity. The aid allocation literature does not provide a consensus on the impact of trade on aid flows (McGillivray and White, 1993).

HYPOTHESISED AID-TRADE CAUSAL LINKS

In summary, three general possibilities can be identified. The first is that trade is a determinant of aid: donors grant more aid to those developing countries which import more from them. This is Case I which can be expressed as the hypothesis that "trade causes aid" and if such causality is found the implication is that trade flows tend to precede aid flows in time. There is no assessment of the impact of aid on the recipient economy: Case I relates to why donors grant aid to one recipient rather than another, and says nothing about the economic merits of the aid. If we observe that aid impacts on trade, the hypothesis that "aid causes trade", the associated economic merits of aid could be positive or negative. On the one hand, the aid may engender trade dependency, which we term Case II: aid causes trade with the donor not because the aid generates growth, but because it establishes a tie with the donor (which is likely to impair recipient growth). On the other hand, if aid contributes to growth, or relaxes a foreign exchange gap, we would expect recipient imports to increase: we term this Case III, where aid creates trade through growth. Put briefly:

Case I: Trade is a determinant of aid allocation; tested as the hypothesis "trade causes aid" (lagged effect of trade on aid).

Case II: Aid generates trade dependency (recipient on the donor); tested as hypothesis that aid and trade are simultaneously determined (tying).

Case III: Aid leads to trade creation via growth; tested as hypothesis that "aid causes trade" (lagged effect of aid on trade).[1]

AN ECONOMETRIC INVESTIGATION

Our attention now turns to econometrically evaluating the preceding hypotheses. Morrissey (1993b) looked at Case II (although data on shares were not used) by estimating the following equation:

$$\Delta X_{ij} = \beta_0 + \beta_1 \Delta M_i + \beta_2 \Delta A_{ij} + e_i \tag{6.1}$$

where X_{ij} is exports from aid donor j to aid recipient i, M_{ij} is total imports into i, A_{ij} is aid from j to i, Δ indicates year-on-year changes and e_i is an error term with the standard properties. A selection of results from estimating (6.1) using pooled cross section data relating to three donors and a sample of sub-Saharan recipients is shown in Table 6.1. These results highlight a number of problems with this approach. First, equation (6.1) ignores historical links between donors and recipients. In the case of colonial ties, for example, there are well known biases tending to result in higher levels of exports (and aid) than would otherwise be the case. The argument for exclusion is that historic links affect (starting) levels but need not affect year-on-year changes; this may or may not be true and could be tested. Second, there is serious difficulty in interpreting the coefficients. Consider the case where an increase in aid directly finances an increase in imports so that $\Delta A_{ij} = \Delta X_{ij}$ implying $\beta_2 = 1$. The coefficient estimates of (6.1), however, will depend on whether ΔX_{ij} displaces other sources or increases total imports. The specification of (6.1) does not allow one to distinguish these possibilities; similar problems apply to less extreme cases.

Table 6.1. Simple Estimates of the Aid-Trade Relationship.
Model: $\Delta X_{ij} = \beta_0 + \beta_1 \Delta M_i + \beta_2 \Delta A_{ij} + e_i$

		β_0	β_1	β_3	R^2	F
France:	Fixed Effects Model		0.091* (13.25)	0.592 (1.43)	0.577	24.21
	Kmenta Model	0.398 (0.98)	0.070* (15.11)	0.376* (4.99)	0.372	98.71
Germany:	Fixed Effects Model		0.212* (6.71)	–0.310 (–1.72)	0.728	45.86
	Kmenta Model	0.182 (0.75)	0.037 (0.65)	0.067* (17.52)	0.422	121.92
UK:	Fixed Effects Model		0.170* (37.89)	0.742 (1.47)	0.738	48.276
	Kmenta Model	–0.75** (–2.23)	0.084* (15.62)	0.508* (4.66)	0.355	91.78

Figures in parentheses are *t* statistics (heteroskedasticity-corrected in the cases of Fixed Effect Model results). The R^2 is adjusted in the cases of Kmenta model results; for the Fixed Effect Model results it is the Buse raw-moment R^2. * denotes significant at the 95 percent level or greater. Sample size is 504 throughout.

Nevertheless, the results in Table 6.1 provide some indication of what to expect. In all cases, unsurprisingly, the change in donor exports followed the trend in total recipient imports. For both France and Germany, the positive constant indicates that their exports were tending to increase, but only for France is there a suggestion that aid contributed to the increase in exports. For the UK, while there is evidence that aid contributed to increased exports, the trend is of declining exports to African countries. The evidence suggests that France used aid to maintain and increase its exports to Africa, the UK used aid to offset the decline in its exports, while Germany did not need to use aid to increase its export performance. Given the problems with the approach, these results, while intuitively appealing, may not be reliable. Our attention now turns, therefore, to a more thorough analysis of the data.

For this analysis we have collected data on exports and net aid disbursements from France, Germany and the UK to a sample of 36 African countries over 1969–92 (for some African countries the end-point is several years earlier). The aid data are from the OECD's *Geographical Distribution of Financial Flows to Developing Countries*, and the exports are in fact imports from each donor as reported in the IMF's *International Financial Statistics Yearbook.* Both sets of data were reported in current $US. To obtain real values we created two series for each variable. Shares referred to below are donor aid and exports as shares of total recipient aid and exports respectively; the ratio series is each of aid and imports as shares of recipient GDP. Here we concentrate on the method and the classifications of donor-recipient pairs according to the three Cases set out above.

The analysis presented here is based on comparing results using the two sets of pairwise data (shares and ratios), with variables:

M_{ij}/M_i: import share: imports by recipient *i* from donor *j* expressed as a share of total imports by *i*;

A_{ij}/A_i: aid share: aid from donor *j* to recipient *i* as share of total aid to *i*;

M_{ij}/G_i: import ratio: imports from donor *j* as a share of *i*'s GDP; and,

A_{ij}/G_i: aid ratio (aid from donor *j* as a share of *i*'s GDP).

The aid-trade relationship has both time and cross-section dimensions. Whether aid is trade creating, and indeed if it impacts on growth, is a dynamic question that must be addressed to time series data. In contrast, the importance of trade as a determinant of aid allocations is an issue of distribution across countries, which must be addressed to cross section data. As the questions we ask combine both elements, it is appropriate to use panel data (where time series for the same cross section are pooled). There are well known econometric difficulties with both time series and cross section data; unfortunately, these are multiplied when the two are pooled. The most obvious problem with pooled cross-section and time series data is that the coefficients are assumed constant over time and across countries. Techniques for dealing with the latter are well established, the most simple approach being to estimate a fixed effects model (as in Table 6.1): a separate dummy variable is included for each country, which picks up any systematic difference between that and other countries (the fixed effect). One may then wish to adjust the estimated fixed effects model to account for heteroskedasticity and serial correlation of the error term (the Kmenta model, as reported in Table 6.1, does this). Such adjustments are standard and reported for our results.

It is now standard in time series econometrics to test for cointegration between the variables under scrutiny. To do this properly would require finding the cointegrating relationship or error correction mechanism for each time series; this can be an arduous task for any time series, and it is beyond our scope to attempt it for over 200 pairwise time series. Furthermore, cointegration tests are based on asymptotic values which assumes long time series; our series are all of fewer than 25 observations which are small (some might say too small), so cointegration tests may not be reliable. Our aim is not strictly to find the cointegrating relationship but to test the order of integration of each pairwise time series so that we can then only pool those countries for which the variables have the same order of integration. Our method follows a number of stages.

The first involved testing for the order of integration of each time series. This is simply a unit root test to identify at what order of integration the variable is stationary. An I(0) variable is stationary in levels (ie. it has constant mean and constant variance around that mean; any shock that causes a deviation from the mean will have only a temporary effect), which does not mean that the level is constant over time (it may, for example, have a trend). An I(1) variable is stationary in first differences (changes), an I(2) variable is stationary in second differences (changes in changes), etc.

The second stage involved identifying those countries for which paired series are of the same order of integration; only variables of the same order of integration exhibit a stable long-run relationship. We then test if they are cointegrated. If so, we know that the error term when one is regressed on the other is itself stationary, hence has constant mean and variance, hence the standard properties of the error term hold and the relationship can be estimated using OLS. If the variables are not cointegrated, this implies the error term is non-stationary and OLS estimates are not reliable.

The third and final stage involved pooling only those countries for which the pairwise variables are of the same order of integration. The merit of this approach is that the countries which are pooled exhibit similar time series characteristics. In other words, if plotted against time the variables for each countries would exhibit similar patterns. It seems reasonable to pool such countries. If the variables for one country are integrated of a different order to those for another country, the time patterns for the two countries will be very different and they should not be pooled.

It is important to emphasise that we test for order of integration purely as a means of selecting countries for use in the pooled analysis. If the pairwise variables are of different orders of integration, that country is excluded from subsequent analysis. For each of the four variables — M_{ij}/M_i, A_{ij}/A_i , M_{ij}/G_i, A_{ij}/G_i — we began with 108 pair-wise (France, Germany and UK each paired with 36 African countries) time series. Put another way, for each of the share (M_{ij}/M_i, A_{ij}/A_i) and ratio (M_{ij}/G_i, A_{ij}/G_i) paired series there were cross section samples of 36 for each of France, Germany and the UK. Once these cross sections are restricted to only those countries for which both paired series (share and ratio) are of the same order of integration, the samples are substantially reduced (and n gives the number of countries in each cross section; for example, for France M_{ij}/M_i and Aij/Ai are of the same order of integration with 13 African countries and for Germany with 15). The 'full sample' pooled results reported in Tables 6.2 and 6.3 refer to pooling all those countries for which both variables were of the same order of integration (regardless of which order).

The sub-samples are when only countries with variables of the same order of integration are pooled together. For example, for France in Table 6.2, equation 6.1 reports the results of the fixed effects model for N=13 African countries for which M_{ij}/Mi and A_{ij}/A_i are of the same order of integration, equation 3 reports the corresponding fixed effects model results for those 5 African countries for which the two variables are I(0), equation 6.5 is for the four countries for which the two are I(1), etc. The relevance of this selection procedure is demonstrated by the results. Again, in the case of France in Table 6.2, although the coefficient on A_{ij}/A_i is not significant for the full sample, it is significant for each sub-sample; for Germany and the UK the coefficient is significant in all cases, but the values differ.

Table 6.2 presents the results of estimating the following equation:

$$\left(\frac{M_{ij}}{M_i}\right)_t = \alpha_I \left(\frac{A_{ij}}{A_i}\right)_{t-1} + \sum_{n=1}^{N} \alpha_{n+1} D_n + e_{it} \qquad (6.2)$$

The α_{n+1} terms are the values of the fixed effects dummies for each country (D_n) for the total sample of N countries in the cross section. We are not actually concerned with the values of these coefficients, but rather with their sign and significance. Excepting some countries for France in Table 6.2 and UK in Table 6.3, all are significant (as indicated by the F test) and positive. This implies that for virtually all countries import shares of a donor are higher than predicted by aid shares alone, and that the precise relationship does differ across countries; effectively, the fixed effects model picks up the effect of omitted variables. Although not reported in the Tables, in virtually all cases there was evidence of heteroskedasticity. This problem, and the possibility of autocorrelation, are corrected in the adjusted fixed effects model, through the following properties

$E(e_{it}^2) = \sigma_i^2$ (imposes homoskedasticity)

$E(e_{it}e_{jt}) = 0 \; (i \; j)$ (ensures cross-section independence)

$e_{it} = \rho e_{i,t-1} + u_{it}$ (corrects for autoregression)

The aid variable is shares lagged one period in Table 6.2, so the results can be assessed as tests of Case III: are aid shares significant determinants of import shares? Equation (6.3) was estimated for current aid but the results were often not significant. The evidence in Table 6.2 suggests that there is a significant relationship between aid and import shares and that both shares are positively related for the three donors. For France, the coefficient is close to 0.6 in all cases, suggesting the import share is almost twice the aid share; for Germany, the coefficient is closer to 0.25, suggesting the import share is almost four times the aid share. This is consistent with the observation from Table 6.1 that France uses aid more actively than Germany in support for exports. For the UK it depends on the sub-sample, and there is no consistent difference in the two groups: N=7 (see row 4) includes three ex-British and three ex-French colonies plus Ethiopia; row 6. is mostly ex-French or Belgian colonies, plus Egypt, Sudan and Liberia. It is mildly suggestive that aid is of less importance to support trade in ex-colonies, but the only solid implication is that France and the UK appear to make more use of aid to support trade.

Table 6.3 shows results of estimating the following equation:

$$\left(\frac{M_{ij}}{G_i}\right)_t = \beta_1 \left(\frac{A_{ij}}{G_i}\right)_{t-1} + \sum_{n=1}^{N} \beta_{n+1} D_n + e_{it} \qquad (6.3)$$

The method of selecting samples and the models estimated are as for equation (6.2). Pooled results were only estimated for sub-samples of at least four countries. As this looks at ratios with lagged aid, it can be interpreted as 'testing' Case III. The basic implication is that the link is not significant for Germany (consistent with our priors). For the UK and France it is significant for a particular sub-sample and the coefficient for the UK of 0.8 (row 3) is slightly higher than for France (0.6 in row 6); both sub-samples include Chad, Egypt, Gabon and Gambia. This is suggestive that aid is quite important to support exports of these two donors to those same African countries. The same model was estimated with the unlagged aid ratio (not reported). In this case the same sub-sample had a significant coefficient of 0.33 for France, only the sub-sample in row 4 had a significant coefficient (of 0.69) for the UK; none of the estimated coefficients were significant for Germany. This lends support to the conclusion that the UK, and to a somewhat lesser extent France, engender trade dependency by using aid to support trade.

Table 6.2. Fixed Effects Model Estimates for Shares Series — Equation (6.2).

Model	France				Germany				United Kingdom			
	α_1	R^2	F	N	α_1	R^2	F	N	α_1	R^2	F	N
Fixed Effects	0.04 (0.73)	0.91	52.49*	13	0.07* (3.02)	0.52	99.94*	13	0.33* (11.45)	0.60	55.47*	13
Adjusted Fixed Effects	0.02 (1.02)	0.95	55.05*	13	0.05* (2.55)	0.93	89.30*	15	0.24* (5.64)	0.66	140.9*	15
Fixed Effects I(0)	0.69* (10.51)	0.67	8.02*	5	0.11* (2.81)	0.36	78.96*	6	0.21* (7.55)	0.71	45.74*	7
Adjusted Fixed Effects I(0)	0.58* (9.90)	0.90	7.14*	5	0.09* (2.84)	0.93	8.53*	6	0.22* (4.91)	0.73	11.32*	7
Fixed Effects I(1)	0.50* (9.95)	0.93	20.40*	4	0.29* (6.82)	0.30	17.62*	9	0.74* (7.35)	0.44	21.54*	8
Adjusted Fixed Effects I(1)	0.57* (18.39)	0.93	3.38*	4	0.27* (7.56)	0.79	17.45*	9	0.68* (9.29)	0.66	14.52*	8
Fixed Effects I(2)	0.40* (9.16)	0.57	10.71*	4								
Adjusted Fixed Effects I(2)	0.59* (13.50)	0.79	6.22*	4								

The cross-section of countries is here broken up by the order of integration of the two variables and estimations are performed separately. The full sample is the sample of all those countries having both variables integrated of the same order, be it I(0), I(1) or I(2). I(0) denotes integrated of order zero, I(1) integrated of order one and I(2) integrated of order two or more. The R^2 reported is adjusted. That for the adjusted fixed effects model refers to the Buse raw-moment R^2.. The F statistics test for the significance of the fixed effects. Numbers in parentheses are *t* ratios. * indicates significance at the 95 percent lever or greater. *N* indicates the number of countries in the cross-section: the usual time period for these countries ranges from 21 to 24.

Table 6.3. Fixed Effects Model Estimates for Shares Series — Equation (6.3).

Model	France				Germany				United Kingdom			
	β_1	R^2	F	*N*	β_1	R^2	F	*N*	β_1	R^2	F	*N*
Fixed Effects	0.003 (0.03)	0.84	136.4*	12	0.13 (1.44)	0.29	80.35*	7	0.69* (3.66)	0.86	72.18*	14
Adjusted Fixed Effects	0.01* (0.13)	0.78	26.96*	12	0.05 (0.75)	0.79	10.03*	7	0.42 (1.73)	0.82	37.27*	14
Fixed Effects I(0)					0.03 (0.28)	0.15	56.47*	4	0.79* (3.47)	0.91	74.10*	5
Adjusted Fixed Effects I(0)					–0.01 (–0.08)	0.71	4.74*	4	0.45 (1.25)	0.83	6.21*	5
Fixed Effects I(1)	0.62* (5.34)	0.68	75.83*	8					–0.33 (–0.55)	0.65	57.61*	8
Adjusted Fixed Effects I(1)	0.58* (7.48)	0.71	12.72*	8					0.32 (0.95)	0.81	11.50*	8

The cross-section of countries is here broken up by the order of integration of the two variables and estimations are performed separately. The full sample is the sample of all those countries having both variables integrated of the same order, be it I(0), I(1) or I(2). I(0) denotes integrated of order zero, I(1) integrated of order one and I(2) integrated of order two or more. The R^2 reported is adjusted. That for the adjusted fixed effects model refers to the Buse raw-moment R^2.. The F statistics test for the significance of the fixed effects. Numbers in parentheses are *t* ratios. * indicates significance at the 95 percent lever or greater. *N* indicates the number of countries in the cross-section: the usual time period for these countries ranges from 21 to 24.

ASSESSING THE DIRECTION OF CAUSALITY

The estimates in Tables 6.1 to 6.3 and the method outlined above relate to how we could try to estimate if there is an aid-trade link; progress on this front will involve more intensive estimation of a more sophisticated specification than (6.2) and (6.3), best tackled through trying to identify the 'demand for imports' equation for each country, and then testing if the aid variable is significant when included. The other issue raised in Section II was whether there is a causal (in a Granger sense) link between aid and trade. Evidence on causality can be used to assess which if any of Cases I, II, or III is most valid (it is possible that all have some validity). Consequently, we estimated the following equations:

$$\left(\frac{M_{ij}}{M_i}\right)_t = \alpha_0 + \sum_{n=0}^{x} \alpha_n \left(\frac{A_{ij}}{A_i}\right)_{t-n} + \sum_{n=1}^{y} \alpha_{x+n} \left(\frac{M_{ij}}{M_i}\right)_{t-n} + \mu_{it} \tag{6.4}$$

$$\left(\frac{A_{ij}}{A_i}\right)_t = \beta_0 + \sum_{n=0}^{x} \beta_n \left(\frac{A_{ij}}{A_i}\right)_{t-n} + \sum_{n=1}^{y} \beta_{x+n} \left(\frac{M_{ij}}{M_i}\right)_{t-n} + \nu_{it} \tag{6.5}$$

$$\left(\frac{M_{ij}}{G_i}\right)_t = \gamma_0 + \sum_{n=0}^{x} \gamma_n \left(\frac{A_{ij}}{G_i}\right)_{t-n} + \sum_{n=1}^{y} \gamma_{x+n} \left(\frac{M_{ij}}{G_i}\right)_{t-n} + \varepsilon_{it} \tag{6.6}$$

$$\left(\frac{A_{ij}}{G_i}\right)_t = \delta_0 + \sum_{n=0}^{x} \delta_n \left(\frac{A_{ij}}{G_i}\right)_{t-n} + \sum_{n=1}^{y} \delta_{x+n} \left(\frac{M_{ij}}{G_i}\right)_{t-n} + \upsilon_{it} \tag{6.7}$$

Evidence of causality from aid to trade (Case III above) would require a finding that α_n in (6.4) and/or γ_n in (6.6) were significant; evidence of causality from trade to aid (Case I) would require finding β_n in (6.5) and/or δ_n in (6.7) to be significant; bi-directional causality could be asserted if α_n and β_n, or γ_n and δ_n were found to both be significant. Contemporaneous causality was tested by having no lagged value on aid in (6.4) and no lagged value on trade in (6.5); if current aid appears to cause current trade we infer that this is evidence of trade dependency (Case II in Section II).

The results are presented in Appendix Tables 6.A1 to 6.A6 and summarised in Table 6.4. Our interpretations rely primarily on the F statistics and *t* ratios reported in the Appendix tables. The first set of results in Table 6.4 refer to equation (6.5) and can be interpreted, where causality is found, as evidence in favour of Case III. All evidence of causality from aid to imports, equations (6.5) and (6.7), excluding the case of contemporaneous causality, are evidence in favour of Case III. Contemporaneous causality in equation (6.5) is interpreted as evidence in favour of Case II. Thus, overall, there are 18 cases offering evidence in support of Case III and 6 offering evidence in favour of case II. Any finding that imports cause aid, equations (6.6) and (6.8), is evidence in support of Case I; there are 24 such cases. There are quite a few cases of bi-directional causality: for Uganda and Rwanda with respect to France; for Algeria with respect to Germany; and for Mauritius and Ethiopia with respect to the

Table 6.4. Causality in Aid and Trade Flows.

	France	Germany	United Kingdom
Aid causes Imports (Shares) (Case III, equation 6.4)	Burundi Central African Rep. Tanzania	Algeria Cameroon Egypt Togo	Central African R Mauritius
Imports cause Aid (shares) (Case I, equation 6.5)		Burkina Faso Congo Kenya Tanzania Zambia	Ethiopia
Aid causes Imports (ratios) (Case III, equation 6.6)	Chad Madagascar Rwanda	Algeria Benin Malawi	Chad Mauritius Rwanda
Imports cause Aid (ratios, Case I, equation 6.7)	Congo Gambia Rwanda	Mauritania Tanzania	Burkina Faso Congo Egypt Gabon Ghana Mauritius
Aid causes Imports (Case II, equation 6.4)	Kenya Uganda	Algeria	Burundi Ethiopia Mauritius
Imports cause Aid (Case I, equation 6.5)	Mauritius Uganda	Algeria Kenya	Ethiopia

UK. Thus, the choice between case I and either of the other cases (which are difficult to distinguish), is finely balanced. There is evidence in favour of all cases.

If we consider the three donors, the issue remains as finely balanced and again there is evidence supporting all possibilities. Particular pairings are quite interesting. Except for contemporaneous causality, which is bi-directional, there is a consistent finding that aid causes imports from Germany to Algeria; an intuitive interpretation could be that Germany uses aid to break into the French ties with Algeria. A similar finding holds for the UK and Mauritius, but this offers no intuitive interpretation. Our conclusion is that there is evidence for all cases and a fuller understanding of the complex aid-trade relationship will require more detailed study of individual donor-recipient relations.

CONCLUSION

The literature on aid policy, and especially on donor motives for aid, abounds with assertions regarding actual (but unproven) and potential reasons as to why aid and trade flows between donors and specific recipients may be linked; this alone validates our attempt to assess the empirical basis for such assertions. The arguments were set out in Section II, which identified three hypotheses to distinguish alternative cases of the aid-trade relationship. The empirical evidence reviewed here offers some evidence in support of all cases, but further detailed analysis would be required to yield any reliable conclusions. Testing for causality using time series data is an advance on looking at descriptive statistics and the results of aid allocation studies, but should be seen as no more than an initial attempt to validate the aid-trade relationship. The available evidence suggests that there is indeed a relationship between aid and trade, but that the specific nature of this relationship can vary between donor-recipient pairs.

The obvious implication for future research is to explore in more detail the nature of specific donor-recipient relationships. We have gone some way towards suggesting the econometric basis for such studies, and more sophisticated modelling techniques could be employed, but arguably the most important advances are those concerning theory. We do not, in the economic literature, have an accepted formal model of the allocation of aid, nor of how aid can act as a determinant of trade flows. Until such models are developed and tested, we cannot adequately understand why observed (statistically) aid-trade relationships take the form they do; even the more sophisticated existing (econometric) analyses are based on the *ad hoc* specification of regression equations. The theoretical model should yield structural equations which are suitable for estimation, or at least a model which can be solved to obtain appropriate reduced form equations. Until such models are developed and empirically validated, only very tentative conclusions can be drawn regarding the links between aid and trade. Nevertheless, we hope we have shown, both in terms of the purported theoretical links and the empirical evidence, that this is a relationship central to the understanding of donor aid policies and the impact of aid on recipient countries.

NOTES

[1] McGillivray and Morrissey (1998) report results from a selection of 15 studies from the aid allocation literature which look at whether trade causes aid. While a number of these studies provide statistical evidence of a correlation between aid and trade, there are important caveats (McGillivray and White, 1992, provide a comprehensive statement). The majority of studies test only for a contemporaneous relationship. This makes interpretation of results somewhat difficult: it may be the case that the correlation is not due to the aid allocation decisions of donors, but the effects that aid has on trade (the direction of causality is therefore ambiguous). There are also data limitations. Each of the 15 studies uses cross section data, and as such implicitly assume that trade has the same impact on aid for all countries included in the sample; that is, the estimated coefficient on the trade variable is restricted to being the same for all recipients in the sample. This would seem an heroic assumption. Finally, and most obviously, the results refer only to correlations and inferences regarding causality cannot be drawn. Nilsson (1996) adopted a very different approach and introduced aid flows into a gravity trade model to test for an aid-trade link between each EU donor and all recipients of EU aid (the sample of recipients thus varied from year to year). The basis of the gravity model is that exports from (donor) j to (recipient) i are determined by the size of the two countries (absolute and per capita GNP) and the physical distance between them. To these core variables were

added bilateral aid flows (from *j* to *i*), multilateral aid (to *i*) and a dummy for members of Lomè to pick up historic links. The results are strongly suggestive of significant links between bilateral aid and donor exports to recipients for Belgium, Germany, France, Italy, Spain and the UK. Nilsson's approach does not, however, allow one to infer anything about the direction of causality. McGillivray and Morrissey (1998) also report results for unpublished studies of whether aid causes trade.

REFERENCES

Andersson, T. and H. Hellstršm (1994), *Links between Development Assistance and Donor Country Exports — the case of Sweden*, SASDA, Ds 1994:58 Report 1, Stockholm: Ministry for Foreign Affairs.

Granger, C.J. (1969), "Investigating Causal Relationships by Econometric Models and Cross Spectral Methods", *Econometrica*, 37, 424–435.

Heller, P. (1975), "A Model of Public Fiscal Behaviour in Developing Countries: Aid, Investment and Taxation", *American Economic Review*, 65, 313–327.

International Monetary Fund (IMF) (1974–94), *Direction of Trade Statistics Yearbook*, International Monetary Fund, Washington.

Jepma, C. (1989), *The Tying of Aid*, International Foundation for Development Economics, University of Groningen.

Jepma, C. (1991), *EC-wide Untying*, International Foundation for Development Economics and Department of Economics, University of Groningen.

Maxwell, S. and H. Singer (1977), "Food Aid to Developing Countries: A Survey" *World Development*, 7: 4, 225–247.

McGillivray, M. and E. Oczkowski (1992), "A two-part sample selection model of British bilateral foreign aid allocation", *Applied Economics*, 24, 1311–1319.

McGillivray, M. and O. Morrissey (1998), *Links between Aid and Trade Flows: A Literature Survey*, CREDIT Research Paper, Centre for Research in Economic Development and International Trade, University of Nottingham, Nottingham (forthcoming).

McGillivray, M. and H. White (1993), "Explanatory Studies of Aid Allocation among Developing Countries", The Hague: *ISS Working Paper No. 148*.

Morrissey, O. (1991), "An Evaluation of the Economic Effects of the Aid and Trade Provision", *Journal of Development Studies*, 28, 104–129.

Morrissey, O. (1993a), "The Mixing of Aid and Trade Policies", *The World Economy*, 16:1, 69–84.

Morrissey, O. (1993b), "Donor Trade Benefits from Aid: Evidence from the EC and sub-Saharan Africa", paper presented to the Aid Policy Working Group: General Sessions, *VIIth EADI General Conference*, Berlin, 15–18 September 1993.

Morrissey, O. (1995), "Politics and Economic Policy Reform: Trade Liberalisation in Sub-Saharan Africa", *Journal of International Development*, 7: 4, 599–618.

Morrissey, O., B. Smith and E. Horesh (1992), *British Aid and International Trade*, Buckingham: Open University Press.

Mosley, P, J. Hudson and S. Horrell (1987), "Aid, the Public Sector and the Market in Less Developed Countries", *Economic Journal*, 97, 616–641.

Nilsson, L. (1996), "Aid and Donor Exports: The Case of the EU Countries", Department of Economics, University of Lund, mimeo.

OECD (1975–94), *Geographical Distribution of Financial Flows to Developing Countries*, Paris: Organisation for Economic Co-operation and Development .

Randal, J. and T. German (Eds) (1994), *The Reality of Aid 94*, London: ActionAid

van Wijnbergen, S. (1986), "Macroeconomic Aspects of the Effectiveness of Foreign Aid: The Two Gap Model, Home Goods Disequilibrium and Real Exchange Rate Misalignment", *Journal of International Economics*, 21, 123–136.

White, H. (1992), "The Macroeconomic Impact of Development Aid: A Critical Survey", *Journal of Development Studies* , 28, 163–240

White, H. and M. McGillivray (1992), "Aid, the Public Sector and Crowding In", in *Two Papers on Aid and Government,* ISS Working Paper, No. 126, The Hague.

APPENDIX — RESULTS FOR GRANGER CAUSALITY TESTS

Table 6A1: Econometric Estimates.

$$\text{Model: } \left(\frac{M_{ij}}{M_i}\right)_t = \alpha_0 + \sum_{n=0}^{x} \alpha_n \left(\frac{A_{ij}}{A_i}\right)_{t-n} + \sum_{n=1}^{y} \alpha_{x+n} \left(\frac{M_{ij}}{M_i}\right)_{t-n} + \mu_{it}$$

	France			Germany			United Kingdom		
Aid Recipient	***l,m***	**F**	***lres***	***l,m***	**F**	***lres***	***l,m***	**F**	***lres***
Algeria (*n*=25)				2,3	16.3*				
Burkina Faso (*n*=23)				2,3	1.79				
Burundi (*n*=25)	1,1	5.12*					3,1	0.0	
Cameroon (*n*=24)				1,2	4.84*				
Central African Rep. (*n*=23)	2,2	3.02*					2,3	2.58*	
Chad (*n*=23)							2,1	2.87	
Congo (*n*=23)	3,1	0.45		3,2	1.39				
Egypt (*n*=25)				2,2	5.53*		3,1	0.15	
Ethiopia (*n*=24)							3,1	1.12	
Kenya (*n*=25)	2,2	1.17		1,1	0.28				
Madagascar (*n*=23)				1,2	0.74				
Mauritius (*n*=25)	2,2	1.97					3,2	3.69*	
Morocco (*n*=25)				1,3	1.67		3,1	–0.21	
Nigeria (*n*=24)				1,2	1.03				
Rwanda (*n*=24)							3,2	2.50	
Sierra Leone (*n*=25)				1,1	0.73				
Tanzania (*n*=25)	3,3	3.15*		1,1	0.20		1,2	3.37*	
Togo (*n*=23)	1,2	2.54		1,3	5.54*				
Tunisia (*n*=25)							1,1	0.0	
Uganda (*n*=24)	2,1	0.08							
Zaire (*n*=24)	3,1	0.34							
Zambia (*n*=24)				1,3	1.86				

l,m denote the optimal number of lags in the first- and second-stage regressions, respectively, using Hsiao's Granger-Akaike procedure. F is an F statistic testing the null that aid does not precede imports. *, when assigned to this statistic, indicates that null is not accepted at the 95 percent level or greater. *lres*, an alternative test for causality, refers to the lagged residuals of the co-integrating relationship. *, when assigned to this test statistic, indicates rejection of the null. x and y in the above equation vary from 1 to 3. Variables in this equation might be differenced once or twice to render them stationary, depending on the order of integration of the variable. The model was not applied to time series with less than 23 observations.

Table 6A2: Econometric Estimates.

Model: $$\left(\frac{A_{ij}}{A_i}\right)_t = \beta_0 + \sum_{n=0}^{x}\beta_n\left(\frac{A_{ij}}{A_i}\right)_{t-n} + \sum_{n=1}^{y}\beta_{x+n}\left(\frac{M_{ij}}{M_i}\right)_{t-n} + v_{it}$$

	France			Germany			United Kingdom		
Aid Recipient	***l,m***	**F**	***lres***	***l,m***	**F**	***lres***	***l,m***	**F**	***lres***
Algeria (*n*=25)				1,1	0.14				
Burkina Faso (*n*=23)				1,2	6.60*				
Burundi (*n*=25)	3,2	0.94					3,1	0.00	
Cameroon (*n*=24)				1,1	1.14				
Central African Rep. (*n*=23)	3,3	1.33					3,2	1.88	
Chad (*n*=23)							2,3	1.45	
Congo (*n*=23)	3,2	2.04		3,2	13.6*				
Egypt (*n*=25)				3,1	–0.08		3,1	1.48	
Ethiopia (*n*=24)							1,3	2.42*	
Kenya (*n*=25)	3,1	1.28		3,3	10.3*				
Madagascar (*n*=23)				1,1	2.91				
Mauritius (*n*=25)	2,3	0.55					3,1	0.39	
Morocco (*n*=25)				2,1	2.64		1,1	0.20	
Nigeria (*n*=24)				3,1	1.10				
Rwanda (*n*=24)							1,1	0.05	
Sierra Leone (*n*=25)				3,1	0.08				
Tanzania (*n*=25)	2,2	1.07		1,1	8.43*		2,1	2.49	
Togo (*n*=23)	2,1	0.05		3,2	2.60				
Tunisia (*n*=25)							1,1	0.07	
Uganda (*n*=24)	2,1	0.84							
Zaire (*n*=24)	1,1	0.14							
Zambia (*n*=24)				1,2	4.31*				

l,m denote the optimal number of lags in the first- and second-stage regressions, respectively, using Hsiao's Granger-Akaike procedure. F is an F statistic testing the null that aid does not precede imports. *, when assigned to this statistic, indicates that null is not accepted at the 95 percent level or greater. *lres*, an alternative test for causality, refers to the lagged residuals of the co-integrating relationship. *, when assigned to this test statistic, indicates rejection of the null. x and y in the above equation vary from 1 to 3. Variables in this equation might be differenced once or twice to render them stationary, depending on the order of integration of the variable. The model was not applied to time series with less than 23 observations.

Table 6A3: Econometric Estimates.

Model: $\left(\frac{M_{ij}}{G_i}\right)_t = \gamma_0 + \sum_{n=0}^{x} \gamma_n \left(\frac{A_{ij}}{G_i}\right)_{t-n} + \sum_{n=1}^{y} \gamma_{x+n} \left(\frac{M_{ij}}{G_i}\right)_{t-n} + \varepsilon_{it}$

	France			Germany			United Kingdom		
Aid Recipient	***l,m***	**F**	***lres***	***l,m***	**F**	***lres***	***l,m***	**F**	***lres***
Algeria (*n*=24)				3,2	5.69*				
Benin (*n*=24)				1,1	5.41*		2,1	0.0	
Burkina Faso (*n*=24)							3,2	1.35	
Central African Rep. (*n*=24)	1,1	0.14							
Chad (*n*=24)	3,3	0.94	−3.1*				2,1	3.21*	
Congo (*n*=24)	3,1	1.69					3,1	1.80	
Egypt (*n*=24)	2,1	2.77					1,1	0.31	
Ethiopia (*n*=24)							1,3	2.17	
Gabon (*n*=24)	3,1	1.89					1,3	2.17	
Gambia (*n*=24	3,1	0.81					1,1	0.16	
Ghana (*n*=24)	2,1	0.32					3,1	2.82	
Madagascar (*n*=24)	1,3	2.81*							
Malawi (*n*=24)	2,3	2.11		3,1	4.68*	−3.3*			
Mauritania (*n*=24)				1,1	1.01				
Mauritius (*n*=24)							3,2	5.24*	
Morocco (*n*=24)	1,2	0.43							
Nigeria (*n*=24)							1,3	1.53	
Rwanda (*n*=24)	1,3	3.02*					3,3	3.99*	
Senegal (*n*=24)				2,2	2.00				
Sierra Leone (*n*=24)	1,2	1.40		1,2	1.68		1,1	0.26	
Tanzania (*n*=24)				1,1	0.00				
Uganda (*n*=24)							1,1	0.18	

l,m denote the optimal number of lags in the first- and second-stage regressions, respectively, using Hsiao's Granger-Akaike procedure. F is an F statistic testing the null that aid does not precede imports. *, when assigned to this statistic, indicates that null is not accepted at the 95 percent level or greater. *lres*, an alternative test for causality, refers to the lagged residuals of the co-integrating relationship. *, when assigned to this test statistic, indicates rejection of the null. x and y in the above equation vary from 1 to 3. Variables in this equation might be differenced once or twice to render them stationary, depending on the order of integration of the variable. The model was not applied to time series with less than 23 observations.

Table 6A4: Econometric Estimates.

Model: $$\left(\frac{A_{ij}}{G_i}\right)_t = \delta_0 + \sum_{n=0}^{x} \delta_n \left(\frac{A_{ij}}{G_i}\right)_{t-n} + \sum_{n=1}^{y} \delta_{x+n} \left(\frac{M_{ij}}{G_i}\right)_{t-n} + \upsilon_{it}$$

	France			Germany			United Kingdom		
Aid Recipient	***l,m***	**F**	***lres***	***l,m***	**F**	***lres***	***l,m***	**F**	***lres***
Algeria (*n*=24)				1,3	0.63				
Benin (*n*=24)				3,3	2.16		3,1	0.07	
Burkina Faso (*n*=23)							2,3	2.78*	
Central African Rep. (*n*=24)	2,2	1.86							
Chad (*n*=24)	1,2	1.35	–0.92				1,2	1.49	
Congo (*n*=24)	3,3	3.83					1,2	3.10*	
Egypt (*n*=24)	1,1	1.96					1,1	16.3*	
Ethiopia (*n*=24)							2,1	0.77	
Gabon (*n*=24)	1,3	1.49					3,1	4.38*	
Gambia (*n*=24)	1,2	4.30*					2,1	1.88	
Ghana (*n*=24)	3,1	2.93					1,3	6.89*	
Madagascar (*n*=24)	1,1	–1.49							
Malawi (*n*=24)	3,3	1.59		1,3	1.44	–0.77			
Mauritania (*n*=24)				1,3	13.8*				
Mauritius (*n*=24)							3,1	3.47*	
Morocco (*n*=24)	1,1	2.09							
Nigeria (*n*=24)							1,2	2.05	
Rwanda (*n*=24)	2,1	3.80*					2,1	0.12	
Senegal (*n*=24)				2,1	0.67				
Sierra Leone (*n*=24)	1,1	0.33		2,1	0.14		1,1	0.10	
Tanzania (*n*=24)				1,1	3.96*				
Uganda (*n*=24)							1,1	0.00	

l,m denote the optimal number of lags in the first- and second-stage regressions, respectively, using Hsiao's Granger-Akaike procedure. F is an F statistic testing the null that aid does not precede imports. *, when assigned to this statistic, indicates that null is not accepted at the 95 percent level or greater. *lres*, an alternative test for causality, refers to the lagged residuals of the co-integrating relationship. *, when assigned to this test statistic, indicates rejection of the null. *x* and *y* in the above equation vary from 1 to 3. Variables in this equation might be differenced once or twice to render them stationary, depending on the order of integration of the variable. The model was not applied to time series with less than 23 observations.

Table 6A5: Econometric Estimates.

Model: $\left(\frac{M_{ij}}{M_i}\right)_t = \alpha_0 + \sum_{n=0}^{x} \alpha_1 \left(\frac{A_{ij}}{A_i}\right)_t + \sum_{n=1}^{y} \alpha_2 \left(\frac{M_{ij}}{M_i}\right)_{t-1} + e_{it}$

	France			Germany			United Kingdom		
Aid Recipient	α_0	α_1	α_2	α_0	α_1	α_2	α_0	α_1	α_2
Algeria (n=25)				0.04 (1.83)	0.12* (2.05)	0.62* (3.43)			
Burkina Faso (n=23)									
Burundi (n=25)							0.02* (3.30)	–5.02* (–2.18)	0.32 (1.64)
Cameroon (n=24)									
Central African Rep. (n=23)									
Chad (n=23)									
Congo (n=23)									
Egypt (n=25)									
Ethiopia (n=24)							0.08* (3.94)	0.48* (2.00)	–0.25 (–0.95)
Kenya (n=25)	0.02* (3.20*	0.27* (2.37)	0.38* (1.98)						
Madagascar (n=23)									
Mauritius (n=25)							0.02 (1.78)	0.13* (4.14)	0.71* (8.20)
Morocco (n=25)									
Nigeria (n=24)									
Rwanda (n=24)									
Sierra Leone (n=25)									
Tanzania (n=25)									
Togo (n=23)									
Tunisia (n=25)									
Uganda (n=24)	0.02* (3.39)	0.99* (3.24)	0.05 (0.25)						
Zaire (n=24)									
Zambia (n=24)									

Results are reported only for those countries for which α_1 is significant. t– ratios are shown in parentheses. * denotes significance at the 90 percent level or greater.

Table 6A6: Econometric Estimates.

Model: $\left(\frac{A_{ij}}{A_i}\right)_t = \beta_0 + \sum_{n=0}^{x} \beta_1 \left(\frac{A_{ij}}{A_i}\right)_t + \sum_{n=1}^{y} \beta_2 \left(\frac{M_{ij}}{M_i}\right)_{t-1} + \upsilon_{it}$

	France			Germany			United Kingdom		
Aid Recipient	β_0	β_1	β_2	β_0	β_1	β_2	β_0	β_1	β_2
Algeria (n=25)				–0.08 (–1.48)	0.51* (2.92)	0.95* (1.89)			
Burkina Faso (n=23)									
Burundi (n=25)									
Cameroon (n=24)									
Central African Rep. (n=23)									
Chad (n=23)									
Congo (n=23)									
Egypt (n=25)									
Ethiopia (n=24)							0.01 (0.49)	0.06 (0.27)	0.31* (1.74)
Kenya (n=25)				–0.01 (–0.17)	0.10 (0.49)	1.04* (2.06)			
Madagascar (n=23)									
Mauritius (n=25)	–0.11 (–0.86)	0.38* (1.91)	3.34* (2.11)						
Morocco (n=25)									
Nigeria (n=24)									
Rwanda (n=24)									
Sierra Leone (n=25)									
Tanzania (n=25)									
Togo (n=23)									
Tunisia (n=25)									
Uganda (n=24)	–0.01* (–2.24)	0.55* (4.58)	0.34* (4.40)						
Zaire (n=24)									
Zambia (n=24)									

Results are reported only for those countries for which β_2 is significant. t– ratios are shown in parentheses. * denotes significance at the 90 percent level or greater.

CHAPTER 7

POLITICISING DEVELOPMENT?
The Role of Participation in the Activities of Aid Agencies

Howard White

INTRODUCTION

Following a steady rise in popularity since the early 1980s, participation has become an important part of the rhetoric of many aid agencies. As Nelson and Wright put it: "in the 1980s discussions begun on why thirty years of conventional, technocratic, top-down forms of development were not working" (1995b: 4). In fact, as illustrated in Part 3 of this chapter, the current flurry of participatory activities may be seen as the third wave of participation since 1945. The first, the Colonial Development Movement which largely died out in the 1960s, had its roots in the pre-war colonial welfare activities of the British and French governments and received substantial support from the U.S.. The second wave in the 1970s was associated with the U.N. system, the move to Basic Needs and the increased focus on rural development, but was much stronger in rhetoric than in practice. The current, third wave, more closely identified with NGOs but also some bilateral agencies, steadily picked up momentum in the 1980s and has been on a roll in the 1990s with the added impetus given by the conversion of the World Bank to the cause. The discussion of trends in participation is preceded in Part 2 by a brief review of why participation is held to be necessary.

Whilst participation has commonly been envisaged as participation by project beneficiaries in project activities, this perspective needs to be broadened in three ways: (1) participation can relate to *any* official activities, i.e. policy as well as projects; (2) participation need not only be in the implementation of policies and projects, but also in their identification, design and evaluation, i.e. participation can occur at any stage of the project (or policy) cycle; and (3) participation need not only include those affected by the policy or project intervention (what are now called primary stakeholders) but also those responsible for the implementation of these activities and other concerned parties (secondary or institutional stakeholders). These three distinctions give rise to a number of possible permutations of participatory activity.[1] It shall be argued in Part 4 that the Bank has in fact restricted itself to a fairly small number of these possibilities. This discussion focuses on the activities of the World Bank not because the Bank is the founder of the participatory movement — it clearly is not — but it is now a major force in that movement, which some claim has hijacked participation from its original route to more radical forms of development intervention. Part 5 offers conclusions, suggesting limitations to participation as currently practiced and what may be done to overcome these limitations.

WHY DOES PARTICIPATION MATTER?

The arguments in favour of participation fall into two broad categories: (1) since the term "beneficiaries" implies that people are intended to benefit from the aid-supported interventions then participation is necessary to identify and best meet their needs; and (2) that project effectiveness is higher in participatory projects than in comparable non-participatory ones. These two arguments are not unrelated. At its most extreme, failure to involve beneficiaries can result in project failure, including instances in which "beneficiaries" protest against the project, as in the case of an urban project in the Philippines described in Section 4 below, or engage in sabotage of project activities such as uprooting saplings in woodlot projects (as documented in Ferguson, 1990).

Critics of the first view-point would argue that beneficiaries are not equipped with the necessary technical knowledge to take part in decisions about design. Burghart (1993) documents how participatory project identification led to the cleaning of the village well with disastrous results. But the developing world is, literally, littered with examples of the technical failures of "the experts" (and even the case described by Burghart reads more like a problem of a well-meaning but inept outsider). This critique is, anyhow, to miss the point. Of course there may be aspects of project design, in sectors such as rural electrification or water supply, for which beneficiaries cannot make the technical decisions concerning project design. But projects in such sectors can involve beneficiaries in planning, and should do where issues of type of service (e.g. home delivery or communal standpipes in the case of water supply), relocation or user charges arise.

The view that participation increases project effectiveness has been put forward on a regular basis by, amongst others, the Operations Evaluation Department (OED) of the World Bank. To take a recent example (World Bank, 1994), a review of agricultural development projects stated that beneficiary participation at all stages of the project cycle is essential, but that projects have often been designed and implemented with little beneficiary involvement. Other work undertaken at the World Bank has systematically examined the link between participation and project outcomes. At the theoretical level, Gerson (1993) explores the foundations in economic theory for arguments for participation, such as overcoming free-rider problems. At the empirical level, Narayan (1995) reports results of an analysis of 121 rural water supply projects in 49 countries, supported by 18 different agencies. Regression analysis showed, after allowing for other factors, participation, particularly when it occurred throughout the project cycle, was a significant determinant of project effectiveness.

Given these arguments in favour of participation obvious questions arise, most notably how should it be done, why it does not occur more often and how to overcome obstacles to participation? These questions underlie the discussion in the remainder of this chapter.

THE RISE (AND FALL) OF COMMUNITY PARTICIPATION

The current emphasis on participation is *not* new, but may be seen as the third "wave" (or fad) of participation in the last 50 years. In this part of the paper these three waves are documented in more detail, with some reflection as to their implications for current participatory efforts.

The first wave of participatory development: the Community Development Movement

Within the context of social programs in their African and Asian colonies the British began to develop the model of Community Development in the pre-war period and applied it more widely after 1945. The French programme, *animation rurale*, was similar. This model was adopted by newly independent nations, most notably India, and USAID and the United Nations began to pour financial and technical resources into the establishment of Community Development programs throughout the 1950s.[2]

Community Development had strong democratic ideals. In India it was seen as the basis for popular participation in the planning process, with development plans being prepared at the village level. For the U.S. the provision of a democratic alternative to communism was a major motivation in supporting the movement. The approach of the U.S. and the U.N., the two most influential bodies in the development of Community Development programs, and that adopted in India and other countries, was to send a trained "multi-purpose village-level worker" to act as a catalyst and assist villagers in formulating their village plans. The worker had basic skills in literacy, health and agriculture and could call on regionally-based technical specialists if required. Matching grants were usually available to implement village projects. By 1960 there were programs in over sixty countries in Africa, Asia and Latin America. At the movement's peak in 1959, USAID employed 105 direct hire and contract Community Development advisors. During the ten years up to 1962 the U.S. gave $50 million to Community Development programs in over thirty countries, and a somewhat smaller amount indirectly though the United Nations (Holdcroft, 1978: 18). However, within three years these programs were closing down and international donor support drying up. After ten years little or nothing remained. Although community development as an activity continues, as a large-scale movement attracting substantial donor support it disappeared. Many younger development workers today (practitioners and academics alike) are unaware it ever existed, and older ones who must know of it through their own involvement seem unwilling to draw out the lessons of this costly failure for current practice. There are, however, several lessons to draw from this experience.

First, the story is an early example of fadism amongst development agencies, who will build up an approach — to the extent that it is virtually a requirement that a country have such a programme in order to receive aid — and then lose interest, leaving the programme to collapse. The second lesson is the extraordinary inability of even the academic development community to learn from previous failures. I first came across the Community Development movement in the paper by Holdcroft

(1978), which compares it with the Integrated Rural Development Projects which were fashionable in the 1970s (and were a part of the second wave of enthusiasm for participation). A literature search revealed a massive literature on the topic from the 1950s and 1960s (and training manuals from the 1940s which, the dated nature of the photos excepted, could well have been from the 1990s), but virtually no references thereafter.[3] Indeed, there is now the convenient myth that development efforts in the 1960s (there is usually no mention of the 1950s at all) relied on a growth-oriented, trickle down strategy (for example, the above quote by Nelson and Wright), thus side-stepping the fact that there was an almost universally adopted bottom-up approach which was a dismal failure. Finally, and most importantly, to the extent that there was a post-mortem on the Community Development movement it pointed to failings that plague current efforts at participation, such as elite identification on the part of community workers, elite capture of "community benefits" (whilst the costs may be shared by all, from the point of view of the labourer the "voluntary labour" of development projects may seem little different to the corveé labour schemes implemented during colonial rule), and that what was called a participatory approach was ultimately a top-down design with a quite narrowly defined role for participation (usually restricted to implementation). Two main issues pervade these problems. First, communities are stratified rather than homogenous, so that "community participation" which ignores divided interests will most likely reinforce existing dominant interests. It should always be asked, who is participating and who do they represent? Second, genuine participatory action on the part of donors requires that they enter a partnership with the community, with agreed obligations on both sides, whereas few donors are in fact willing to relinquish their own power in the aid relationship.[4]

Although these weaknesses were identified at the time, recognition of the approach's shortcomings did not lead to its revision and improvement but rather, has rather often regrettably been the case with donor agencies, to its total abandonment. The collapse of the programme was hastened by the spectre of famine in Asia and the promise offered by the propagation of Green Revolution technology through an unashamedly top-down approach. However, it was only a few years before voices for participation again began to be heard.

Basic needs, radical rhetoric and rural development: a second wave?

In December 1969 the U.N. General Assembly adopted the Declaration on Social Progress and Development, Article 5 of which emphasized the importance of participation in the development process. Two later U.N. publications on participation mapped the continued interest of the U.N. in this issue: "Popular Participation in Development" in 1971 and "Popular Participation in Decision Making for Development" in 1975. By 1980 the importance of participation was such that it was placed at the core of the development process in the definition adopted in the launching of the Third U.N. Development Decade: "the ultimate aim of development is the constant improvement of the well-being of the entire population on the basis of its full participation in the process of development and a fair distribution of the benefits therefrom" (quoted in U.N. 1986).

Support for participation was evident throughout the U.N. system in the 1970s and early 1980s; for example the call for participation in urban planning made in the Vancouver Plan of Action adopted at the UN Conference on Human Settlements, the role of participation in the 1978 Alma Alta "Declaration on Primary Health Care" supported by UNICEF and WHO, the FAO-sponsored People's Participation Program founded in 1982, the UNESCO conference Participation in Rural Development held in Lima in 1978, and the efforts of ILO associated with its promotion of Basic Needs. Although bilateral agencies also paid attention to the issue — for example a mention in the UK 1975 White Paper and a USAID policy statement on participation in the same year — in retrospect this second wave was driven by rhetoric at international conferences rather than wide-spread changes on the ground. Shepherd (1983) reviews ILO's experience in urban development and Rahman (1987) that in rural development, and both papers illustrate the tendency to rhetoric rather than practical advice. More generally, Esman and Uphoff concluded toward the mid-80s that "local organizations have not figured centrally in most of the literature, strategies, or policy formulations for rural development" (1984: 42). However by that time the ripples of the third wave could already be seen.

From beneficiary to stakeholder: the third wave of participatory development

This third wave had two origins. First, was a more concerted effort by bilateral donors to adopt participatory techniques: such as Sweden from 1980, and the participatory adaptation of the logical framework, known as ZOPP by the German agency GTZ (GTZ, 1988). Second, a rising share of aid was channelled through non-governmental organisations (NGOs) during the 1980s: this phenomenon was to an extent part of the drive toward more participatory development, but also helped fuel it. Donor funding has led to a proliferation of grassroots organisations in developing countries, adding further weight to calls for participation: as at the Arusha Conference in 1990 with representatives from over 500 African organisations (Nelson and Wright, 1995b: 3).

During the 1990s this third wave has engulfed the World Bank. Although, as is documented below, there was a steady increase in participatory aspects to Bank activities in the 1980s, the formation of the Learning Group on Participatory Development in 1990, subsequent publication of the Participation Source Book (World Bank, 1995) and participatory activities associated with poverty assessments have moved the Bank to centre stage in the participation debate.

The Source Book introduced stakeholder analysis to the Bank's work and the development community at large, and thus broadened the terms of the participation debate. Previously, the term participation had most often been used synonymously with community participation — that is the participation of the general public in matters of policy and project planning and implementation. But stakeholder analysis implies that participation should also apply to the involvement politicians, government officials and representatives of civil society organisations in these processes. In the case of the Bank it is these first two groups which have been dominant, so that there is a close match between the Bank's adoption of participation and the concern for "ownership" which also emerged in the early 1990s. That the Bank should be concerned with the participation of these secondary stakeholders is no bad thing: but it clearly should not be at the expense of giving voice to primary stakeholders, which many would see as being what "real participation" is about. The next part of this paper explores the participatory practices of the Bank in more detail, and examines, *inter alia*, to what extent such a concern is valid. The discussion also leads to an assessment as to whether the third wave of participation can be expected to achieve more than did its predecessors.

PARTICIPATION IN WORLD BANK ACTIVITIES

There is scope for participation in the activities of donor agencies at several levels. Most of the participation literature concerns participation in projects. But donors also support sector and economy wide policy changes with programme aid, and undertake various sectoral and economic analyses (in the World Bank's terminology the latter are called Economic and Sector Work, ESW). There is also the issue of participation in setting the aid agency's agenda at the global level. These agencies are of course accountable through their own parliaments, though several try to involve various stakeholders (NGOs, academics etc.) in their policy discussions. No donor has made any substantial effort to extend to involving recipients at any level in the process of aid policy planning. Indeed, it is notable that the global forum for aid policy is the donor's club the Development Assistance Committee (DAC), although UNCTAD tried unsuccessfully to assume this role in the 1960s. In this paper the discussion is restricted to policy and projects at the level of individual recipients (called borrowers by the Bank).

Participatory analysis of policy change

The World Bank has always conducted sectoral analysis and reported on the general state of economic development amongst borrower countries. However, as is widely documented elsewhere (e.g. Mosley *et al.*, 1991), during the 1980s the receipt of aid funds (called programme loans and credits[5]) was made conditional upon undertaking policy reforms. By the end of the decade, most bilateral donors had hitched their own programme aid to the conditionalities of the World Bank and the IMF (see Hewitt and Killick, 1996).

Participation can take place in any (or none) of the design, implementation and evaluation of reform programmes and the participation may be that of government officials, representatives of civil society or "the people". The design of World Bank reform programmes is a largely non-participatory process. The framework for these reforms in the Policy Framework Paper (PFP), drawn up by the World Bank and the IMF in Washington, although at least nominally adopted by government. A PFP typically covers a three year period, during which there will be a series of adjustment loans (usually scheduled to be disbursed over the course of one year but more often actually disbursed between one and two years) which contain more detailed conditions in accordance with the objectives and targets given by the PFP. The PFP and subsequent loan agreements are the subject of negotiation between the World Bank and government. But at this stage only a narrow range of government officials will be involved, and the Bank is usually reluctant to share too much with its donor "partners" who are also funding the adjustment effort. However, by the early 1990s there was concern over lack of recipient "ownership" of these programmes which has led to efforts to, at least formally, put more onus on government in policy design.[6] However, participation on a wider scale is left for implementation.

Participation has to be widened for implementation, since a wider range of agencies and officials are involved in implementing the reforms (which can range over several agencies) than are in the negotiation process. It can thus happen that technical ministries are charged with implementing reforms for which they have had no input into the design process. Rather unsurprisingly, this can be a problematic procedure on account of both stubbornness borne by resentment on the part of responsible officials and because of genuine technical programmes unforeseen by those with less experience of the sector. References can be found in various World Bank documents to the importance of involving implementing agencies in the design process, but this practice is far from widespread. The World Bank's support to adjustment in Ghana in the late 1980s provides one example. There was a perception that the reforms, which started in 1983, were "running out of steam": the early, "stroke of the pen" reforms, had been pushed through by the highly committed and capable economic team at the centre of government, but these top officials lacked a similarly talented and committed middle-rank cadre to carry through the more detailed reforms. A series of workshops was therefore held around the country to "explain" the reforms to people to gain their support for the process — but not to allow them to input into the design of the programme itself.

The process by which wider participation takes place only after agreement has been reached between government and the World Bank has not been changed by the emergence of democratic institutions in many developing countries (which has itself has been supported by donors). With no apparent sense of irony, the conditionality for one African country required "Parliament to pass the new Land Act". Whilst it may be reasonable to ask government to introduce an act to Parliament (if somewhat naive to believe such a fundamental measure can be got through with the minimum of consultation), it is rather at odds with notions of ownership, let alone democratic government, for an outside agency to require Parliament to pass certain pieces of legislation. It is almost needless to add that Parliament was not so compliant, and Bank staff had to seek a waiver from their Board to disburse the funds without this condition having been met.

In the absence of democratic institutions it is problematic to identify the best means of participation for policy dialogue. Various attempts have been made to involve agencies such as NGOs, but these "self-appointed representatives" of civil society are often political in nature. Even where a multi-party system exists then, at least in sub-Saharan Africa, there is an absence of genuine debate over policies, both within the political system and in the press. Opinion polls may fill this gap, but the infrastructure does not exist to support them in much of the developing world, again notably in Africa (but they are used in Latin America).[7] Participatory analysis of policy issues can fill this gap.

Three areas in which participatory analysis has or may be used by the World Bank can be identified: (1) the use of participatory techniques in sector studies; (2) Participatory Poverty Assessments, which are the most important example of the first category and so warrant separate mention; and (3) participatory analysis of policy reforms. Each of these is now elaborated upon.

The main plank of the Bank's Economic and Sector Work (ESW) is the Country Economic Memorandum (CEM), but reports are also produced on a regular basis on other sectors, and more general topics such as gender and the Poverty Assessments, the latter of which is discussed below. There are examples of participatory approaches to these studies — for example, Gandhi's (1995) contribution to the *Participation Handbook* on the Women in Development Sector Strategy in Morocco and Saran (1995) on the Education Sector Credit in Yemen. CEMs draw on these various sector reports and so draw on participatory analysis to the extent is has been carried out at these earlier stages: for example the Ghana Poverty Assessment (World Bank, 1996) summarises the results of the poverty profile in the PPA. However, the writing of CEMs is not itself a participatory process, and the results of participatory analysis are filtered by development professionals: participation does not extend to the interpretation and application of the results of participatory work.

Poverty assessments (PAs) were introduced following the launch of the World Bank's New Poverty Agenda with the 1990 *World Development Report*. An assessment is intended to address three key themes: who the poor are (the poverty profile), the causes of poverty, and a poverty reduction strategy. Increasingly participatory poverty assessments (PPAs) have been included as a part of the exercise (for a more general discussion of these see World Bank, 1993; Carvalho and White, 1997; and Hanmer *et al.*. 1997: Appendix IV).[8] These PPAs vary greatly in content and quality, but the best of them (such as those prepared for Ghana, Kenya and Zambia) draw on the full range of participatory techniques, such as wealth-ranking exercises, mapping and seasonality diagrams, developed under the heading of Participatory Rural Appraisal (PRA, see Chambers, 1994). A review of African poverty assessments concluded that, despite these variations in quality, they were in general a worthwhile addition to the analysis presented in PAs adopting more traditional techniques. However, it appeared that the main PA most frequently drew on PPAs where their findings could be used in support of the argument being made, whereas conflicting information was disregarded (Hanmer *et al.*, 1997: IV.14–15). Moreover, few PPAs explicitly addressed the issue of attitudes of the poor to the economic reforms being undertaken. Of course the impact of specific reforms was addressed where they were felt to be of especial relevance to the poor: user charges in social services being the main example. It was felt by many respondents that such charges restricted access to health and education, and a robust finding from PPAs was that exemption schemes for the poor were not working, at least in part on account of petty corruption.[9]

Work sponsored by donors other than the World Bank has been explicitly concerned with popular perceptions of reform. Booth *et al.* (1993) used focus groups from a range of communities across Tanzania to examine attitudes to economic and political reform, as did Bratton and Liatto-Katundu (1994) for the case of Zambia, and Booth *et al.* (1995) on social sector reform in Zambia. These studies report rather different findings with respect to economic liberalisation. In Tanzania there is widespread support, including amongst the rural poor (especially women), for policies which put goods back on the shelves — although the study also questioned whether the production response that was occurring in the villages was of the sort which could sustain growth. By contrast, Bratton and Liatto-Katundu reported that attitudes to economic reform were mixed, but concluded that "one finding is clear: Zambia's MMD government has yet to build a basic understanding, let alone a popular support, for its radical programme of restructuring" (1994: 549).[10] On the specific issue of cost recovery in health, Booth *et al.* (1995) found a widespread opinion that the poor could not afford to pay the new charges, but also a feeling that those who could pay should. However, more recent studies in Zambia (summarised in PAG, 1997) suggest a growing acceptance of user charges.

The various studies find less difference between the two countries with respect to peoples' attitudes to political liberalisation. There is not very strong evidence to support the view that democratic rights are viewed as an essential element in welfare, except in the negative sense that some Zambians resented having been forced to vote by the party youth under the UNIP regime.[11] Ignorance of the workings of the new system, in large part because of seeing government and party as the same (as had indeed been the case for most the time since independence), was evident in Zambia. In Tanzania, more people were openly hostile to the introduction of multi-party democracy, which was seen as causing unnecessary divisions and potential conflicts.

The conclusions from this discussion of participation in the policy process is that is has nearly entirely been restricted to secondary stakeholders, and that attempts to involve these stakeholders in policy design have in most countries been at best only partially successful.[12] The Bank has not made a systematic attempt to canvass opinions of the poor on the impact of economic reforms, and where such information has emerged from PPAs it as been used in a limited way. These comments are not to deny that there has been a shift between the 1980s and 90s toward a more participatory-orientation. But, so far as policy analysis is concerned, it still has some way to go. Is the same true of project activities?

Participation in development projects

In the case of a Bank-supported urban upgrading project in Indonesia in the 1970s "many learned about [their relocation] the day the bulldozers appeared at their front door" (consultants' report on project, quoted in Ayres, 1984, p.192). Since that time, participation has certainly increased, though the impact of much of this has historically been constrained by: (1) restricting participation to the implementation phase of the project cycle; and (2) adopting participation to increase the efficiency with which pre-determined project objectives are achieved (most notably cost-sharing) rather than allowing participants to shape project activities. Examples of these points may be made with reference to two urban projects.[13]

The Lusaka Upgrading and Sites and Services Project involved the relocation of settlers from a traditionally volatile area, which was achieved peacefully. A World Bank Staff Working Paper reviewing the extent of participation in this and three other low-income shelter projects saw this peaceful relocation as the major achievement of having had a participatory component to the project (Keare and Parris,

1982). The paper also mention the establishment at the planning stage of Road Planning Committees to make modifications in proposed road layout (*ibid*, 1982: 90) In contrast, Moser discusses the role of the committees as follows:

> The formation of a Road Planning Group undoubtedly made a more interactive form of participation possible, increasing the opportunities for feedback to the implementing agency. However, the fact that 36 elected part officials were taken as representative of the community, and insufficient proper meetings were held meant that in reality only a minority view was heard. This was particularly problematic for women, who were not consulted at all, since the relocation of roads had a drastic effect on their domestic responsibilities. (Moser, 1987: 317).[14]

A survey of the project area revealed that the majority of the inhabitants were unaware of the existence of the committees. These contrasting perspectives are explained by the authors having different implicit objectives for participation. The position taken by Keare and Parris is that participation made the project "work" — the participants moved without undue fuss and some form of agreement was even reached on aspects of project design. However, from a perspective that places more emphasis on the satisfaction of beneficiary needs, participation failed: it was not able to ensure that the views of the less powerful were taken into account.

A more striking case of where there are conflicting stories of the same project is the Philippines I Project to upgrade the Tondo Foreshore Area. Keare and Parris comment that:

> consultation with barangay leadership and community groups has led, as in the case of Zambia, to the circumvention of major social disruptions during the reblocking process... The Philippine evaluation team has noted that a marked passivity characterizes group meetings were project plans are discussed; Tondo dwellers seem regularly to follow barangay leadership in declaring preferences for particular services or procedures, even where these involve significant disruptions in reblocking their homes (*op. cit.*, 1982: 90–91).

In contrast the discussion of the project by Ayres (1983:186–88) focuses on the difficulty faced by project officers in choosing who represented the people: the barangay leadership (created by the Government following the imposition of martial law) or the very active Zone One Tondo Organization (ZOTO). ZOTO had, for example, organized a series of protests and marches in 1976 for the widening of the drainage canals. Ayres says that the response of the project officers was to "leave it to the people", who were given a choice of three upgrading schemes. All groups voted for the most expensive reblocking option. Ayres quotes a project officer as saying that that shows what happens when the Bank "goes overboard" on community participation (1983:188). Turning finally to an account of the project from a more radical perspective we find yet another story (Bello and Bielski, 1982), which describes ZOTO as a federation of 113 organizations formed to struggle against evictions during the sixties and the barangay leadership as a form of secret police. ZOTO had been active in opposing the Government's housing program and argued for upgrading, as was eventually promoted by the Bank. Barangay leaders, were not part of the formal government structure, but had a role in keeping an eye on possible dissenters. A consultants' study for KfW found that many barangay leaders did not see their role as a consultative one, but simply of handing decisions down to the people. Furthermore, many were unaware of the three choices, whilst others were seen to have forced the more expensive option on residents (a fact admitted in a quote from the then Urban Division Chief, *ibid*: 114–15).[15] Bank officials seem to have been in a genuine quandary, even on the admission of Bello and Bielski, since they thought that they were having successful discussions with ZOTO, who would then turn around and say they were against the project. The Government did not sit back during all this and do nothing. Seven thousand people were arrested at a 1976 "People's Conference" organized by ZOTO to air grievances. The following year the group's leader was arrested and tortured. It is perhaps not so surprising that, as Keare and Parris put it, "a marked passivity characterized group meetings".

These experiences with urban development should not be taken as evidence that the Bank's involvement with participation in the 1970s and 80s was always misguided. There were, for example, relative successes with pastoral associations in livestock projects in Zaire and the Central African Republic.[16] The Ituri Livestock Development Project in Zaire, which began in 1977, aimed to promote pastoral associations to manage dips and organize communal grazing. The management of the Project Unit placed a strong emphasis on group activities through the extension services and, by 1979, 50 associations — called Promotion Pour la Defense de l'Elevage, PRODELs — had been formed. (By then membership had been made compulsory, but it was already high before this). The main attraction to producers proved to be improved access to veterinary drugs and services that membership of a PRODEL gave them. But the PRODELs also came to play a vital role in giving their members a voice in successfully resisting attempts by more powerful individuals to appropriate communal land. In 1979 a Federation of PRODELs was formed: the Association des Cooperatives d'Eleveurs de l'Ituri (ACOOPELI). Although the formation of ACOOPELI was unforeseen at appraisal it has come to be central to the success of the project, taking over activities, such as the management of the abattoir, which had originally been entrusted to the Government's livestock parastatal, ONDE, but which had proved to be ineffective.

The Central African Republic Livestock Development Project, started in 1980, provides another example of a herders association assuming implementation responsibilities. The original project design relied heavily on the Government's Livestock Service. But after two years no progress had been made and the project was redesigned, with the institutional emphasis shifting to the National Association of Central African Herders (ANEC). Although set up by Government, ANEC was a private organization supporting itself entirely from membership fees (in 1985 65 per cent of all herders were paying fees). ANEC proved an effective implementing agency — especially in the sale of veterinary drugs, achieving a level over 500 per cent of the appraisal objective. However, ANEC which was created as a national organization, rather than growing from the grassroots as did ACOOPELI, and has problems in articulation with its members, a problem exacerbated by the domination of the organization by its better-off members.

Whilst, participation may occur at any stage of the project cycle, the examples discussed so far show it to have been concentrated in implementation, thus necessarily limiting the objectives which may usually be achieved through participation. However, there is some evidence some change in Bank practices, both with respect to project identification and evaluation.

Within broad parameters local communities may be involved in project identification, particularly in the context of what are now called Social Funds.[17] Examples of World Bank-supported Social Funds with participatory allocation mechanisms include the Nepal Rural Water Supply and Sanitation Project, the Albania Rural Poverty Alleviation Project, and the Zambia Social Recovery Fund. The nature of the participation in such projects varies, but the most common model is of a Social Fund which is an autonomous body which that distributes funds to local councils and NGOs to implement approved projects. There is an emphasis on projects being demand-led, i.e. requests arising from communities or organisations themselves, which clearly has advantages in terms of ownership, but the obvious disadvantage of further marginalising the already marginalised. More generally, the transparency with which funds are allocated and used is an issue that should perhaps receive more attention than it does.

Formerly called beneficiary assessment (BA), participatory evaluation of projects has emerged at the World Bank since the early 1980s. The approach is particularly identified with the work of Larry Salman, whose work on participant observation as an evaluation technique (reported in Salmen, 1987) was a seminal contribution, but also Michael Bamberger (1986) and Michael Cernea (1987). A review of Bank experience in the late 1980s identified 19 projects using BA and another four for which it was planned (Salmen, 1989), whereas a similar exercise in the mid-90s listed 59 projects which had used BA (Salmen, 1995).[18,19] This is a dramatic increase, although still representing only a small share of Bank lending.

In the case of projects, unlike in the case of policy, the World Bank has involved primary stakeholders, usually relying on local intermediary organisations for this purpose. The focus of participation has been at the implementation stage of activities: though there are indications that this is changing over time, projects with participation in design and evaluation remain a small percentage of total Bank projects. The framework for participation thus remains one in which it is used to increase the efficiency with which pre-determined objectives are met.

CONCLUSIONS

The title of this paper "politicising development?" is deliberately tongue in cheek. Development is always and everywhere an unambiguously political process. Conceived as a tool for empowerment, participatory development by aid agencies can shift the balance of power in favour of the poor. As Nelson and Wright say: "participation, if it is to be more than a palliative, involves shifts in power" (1995b: 1). The analysis of participation as practised in World Bank policy advice and project activities suggests that it tends more to the palliative than the power-shifting end of this spectrum. This finding is not unique to the World Bank but could be drawn from an analysis of other official donors (see, for example, Eyben and Ladbury, 1995).[20]

Why have agencies' participatory endeavours been disappointing? There are two, related, sets of answers to this question. The first concerns constraints with the agencies themselves to the adoption of participatory practices. The second the inherent problems in achieving participation.

Aid agencies operate under various constraints. The first is that the aid programme is used to meet various objectives of the donor government, of which development is just one (albeit often the most important). The second is that the requirement of public accountability in the donor country necessitates that the donor to some extent dictate the terms and nature of the aid it gives: USAID is the most hamstrung of official agencies being subject to numerous Congressional resolutions, but the point applies more generally. Third, are operational and bureaucratic pressures within agencies which mitigate against participatory practices. The most frequently cited such pressure is the need to disburse funds, but a rigidly applied or overly bureaucratic planning or monitoring system can have the same effect. Hence, reform of agency structures is required if participatory practices are to make headway. Such a reform strategy should comprise the following components: (i) identify and eliminate constraints such as the pressure to disburse (such a move has been initiated in the Bank in recent years); (ii) improving access of poverty-oriented lobby groups to donor decision making processes; (iii) increased utilization of a multi-disciplinary approach at the field level; and (iv) increase the "participation consciousness" of development professionals (for example, the scheme of temporary residence of Bank staff in low-income areas in developing countries introduced under the Bank's latest President, Wolfensohn). While these steps are usually necessary pre-requisites for successful participation they are not, in general, sufficient conditions, since the neglected history of donor-supported participation points to genuine problems in achieving it.

The problems in participation were mentioned as lessons to draw from the failures of the Community Development Movement. These lessons essentially come down to the fact that communities are not homogenous, but socially differentiated entities riven by conflicting interests. There will be existing formal and informal group structures, and an understanding of these social realities in each specific situation is a pre-requisite for planned participatory interventions. Difficult issues then arise as to the extent to which existing structures are utilised, though these may well be elite-dominated (but if excluded they can take over activities anyway, or failing that sabotage them). These structures may also correspond to national divisions (ethnic or religious) and so draw the donor unwittingly into the political arena. The undoubted strides that have been made in developing participatory techniques in the decade or so, do not provide answers to the problems raised by the political nature of development. More explicit recognition of this fact by aid agencies would be a start.

REFERENCES

Ayres, Robert L. (1983) *Banking on the Poor: The World Bank and World Poverty* [Cambridge, Mass.: MIT Press].

Bello, Walden and Vincent Bulski (1982) "Counterinsurgency in the City" in *Development Debacle: The World Bank in the Philippines* by Walden Bello, David Kinley, Elaine Elinson. Bello, Walden F. (San Francisco, CA: Institute for Food and Development Policy).

Bamberger, Michael (ed.) (1987) "The Role of Community Participation in Development Planning and Project Management", *EDI Policy Seminar Report No. 13* [Washington D.C.: EDI, World Bank].

Booth, David, Flora Lugangira, Patrick Masanja, Abu Mvungi, Rosemarie Mwaipopo, Joaquim Mwami and Alison Redmayne (1993) *Social, Economic and Cultural Changes in Contemporary Tanzania: a people-oriented focus* [Stockholm: SIDA].

Booth, David *et al.* (1995) *Coping with Cost Recovery* [Stockholm: SIDA].

Bratton, Michael and Beatrice Liatto-Katundu (1994) "A Focus Group Assessment of Political Attitudes in Zambia" *African Affairs* 93 535–563.

Burghart, Richard (1993) "His Lordship at Cobblers' Well" in Mark Hobart (ed.) *An Anthropological Critique of Development* [London: Routledge].

Carvalho, Soniya and Howard White (1997) "Combining the Quantitative and Qualitative Approaches to Poverty Measurement and Analysis: the practice and the potential" *World Bank Technical Paper No. 366* [Washington D.C.: World Bank].

Cernea, Michael M. (1985) *Putting People First: Sociological Variables in Rural Development* [New York: Oxford University Press].

Chambers, Robert (1994) "The origins and practice of participatory rural appraisal" *World Development* 22 959–961.

Charlick, Robert (1980) "Animation Rurale: Experience with 'Participatory' Development in Four West African Nations" in *Rural Development Participation Review*, I(Winter),

Curtis, Donald (1995) "Power to the People: rethinking community development" in Nelson and Wright (1995a).

Esman, Milton J. and Uphoff, Norman T. (1984) *Local Organisations: Intermediaries in Local Development* [Ithaca: Cornell University Press].

Eyben, Rosalind and Sarah Ladbury (1995) "Popular-participation in aid-assisted projects: why more in theory than in practice?" in Nelson and Wright (1995a).

Ferguson, James (1990) *The Anti-Politics Machine* [Cambridge: Cambridge University Press].

Gandhi, Suniat (1995) "Morocco: Women in Development Sector Strategy" in World Bank (1995a).

Gerson, Philip (1993) "Popular Participation in Economic Theory and Practice" *HRO Working Paper 18* [Washington D.C.: World Bank].

GTZ (1988) ZOPP. An introduction to the method. [Eschborn: GTZ].

Hanmer, Lucia, Graham Pyatt and Howard White (1997) *Poverty in sub-Saharan Africa. What can we learn from World Bank Poverty Assessments?* [ISS/ISSAS: The Hague].

Hewitt, Adrian and Tony Killick (1996) "Bilateral Aid Conditionality and Policy Leverage" in Olav Stokke (ed.) *Foreign Aid Toward the Year 2000* [London: Frank Cass].

Holdcroft, Lane E. (1978) "The Rise and Fall of Community Development in Developing Countries, 1950–65: A Critical Analysis and an Annotated Bibliography".

Keare, Douglas and Parris, Scott (1982) "Evaluation of Shelter Programs for the Urban Poor: Principal Findings", *World Bank Staff Working Paper No.547* [Washington D.C.: World Bank].

Maxwell S. and Riddell R. (1998) "The Concept of Partnership in the White Paper", *Journal of International Development* 10(2), 257–268.

Mosley, Paul, Jane Harrigan and John Toye (1991) *Aid and Power* 2 volumes [London: Routledge].

Narayan, Deepa (1995) "The Contribution of People's Participation" *ESD Occasional Paper Series No. 1* [Washington D.C.: World Bank].

Nelson, Nici and Susan Wright (eds.) (1995a) *Power and Participatory Development: theory and practice* [London: Intermediate Technology Publications].

Nelson, Nici and Susan Wright (eds.) (1995b) "Participation and power" in Nelson and Wright (1995a).

Oxford Policy Management (1996) "Sector Investment Programmes in Africa: issues and experience, evidence from case studies", paper prepared for SPA seminar on SIPs, 16th December 1996.

Paul, Samuel (1987) "Community Participation in Development Projects: the World Bank Experience", *World Bank Discussion Paper No. 6* [Washington D.C.: World Bank] (also reproduced in Bamberger, 1988).

PAG (Participatory Assessment Group) (1997) "Summary paper for workshop to disseminate findings from participatory analysis" [Lusaka: PAG].

Rahman, Md. Ainsur (1987) "Participation of the Poor in Rural Development: Approach and Experience in an ILO Effort" in Bamberger (1987).

Salmen, Lawrence (1987) *Listen to the People: Participant Observation Evaluation of Development Projects* [New York: Oxford University Press].

Salmen, Lawrence (1989) "Beneficiary Assessment: improving the design and implementation of development projects" *Evaluation Review* 13(3) 273–291.

Salmen, Lawrence (1995) "Beneficiary Assessment: an approach described" *Environment Department paper No. 23* [Washington D.C.: World Bank].

Saran, Yogendra (1995) "Republic of Yemen: Education Sector Credit" in World Bank (1995a).

Shepherd, Andrew (1983) "The ILO Experience: Mass Community Participation in Decision-Making for Basic Needs" in Caroline Moser (ed.) "Evaluating Community Participation in Urban Development Projects", *Development Planning Unit Working Paper No. 14* [London: University College].

United Nations, Department of International Economic and Social Affairs (1986) *Popular Participation in Selected Upgrading Programmes in Urban Area* [New York: UN].

White, Howard (1989) "Community Participation in Development Projects: Problems and Prospects", mimeo, World Bank.

World Bank (1993) "Participatory Poverty Assessment" *HRO Dissemination Note No. 13* [Washington D.C.: World Bank].

World Bank (1994) *1992 Evaluation Results* [Washington D.C.: World Bank].

World Bank (1995a) *World Bank Participation Source Book* [Washington D.C.: World Bank].

World Bank (1995b) *Ghana: Poverty Past, Present and Future* [Washington D.C.: World Bank].

NOTES

[1] The three distinctions made here suggest a three dimensional matrix with 16 cells. The axis of this matrix are policy/project; identification/design/implementation/evaluation; and primary/secondary stakeholders. (Of course the number of cells increases if the project cycle is more elaborated or if secondary stakeholders are further subdivided). The argument in this paper is that only two or three of these 16 cells are filled with any significant amount of activity.

[2] See Holdcroft (1978) for the history of Community Development and Charlick (1980) on *animation rurale.*

[3] There are exceptions to this statement, a recent one being Curtis (1995) (who however sees more continuity between the Community Development Movement and current activities than is suggested here).

[4] Partnership has become an important issue in the later 1990s — as exemplified by the White Papers issues by the governments of Sweden and the United Kingdom in 1997. The point being made in this paper may also be made in relation to these new policy statements: i.e. partnership implies that donors should be willing to enter into binding contractual obligations with recipients (see Maxwell and Riddell, 1998).

[5] In Bank terminology funds from the IDA window (available to low-income countries) are called credits, whereas those from the main IBRD window are loans (and are indeed insufficiently concessional to qualify as ODA).

[6] In particular speeches made by the then World Bank Vice President for the Africa Region, Edward Jaycox, called for an end to the Bank writing programmes for countries. Implementation of the policy of "recipient ownership" has been rather more uneven, with at least one reported case of an African Minister of Finance being told "unless you say you own this programme then you won't get the money".

[7] See, for example, the report in *The Economist* of Latin American perceptions of democratisation ("Brightening up" *The Economist* 4th April, 1998: 56).

[8] The discussion here concerns the role of PPAs in the PA, though other aspects of participation are also pertinent to PAs. Notably, a considerable effort was made by the World Bank to encourage local ownership and use of the Zambia PA through a series of workshops. A review of this process found that the PA was, however, still seen as a "Bank product", with a number of those interviewed pointing out that consultation did not mean ownership as the Bank still set the terms of reference and the agenda for the discussion of recommendations.

[9] However, the proposed policy response in most Assessments was to improve publicity for exemptions, not to tackle the corruption problem.

[10] However, another observer of the political scene believes that the Tanzanian finding also hold for Zambia, and reports that Bratton's own view has shifted toward this position (personal communication from Jan Kees van Donge).

[11] The survey of Latin American attitudes mentioned in note 7 found support for democratisation by between 21 and 86 per cent (Peru and Uruguay respectively).

[12] The current fashion for Sector Investment Programmes (SIPs) predicates that donors should fund programmes designed by government, thus ensuring recipient ownership. However, existing reviews of SIPs (e.g. Oxford Policy Management, 1996) find them to be donor-driven, a tendency which may be expected to increase as SIP's status as "flavour of the month" means that each country will be required to have one, irrespective of if the pre-conditions for a recipient-designed SIP are in place (or to allow the time necessary for this to happen).

[13] These examples are taken from White (1989).

[14] Narayan (1995) reports that a failure to involve women has been a common feature of the projects studied in his review of 121 rural water supply projects, of which only 17 per cent achieved high levels of involvement by women.

[15] Yet, according to another Bank source it was the community that first raised the possibility of reblocking (Paul, 1987).

[16] However, these examples are drawn entirely from Bank sources, and so should be treated with some caution in the absence of independent verification.

[17] Similarly, the European Union supports micro projects in various countries, where the decision as to the use of funds involves some form of local participation

[18] Over one third (20) of the 59 projects were in the Population, Health and Nutrition sector, followed by education and agriculture (9 each), urban development (8) and Social Action Programmes (5 each).

[19] Other donors have also turned toward participatory evaluation in the 1990s. For example, the evaluation of British assistance to slum improvement in Calcutta (which includes an explicit discussion of the advantages of the participatory methodology). The Netherlands has eschewed a participatory approach to evaluation until very recently, but has now undertaken two "perception studies"—one in Bolivia and the other on the Dutch volunteer organisation, SNV— the results of which are not yet published.

[20] Which is not to imply that NGOs are necessarily more successful in this regard.

CHAPTER 8

TECHNICAL EXPERTISE AND INDIGENIZATION

L.S. Wilson

INTRODUCTION

The problem of "indigenization" of foreign aid projects involving technical assistance is a serious one for both donors and recipient counties. A common type of aid project involves the provision of foreign expertise, very often from the donor country, to the government of a LDC. Typically a main goal of such projects will be training, such that eventually indigenous expertise will be available and the donor can withdraw, leaving the project operating successfully without aid. Frequently, however, this final stage, turning the project over to local expertise, is not successful for a variety of reasons. We want, here, to explore the various approaches that have been taken to this problem, the reasons many of them have been unsuccessful, and the approaches that might most likely work.

One of the symptoms of this problem is that there continues, in many developing countries, to be a large number of expatriate advisors and managers in governments bringing charges of a sort of "neo-colonialism" from some. There is also the anomaly in some developing countries of there being a significant number of nationals of the recipient country working outside the country while nationals of the donor countries provide services and skills that these people would be able to provide. The donor country nationals most often work at high wages which would be enough to lure the recipient country nationals home.

This type of assistance makes up a small but significant portion of total aid. Cassen and Associates (1986), in their study for the Task Force on Concessional Flows set up by the Joint Ministerial Committee of the Boards of the World Bank and the International Monetary Fund, determine that "technical cooperation" in total makes up more than one-fifth of total overseas development aid given by the OECD countries. Not all technical cooperation, of course, generates the types of problems discussed here, some, for example, is made up of direct scholarship support that is not part of institution building. Cassen and Associates, however, estimate there were 150,000 "external advisors, consultants, seconded expatriates and other 'experts'" (p. 198) employed in LDCs at the time of their study.

This topic has been discussed before and some of these approaches have been explored, most particularly in Cohen (1992) and Wilson (1993). These papers, however, are not so general but rather were primarily concerned with criticising a particular approach being considered for indigenizing projects in Kenya. More general discussions can be found in works on "capacity building" by Haddow (1982), Berkman (1990), Cohen (1991), Wai and Rice (1991), Bossuyt et al (1992) and Berg (1993).

Both the Wilson and Cohen papers present rather critical views of technical assistance projects of this type, perhaps because they were both written with a particular project in mind. Here we want to look more closely at the other side of the discussion. We want to explore in more detail arguments *for* donor intervention in these markets in order to see if they counter-balance the arguments made previously. It is hoped that a more detailed analysis of these arguments will yield some policies which will better work to indigenize than the policies that have typically been pursued. A variety of arguments will be studied, mainly around the theme that there are market failures in the recipient countries that donors, being from "outside", can correct for. The implications of these arguments for project design will be drawn.

POLICIES AND GOALS

When one looks at the set of goals implicit in many aid projects there often seems a confusion of purposes and expectations [see Bigsten (1998)]. All projects, of course, have as their purpose improving conditions in the recipient country. Technical assistance projects however often have the additional expectation that they will somehow be taken over by the host country and it is here that expectations do not always seem well formed.

Projects typically begin with the donor supplying resources from abroad with the expectation that over time the recipient country will be able to take over. It is often not so clear, however, what has to change in order that this be able to happen. Is the country short of resources? Of all resources or just specific ones? Are there resources in the economy as a whole but not available to the government or the group who are to take over the project? There may, for example be only a rudimentary tax system. Does the country have the resources but for some reason not put sufficient priority on the donor's project? If these are problems what will change?

Very often donors, enthusiastic about their own projects, do not have these things well thought out. How much of an increase in overall resources will be necessary before the recipient country can take over the project? How realistic is it to expect this to occur in the donor's time frame? How many other demands on these resources will there be? Sometimes the donor expects the example or experience of the project to lead to a reallocation of resources within the country. How is this to occur? Why are not resources well allocated already?

In general, it is argued below, that many projects fail to be indigenized because of a confusion or lack of realism in these expectations about where resources are to come from. Indeed in some cases the donor may be misguided to believe that his project can be taken over in any reasonable time period. In the next three sections these issues are discussed in detail.

RESOURCE TRANSFER FROM ABROAD

Traditionally technical assistance projects have been based on the idea that the recipient country is short of resources, either of a specific type or overall. The idea, therefore, has been for the donor to provide these resources, typically with some sort of expectation that the recipient country will eventually be able to meet its own needs in some way, leaving the donor able to withdraw from the project. This approach differs from one that has become more popular recently where the donor feels the recipient economy has the resources but that these are just not well allocated. In this latter case, to be discussed in the next sections, the donor's purpose is to help with, or in some cases even force, some new, hopefully more efficient, utilization of the resources already available in the economy.

Some projects, of course, have a natural life and come to an end, and thus don't need taking over, the building of a road or some other type of infrastructure for example. Even these sorts of projects, however, often require skilled people for maintenance. The donor may thus be involved for longer than just the initial capital building period and there will still be the need to eventually turn the project over to local staff.

There are a variety of ways in which donors might expect circumstances in the recipient country to improve thus allowing them to leave, turning projects over to local expertise. In general these improvements must be in the form of relaxation of whatever constraints kept the recipient country from undertaking the project in the first place. These constraints could be of several types. There could be a shortage of resources overall, the country could just be poor, have many demands on its resources, and not give the particular project enough priority to undertake it given the resources available. The country could have enough resources overall but, if the project is within government, the government itself could be starved for resources. Finally there could be a shortage of some specific types of resources necessary for the project.

This last type of shortage is very often in the form of a shortage of particular types of skilled manpower, well trained economists, engineers, or veterinarians as examples. Growth in the economy, the standard of living and the education system might correct this but we can expect this to take a long time. Projects often, therefore, incorporate training programs. A difficulty with these, as we will discuss further below, is that the donor's project may not be the only demander of the newly trained skilled workers. These workers may be attractive to employers outside the recipient country, perhaps in the country where they are trained, and thus it may be difficult to get them to return. Within the country, if the donor's project is within government, the private sector may have demand for these skills as well. In many countries for example bank regulation is weak because of the government's inability to compete with the private banking sector for staff. Finally, the donor's project may not be the next priority for government and workers may be assigned elsewhere within the public sector. Many may, therefore, need to be trained before the recipient country government or economy would choose to assign them to the specific donor's project. This problem of reallocating skilled workers across employers within the country is discussed below.

More generally, donor funding might be necessary because, in some way, the country may not be able to afford to provide the service for itself. In these cases the donor may expect that with development and rising incomes this problem will be resolved. The constraint could be in the nature of an overall shortage of resources or, if the project is within government, an inability of the government to get access to these. It is possible, for example, that the society might in principle be able to afford a service but because of a poorly organized tax system government itself could be unable to afford the resources. In this case the donor might expect an improvement in the tax system to allow the government to take over the funded project.

These latter types of expectations, that income would grow or the tax system be improved, must be seen to take a long time. If these are the routes thorough which the donor hopes the recipient country will be able to take over and run the project on their own then the donor must be prepared for this.

One of the attractive features of the traditional approach, the supplying of new resources into the system, is that there should be benefits to the recipient country whether the project is well chosen or not. While it is obviously best that aid money be spent in the most efficient way possible, if mistakes are made, say if the donor is not well informed for some reason, it is likely that the project chosen will still yield some net benefit.

Mistakes can be of different sorts and this will have implications and likelihood that the recipient government will be willing to take a project over and "indigenize" it. In Figure 8.1 the distance OS along the horizontal axis can be taken to be the indigenous supply of the resource to the local economy or to the government depending on the particular problem. Distance OS, for example, might represent the number of economists the government of the recipient country is able to hire at some politically feasible wage rate. The curve MB represents the marginal benefit of additional resources, in the example of additional economists to the government. In the diagram it is assumed that the recipient government has allocated the resources efficiently, to the highest MB activities. In this case the best use of additional donor provided resources would be to take on the next highest MB activities, in the diagram, those between S and A. These, being the next priorities of the recipient when resources come available, are also the most likely to be taken over thus allowing the donor to turn over the project and leave.

Figure 8.1.

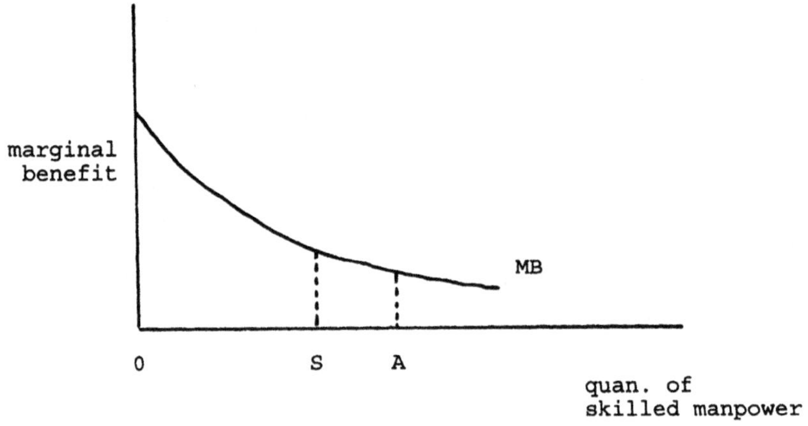

Several types of error are possible. The recipient government itself may not have resources well allocated. In Figure 8.2, for example, the amount of resources B to C might, instead of being optimally allocated, be used for projects yielding lower MB, say those in the range A to D. If this is the case donor resources are best used in that range omitted by the recipient, providing benefits in the range MB_B to MB_C, but even if they are not used over this range they will still yield a positive MB in the recipient country.

The donor may also not pick optimal projects. In the context of the diagram the donor might, for example, pick projects in the O to S range duplicating work already being done by the recipient country. If this is the case, and the recipient country and economy operate efficiently, then their resources can be moved to the next best alternative use, say in range S to A and thus best use will still be made of the aid.

Alternatively, the donor may pick projects which would not be the next priority of the recipient government. The donor might pick projects in the A to D range in Figure 8.2 for example. These projects will still be useful in that they have a positive MB to the recipient country, although not as high a one as if the optimal projects had been picked, but importantly here these projects will not be so easily indigenized. Assuming the recipient government correctly allocates resources and knows what it is doing, as resources come available they will not be assigned to taking over projects in the A to D range but rather to taking on those currently not being done in the S to A range.

This may well be the main reason recipient governments fail to take over projects that donors fund. The projects may be attractive to the recipients and they may be glad to have the resources and the help they provide as these projects have positive marginal benefits. At the same time, these projects may not necessarily be the next priority for them when their own resources come available. Thus, when the donor leaves, their project will not be taken over. Even when the donor trains workers specifically for their project, if these workers are scarce in the economy as a whole, they may not be more than temporarily assigned to the project.

Figure 8.2.

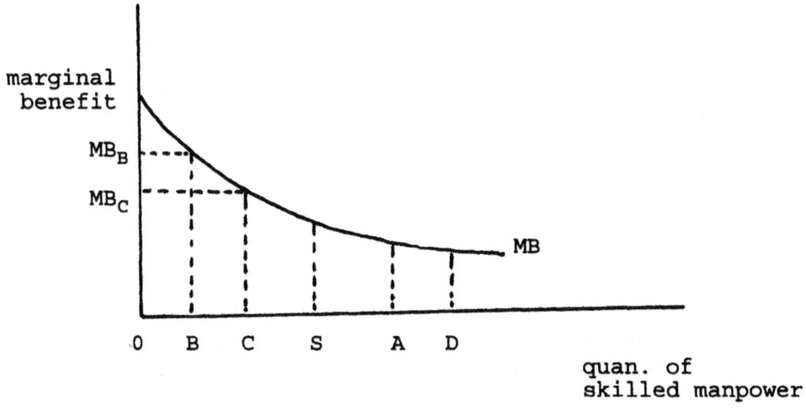

This is made more difficult by the possibility of differences between the donor and the recipient about priorities and by the possibility of strategic behaviour on the part of the recipient. It is clear that the recipient has an interest in claiming that the level of resources is not sufficient to take over the donor's project if the expectation is that the donor will then stay on. The donor will thus have difficulty in knowing whether they can leave, confident their project will be taken over, or not.

In Figures 8.1 and 8.2 the MB curve might also be taken to represent the marginal benefits of a resource to the economy as a whole, the marginal benefit, say, of another economist to the recipient country economy as a whole. If this is the case the analysis above continues to be applicable. The economy as a whole, if it operates reasonably efficiently, will allocate resources to their most useful purposes. New resources provided by a donor will be best used in the next highest MB purposes. Mistakes are possible. There may be some impediments to efficient resource allocation in the recipient country or donors may not chose the highest MB project not otherwise being done.

This analysis has implications for donor funded training programs. Unless the donor's project is the next priority of the government, or the economy as a whole, for the allocation of the skilled manpower being trained, the donor cannot expect to keep these workers. It would be inefficient for these workers to be assigned to lower priority uses. This may explain why many donors have the experience of seeming to train more workers than their specific projects need and yet not having these projects taken over.

Second, a well functioning economy would assign workers according to where they are most useful across the whole economy, including the private sector. Donors often have the problem that they train workers for their specific project or to strengthen the public sector, only to have these workers move elsewhere. If the local economy is functioning well, and the problem is one of an overall shortage of resources, then this may not be a bad thing. It could be, of course, that the local economy is not allocating resources efficiently and this is the problem we discuss in detail in Sections IV and V below.

Third, the way training is undertaken will have implications for its impact on the supply of the workers to the local economy and to the project. First, as we discuss further below, one of the problems of supply is the ability of skilled manpower to compete internationally. Workers who have these opportunities will be more or less willing to work abroad according to their degree of "home attachment" and this, in turn will depend to some extent on where and how they are trained. Workers who have the experience of living abroad, while being trained in a developed country for example, may be less likely to enter the recipient country labour force. This may mean that if the donor can develop training programs which do not involve sending the trainees abroad there will be a better chance of retaining them.

Similarly, the nature of training and credentials will have an impact on the trainees' mobility. Specific training which makes the worker useful for the donor's project but which is not so generally applicable be make it more likely the project can retain the trainee. This is the case both for competition from international employers and other employers within the country. Some donors have therefore tried to develop training schemes which expressly do not result in degrees or credentials which signal to other potential employers how valuable the worker is.

Many training programs also include some bonding of trainees to the government or more specifically to the donor's project. This may not work well in that it is difficult to force workers to stay and perform in jobs where they do not wish to be. Secondly, again if the economy is doing a good job of allocating resources, if the problem is primarily one of an overall shortage, then not allowing the market and government to best allocate the newly trained worker may be sub-optimal.

In summary, then, this traditional approach, where the main theme is supplying extra resources into a resource scarce economy, is likely to always do some good. Most good will come of it if the local economy is already allocating resources well and if the donor and recipient can agree on the next highest priority areas. If this is the case, and projects are in the next highest priority areas the donor will have reasonable success in turning the project over as this would be the next use the recipient government would put resources which come available to. In many cases the extra resources will take a long time to come available — a general shortage of income or foreign exchange for example, and the donor might expect to have a long involvement.

REALLOCATION OF EXISTING RESOURCES

A particular approach to indigenization deserving of special attention is that around reallocating, rather than supplying new, resources within the recipient country. There are several reasons why this approach has received attention recently. In the main, however, it can be thought of as part of the more fundamental ideas of "capacity building" or "restructuring" which generally place emphasis on efficient use of the resources available rather than on the supplying of additional amounts. In these approaches, the developing economy, while it may still be resource scarce, is seen as not using the resources it does have effectively. Aid donors therefore see it as more important to press for the reallocation of the resources already existing within the country than to supply more. Donors might, for example, believe that a particular type of skilled man-power is somehow being mis-used. More particularly, as discussed above, many donors have been in the position of having trained large numbers of people to the skills necessary for their particular projects but none-the-less finding that their projects cannot yet be turned over to local staff.

These ideas may be correct and, in addition, whatever the level of resource availability in the recipient country, efficient allocation of resources is important. At the same time there are dangers that the donors will, themselves, force misallocation as the information requirements for this type of policy are high. One must know where the resources are being re-allocated from and in many cases why the sub-optimal allocation is occurring. It is also harder to design solutions which are permanent in that they will survive the departure of the donor.

From the donor's point of view this could be thought of as a type of second-best problem where for some reason, in absence of donor intervention, resources are not being put to their first best use. Optimality requires that the marginal benefit (MB) of an additional unit of the resource, say an additional skilled worker of a specific type, be equated across uses. Workers might, for example, be split between the public and private sectors and optimality requires that the marginal benefits be equated between the two sectors.

What distortions could occur in these markets? One set of possibilities is that too few of the available resources would be in the public sector, or more narrowly in government, and too many elsewhere in the economy. Resources might also be misallocated within government or within the broader public sector. Finally, there is the idea that resources might be misallocated in some way internationally with too few of the recipient country's nationals working within the country and the gap being made up with expatriate workers.

What might cause these misallocations? A main cause is an inability of the government to pay the market wage, at least for some types of workers, defined in some way. Highly skilled workers, say workers with good quality Ph.D.s for example, face an international market and competing in this market might be politically impossible. Governments may be able to justify the purchase of some commodities at international prices, cars, trucks and other machinery for example, but it may be perceived as too inequitable to pay some workers wages many times what others, without international opportunities, could earn.

These workers need not be located outside the recipient country. There may be employers outside government, but located in the country, who can pay much higher wages. The private sector might not be constrained by such a strong sense of equity. In many LDCs there is significant employment in international organizations and these are often constrained to pay international rates whatever local conditions. There are often many consulting opportunities for these organizations as well and workers may find it attractive to work in consulting even though this may require periods of not being directly employed.

These wage distortions may cause distortions in choice of techniques and inefficiencies beyond just too few skilled workers being employed. If these workers are seen as costing little, even though there is a scarcity of them, there may be a reluctance to look for alternative, perhaps capital intensive, ways of being more efficient overall.

There is often a sense that the overall government budget constraint is too binding for proper resource allocation. Even given the overall constraints of the economy, resources may not be well allocated, at least by some definitions, because the government may not be able to get access to funds, say because of a poor tax system. In these cases then, where the "shadow price of government revenue" is significantly above one, somehow transferring spending power from the private to the public sector, without incurring the normal dead weight loss of the tax system, would improve resource allocation. This may manifest itself in the sense that skilled workers may seem less valuable in the private sector than they would be in the public one and yet the public sector seems unable to get the funds to hire them.

Finally resources could be misallocated within the public sector. There are many possibilities here. Within government itself the process of allocating the skilled workers may be corrupt or be subject to nepotism. Some jobs may be more attractive to workers than others, say they might be urban rather than rural, and yet this may not match where workers would be most usefully sent. Individual Ministers or government officials might be powerful and demand more than is optimal.

The public sector typically includes more than just government. There may be parastatals of various types and universities and colleges as examples. The constraints on these employers may not be the same as on government itself yet government may directly fund these organizations. Again, then, if one part of the public sector is treated differently from another, such that the budget constraint is less binding in one than the other, resources may be misallocated.

This type of misallocation is difficult for donors to deal with as it ostensibly represents a difference of opinion between the donor and the recipient country about allocation. The donor therefore runs the risk of being seen to be, or actually being, paternalistic, in trying to force a different allocation within the public sector than the government itself has chosen. At the same time, some of these problems may not be fully under the control of the government, it may not adequately be able to deal with nepotism and corruption for example, and it may welcome an external agency helping it to better assign its staff.

Many of these difficulties are in the nature of second best problems. Modelling this explicitly makes it possible to see some of the issues which might arise in trying make corrections in order to move closer to the first best allocation. It allows us to discuss the policies which might be pursued by donors and the possible benefits and pitfall of these.

Assume two local markets and an international market for a particular type of skilled worker. In the local market workers can either work for the government, at wage w_G, or as consultants to international organizations and firms. These international organizations pay international rates of w_C and there are a fixed, exogenously determined, number of man-days of work available of N_C. Workers must work in one market or the other, i.e. government workers cannot get time off to consult when the opportunity arises. We assume the consulting work is spread evenly among those who chose to work as consultants, i.e. there are none of the problems of job turnover, etc. as discussed in the Harris-Todaro literature [see Mazumdar (1976), Milne and Wilson (1992)]. There are L_C workers who choose to be consultants, thus

$$L_G + L_C = L \tag{8.1}$$

where

L_G	is the number working in government, and
L	is the total supply of skilled workers.

These workers will be allocated across the two types of jobs so that

$$w_G = w_C N_C/L_C = w_C N_C/(L - L_G) \tag{8.2}$$

Thus

$$L_C = w_C N_C/w_G$$

and

$$L_G = L - w_C N_C/w_G$$

Total "unemployed resources" will be $L_C - N_C$ or a rate $(L_C - N_C)/L$.

This model stylizes the view that resources are misallocated between the public and private sectors, in this case because of several sets of rigidities. First, government wages are fixed, perhaps, as discussed above, because, for equity reasons, the state is unable to pay the higher rate necessary to attract the skilled workers. Second, the consulting sector pays fixed, externally set, wages and has a limited number of man-days of work available. Finally, as we have characterized it here, workers must be in one sector or the other. Workers cannot work for government and take time off to do the higher paying consulting jobs when they come available. The result of this, therefore is that there are unemployed resources. In Figure 8.3 below, based on Basu's treatment of the Harris-Todaro problem [see Basu (1984), p.73], we see both types of inefficiency. Line H represents the rectangular hyperbola

$$w_G(L - L_G) = w_C N_C \tag{8.3}$$

derived from equation (8.2). The right-hand side of the equation is a constant, given our assumptions., thus the fixed w_G determines the number of workers in consulting, $L_C = (L - L_G)$. We see that in equilibrium the MB_G of another worker in government exceeds the wage rate and thus that MB is not equal to marginal cost to the government. It would be efficient for the government to offer more to attract more workers. As well there are a number of "unemployed" workers $(L_C - N_C)$ so that some resources are not being used productively at all. Both of these represent a misallocation of resources.

The total supply of skilled workers to the economy will also be determined by w_G. These workers have the alternative of working internationally at some wage w_I — this might be, for example, in a developed country or for an international organization. Assume however that these workers have some "affinity" for their home country

Figure 8.3

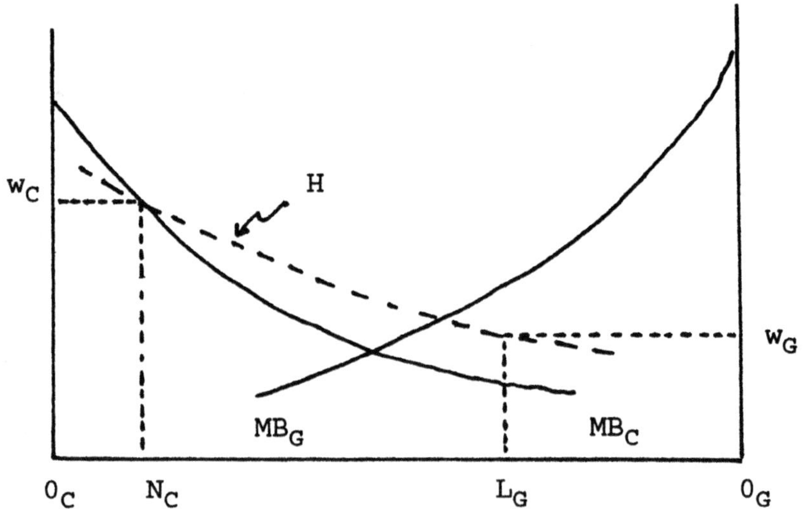

such that they would be willing to work there for less than they could command internationally. This "affinity" is distributed over some range, not everyone would demand the same premium to stay abroad. For a given local government wage, therefore, all those workers with "home attachment" or "affinity" stronger than a certain level will chose to return to or stay in the home country. If we define variable "h" as the "home attachment" and assume it is distributed as, say, in Figure 8.4, then

$$w_G = w_I(1 - h_E)$$

defines the value of the home attachment, h_E, at which a skilled worker will just be indifferent between coming home and living abroad. Thus all those with home attachment greater than h_E will choose to live in the recipient country. An increase in w_G will lower the equilibrium h_E, increasing the number who wish to be in the home country. Thus for a distribution of h as pictured in Figure 8.4, the supply curve of the skilled labour to the country will be as in Figure 8.5 and L will be $L(w_G)$ with $L'(w_G) > 0$. The supply of labour to government will thus be

$$L_G = L(w_G) - w_C N_C / w_G \tag{8.4}$$

The model specifies both the supply of the skilled workers in the recipient country and also how these are allocated — in this case the supply of workers to the public sector. It also yields two types of inefficiency in allocation. First is the amount of underemployment in the private, consulting, sector. At any time a number of workers are not employed at all except in searching for high paying consulting jobs. Second is the inconsistency between the wage paid and the marginal benefit of extra workers to the government, the fact that the government is not able to pay up to where marginal cost equals marginal benefit. Both these inefficiencies represent stylized cases where donors would feel a need to press for reallocation rather than, or in addition to, greater supply. The model allows us to discuss at least some of the forms of distortion and misallocation that may exist and various policies for dealing with this.

As depicted, the misallocation is in the nature of a second-best problem where wages in the economy are not set to the right levels. Correction can be of two forms

Figure 8.4

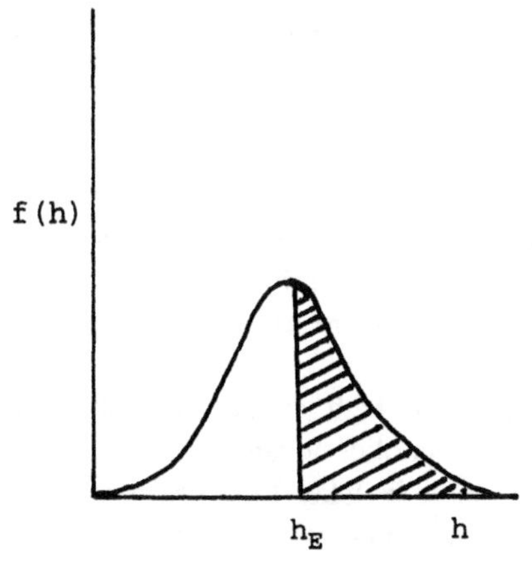

Figure 8.5

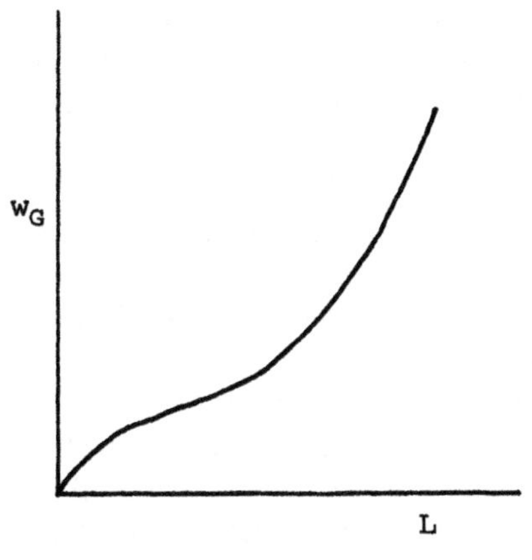

— first the removal of the original distortions or second, where this proves impossible, the introduction of compensating distortions elsewhere.

In the model there are too few of the skilled workers in the government sector and too many in consulting. In addition, because w_G does not equal MB_G, there are too few skilled workers in the country as a whole. An obvious way of correcting these problems is to raise w_G for this group of workers. The question then becomes — why does the government pay too little and what can be done. In some cases this is administrative. The average national income is low, less skilled workers who have no international market can command only low wages. Government then, on the grounds of equity, either with other civil servants or with workers in general, may feel they cannot pay the high wages necessary to equate w_G to MB_G and attract the skilled workers they need. In this case the first best solution is clear — the government needs to be less concerned about equity. There may be many reasons, however, why this is difficult or impossible.

One strategy for government in these circumstances is remuneration in forms other than as direct wage payments — interest free loans, training, trips abroad, the promise of a lucrative future position in a parastatal or elsewhere where the government has influence, etc. Even these however may create resentment over inequity. A role donors can play, with respect either to direct wage income or these other forms of remuneration, is to "take the blame" for the perceived inequality. The recipient country government may therefore be happy to agree to have the donor allocate its funds to these purposes — perhaps even while publicly complaining about the apparent inequity. In this case, therefore, where the recipient country government cannot be seen to pay the high wages necessary to attract skilled workers the donor can help by being perceived as the source of the inequality. At the same time, as we will see below, there are potential difficulties with this that the donor needs to be cautious about

Closely related to this is the problem of a poor tax base. As discussed above a poor tax base might imply a high shadow price of government revenue such that while the society as a whole could afford resources, the government could not. This gives the result, or the impression of the result at least, that resources are misallocated between the private and public sectors. In this case the public sector will appear to under-utilize all inputs and types of labour, not just skilled workers. The solution to this is a relaxation of the overall government budget constraint. In the short run this can be done by aid for general budget support. In the longer run, though, the overall tax system must be improved to lower the shadow price of government revenues relative to resources in the society in general.

A first best solution, then, would be for the government to raise wages. For various reasons this may be difficult. In some cases it may be possible for a donor to assist in solving the problem with general budget support or by taking blame for inequitable pay schemes. As we will see below however there are potential problems with these approaches.

A second source of distortion are the disequilibrium high wages paid in the consulting or private sector. In the model this leads to a pool of underemployed workers queuing for those jobs. As modelled, this sector could be taken to represent particularly employment by international organizations and donors who are under pressure to pay "international" wages. This misallocation could be directly corrected through these organizations lowering wages offered towards those offered by government.

In many cases the justification for international organizations paying these high wages is similar to the justification of the local government for not doing so, a concern for inequality. In the case of the international organizations it is argued that if they must pay a certain wage in rich countries for skilled workers then they must do the same thing world-wide. Just as with the too low government wages, this causes a misallocation of the skilled workers within the recipient country.

As we will discuss further below, it is sometimes argued that these organizations, by paying international level wages, attract workers from outside the country but in this model this will not be so. Migration to the country is determined by the expected wage which is the full time wage of the government employee. Higher wages in the consulting sector only cause more workers to choose to work in that sector, lowering the probability of any individual in that sector being employed.

Finally, the actual number of consulting jobs determines the amount of misallocation as well. In Figure 8.3 above we have shown the consulting sector as facing exogenously fixed wages but hiring along its marginal benefit curve. This might not be the case, the number of "man-days" might also be determined exogenously without direct reference to marginal benefit. Lowering the number of jobs, of man-days of employment offered, will, like lowering consulting wages, also reduce the portion of the work-force who will choose partial employment in the consulting sector.

One set of solutions, then, is what we can think of as moving to first-best by eliminating distortions. For some of these possibilities the role of donors or outsiders is limited. In others however, the existence and support of donors can help — "taking the blame" for what might appear to be inequitably high wages for certain types of skilled workers or offering general budget support are examples.

SMALL PROJECTS

Donors' attempts to indigenize are often made at more of a project level than out of concern for the civil service as a whole. Donors start up a particular project, provide expertise from their own nationals and plan that in the longer run local expertise will take over. Indeed the project is typically not seen as successful until this happens. The types of policies used to pursue this goal can have serious impact on the rest of the economy and the civil service and in that way can be thought of as types of second best policies. The interaction, therefore, between the reallocation of existing skilled workers within the economy, towards the project, and the separate goal of improving over-all allocation is important.

There are a number of dangers to this type of policy because, in the main, they involve the shuffling of existing resources around within the economy rather than the supplying of new ones. As discussed in Section III, if the local economy is allocating resources correctly and the donor has picked the project which would be the next priority of the recipient country, then, as resources come available, the project will be taken over as the donor leaves. If this is not to be the case then there must be some problem — the donor has different priorities from the recipient or the recipient economy is not allocating for the best.

The first and most obvious danger is simply paternalism, that the donor and the recipient disagree on what is best and the donor is trying to impose its priorities. The recipient country may be, as discussed in Section III, happy to receive the aid but not see the donor's project as its next priority. If, in this case, the donor undertakes some actions to reallocate local resources it will be a move away from what the recipient sees as optimal. There are several possibilities here. One is that the donor is misguided, the recipient's priorities are correct, and any reallocation is for the worse.

In general this seems a reasonable probability. One needs particular reasons to believe the local government does not allocate for the best. Similarly we think of the private sector as efficient and not employing workers to the point where wages exceed benefits. It may seem that the government is short of particular types of expertise but it must be kept in mind that the country is poor — as an aid recipient — and all resources will be scarce. A first point then is that donors must be careful in forcing reallocation towards their projects. It may be that resources are scarce everywhere in the economy rather than just in the area of their particular project. Before reallocating, then, one needs to know, not just what the benefits of having expertise in your area are, but also what the losses of moving expertise from elsewhere will be. Attempts to reallocate existing resources within the country, rather than just to supply more, thus require a good deal more information to be beneficial.

A frequently used policy is to pressure the recipient government to reallocate towards the donor's project. This might be done, for example, by tying other aid to the "success" of the particular project. If this is to be optimal over all the donor must know that not only are the resources well used in their project but also that they are better used in their project than in the alternative use they would be put to.

Having made this caution, it is none-the-less true that in many cases resources will not be optimally allocated within the recipient country. This could be both within the public sector and between it and the private one. As modelled above, for example, too few resources were in the public sector and some were underemployed. There are also possible causes of misallocation beyond those in the model. The government or its officials may be corrupt or there may be nepotism within the administration. It may also be, more fundamentally, that the government does not have the administrative capability to properly choose the optimal allocation of resources — indeed some technical cooperation projects are to improve this very capability. A donor might, therefore, well feel the allocation could be improved upon, and that some of the underemployed resources could be used to allow the recipient country to take over the donor's project.

We can see, however, from the specific, but representative, case of the model above that the donor must be careful of what policies it pursues. Some policies can be seen to be clearly successful, others not. As discussed above, one possibility is for the donor to provide general support for increases in wages for the skilled workers in question within the government as a whole. The donor might assign some of it's general, budget support, aid to this goal, with the recipient government's acquiescence, in order to help the government, by "taking the blame", with the political issue of the inequality which will arise from these high wages for the skilled. This is a particular example of "tied aid" where the "tying" would be with the private, but perhaps not public, agreement of the recipient. From equation (8.4) we see that this will bring more of these workers into government, both from the underemployed in the consulting or private sector and from outside the country. Some of these workers could be assigned to the donors project although the considerations of whether this is the best use of them discussed above are still relevant. This is a policy, then, that could lead to an overall increase in efficiency with less workers underemployed in consulting and more skilled nationals in the country.

More complicated, however, are schemes to attract workers to the donor's specific project by paying just those specific workers high wages. One can see why this policy might have an appeal. It is far cheaper than subsiding all the skilled workers in the public sector. The donor can see the misallocation of workers queued up for consulting jobs and underemployed. Indeed, the donor might even have paid for some of these workers to gain the skills allowing them to do this. The donor might not see the local government as being able to optimally allocate workers, even with the donors general support. It may seem a simple solution, therefore, to offer wages competitive with the consulting sector and attract some of these workers back to government and to the donor's project.

There are dangers to this however and the importance of these depends very much on how this is done and, as a result, where these workers come from. A simple scenario is one in which the donor offers international level salaries, in hopes of attracting back some of the nationals working abroad as well as the underemployed in the consulting sector, and advertises generally taking the best candidates from all sources — within government, the private sector, and from outside the country. A possibility in this scenario is that the donor will be seen as attempting to compete directly in the market for consultants and thus that the donor's jobs will be seen as the same as these. In equation (8.4) this will be represented by an increase in variable N_C with the result that w_C/w_G workers will leave government and move to consulting and no new workers will be attracted into the country. In other words, not only will as many workers as the donor requires come out of the rest of the government sector but more than this number will leave government, some to join the pool of workers who are underemployed in the consulting sector.

In the model case, at least, there is no implication that the workers within the government are not optimally allocated, only that there are too few of them and too many in the private sector. In this case, therefore, where the workers are drawn randomly out of government to the donors project we can expect that resources will be less well allocated than before. If the economy is as described in Figure 8.1 in Section III, where the limited government resources are assigned to the top priority projects, with the donor picking up the next most useful jobs, then any movement of skilled workers from their roles in government to the project or the private sector will be on average for the worse.

This case, of course, is a special one and meant to show the dangers possible. None-the-less it is fairly realistic so if the donor hopes to avoid these problems special care must be taken. A great deal depends on the perception of those in the job market with respect to the likelihood of getting the jobs. In the example above, the donor's jobs are seen as consulting jobs which those choosing consulting as a career expect to have a reasonable chance at. Thus w_C/w_G will move for each job created. There are other possible perceptions however. An alternative is that the donors hirings are taken at random from the three sources — government, the consulting sector, and abroad — in such a way that the other workers in the economy then realize that the jobs are filled and that they have no chance at them. In this case the number of consulting jobs, N_C, will not be seen to change nor will the number in the country net of those brought in to work on the project (as w_G is unchanged). In this case, then, the workers will be drawn from new migrants and the government, depending completely on how many the donor hires from abroad. The number in consulting will not change however, and, to the extent that the donor hires from those in consulting, workers will leave government to join that pool.

The case with the least impact locally will be where the donor hires *only* from abroad, making it clear they will never hire from the local consulting community or from within the government. This is difficult of course as it requires discrimination against nationals who may differ from those abroad, not in ability, but only in the degree of "home attachment".

A final case which might be practical but which seems little tried is to make the donors higher paying jobs available to all the skilled workers within government. In this case a government worker would then see his wage not as w_G but as some expected wage $E(w_G)$ made up of w_G and w_D, the donors wage level. In this case

$$L_G = L[E(w_G)] - w_C N_C / E(w_G) \quad (8.5)$$

and, as $E(w_G)$ will be greater than w_G, we can expect both migration of skilled workers to the country and less underemployment in consulting. The donor would have to experiment with w_D in order to ensure that the number in the rest of government was not reduced.

In summary, it is only under quite specific arrangements that a donor funded project paying above government wages will improve the allocation of skilled labour in the economy.

- Hiring in the open market at consulting level salaries will result in all workers (net) coming from the government except those specifically recruited from abroad.

- There is danger that if the donor's jobs are seen as "consulting" jobs, where only those who are in consulting and thus out of government have the possibility of employment, more will leave government for consulting than the donor hires because of the Harris-Todaro like pool of underemployed in consulting.

- If the donor can discriminate and hire only from abroad, even though there may be well-qualified candidates locally, the donors project will be staffed by nationals and there will be no impact on the other sectors.

- The donor could work towards a second-best improvement by making its higher paying jobs available on some sort of probabilistic or rotational basis to all the skilled workers in the public sector. This would raise expected government wages and draw more people into that sector.

The model is stylized but captures at least some of the main features of the problem. Government internal misallocation is not modelled but is discussed above. The consulting, private, sector is particularly stylized, however, in that there will be many non-government employers — an international public sector — local offices of UN agencies for example — international and local private firms, and a local public sector outside central government — the universities and colleges and parastatals for example. In many LDCs it is the last group, the universities and parastatals, that lure the most skilled workers from government as the constraints on salary equity seem less binding. It is worth noting though that in some sense this sector is still under government control and if too much skilled manpower is allocated there it should be within government control to correct for this misallocation. At the same time, however, expressly because these "outside government" government agencies do seem less bound by equity considerations with the rest of the public service the proposal is sometimes made that the government skilled worker shortage can be solved by setting up "research groups" outside narrow government.

It is only in the latter two cases, where the donor discriminates in favour of hiring abroad or where the donor's jobs are seen as available to all civil servants on a rotational basis, that we get an improvement in allocation.

Finally, we should note an important feature of all these proposals. This is that all are dependant on donor funding, they are corrections for misallocation of resources which depend on the continuing support of the donor financially. In this sense then they may not represent full indigenization. The donor will have been able to withdraw it's own expatriate workers and turn the project over to skilled nationals but it will not be able to see the project as complete and withdraw entirely. In the longer run the donor must have some further expectations about being able to withdraw funding to extricate themselves entirely. As discussed in Section II above, there are various ways this might happen. The financial position of the government of the recipient country may improve, through GDP growth or an improvement in the tax position, or the number of skilled workers might increase. These things might happen with support of the donor through training or administrative assistance. Donor support for many projects is fairly long term in nature, there are Canadian International Development Agency projects in East Africa which have been in place for more than twenty years.

The project might also change preferences and priorities in various ways. The existence and example of the project may make the recipient government more aware of the importance of the type of work being done and induce them to take the project over when the donor leaves. Government ministers, for example, will get used to being well briefed for international conferences and will realize they can not be without this even if the donor withdraws. The recipient government may have lacked basic planning and organizational ability and so have had difficulty setting priorities. Donors may provide technical assistance at this basic level and thus leading to reallocation of resources. Technical cooperation to governments can be thought of as transferring the technology of government, thus new ways of doing things will be learned and continued with after the donor withdraws. In some cases there is a type of administrative inertia — bureaucratic power bases form and it is difficult to transfer resources around. A donor may be able to force this. Then, when they depart, they will leave in place the new structure which itself will be resistant to change and thus unlikely to go back to the old ways.

Similarly skilled workers may also change their preferences. Government work might come to be seen as more productive and useful and thus more attractive to those underemployed in consulting. Luring back recipient country nationals from abroad with high initial salaries may change their "home attachment" so that when the donor funded higher paying jobs end they still chose to stay in their country. These sorts of changes would increase the number of skilled workers available to the government.

SUMMARY

A main theme of this paper is to stress the differences between the traditional form of aid, the supplying of new resources into the developing country, and the newer view of forcing the reallocation of existing resources within the country. The traditional approach is one that requires far less information about the recipient economy. New resources can generally be seen as having a benefit whether they are optimally allocated or not. It is, of course, better to allocate these resources to higher, rather than lower, marginal benefit uses, but as long as the marginal benefit is positive the resources will improve welfare.

At the same time, if projects are not carefully chosen from among those with the highest priority in the recipient country, then the recipient country will be reticent to take them on themselves and the donor will have difficulty turning their project over to local operation. Thus, even as more resources come available, the donor may find that it will be impossible to leave with confidence that their project will continue. This is particularly a problem where the donors have themselves contributed to relaxation of the resource constraint and feel, naturally, that those new resources should be assigned to their project. Projects often, for example, include training of local people and the donors are then upset to see these skilled people being assigned elsewhere. The inability of donors to successfully pick the next highest priority projects for the recipient country may well explain the lack of success in indigenization.

This can be made especially difficult by the incentives which the recipient country has to claim that, whatever has happened, resources are still not adequate so that the donor's will continue with the project. The donor may thus feel the recipient will always be strategic in their claim that they cannot yet take over the project and this makes getting a true sense of how binding the resource constraints are difficult.

The newer approach, of attempting to force reallocation of existing resources to improve efficiency within the country, is more difficult. This is because it requires much more knowledge of alternative resource uses. In the traditional approach the donor knows that, wherever allocated, his contributions will be of benefit and improve welfare. This is less clear where the goal is to move resources from one activity in the economy to another. One needs to know the value of the new use, where the resources will come from, and how valuable they were there. Much of the discussion in Sections IV and V was of the difficulties of doing these things.

REFERENCES

Basu, K., (1984). The Less Developed Economy: a Critique of Contemporary Theory, (Basil Blackwell, Oxford).

Berg, Elliot J., (1993). Rethinking Technical Cooperation: Reforms for Capacity Building in Africa, (New York: Regional Bureau for Africa, United Nations Development Programme and Development Alternatives).

Berkman, Steve (1990). "Technical Assistance in Africa: How it Works and Doesn't Work", Internal Memorandum for AFTED, World Bank, Washington, D.C.

Bigsten, A. (1998), "Can Aid Generate Growth", This volume.

Bossuyt, J., Laporte, G. and van Hoek, F. (1992). "New Avenues for Technical Cooperation in Africa: Improving the Record in Terms of Capacity Building", European Centre for Development Policy Management, Maastricht, The Netherlands.

Cassen, Robert and Associates (1986) Does Aid Work?, Clarendon Press, Oxford.

Cohen, John M.(1991). "Expatriate Advisors in the Government of Kenya: Why They are There and What Can be Done About it", Development Discussion Papers, 376, Harvard Institute for International Development, Cambridge, MA.

Cohen, John M.(1992). "Foreign Advisors and Capacity Building: the Case of Kenya", Public Administration and Development, XII (1992), 493–510.

Haddow, Paul S.(1982). "The Post Graduate Training and Utilization of Professional Planners and Economists in the Government of Kenya: Recommendations to the Government and donor Agencies" (Report Prepared for the Ministry or Economic Planning and Development and the Canadian International Development Agency, July 1982).

Milne, W. and L. S. Wilson, (1992), "A Labour Turnover Model of Unemployment in Kenya", mimeo.

Mazumdar, Dipak (1976), "The Rural-Urban Wage Gap, Migration, and the Shadow Wage", Oxford Economic Papers.

Wai, Dunstan and Rice, Gerald T. (1991), The African Capacity Building Initiative: Toward Improved Policy Analysis and Development Management, The World Bank, Washington D.C.

Wilson, L. S., (1993), "Kenyanization and African Capacity 'Shuffling'", Public Administration and Development, Vol 13, pp. 489–499.

III

Case Studies:
The Donor Experience

CHAPTER 9

DANISH AID POLICY:
Theory and Empirical Evidence

Finn Tarp
Christian F. Bach
Henrik Hansen
and
Søren Baunsgaard[1]

INTRODUCTION

Much of the academic literature on foreign aid and development has focused on estimating aid needs or assessing aid effectiveness. In contrast, the aid allocation literature — summarised in McGillivray and White (1993) — deals with issues such as the determination of the size of the overall aid allocation and the motives of individual donors. These studies are not only of interest on their own account. A more profound understanding of the impact of aid on development cannot be achieved without clarifying how much aid is given, to whom it is channelled, and how it is composed.

This chapter analyses how Danish aid policy has evolved since the early 1960s. This is pertinent due to the widespread perception that the aid policy of Denmark together with other like-minded countries such as Norway, Sweden, the Netherlands, and Canada is driven largely by the development needs of poor countries. A formal model for the country allocation of Danish bilateral aid commitments is also proposed, and it is argued that there are two key steps involved in the aid allocation process. The theoretical model underpins a cross-country panel data analysis, which is applied to derive conclusions about the significance and parameter signs of the different officially stated motives behind Danish bilateral aid allocations during the period 1976–94.

Following this introduction, Section II provides a descriptive analysis of Danish aid in a historical and international comparative perspective. In Section III, the formalised model of how Danish bilateral aid is distributed among recipient countries is put forward. This framework is made quantifiable in Section IV, and the empirical analyses are summarised in Section V. Conclusions are drawn in Section VI.[2]

DESCRIPTIVE ANALYSIS

Danish international development assistance emerged in the cold war atmosphere of the late 1940s. Multilateral contributions were made to the UN Expanded Programme of Technical Assistance (EPTA) from 1950, and limited financial support was also provided in the 1950s for bilateral purposes. An institutional framework for the administration of Danish aid was established in 1962 under the aegis of the Ministry of Foreign Affairs, and during the following three decades total official Danish aid grew consistently. The UN official development assistance (ODA) target of 1 percent of GNP was therefore reached in 1992. This development is in sharp contrast to the profile of total DAC aid that remained between 0.30–0.35 percent of GNP during the period 1976–92, after which it fell to around 0.26 percent in 1995. This decrease reflects in particular the pronounced drop in American aid allocations.

Another characteristic of Danish aid includes the more or less equal shares of multi- and bilateral aid. Multilateral aid has been much larger in relative terms than what is commonly seen within DAC. In fact, the UN has remained one of the cornerstones of Danish foreign policy for decades, and Danish aid policy has tried to ensure that the aid giving process took place in a way that would minimise recipient country economic and political dependence on individual donors. Respect for the wishes and priorities of recipient countries and abstaining from linking aid with political conditionality were guiding principles for Danish aid from the early years. However, these principles have been increasingly challenged since the 1980s. Other channels for Danish multilateral aid have included the World Bank (including IDA), the Regional Development Banks, and since the early 1970s assistance through the EU has gradually come to play an important role. Consequently, whereas 80 percent of Danish multilateral aid was channelled through the UN in previous decades, this share is now around 50 percent.

In the implementation of Danish bilateral aid a range of NGOs have been active. In 1995, for example, they were responsible for implementing 16.7 percent of total

Figure 9.1. Concentration of Danish Aid flows, 1960–95.

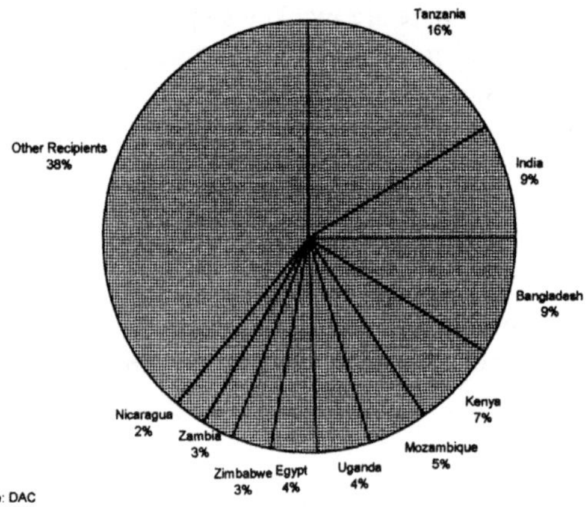

Source: DAC

bilateral Danish aid (Danida, 1997 p. 107). The NGOs have also played a vocal role in influencing the principles of Danish aid, and they have helped maintain a high level of political and general public support to the aid programme. In addition, one does find a set of moral and idealistic motives, concerned with helping poor people in need, behind official Danish aid policy. Accordingly, India, Tanzania, Kenya, and Bangladesh (Figure 9.1) received more than 40 percent of all Danish bilateral assistance from 1960 to 1995. Yet, it is also characteristic that the concentration of Danish bilateral aid (measured by the share of the five and ten most important recipients) has shown a downward trend over time.

Physical infrastructure and modern agriculture were the main areas identified for Danish bilateral support in the beginning in line with the then influential modernisation approach to development. Nevertheless, it was not until 1971 that a law on development co-operation was put in place, in which the official goals of Danish aid were formalised. This Act has since been revised several times, but paragraph 1, which has by now remained unchanged for more than 25 years, continues to affirm that the overriding aims of Danish aid are: (i) economic growth, (ii) social progress, (iii) political independence, and (iv) the promotion of inter-cultural understanding and solidarity. It is also central in Danish policy statements that the fundamental principles of the UN are to be respected in the development process.

While the legal underpinning of Danish aid has remained unchanged, it has nevertheless been subject to repeated public debates, and policy statements have evolved in distinct ways. In fact, the development strategies behind Danish aid policy reflect quite closely how development thinking has been changing over the years on the international scene. While "growth and trickle-down" thinking was influential in the 1950s, the 1960s and the early part of the 1970s "redistribution with growth" and "basic human needs" (BHN) approaches came more into focus in Danish aid from the mid-1970s. From 1975, poverty reduction started occupying centre stage, and at the same time "women in development" appeared as a first cross-cutting issue of Danida in line with UN principles and thinking (Estrup, 1995). It is also illustrative that official statements by Danida in the late 1970s emphasised that bilateral aid should concentrate not only on the poorer developing countries but be implemented in such a way that it benefited poorer groups of people. Integrated projects with a clear focus on the poor became a common tool, to which reference was made. Moreover, the increasing relative importance of social infrastructure and services and the decreasing importance of production sectors in the late 1970s, as reflected in available data, appear as a response to the greater importance of BHN considerations in official policy statements from 1975.

A major review of the principles behind Danish aid was undertaken in the early 1980s, following the publication of the report of the influential Brandt Commission (Brandt et al., 1980). Several changes in the aims and principles guiding Danish aid were indeed formulated in the 1982 "Bang-report", but no substantial political changes were pursued (Nyboe-Andersen, 1986 p. 7). Collaboration with the four main recipient countries at the time was supported politically, and no decisions were taken on adding new countries. In sum, during the earlier parts of the 1980s, BHN and social sector concerns continued to influence Danida thinking. Little by little more attention was paid to the need for pursuing macro-economic policy reforms and structural adjustment across a large number of developing countries, and the debt crisis became a major issue in international debates. However, Danida bilateral aid did not really change focus, and programme aid continued to make up a very small share of Danish aid. Moreover, Danida has generally been more favourable to a human face approach to adjustment (Cornia, Jolly and Stewart, 1987) than to the more orthodox liberalisation and reform packages, pursued by the IMF and the World Bank during most of the 1980s — as discussed in Tarp (1993). Accordingly, during the period 1988–94, total Danish balance of payments (BOP) support (i.e. programme assistance and action related to debt) remained low, at only DKK 2.2 billion or approximately 8 percent of the Danish bilateral aid budget for the whole period. Only a limited part of this support was explicitly linked to policy conditionality, which has gained increasing support in more recent years. The single major programme initiative during this period was the 1987 debt relief operation, in which the debt owed to Denmark by a number of Danish aid recipients was cancelled.

Environmental issues were added as a second Danida cross cutting concern, following the Brundtland Commission Report (Brundtland et al., 1987). Promoting "social development and sustainable growth", while at the same time paying more attention to "human rights", were also included in 1988 as explicit objectives in a "Danida Action Plan". Subsequently, in 1989 the Foreign Policy Committee of the Danish Parliament established a checklist of seven criteria to guide the selection of so-called programme countries to receive bilateral aid (Estrup, 1995). These criteria can be summarised as follows:

1. The economic and social level of development and developmental needs and plans.
2. The level of aid from other bilateral and multilateral donors and the ability to absorb and make use of aid.
3. The possibilities for promoting sustainable development through policy dialogue.
4. The possibilities for furthering human rights in accordance with internationally agreed standards.
5. The possibilities for addressing gender imbalances.
6. Previous experiences of Danida from bilateral aid collaboration with the country in question.
7. The possibilities for furthering the involvement of Danish business and employment.

In relation to the seventh criteria the parliamentary committee highlighted that it should only be considered after the first six dimensions were addressed. However, other potential trade-offs were not addressed, except that poverty reduction was retained as the overarching goal. Moreover, while the above list does not make reference to political conditionality, the goals of "good governance and democracy", nevertheless started appearing in a variety of Danida documents, including the 1994 Danida "Strategy for Danish Development Policy towards the Year 2000", accepted by Parliament in March 1994. As such Danida now operates with three cross cutting concerns: gender imbalances, environment, and democracy and human rights. They are, however, all perceived as dimensions of the poverty reduction goal, and imply that while the need for economic growth is recognised, it is at the same time held that growth may not itself reduce poverty.

Key features of the strategy report just referred to also include a concentration on 20 programme countries, mainly located in Africa and South Asia, and a focus on a few (two to four) sectors in each of these countries. Consequently, sector support programmes are of increasing importance as compared to the traditional project mode of aiding developing countries. Renewed attention to the importance of the agriculture sector is also appearing alongside the social sector focus of previous years. In line with the changing balance between the role of the state and the private sector in development, policy statements also pay increasing attention to "supporting the private sector".

In accordance with stated goals, Denmark has over the years consistently concentrated its bilateral aid on the poorest developing countries (Figure 9.2.1). In fact, the average GNP per capita of recipients of Danish aid has typically been at a level of only half that of the average for total DAC aid receiving countries. In addition, the average income level of recipients of aid from the group of like-minded donors has occupied the middle ground except in 1986. Similarly, Danida has typically supported countries with a relatively low life expectancy as compared to the other two groups (Figure 9.2.4). When it comes to GNP growth, it is difficult to discern any important differences between the three groups of aid recipients just referred to. Instead, it would appear that recipients of Danish aid have actually followed a growth path in per capita terms, which is almost identical to what happened in the group of countries receiving aid from DAC as a whole. This pattern is, in turn, replicated for the group of aid recipients receiving aid from the like-minded countries (Figure 9.2.2). However, since countries, which receive aid from Denmark, are on average poorer than those who receive aid from, for example, DAC, total growth has undoubtedly been somewhat higher in the typical Danida country as population growth is relatively high. As regards political and civil rights of the average recipient country, referred to in the fourth criteria in the Danida checklist, it is clear that Denmark scored rather poorly until the late 1980s. However, since then it appears that the increased focus on human rights has put Danish aid more in line with that of aid from other sources (Figure 9.2.3).

The quality of policy in aid receiving countries has attracted increasing attention in recent years, and is likely to continue to do so following World Bank studies such as that of Burnside and Dollar (1997). They argue that careful examination of experience with foreign aid shows that aid is an effective investment when the economic policies of a recipient country are sound. In their analysis, they rely on an index of inflation, the government budget deficit, and the degree of openness of the economy; and an overall index of sound policy is derived on this basis. As is clear from Figure 9.3.1–9.3.4, economic policy in countries receiving Danish aid has been close to that of countries supported by DAC and the like-minded group, at least when it comes to inflation and the government budget deficit. Yet, the typical country aided by Danida has generally been a little less open than the other two groups. As such the overall

Figure 9.2. Characteristics of aid receiving countries.

Figure 9.2.1. Nominal Income of average recipient country

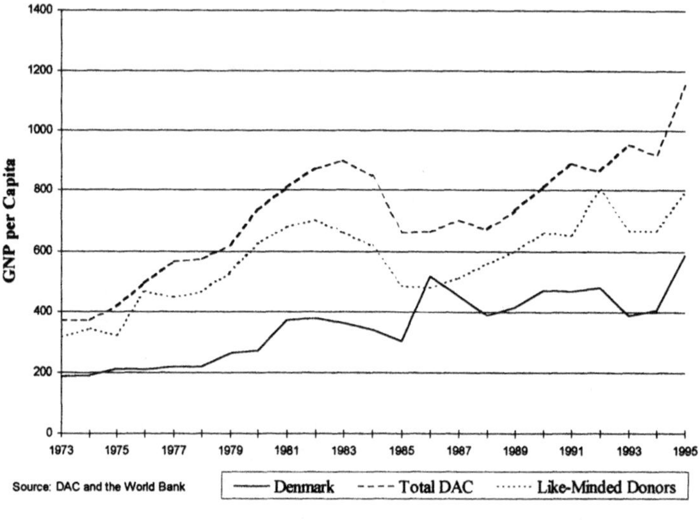

Figure 9.2.2. Real GNP per capita growth of average recipient country

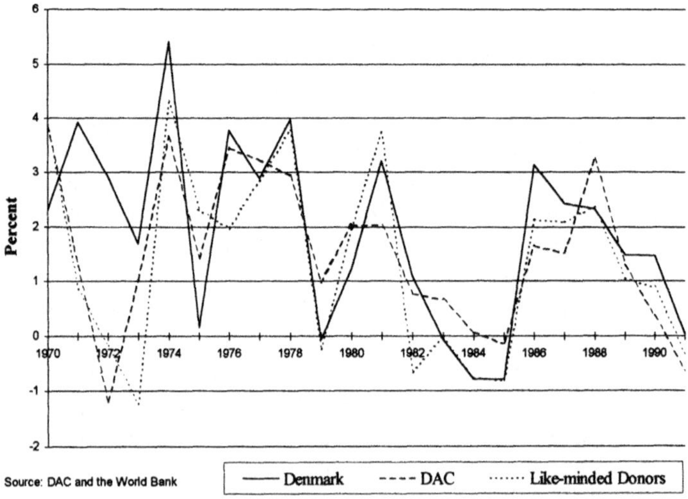

Notes: Figure 9.2.1. The increase in GNP per capita in 1995 can be explained by the depreciation of the US $ and increases in aid to relatively affluent countries in Eastern and Central Europe.

Figure 9.2 *(continued)*. Characteristics of aid receiving countries.

Figure 9.2.3. Political and civil rights of average recipient country

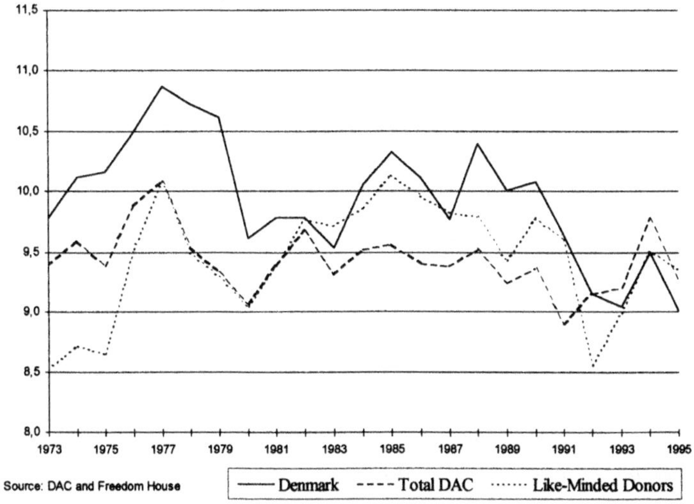

Figure 9.2.4. Life expectancy of average recipient country

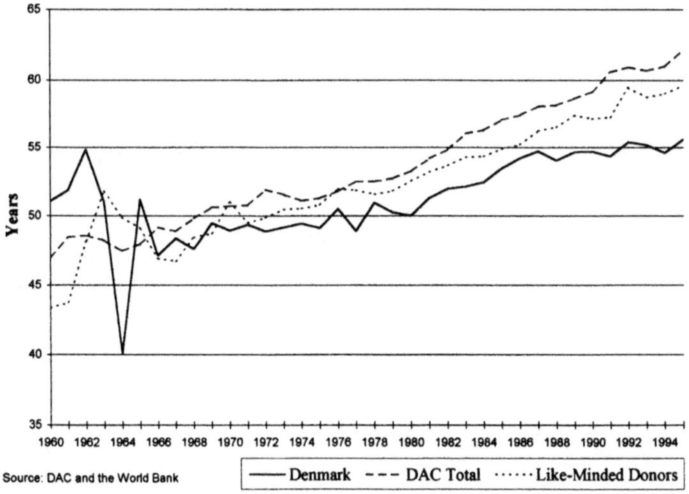

Notes: Figure 9.2.3. Higher Values of the index, which goes from 2 to 14, imply lower rights.

Figure 9.3. Policy indicators.

Figure 9.3.1. Annual inflation of average recipient country

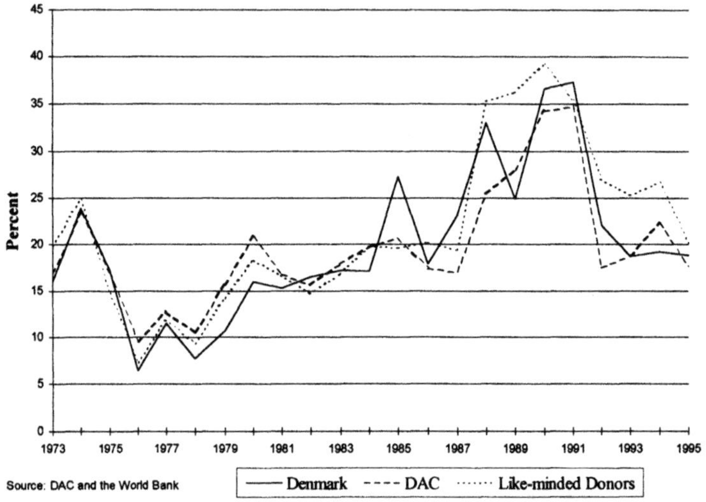

Figure 9.3.2. Government budget deficit of average recipient country

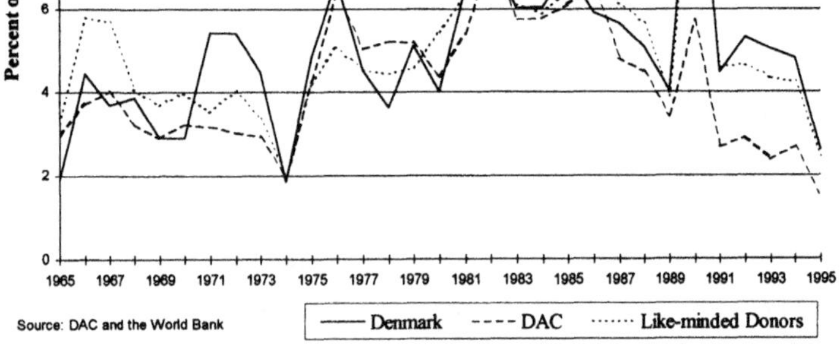

Figure 9.3 *(continued)*. Characteristics of aid receiving countries.

Figure 9.3.3. Degree of openness of average country

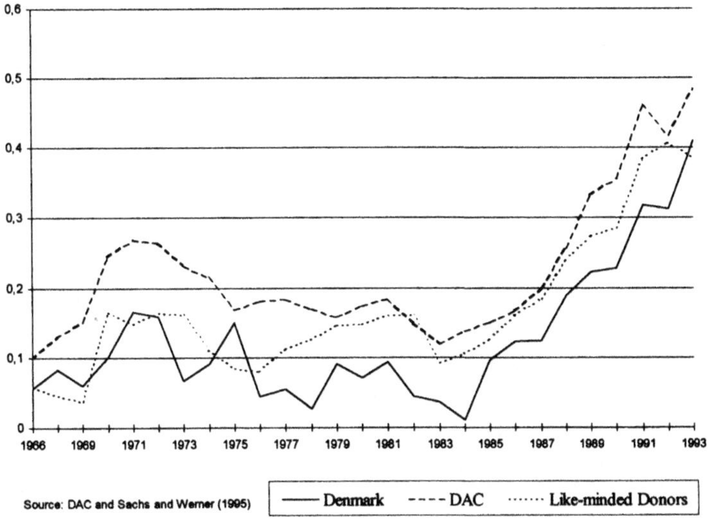

Figure 9.3.4. Value of policy index of average recipient country

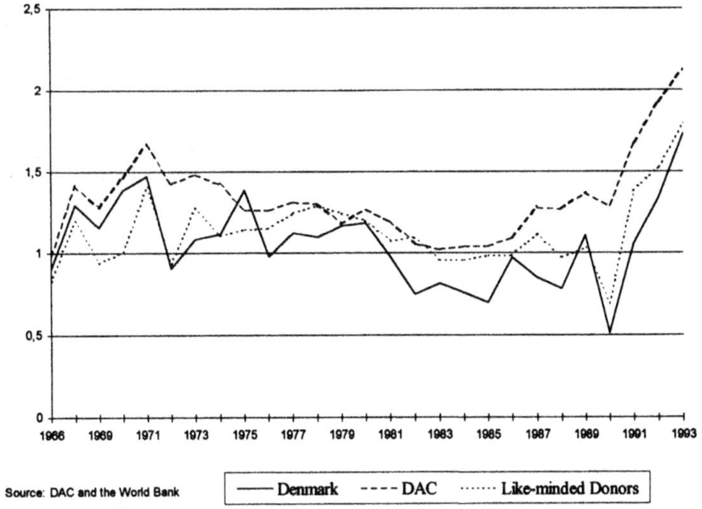

Notes: Figure 9.3.3. Openness is measured with the Sachs and Werner dummy variable where the value 1 indicates an outward-oriented trade policy. Figure 9.3.4. The policy index is calculated according to the Burnside and Dollar (1997) formula: Policy = 1.3 + 5.4 * Budget Surplus – 1.4 * Inflation + 2.1 * Openness.

value of the policy index of the average Danish aid recipient has over the years been on the low side, in particular during the 1980s. This is in all likelihood mainly due to the fact that poorer countries are relatively more dependent on taxes on international trade. The results of Burnside and Dollar are still subject to debate, but the above observations do highlight that it is sensible for Danida to monitor and analyse closely the quality of overall policy-making in the countries that receive Danish aid.

Turning to the level of aid as a share of GNP in the average recipient country (Figure 9.4.1) only minor differences can be identified until the mid-1980s among Denmark, the group of like-minded countries, and DAC. If anything, the typical recipient of DAC aid had a slightly higher aid inflow than what was the case for Danish aid recipients. However, this characterisation has since been modified significantly. In the late 1980s and the first half of the 1990s the typical aid receiving country had a much higher aid/GNP ratio than in previous decades. Moreover, already from 1986 Denmark started to focus its aid on countries with relatively high aid/GNP ratios (such as Tanzania and Mozambique) and even more so than DAC. The impact of aid in highly aid dependent countries is therefore a subject which is highly relevant for Danida to grapple with. When it comes to net private capital flows, there is, however, little indication that Danish aid recipients differ from the typical DAC case (Figure 9.4.2). Net private capital inflows, which were generally small as a share of GNP, but nevertheless positive from 1968 onwards, decreased in the early 1980s and even turned negative in the early 1990s. Since then a hesitant recovery has been recorded, but the inflow remains below 1 percent of GNP.

In sum, the level of total Danish aid has been and remains exceptionally high as a share of GNP when compared to that of other donors. Moreover, Danish aid has certainly tried to adhere to the first criteria in its programme country checklist, and the importance of human rights (fourth criteria) has been increasing. It is, however hard to find any special characteristics in the profile of a typical Danish aid recipient when it comes to the Burnside-Dollar index. Thus, the data presented do not support claims that Denmark has generally supported countries that pursue policies, which are less sound, than what can be said for aid receiving countries in general. To this end it must be stressed that the group of countries for which data for the policy index are available is much smaller than the group of countries that actually receives Danish aid.[3] Similarly, Danish aid recipients have not been much different from other aid receiving countries when it comes to aid and net private capital flows as a share of GNP, although an interesting increase in the aid/GNP share can be noted in recent years. This indicates that Denmark is focusing on countries that are relatively aid dependent, which is potentially in conflict with the second criteria on the checklist. As regards, the third (environment), fifth (gender), sixth (previous experience), and seventh (Danish business interests) criteria on the checklist, it is difficult to generalise on the basis of the data used in this study. Yet, further observations on Danish business interests are included in subsequent sections. A final distinguishing characteristic of Danish aid is that in 1995 some 41 percent of bilateral Danish aid went to African countries South of the Sahara as compared to only 26 percent for total DAC aid.

Figure 9.4. Aid and net capital inflows.

Figure 9.4.1. Total net aid received by average recipient country

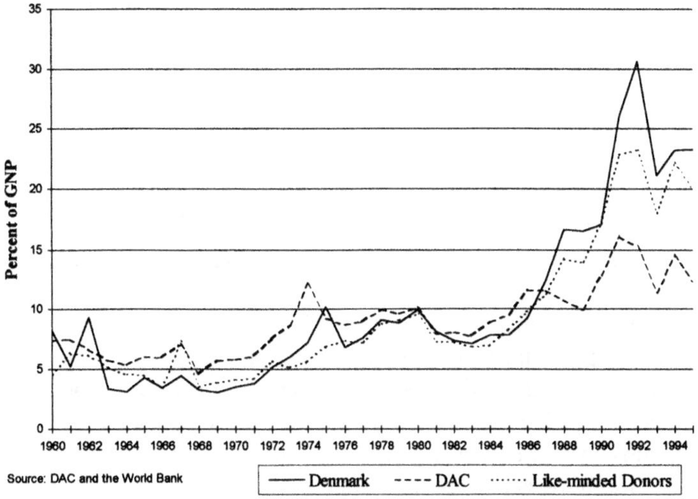

Figure 9.4.2. Net private capital inflows received by average recipient country

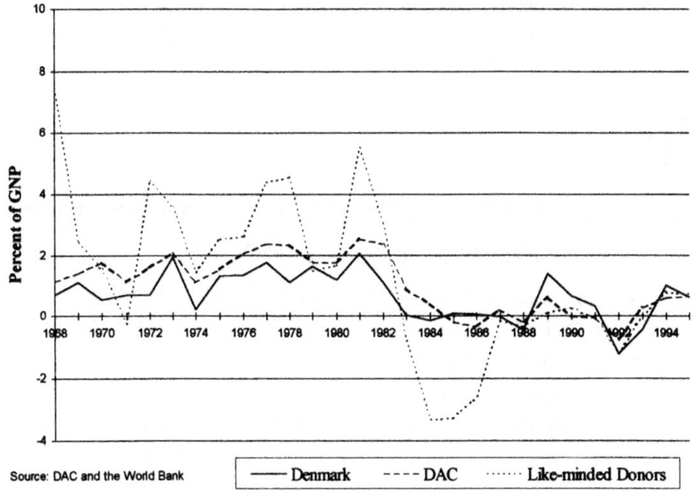

A TWO-STEP MODEL OF AID ALLOCATION

In order to assess to what extent officially stated criteria have guided actual Danish development assistance, a specific model of aid allocation is needed. The model put forward here is based on the approach to aid allocation formulated by Dudley and Montmarquette (1976). Accordingly, the aid-giving process is modelled as a two-step decision procedure involving (i) the choice of recipient (eligible) countries, and (ii) decisions on the actual levels of aid to be received by the selected countries. The model by Dudley and Montmarquette is extended through an explicit separation of the two steps. Moreover, second step decisions are conditional on the selections made in the first step. In a Danish context it can certainly be hypothesised that the underlying political process in country selection differs from the process leading to decisions about aid allocation in the second step. Parliament takes an active stance in the choice of aid recipients, whereas Danida has in all likelihood a stronger hand in actual aid allocations, which involve operational planning and a range of day-to-day decisions. In addition, the composition of interest groups, being active in the first step in influencing policy makers will differ from the composition in the second step. "Loosing groups" from the first step will drop out in the second step, and some interest groups will only be active in the second round. Moreover, it is unlikely that the lobbying influence of participating interest groups is the same in the two steps.

In the first step of the aid allocation process, decision-makers concentrate solely on whether a specific country is eligible as a recipient of aid or not. This decision is based on an eligibility index, summarising the various donor criteria. Such an index can be constructed in many ways. In the present model a geometric version is used, so the index value for country j in year t is given by

$$I_{jt} = \prod_{h=1}^{H} x_{jt,h}^{\alpha_h}. \tag{9.1}$$

Here, $x_{jt,h}$, $(h = 1,...,H)$ refers to different country specific indicators mirroring existing donor motives. The weight assigned to each indicator, α_k, has a dual role, reflecting both the relationship between the indicator and the motive and the relative importance of the motive. Hence, it is not possible to evaluate the importance of a motive from the size of the weight. It is, however, possible to evaluate the importance of the indicator in the decision process.[4]

Using the eligibility index, country selection decisions can be formulated with reference to a simple threshold value, which may be constant over time or change in a pre-specified way. Thus, the decision rule can be given as

$$S_{jt} = \begin{cases} 1 & \text{if} \quad I_{jt} \geq c \cdot B_t^{-\alpha_{H+1}} \\ 0 & \text{if} \quad I_{jt} < c \cdot B_t^{-\alpha_{H+1}}, \end{cases} \tag{9.2}$$

where $S_{jt} = 1$ specifies that country j should receive aid in year t, c is a constant, and B_t is the total aid budget in year t. If $\alpha_{H+1} > 0$ the threshold value depends on the total budget while it is constant if $\alpha_{H+1} > 0$. Accordingly, potential recipients are ranked by the eligibility index, and only those with a value greater than or equal to the threshold line are chosen as recipients.

When all indicators are strictly positive a log-transformation can be applied resulting in a log-linear decision rule

$$S_{jt} = \begin{cases} 1 & \text{if} \quad \sum_{h=0}^{H+1} \alpha_h z_{jt,h} \geq 0 \\ 0 & \text{if} \quad \sum_{h=0}^{H+1} \alpha_h z_{jt,h} < 0 \end{cases}, \tag{9.3}$$

where $\alpha_0 = -\log(c)$, $z_{jt,0} = 1$, $z_{jt,h} = \log(x_{jt,h})$ for $h=1,...,H$, and $z_{jt,H+1} = \log(B_t)$. This formulation of the first step decision will be used in the empirical analysis.

In the second step, decision-makers concentrate on the allocation of the total aid budget, taking country selection as given. Following Dudley and Montmarquette (1976) and Trumbull and Wall (1994), the objective function in the aid allocation step is given by a direct addilog function. Hence, the aid allocation problem may be formulated as:

$$\begin{aligned} &\max \sum_{j=1}^{s_t} W(a_{jt}) = \sum_{j=1}^{s_t} a_{jt}^{\delta} J_{jt} n_{jt}^{\theta}, \quad 0 < \delta < 1 \\ &\text{subject to} \quad B_t = \sum_{j=1}^{s_t} a_{jt} n_{jt}, \\ &\qquad\qquad\quad J_{jt} = \prod_{k=1}^{K} x_{jt,k}^{\gamma_k}, \end{aligned} \tag{9.4}$$

where s_t is the number of countries chosen as aid recipients, a_{jt} is per capita aid, and n_{jt} the population in country j in year t. The indicators for donor motives are again summarised in an index, J_{jt}, which is used to assign a donor value to the allocation. The weights in the index, γ_k, have the same characteristics as the weights in the eligibility index, but they need not coincide.

Assuming strictly positive indicators, the solution to the aid allocation problem leads to a log-linear model for the aid allocated to each selected country

$$\begin{aligned} &\log(a_{jt}) = \beta_0 + \sum_{k=1}^{K} \beta_k \log(x_{jt,k}) + \beta_{K+1} \log(n_{jt}) + \tau_t, \\ &\beta_0 = \frac{\log(\delta)}{1-\delta}, \quad \beta_k = \frac{\gamma_k}{1-\delta}, (k = 1,...,K), \quad \beta_{K+1} = \frac{\theta - 1}{1-\delta}, \quad \tau_t = \frac{\log(b_t)}{1-\delta}, \end{aligned} \tag{9.5}$$

where b_t is the value of a marginal increase in the total aid budget.

Equation (9.3) and (9.5) specify the decision rules, or guidelines, in the aid allocation model. In the empirical analysis in Section V, the same set of indicator variables will be relied on in the two steps, and it is investigated whether their impact is the same in the two steps.

QUANTIFYING THE MODEL

In Section II a checklist of officially stated criteria to be used in the selection of programme countries was identified. In the following it is taken for granted that these broad goals adequately capture the complex process of interaction among interest groups and policy makers. This is sensible since NGOs as well as business interests and political parties have all played an active role in formulating Danish aid objectives, and frequent reference is made to these criteria in public discussion. Nevertheless, individual actors may well have considered other more sophisticated variables and indicators in the process. Moreover, their priorities are likely to have been more narrowly focussed. Such dimensions are best studied in country specific analyses from which it may, however, be difficult to generalise. The present cross-country analysis aims instead at identifying the broad and generalised characteristics of Danish aid allocation decisions. Therefore, the analysis is based on relatively few, quantifiable explanatory variables, available for a majority of the aid recipient countries, and the main objective is to obtain results about the statistical significance of Danish aid motives and their positive or negative influence on aid allocations.

All the developing country characteristics listed below should, in principle, be included as explanatory variables in cross-country econometric modelling of Danish bilateral aid allocations along the lines set out in Section III:

1. Level of development and poverty.
2. Level of support from other donors.
3. Absorptive capacity (a euphemism for recipient country ability to use aid productively).
4. Environmental policy.
5. Democracy and human rights.
6. Gender imbalances.
7. Experiences from past collaboration.
8. Danish business and employment interests.

For practical as well as methodological reasons it has not been possible to establish quantified indicators for all of the above variables. In particular, data limitations imply that indicators for environmental policy, gender imbalances, and experiences from past collaboration, cannot be derived for an acceptable number of countries and years in the period under study here. Thus, they are not considered in what follows. As regards the remaining characteristics, the following mapping is used.

First, GNP per capita and life expectancy are chosen as indicators of the level of development and poverty in recipient countries. Secondly, total gross aid disbursements from other donors is used to measure the level of aid originating from non-Danish sources. This variable captures both the possibility that Denmark may choose to reduce aid to countries, which are heavily supported by other donors, and alternatively that Denmark may act in accordance with the donor "band wagon effect". Thirdly, absorptive capacity is measured through the level of private capital inflows. This indicator is certainly subject to debate since it is implicitly assumed that private investors are capable of assessing the capacity of recipient countries to use foreign capital wisely (including public resource transfers such as aid), and that they act accordingly. Thus, as an additional way of trying to capture the impact of the broad and difficult concept of absorptive capacity, growth of GNP per capita is included as an explanatory variable.[5] Fourthly, the "Freedom House" index of political and civil rights is used to represent democracy and human rights. Higher values of this index indicate fewer rights on a scale from 2 to 14. The final item in the list, Danish commercial and similar interests, is represented by Danish exports to a given recipient. In accordance with the second step of the theoretical model and existing aid allocation literature, the Danida criteria are supplemented with the total population of the recipient countries. Finally, a regional dummy for Eastern and Southern African countries is included to investigate if there has been a systematic bias favouring these countries compared to other potential aid recipients.

Decision-makers in donor countries face information lags. Therefore, the recipient country indicators are lagged. Here, averages of the indicator values lagged one and two years are used as explanatory variables. Moreover, in order to reduce heteroscedasticity problems, private capital flows, aid from other donors, and exports are all measured per capita and, in the second step, all variables are scaled by the average of the variable for all countries in the given year's sample.[6] The last transformation removes the time specific effect, τ_t, in equation (9.5).

It is not evident which category of aid should be used to represent the dependent variable. However, Danish bilateral development assistance *commitments* are chosen in preference of the various *disbursement* variables regularly used in the literature (see McGillivray and White, 1993). This is done as commitments are seen as a more accurate measure of donor supply.

EMPIRICAL ANALYSIS

The initial data set, also relied on in Section II, comprise 148 countries covered by the OECD/DAC data set on aid distribution for the period of 1960–95. Due to data limitations, however, this set had to be cut down to an unbalanced panel with 1,768 observations of 132 countries during the period of 1976–94. A list of data sources is included as Annex 9.1.

In the econometric analysis an error component structure with country specific effects is used in both steps in which the two error components in each step are assumed to be independent and normally distributed. The country specific effects are mainly included to capture unobserved country specific preferences or needs and, to some extent, experiences from past collaboration, but the country specific error term may also capture a temporal persistence in the aid allocation. As these conceptually different effects are difficult to distinguish empirically, no attempt will be made to interpret the country specific errors.

Another potential econometric problem is simultaneity between the total amount of aid available for distribution and that allocated to each country. This could be acute if either total aid or the distribution between bilateral and multilateral aid depend on an assessment of need or donor interest in recipient countries. In the current context, this problem is assumed to be minor, as the distribution between bilateral and multilateral aid has remained fairly constant.

Based on the assumption of normally distributed errors the parameters in equation (9.3) are estimated using a one-way random effects probit model:

$$\begin{aligned} &\Pr(S_{jt}=1)=\Pr\{\alpha' z_{jt}+\mu_j+v_{jt}>0\} \\ &\mu_j \sim IIN(0,\sigma_\mu^2), \quad \nu_{jt} \sim IIN(0,\sigma_\mu^2). \end{aligned} \tag{9.6}$$

In the second step, a_{jt} is only observed if $S_{jt}=1$ implying that step two of the aid allocation process is dependent on step one. To clarify the empirical method applied to address this dependency, a latent variable, a^*_{jt}, can be created by calculating second step values for all potential recipients using equation (9.5). With an error component structure including country-specific effects, η_j, as well as an idiosyncratic error term, ε_{jt}, it follows that

$$\begin{aligned} \log(a^*_{jt}) &= \beta_0+\sum_{k=1}^{K}\beta_k \log(x_{jt})+\beta_{K+1}\log(n_{jt})+\eta_j+\varepsilon_{jt} \\ &\quad \eta_j \sim IIN(0,\sigma_\eta^2), \quad \varepsilon_{jt} \sim IIN(0,\sigma_\varepsilon^2). \end{aligned} \tag{9.7}$$

From this, the observed amount of aid allocated to country j in period t is established by

$$\begin{aligned} a_{jt} &= a^*_{jt} \quad \text{if} \quad S_{jt}=1 \\ a_{jt} &= 0 \quad \text{if} \quad S_{jt}=0 \end{aligned} \tag{9.8}$$

The second step in the theoretical model describes the amount of aid given to a specific country, conditional on the information that the country has been chosen as eligible for aid. Thus, the model actually establishes $E(a_{jt} \mid D_{jt}=1)=E(a^*_{jt} \mid D_{jt}=1)$. If error terms from the two steps are correlated, Ordinary Least Squares estimation of the parameters in the unconditional model will result in selection bias. The conditional model resembles what Greene (1987) denotes “An incidentally truncated model”. When the two error terms, ε_{jt}, ν_{jt}, are normally distributed with correlation parameter ρ, the conditional model is given by

$$\log(a_{jt|D_{jt}=1}) = \beta_0 + \sum_{k=1}^{K} \beta_k \log(x_{jt}) + \beta_{K+1} \log(n_{jt}) + \beta_\lambda \lambda_{jt} + \eta_j + \varepsilon_{jt},$$
$$\lambda_{jt} = \frac{\phi(\sigma_v^{-1} \alpha' z_{jt})}{\Phi(\sigma_v^{-1} \alpha' z_{jt})}, \quad \beta_\lambda = \sigma_\varepsilon \rho. \tag{9.9}$$

The model is estimated using the Heckman two-step procedure, where λ_{jt} is calculated for each observation on the basis of the first step probit estimation and included in the second step regression as an explanatory variable.[7]

A key result of this study is, as shown in Table 9.1, that explanatory variables, which are statistically significant in the first step, have a statistically significant impact in the second step. In addition, parameter signs are identical in the two steps. Hence, there is consistency between the criteria governing country selection and the amounts committed. The only exception is the life expectancy variable, which is significant with the expected negative sign in the first step while insignificant in the second step. Once a country has been selected it is therefore not likely to receive more aid as a consequence of low life expectancy.

Turning to variables, which are significant in both steps, it can first of all be noted that GNP per capita has the expected negative impact on aid allocations. In line with the descriptive analysis in Section II, it is therefore clear that Danish aid policy has indeed been poverty oriented. Poorer countries have had a bigger chance of being selected, and once selected they have received more aid. Similarly, aid from other donors has been a significant variable in Danish aid with a positive sign in both steps. Hence, there is indication that the "band wagon" effect has been at work in Danish aid allocations. As such Danish aid policy has tended to augment the amount of aid going to recipients that already receive aid from elsewhere. In addition, Danish aid decisions have been affected by economic performance as measured by the growth variable. High growth in the past has tended to increase the probability of being selected and amounts of aid allocated have also gone up as a result of higher growth. As pointed out in Section II, sound macro-economic policy — along "Washington consensus" lines of thinking — has not been used as an explicit criterion for giving aid in the past. However, if sound macro-economic policy is a precondition for growth — as recently argued — Denmark has in practice been more inclined to support countries with sound policies.

The civil and political rights variable has a statistically significant negative impact in both steps. This indicates that good human rights policies have been important as a screening criterion in the selection of countries as well as in decisions about the amount of aid to allocate. Thus, Danish reactions to changes in human rights have taken various forms. Former aid recipients have been excluded due to worsening human rights and vice-versa for countries, which were previously excluded. In addition, aid committed to countries actually chosen in the first step has been affected by their human rights performance. Thus, it would appear that the principles of constructive dialogue, has been adhered to by Denmark, at least up to a point. This implies that a donor remains in an aid receiving country in spite of some human rights violations

Table 9.1. Two-Step Regressions.

	Probit Estimation			Linear Regression		
	Estimate	*z*-value	*p*-value	Estimate	*z*-value	*p*-valu
GNP per capita	–0.11	–3.65	0.00	–0.81	–5.59	0.00
Life expectancy	–0.37	–2.77	0.01	–0.18	–0.27	0.79
GNP per capita growth	0.18	2.28	0.02	1.24	1.94	0.05
Civil and political rights	–0.15	–3.27	0.00	–0.59	–2.66	0.01
Exports	0.05	3.43	0.00	0.37	5.46	0.00
Total population	10.97	0.52	0.60	0.10	0.58	0.56
ODA from other donors	0.10	7.41	0.00	0.55	4.56	0.00
Private net capital flows	10.80	0.51	0.61	0.19	1.24	0.21
Eastern and southern Africa	0.33	5.42	0.00	1.80	4.91	0.00
Heckman's λ				1.60	21.56	0.00
Total ODA budget	0.09	4.02	0.00			
Obs.		1768			598	
Countries		132			70	
R^2		—			0.52	

Table 9.2. Actual and Predicted Outcomes in Probit Model.

	Predicted		
Actual	0	1	Total
0	1070	120	1190
1	310	268	578
Total	1380	388	1768

and tries to have an impact through the amount of aid allocated. Also the export variable is statistically significant in both steps and it has the expected positive sign. It follows that if Danish exports to a given country increase, then the chance of it being selected improves subsequently. Similarly, the amount of aid received will tend to increase. As such Danish commercial interests appear to have played a role in Danish aid allocations, and it is highlighted that with the chosen lag structure, this analytical result does not reflect the presence and effects of aid tying. Moreover, Table 9.1 demonstrates that when the total aid budget increases, the probability that countries are selected is larger (ceteris paribus), and there has been a consistent regional bias which has favoured countries in Eastern and Southern Africa at the expense of countries belonging to other regions.

The population and private capital flow variables are insignificant in both steps. This means that smaller countries do not receive more aid per capita than larger countries or vice-versa. Thus, the "small-country bias" does not seem to be present in Danish aid allocation. Both Dudley and Montmarquette (1976), and Trumbull and Wall (1994) reached similar conclusions for DAC members, but it is in contrast to widely held beliefs in the literature. The most likely explanation for the result is that the inclusion of other explanatory variables removes the perceived tendency to allocate more aid per capita to small countries. Moreover, as the population size of a country does not affect the probability of being selected as an aid receiving country a large population does not per se increase the value of the eligibility index relied upon in the selection process. Since private capital inflows are insignificant in both steps there is no indication for private capital inflows to have played a major role in the aid allocation process. This is not in accordance with stated Danish aid policy if this indicator is accepted as a valid measure of absorptive capacity. However, it could be argued that Danish aid has intentionally been directed to countries which have had limited access to international private capital. If this is a correct interpretation the result appears more in accordance with the general aims of Danish aid policy.

CONCLUSIONS

It is concluded that this study has captured critical aspects of the Danish aid process. Many of the parameters in focus here are statistically significant with the expected sign, and there has been a high degree of consistency among decisions in steps one and two of the Danish aid allocation process. From the empirical analysis it also follows that officially stated aims and criteria have guided Danish aid. Developing country needs and socio-economic characteristics have certainly influenced Danish bilateral aid allocations alongside commercial interests and — increasingly — political pre-occupations with human rights. The officially declared focus on allocating aid to the poorest among the developing countries is a particularly striking and consistent feature of Danish bilateral aid in international comparative perspective. It is however also noteworthy that there has been a consistent Eastern and Southern African bias in Danish aid allocation decisions.

Another characteristic of Danish aid allocations is that the "small country bias", according to which smaller countries tend to receive more aid per capita than larger countries, is not present in the data. In contrast, there is evidence of the "band wagon effect", which indicates that Denmark tends to supply more aid to countries that are increasingly favoured by other donors. Finally a very high share of total Danish aid is channelled to recipient countries through the multilateral system of agencies, which assumedly pay a relatively high degree of attention to recipient needs rather than donor interests. In spite of the above conclusions about the motives driving Danish aid, it is highlighted that no simple implications can be derived on the basis of this study about the effectiveness of Danish aid.

ANNEX 1. DATA SOURCES

The following variables were all taken from the World Bank WDI-database:

- **GNP per capita.** A country's GNP divided by its population, calculated by the World Bank in US$ according to the Atlas method.
- **GNP per capita growth.** Yearly growth in a country's GNP per capita.
- **Life expectancy.** Average life expectancy of adults in a given country.

The following variables were all taken from the DAC CD-ROM version of "Geographical Distribution of Financial Flows to Aid Recipients":

- **Population.** Total Population in a given country.
- **Danish ODA commitments.** Total Overseas Development Assistance committed by Denmark to a specific country.
- **ODA from other donors.** Total Overseas Development Assistance disbursements from DAC Donors excluding Denmark.

These two variables were kindly provided by the organisation "Freedom House":

- **Civil rights.** This index is the Freedom House/Gastil measure of the civil rights of a country's citizens.
- **Political rights.** This is the Freedom House/Gastil measure of political freedom in a given country.

Finally, "Danmarks Statistik" provided the following variable:

- **Exports.** Danish exports of goods (f.o.b.) to a certain country.

REFERENCES

Andersen, P. Nyboe. "Dansk Bistandstænkning og -Praksis i 25 År." *Danida Annual Report 1986.* 1986.

Baltagi, B. *Econometric Analysis of Panel Data.* New York: John Wiley & Sons. 1995.

Burnside, C. and Dollar, D. "Aid, Policies, and Growth." *World Bank Working Paper no. 1777,* Washington, 1997.

Brandt, W. et al. "North - South: A Programme for Survival." *Report of the Independent Commission on International Development Issues.* Cambridge: MIT Press, 1980.

Brundtland, G. H. et al. "Our Common Future. World Commission on Environment and Development." Oxford: Oxford University Press, 1987.

Cornia, G. A., Jolly, R., and Stewart, F. "Adjustment With a Human Face." Oxford: Clarendon Press, 1987.

Danida. "En Verden i Udvikling. Strategi for Dansk Udviklingspolitik Frem Mod år 2000." *Ministry of Foreign Affairs, Danida.* 1994.

Danida. "Evaluation Report. Poverty Reduction in Danish Development Assistance." *Ministry of Foreign Affairs, Danida.* 1996.

Danida. "Danidas Årsberetning." *Ministry of Foreign Affairs, Danida.* 1997.

Dudley, L. and Montmarquette, C.M. "A Model of the Supply of Bilateral Foreign Aid." *American Economic Review*, Vol. 66, No. 1, pp. 132–142. 1976.

Dudley, L. and Montmarquette, C.M. "The supply of Canadian Foreign Aid: An Explanation and Evaluation." *Economic Council of Canada.* Quebec 1978.

Estrup, J. "Politiske Betingelser i Dansk Bistandspolitik." *Økonomi og Politik*, No. 2. 1995.

Greene, W. H. *Economic Analysis,* 3rd edition. New Jersey: Prentice Hall, 1997.

McGillivray, M. and White, H. "Explanatory Studies of Aid Allocation among Developing Countries: A Critical Survey." *Working Paper Series No. 148.* Mimeo, April 1993.

Tarp, F. "Stabilization and Structural Adjustment." London: Routledge, 1993.

Trumbull, W. and Wall, H. "Estimating Aid-Allocation Criteria with Panel Data." *Economic Journal*, Vol. 104, July, pp. 876–882. 1994.

NOTES

[1] The authors are grateful to World Bank staff and the Freedom House for some crucial data. Helpful comments from Rasmus Heltberg, Peter Hjertholm and Steen Asmussen are gratefully acknowledged. The same goes for participants at the Meeting of the Danish Economic Society at Hindsgavl on 9–10 January 1998. The usual caveats apply.

[2] A more elaborate version of this chapter is available as Discussion Paper 98-06, Institute of Economics, University of Copenhagen.

[3] The share of total bilateral aid going to the group of countries for which data are available to construct the Burnside-Dollar policy index was in some periods only 35–40 percent in contrast to the much better coverage for other indicators used in this chapter. This implies that conclusions emerging from Figure 9.3 must be interpreted with due care. The problem of data availability is particularly pronounced with regard to public sector budgets and the Sachs-Werner dummy for openness of the economy.

[4] As discussed in Section II the relative importance of the official criteria may have changed over time. This should be reflected in changes in the weights. The weights are treated as constant parameters here.

[5] Absorptive capacity is particularly hard to capture in empirical analyses as it reflects the composite impact of the complex environment in which aid is disbursed. Thus, the quality of economic policy making as well as other economic and institutional fundamentals all impact on absorptive capacity.

[6] These transformations of the data are also used in Trumbull and Wall (1994).

[7] From Table 9.1 it can be seen that Heckman's λ is significant. This indicates that there is correlation between steps one and two as one would expect from the outset.

IV

Case Studies:
The Recipient Experience

CHAPTER 10

CAN AID GENERATE GROWTH IN AFRICA?

Arne Bigsten

THE PROBLEM

The objective of aid is to improve the standard of living of poor people. Long term, and sustainable welfare improvements require economic growth. The link between aid and growth is complex, so it has been difficult to measure the growth impact of aid. The problem is to measure the impact, while controlling for other factors that influence growth. However, there are some recent econometric analyses that deal quite effectively with the issue.

This chapter aims to do three things. First, there is a brief discussion about growth determinants in Africa. Second, against this background we review various types of evidence about the impact of aid on growth. Third, based on the evidence we discuss the implications for aid to Africa from different perspectives. Should aid continue, and, if so, what kind of aid and what type of aid relationship may be effective. The chapter ends with some concluding remarks.

WHAT DETERMINES GROWTH?

The rate of growth of any economy is determined by the accumulation of physical and human capital, the efficiency of resource allocation, and the ability to acquire and apply modern technology. What is required for faster growth is change in the economic environment that facilitate both the accumulation of production factors and their efficient allocation, and the introduction of better technologies. There is by now extensive evidence that this requires economic policies at the micro level to develop and sustain efficient markets, while macro policy must be geared to guarantee macroeconomic stability. An efficient economy also requires a supporting environment of efficient institutions.

Investment is a necessary, but not sufficient, condition for growth. A major aim of recent African adjustment programmes has been to increase private sector investment, but uncertainty and lack of credibility as well as low returns have held it back. Still, the macroeconomic environment has been improved in a number of countries, and this will, if the improvements can be sustained, help revive investment.

There have been large distortions in the incentive structures in many African economies, and that consequently resources have been poorly allocated. The reform programmes have reduced distortions, but, so far, the growth impact has been limited. Adam and O'Connell (1997) note that there exist distortions which affect the composition of investment. Typically policy favours public over private investment, foreign over domestic, and import-substituting industry over export agriculture. There is also a differential treatment of investment in non-taxed informal and taxed formal activities. These distortions have been reduced somewhat, but they still distort resource allocation and reduce growth.

A central question is why growth supporting institutions develop. A government which is primarily concerned with its own survival does not necessarily set up ownership rules that are good for economic growth. With special interest politics at centre stage, there is bound to be static inefficiency due to distortions, investors are going to be cautious, and resources are going to be wasted in rent-seeking activities.

In African economies there is a very pervasive influence of politics on economics. Many discretionary policy interventions have paved the way for corruption and rent-seeking (Bigsten, 1993), and elites have also used the system to allocate rents as a means of securing their power positions (Bigsten and Moene, 1996). Adam and O'Connell (1997, p. 17) conclude from their analysis of the relationship between taxation and investment that "the distortionary effects of tax and uncertainly emanate in the main from the structure of political regimes in African economies, and that these structures may act as an impediment to rapid evolution of institutions which otherwise might mitigate the effects of politically motivated uncertainty on investment and growth."

A notion that appears many times in the analysis of the Asian miracle is "shared growth", that is, the mass of the population must see the benefits if they are going to participate actively. It is not only the general citizen who must be included, but also the ruling elite must tolerate competing elites. The fear of opposition and desire for total control has stifled many initiatives in African countries. For shared growth to come about, there is need for a bureaucracy of high quality, which is sufficiently insulated from vested interests. Such an institutional set-up is not easily created, but the opening up of the political arena should support such a change.

Growth is thus determined by investment in physical and human capital, technical progress, and the effectiveness of resource allocation. Changes in these factors do in turn depend on the character of the policy environment, institutions and governance. We will discuss the impact of aid on these variables, and we will also consider how the character of the aid relationship affects the growth impact of aid.

TWO DECADES OF STAGNATION

During the 1980s and first half of the 1990s per capita incomes in sub-Saharan Africa fell by 1.3% per year. Africa stands out as the worst performing region in the world. African economies have invested a smaller share of GDP than comparable regions, and a smaller share of investments has gone to the private sector. One third of the growth gap vis a vis other LDCs may be explained by lower investment rates, but the remaining two thirds were due to slower productivity growth (Collier and Gunning, 1997). Investment in Africa seems to be less efficient that investment in comparable regions. It is estimated that incremental capital output ratios are one quarter of those in East Asia and between half and two thirds of those in other LDCs (Adam and O'Connell, 1997).

So what are the characteristics that set Africa apart? First, private agents in Africa face atypically high risks and poorly functioning governments. Taxes and tax like distortions are high and volatile. The natural environment in Africa is very risky, and there are also risks associated with the difficulty in enforcing contracts. Institutions that reduce the costs of contract enforcement and other transaction costs have not yet evolved. Few of the risks are insurable because of asymmetric information. Firms are less diversified, which means that they are highly exposed to shocks. In some cases they may be physically unable to honour contracts. These difficulties have created a behaviour that in some instances is detrimental to growth. In a high risk environment without formal insurance and credit markets, agents try to protect themselves for example via diversification, accumulation of assets for consumption smoothing, and by building informal insurance arrangements. High risk, poor public services and lack of social capital combine to constrain growth.

A major factor behind the lack of investment response to economic reforms undertaken in Africa during the 1980s and 1990s is the high risks associated with investment in Africa. The risk rating of the Institutional Investor for Africa has actually deteriorated over time from 31.8 in 1979 to 21.7 in 1995 (on a scale from 0 to 100). Increasing uncertainty tends to make investors avoid irreversible investments (at least for a while) and try to achieve ex ante consumption smoothing. Particularly in African agriculture self-insurance mechanisms are prevalent, and these tend to lower growth. Investors choose to go for liquid and safe investments, with negative consequences for growth. One issue of interest in this context may then be to what extent aid can help reduce risks and to increase stability. Here, however, it has been noted that the high aid inflows may have reduced the ability of genuine reforming governments to signal their intentions of sustained reform (Rodrik, 1989), which has meant that investor confidence has not been built up.

There is also a time consistency problem. Ex post it may be beneficial for governments to change their decisions about, for example, tax rates. To the extent that firms realize that this may happen, they may try to protect themselves by shifting away from savings to consumption or to less taxable forms of capital. This lowers investments and the growth rate. Political structures that stimulate predatory behavior aggravate the time consistency problem.

Other reasons for low investment during the reform period may be that the countries started from a disequilibrium capital stock, or that it takes a long time to build up confidence after civil war. If aid can help guarantee stability, it may make the countries more attractive to foreign or domestic investors.

CROSS-COUNTRY EVIDENCE ON THE IMPACT OF AID ON GROWTH

As a share of GDP Sub-Saharan Africa receives nearly five times more aid than any other region. The share of aid to GDP was on average 16% in 1994. It was as high as 101% in Mozambique and 30% in Tanzania. One reason for the high gross flows is, of course, the high debt burden that was accumulated by many countries from the mid-70s onwards. A lot of this has had to be written off or converted to soft loans, and this has required large gross flows of resources, a large part of which then has flown back to the international financial institutions, the World Bank and the IMF. For example, while Zambia in the early 1990s received an annual gross inflow of close to $1,500 million, the net ODA was only about $300 million (Bonnick, 1997, p. 115). The share of debt service to exports was 174% in Zambia in 1995. The increasing aid dependence is contrary to the long-term aim of donors, which is to increase self-reliance and to get to a point where countries can grow from their own resources. Aid dependence has a range of effects that might be detrimental to long term development efforts.

Africa would be in a position to reduce its aid dependence if it had better access to the international private capital markets, but in spite of dramatic increases in flows to the LDCs generally, Africa has been passed by. Investors view Africa as a capital hostile continent, and even Africans themselves hold vast sums of money outside the continent (Claessens and Naude, 1993). Aid to some extent may compensate for this, but the aid flows are not a perfect substitutes for private investment resources, which normally come on other conditions and together with technological skills and other forms of knowhow.

What kinds of effects of aid on growth are possible to discern? One possible approach is to distinguish between direct and the indirect effects of aid. The direct effects alter production, incomes or consumption as a direct consequence of some project or intervention, while the indirect effects are less easily identified. Aid to public sector projects, for example, releases resources which can be used for cuts in taxation and borrowing, or increases in expenditures. The private sector is indirectly affected, for example, via changes in relative prices. Aid may also affect the policy environment. Both via direct and indirect channels aid may have an effect on investment. Since the long term aim of aid is that the recipient country should grow from its own resources, the impact of aid on domestic resource mobilization is also essential. Domestic savings and tax efforts are two important variables to consider. Another concern is the development of exports, which in the longer term is a necessary prerequisite for self-sustained growth. Via Dutch Disease effect aid may make exports less competitive and aggravate the inward orientation. However, during the recent period of economic reforms the appreciation effect of aid has been counteracted by the effects of the liberalization of the foreign exchange market (see e.g. White, 1998).

Many authors have tried to use simple regressions to establish a link between aid and growth on some cross-section of countries, but the result has generally been that there is no significant correlation between the amount of aid and growth (Mosley, 1987, Riddell, 1987, White, 1992, 1998). At the same time, project evaluations show that the majority of projects are successful. This conflicting evidence has been referred to as the macro-micro paradox. One explanation of the paradox could be that the direct effects of aid are positive, while it tends to have negative indirect effects.

Neither Mosley, Hudson, and Horrel (1987), nor Boone (1994, 1996) were able to find any significant growth effect of aid in cross-country regressions. The most ambitious attempt at measuring net effects on growth is due to Burnside and Dollar (1997), who use a more sophisticated approach than previous analysts and model explicitly the interactions among aid, policy, and growth. The main question that they address is whether the effects of aid on growth depend on the policy environment. They also consider whether donors allocate aid in favour of countries with good policies and whether aid has affected policies.

Burnside and Dollar use two stage least squares to estimate simultaneously equations for growth, aid, and policy. By making identifying assumptions about the exogenous determinants of aid, policy and growth, they can determine the separate effects of aid and policy on growth. They are also able to test whether aid influences policy or vice versa.

The explanatory variables also include an index of institutional quality that captures the role of property rights and the efficiency of the government bureaucracy. They further introduce a variable for ethnic fractionalization, which has turned out to be significant in other regressions, the frequency of assassinations to measure civil unrest, and a variable for inefficiency of the financial system. The policy variables are trade openness (a dummy due to Sachs and Warner, 1995), inflation, the share of the budget surplus in GDP and the share of government consumption in GDP. Education was not significant when tried.

They obtain robust results with regard to the impact of institutional quality, inflation and trade openness. Government consumption had a weakly negative effect. When aid was entered directly it had no significant effect. When it was interacted with the policy index, however, it was significant. The authors allow for the fact that aid is skewed towards poorly growing countries by instrumenting aid with population and donor interest variables.[1]

The study does show that aid has positive effects on growth in the good policy environment, while it does not work in distorted environments. When one controls for aid allocation more aid goes to countries with good policies. This is particularly true for multilateral aid, while bilateral aid is more steered according to donor interest variables. Government consumption increases with bilateral aid, but it is not possible to show that aid that increases government spending has a positive growth effect.

There does not seem to be any systematic impact from aid to policy. For example, in Ghana good policies were rewarded, while in the case of Zambia aid increased between 1970 and 1993, while policies deteriorated throughout. It appears, however, to be the case that donors do reward good policy.

Burnside and Dollar thus found that aid significantly increased growth in good policy environments (measured by a composite measure of macroeconomic policies), had no effect in average environments and was actually damaging in bad policy environments. The evidence on the impact of aid on investment is mixed, but there is no clear evidence that aid contributes significantly to higher private investment.

There are, of course, limits as to what you can establish on the basis of cross-country regressions using highly aggregate data. It may well be that such regressions fail to pick up some of the positive effects suggested to exist by micro evaluations. Still, it is hard to argue that aid has, so far, been very effective in stimulating growth in Africa. The evidence suggesting that this poor result to a high degree is due to the type of economic policy and the institutional environment seems convincing. We will discuss the implications of this insight for aid below.

THE CASE OF TANZANIA[2]

Tanzania is one of the major recipients of aid in Sub-Saharan Africa. It is also a country that has had a high profile internationally and which has pursued a high interventionist development strategy. The result of this has been disappointing, however. Official GDP estimates suggest that real incomes per capita in Tanzania are not much higher now then they were in 1970. The pattern is one of stagnation over the 1970s, dramatic reduction in incomes during the crisis period of 1979–85, and slow but definite growth during the reform period starting in 1986.

What can one say about the effect of aid on growth determinants in Tanzania? If we first consider physical capital formation, it is obvious that aid in the 1970s contributed to a high investment rate, but because of the inward-looking, state-directed strategy, the quality of investments became low. Investments declined only moderately in the crisis period, although capacity utilization fell dramatically. Finally, there has been a dramatic increase in capital formation since the reforms started in the mid-1980s. The quality of investments is higher than in the previous period, but still generally low. This may be due to the fact that there still have been only relatively small changes in ownership and the orientation of investment, that is, parastatals still play a large role.

Early attempts of donors to support industry directly did not fare well, and there has been a shift from direct support to indirect support of productive activities. A substantial share of aid has therefore in recent years gone to investments in, and rehabilitation of, economic infrastructure. These investments show good returns, and they also help to create an enabling environment for economic activities. It seems obvious that aid has made it possible for Tanzania to achieve higher investment rates than what would otherwise have been possible.

The major areas of human capital formation that are relevant are health and education. Although the results of projects in these areas have been mixed, the projects undertaken contributed to the early improvements in the supply of skills in Tanzania. Unfortunately, it has been difficult to sustain the advances and many of the achievements of the 1970s have since been eroded. The budget support provided in recent years has at least helped to contain the decline of the public educational system, but it is certainly in a very poor state.

Apart from transferring external resources into the country, aid also has an effect on policy formation. This indirect effect may at times be more important than the direct resource transfer effect. It could be both positive and negative. Aid in the 1970s and in the first half of 1980s indirectly supported a strategy that later turned out to be unviable. Donors gradually became more and more critical in the early 1980s, particularly with regard to the appreciated exchange rate. For example, Sweden was reluctant to join in the critique and, together with other sympathetic donors, Sweden probably helped make it possible for the traditionalists in the Tanzanian government to delay economic adjustment. In this period it is therefore probably fair to say that, although the direct effects of aid were positive, these were counteracted by the negative indirect effect of preserving a policy regime detrimental to growth. The latter effect is impossible to quantify. Still, the costs of delayed reforms may have been substantial. However, since about 1986 aid has increased in support of market reforms, and for this period the impact of aid on the policy environment has instead been decidedly positive. The donors in this period have been essentially in agreement about the requirements for aid to Tanzania.

Much of the aid in recent years has been geared to support the economic reform programme. Poor governance is obviously a severe problem in Tanzania today, and the poor quality of the public administration must certainly have retarded economic growth. Efforts to support public sector management probably have been beneficial, but such effects are hard to measure.

The ability of the country to sustain long-term economic growth and to reduce its current, very high aid dependency will depend on the levels of domestic savings, tax revenues and export performance. The domestic savings rate appears to have gone down during the recent aid boom, but the data is very shaky. Still, this is the effect one would expect to see. It should be noted, however, that at the same time there has been an investment boom, so there has not been any dramatic increase in the consumption share.

Finally, we have the issue of export performance. There is considerable evidence showing that export success is closely related to economic growth, and if aid has effects that are detrimental to exports, this is a serious problem. The focus of the discussion has been the so called Dutch disease effect, which is that aid inflow leads to an appreciation of the real exchange rate. During the Nyerere years the whole policy package was highly biased against exports, but this package was basically not aid driven. Still, by making it possible to finance imports, aid did support an overvalued exchange rate, and it probably also helped extend the period of inward orientation. In the first years of the reform period, aid increased dramatically, while at the same time the real exchange rate depreciated a lot. Then aid supported pro-export reforms. Now the exchange rate is market determined, which means that aid inflows will tend to have an appreciating effect on the exchange rate.

Looking at the growth record of Tanzania, it is hard to argue that aid has had a positive effect on economic growth over the period as a whole. The country for a long time followed a development strategy that turned out to be unviable, and the economy has also been exposed to a series of external shocks. It is not possible to disentangle the overall growth effect of aid in this context. We have looked at the relationship between aid and the factors that are important for economic growth. We have pointed out that the direct effects of resource transfers in most cases are positive, although the effects have often been smaller than expected. We have then argued that the indirect effects on policy are very important. Here, it is possible that the aid of Sweden and other like-minded donors made it possible to delay adjustments in the first part of the 1980s, and thereby exerted a negative influence on growth. Since the mid-1980s, however, this situation has been reversed, and aid has supported sensible policy changes. It is reasonable to assume that the growth effect of aid in this new environment has been positive.

OWNERSHIP AND SUSTAINABILITY

A major concern of recent analysts of aid and development has been the high degree of external control of reform programmes, and the limited domestic commitment. Zambia is a case in point. During the 1980s the lending of the World Bank and also other donors focussed on balance of payments support for structural adjustment. The government for each new programme agreed to undertake reforms, but in the end it did not. The country was unable to diversify exports and to increase growth.

The Chiluba government that took power in 1991 has brought inflation under control and restored the discipline in debt management. Privatization, diversification of production, rehabilitation of economic infrastructure and improvements of social services has been harder to bring about, and poverty has increased. By August 1992 debt had fallen by $1.5 billion to $6.5 billion due to Paris Club rescheduling and debt cancellations by bilateral creditors. Larger IDA commitments have reduced the debt service burden. Commercial and short-term debt has been reduced through debt-buy back operations that reduced the exposure to London-club debtors. Also Paris Club creditors have provided significant debt relief. Zambia's credit worthiness has improved and arrears have been reduced.

The World Bank's own evaluation of its assistance to Zambia concludes that too much emphasis has been put on short term stabilization and too little on long-term growth, and that there has been insufficient and unrealistic analysis of the political situation as well as overoptimism.[3] When evaluating different projects undertaken in Zambia the Bank concludes that portfolio performance compares unfavourably with the region and bank lending overall. Many projects had poor sustainability ratings. Particularly projects in agriculture have had very unsatisfactory results.

The evaluation of bank lending concludes that successful projects have tended to a) be small and not management intensive; b) have appropriate technology; and c) use foreign contractors/consultants and involve some training of nationals. The unsuccessful projects, mainly in agriculture, a) depended on weak administration and management; b) required counterpart funds; c) suffered from imperfect delegation of authority; and d) presented coordination problems among agencies with unclear responsibilities (Bonnick, 1997, p. 8).

These results are rather typical of the problems that have faced donors in Africa. When projects are in a limbo between donors and recipients and no one is fully responsible, they tend to perform poorly. One way to go is then for the donor to take full control. Then they can make the projects work for the period that they are in charge, but the sustainability of the projects in the longer term is highly uncertain. The alternative approach is to put responsibility more squarely with the recipient, which should enhance project sustainability. The Bank and other donors have in recent years attempted to increase Zambian ownership of the development programmes, by giving the Zambian authorities a greater responsibility for coordination and implementation. The pattern is the same throughout Africa, but the results are as yet uncertain.

An interesting analysis of sustainability has been undertaken by Paldam (1997), who has revisited Danish bilateral projects in nine countries five years after their completion. He has constructed a scale according to which has ranked the degree of project success. He tries to figure out whether it was worthwhile to undertake the project or not, but notes that it is hard to evaluate the projects against the multiple, unweighted, vague and qualitative goals of Danish aid. The main result is that the average project is barely worth undertaking. The likelihood of failure increases very strongly if the project either is done in Africa, is in agriculture, or is done within a parastatal arrangement. Social sector projects do better. There is also some weak evidence that NGO projects do better and that small projects are more often successful than large ones. The environment of the projects is also believed to be important, but the limited sample size make it impossible to show this conclusively.

Paldam reaches the depressing conclusion that "the average project in Africa fails" (p. 10). He notes two obvious aspects of the Africa-problem. There is a maintenance problem. It is very hard to organize maintenance activities in Africa in an effective way, which means that projects deteriorate much faster in Africa than elsewhere. This is of course revealed in an evaluation that takes place five year after the completion of the project. Second, there is again a project-ownership problem due to the long periods of high degree of aid-dependence.

Since the analysis essentially covers projects that were completed in the late 1980s, it is somewhat uncertain whether the results from that period are a good guides as to what donors could achieve today. First, there has been a process of learning by doing, that is donors have learnt from past mistakes. Second, there have been extensive macroeconomic reforms in Africa creating a much less distorted and more liberal economic environment. This would make it easier to undertake projects as we have noted above.

AID AND GOVERNANCE

The recent debate on Africa's poor growth performance has tended to shift the focus away from the failure of policy as such to a discussion of the failure of the African state. This has meant that the aid relationship has changed from a non-paternalistic one to one with extensive conditionalities and strict economic and political monitoring. While donors still are concerned with projects and macro policy, the development of political and market institutions are now much more in focus. Early critics of foreign aid, like Bauer and Friedman, argued that the development problem was not one of capital shortage, since that would have been solved by private capital markets, but one of shortcoming in political and economic institutions. Shortages of physical and human capital were just symptoms of these systemic shortcomings. They also argued that with poor institutions aid would be wasted or even inimical to growth by strengthening the position of the government against rival domestic constituencies. Adam and O'Connell (1997) note, however, that the government may hold back growth also by failure to intervene, for example, to provide public goods.

Governments set the incentive regime and provide services. On both these counts African governments have performed poorly. How did the economic policies and the provision of public services evolve, and what role did aid play in this context?

Generally the environment has been anti-agriculture, and the elite that has been in power has generally been able to control the political scene without being challenged by the rural population. It was, however, under some pressure from its own narrow base of supporters. The external pressure for change was mostly weak. Instead aid probably even contributed to the insulation from pressure for change. It was eventually only the failures of the policy that forced changes. Government revenues fell drastically in several countries. Public salaries fell as employment in the sector increased. Aid inflows could not compensate for this, and eventually donors became unwilling to support government policies which were considered to be counterproductive.

However, often when reforms were undertaken they were followed by urban protest and policy reversals. The governments need to find domestic or external restraints on policy relapse. The use of domestic agents of restraint have proven difficult in Africa. Donors and the international financial institutions may help to guarantee the sustainability of reforms and to protect governments from domestic vested interests.

The level of public expenditures to GDP is generally higher in African countries than in comparable countries elsewhere. This does to a high degree depend on the inflow of aid, which typically tends to increase government consumption. There is no clear evidence that this contributes to long term growth, although one would suspect that, for example, improvements in human capital through education and health service provision should have beneficial long term effects.

Transport costs are considerably higher in Africa than in other regions. Electricity costs are higher than elsewhere and water supplies are unreliable. Projects in education have performed badly. Why is this? Partly the reasons are the same as for the private sector, that is a bad policy environment, which contributes to the low returns to public projects. Moreover, the government uses the public sector to further their own private interests and to build political support. Extensive corruption makes it hard to create an efficient system.

THE CHARACTER OF GROWTH ENHANCING AID

Can aid be growth enhancing in the African environment? Yes, the evidence above suggests that this is the case if there is a conducive policy environment. The last few years of structural adjustment have seen considerable improvements in the policy environment, and the private sector is slowly coming alive. However, progress with regard to institutional reform has been relatively slow. There are worries about the lack of transparency and good governance, although the process of reform and democratization should over time help improve the situation. A crucial issue for donors is thus how the relationship between them and the recipient countries should be set up to create and sustain a good environment for growth. We will here very briefly review a set of aspects that a donor needs to consider.

When deciding on the amount of aid to allocate to a country, one needs to consider the absorptive capacity of the recipient. We have noted the poor state of the civil service in most African countries, while at the same time arguing that an effective civil service is a necessity. The direct approach is to try to help reform the system so that it can cope with the aid inflow. Second, one needs to use aid forms that are administratively simple and do not overburden the apparatus. Third, one could seek alternative channels for aid. In a situation with poor administrative capacity and a large debt burden it would also make sense to shift resources to debt service. This will make it possible for the recipient country to use more of its own resources for development, at the same time as reduced debt should stimulate private investment.

Donors should always ask where aid does have its comparative advantages. Where can aid be effectively used, and where is it better to leave the activity to domestic agents? Many African governments are overstretched. They cannot finance the whole public sector structure and pay the wages that are required for effective work in that sector. Donors should therefore be wary of creating new public sector institutions, but should instead concentrate on strengthening the core network. To improve public sector performance, there needs to be civil service reform. Politically, a reduction of the civil service is very difficult, because of retrenchment costs etc. Donors could support the reform process by helping to finance retrenchment or the cost of severance payments of redundant civil servants. This will be very healthy in the long term, and will also put a little capital in the hands of individuals who might do something productive with it. A similar opportunity exists in supporting retrenchment of workers and managers in downsized or privatized parastatals.

Sustainability of activities is the major worry with regard to project aid to Africa. All support requires careful assessment of affordability, given the level of external support likely to be forthcoming. If inconsistent and unsustainable standards of service provision are to be avoided, a sector approach is usually preferable to project aid.[4] In situations where recurrent costs are a serious problem, donor support is especially appropriate for programmes which require higher expenditure now to permit lower expenditure later, and which therefore to some extent have their sustainability built in: Privatization, civil service retrenchment and infrastructure rehabilitation are examples of this.

Balance of payments (or budget) support may be an appropriate way of channelling money into economies where there is limited ability to absorb new projects at the same time as there are serious recurrent cost problems. It is important that countervalues are paid consistently. Failure to pay up undermines the stabilization efforts and softens the budget constraint. Budget support as well as support to projects on the priority list of the government, is essentially support to the government policy package. Given that this is the form of aid, the donor cannot shift the structure of expenditure directly. If this is to be achieved, he must instead specify conditions for minimum shares going to certain expenditures, or put a ceiling on other types of expenditures. Primarily one should consider expenditure shares for education and health. This should, however, not be done by individual donors unilaterally. Like with other general conditions of this nature, there should be coordination among the bilateral donors and the IFI's, for example in the context of the Public Expenditure Reviews.

Still, there are fairly strict limits as to how far donors can change the priorities of a recipient government. If they push through a programme that does not match the government's own priorities, the sustainability of aid activities will be undermined. Activities on which the government puts low priority run a high risk of decline once donors withdraw support.

Another type of public good, apart from education and health services, that it is worthwhile to support is the transport network. An extension and improvement of the road network in the peripheral areas would contribute significantly to the incomes of poor rural groups. This is a group for which it has turned out to be hard to find efficient forms for such support. This type of investment could crowd in investments, in the tradable sector. What will be the main issue in this area is, of course, whether the recipient government at different levels will have the capacity to maintain the extended network in the future. Capacity-building here would thus have to focus on strengthening the relevant institutions in this area. Support to economic infrastructure in general, not just to roads, often seem to work well, although one may at times be worried about the efficiency of the institutions or firms that are to handle the investments once they are there. Close attention should be given to the need for commercialization or privatization of the organizations involved.

We have noted the problem of currency appreciation (Dutch Disease). The first best response is not less aid, but production subsidies to firms in the tradable sector, or simply export subsidies. One could consider export promotion in the form of both price and non-price incentives. Alternatively, one could try interest subsidies, that is, the introduction of a subsidy to banks to make it possible for them to charge lower interest rates for exporting firms. For this to be effective, however, the government must have the capability to handle it and the integrity to allocate the money on merit.

Donors should not try to do too complex things. It is too complex to intervene directly into production activities, be it agriculture or industry. It requires too much local knowledge. Donor interventions related to production should instead be directed to the creation of an enabling environment for the private sector. This may of course include the creation of institutions that can provide finance for the private sector, but the allocation of these resources should be left to the market. The private sector needs to be strengthened. One way to do this would be to set up charitable trust funds, support some venture capital institutions, or even support local banks. These could then function as financial institution that places its money in projects on a commercial basis. This would be one way to channel money into a country, without using the governmental channels or competing with them.

Aid may also help recipient countries to deal with risk. Many economies are, for example, exposed to uncertainty, and incomes may fluctuate due to swings in commodity prices or commodity production or because of international cycles. The recipient may therefore choose to use aid for consumption-smoothing, rather than for investment, when the economy is facing problems. This should also be acceptable to the donor, when there is an emergency situation with, for example, drought and the threat of starvation. The fact that aid is available for such insurance may be growth enhancing, since it relieves the recipient country of the need to choose self-insurance strategies, that would have a cost in terms of growth.

A CHANGING AID RELATIONSHIP

In the previous section we have noted a range of aspects that a donor needs to consider when devising an aid programme. However, since we have noted that the economic policy environment is crucial to the success of aid, the donor must also tackle the issue of how the relationship between donor and recipient affects the outcomes. Given the analysis above it seems reasonable to assume that this may be crucial to the degree of success of the aid programme. This issue is harder to deal with than the one about types of aid, so the discussion here has to be somewhat speculative.

We have noted that it is desirable that the recipient governments "own" the development programmes to a higher degree than they do at present. To achieve this, donors should delegate more responsibility to the recipients, while at the same time creating an incentive structures for good behaviour. At present, the donors feel a conflict between this type of solution and an effective handling of the projects that they finance. It is definitely the case that donors can take full control over projects and get them to work, but what will the long term implications of this be? Can effective project islands survive and have positive indirect effects on the surroundings, or does the hostile environment eventually force a project collapse? After all, well functioning projects in a failing overall structure are not proof of a good aid programme. This is particularly true in areas normally covered by government ministries, where an important output of any project should be a strengthening of government capacity to formulate and execute similar endeavours.

Project documents should include a discussion of how and when the withdrawal of support is to take place. All projects that start should have a specified endpoint in time (or an argument for indefinite or very long-term support).They should define the responsibility of the recipient. If the Government is not willing to commit itself, the project should never start. For the commitment to be credible, a greater share of the project cost should be covered by recipient from the very start.

Due to weak institutional capacity it has often been difficult to realise the aim that the recipient should handle projects. Responsibility for implementation has therefore at times been taken away from the recipient government. There is an obviously a conflict between giving responsibility to the recipient, and financial accountability. Ex post conditionality, that is a broader evaluation of results with pre-specified indicators, can provide strong incentives for reforms, and for a reestablishment of the government's reputation. However, donors should probably not shift completely towards ex post conditionality. There is also a role for ex ante conditionality — not least in terms of providing a means of transfer of advice and expertise and providing some pre-specified contractual obligations, but also for the reasons about the creation of constituencies which will "punish" governments for reneging on ex ante commitments. It is best to think of the aid and conditionality relationship as a two part contract with prior payments within a state-contingent ex ante-conditionality framework and then further aid flows based on ex post considerations.

With a shift in this direction, donors would need to work out a new type of guidelines for monitoring and auditing, since this would have to be of another form than current project evaluations. One could use simplified procedures for accounting, e. g. in terms of broader criteria of programme implementation. There is also a need for improving the design of ex ante conditionality to focus more on state-contingency in contracts. There are two important reasons for this. First, if conditionality is not state contingent then the typical conditionality contract will reward good luck and punish bad luck. If the donors are not in a position to separate good luck from "effort" then ex post conditionality will reinforce this, and there will be a bias in the allocation of aid money towards those enjoying good luck. The second reason is that the most convincing arguments for a shift towards ex post conditionality revolve around the question of reputation. Part of the inability to generate reputations is that the ex ante conditionality, which is not state contingent, typically does not allow any revelation of effort or commitment for the reasons discussed above. Credible governments have an incentive to demonstrate commitment or effort and this can be achieved better with state contingent contracts.

There will be some need for donor coordination also with regard to ex post conditionality. What is required is to find the appropriate balance between ex ante and ex post. For example, governments may have cash flow problems such that although they are committed to reform they are unable to implement reforms without additional aid resources provided ex ante. Similarly, although ex post conditionality does not' specify conditions for the potential recipient, it is still important that the rules of the game are made clear and that they are internally consistent between donors.

A shift towards ex post conditionality would also make it easier to allocate aid as general budget support, which we have argued may be desirable for a number of reasons. In the case of ex post conditionality, once the decision to disburse is made — ex post — the donor must logically relinquish any claim on how the resources are allocated within the country. If the government is truly of the "right type" then it will manage the resource flow and the countervalue funds in a manner consistent with the wishes of the donor. If the recipient government spends it all on non-productive expenditure, inflation and patronage, then (a) the donor has misjudged the type of the country and (b) the country will not win the contest for aid money the next time. With the ex post approach the rules of the game will allow the donor to distinguish good and committed governments from bad ones.[5] A shift towards a general form of support, giving the recipient government increased responsibility and ownership could help restore the quality of government. However, if this approach is chosen, then the donor must be prepared to walk out if the situation deteriorates sufficiently. Here, however, we have another time inconsistency problem, sometimes referred to as the Samaritan's Dilemma. It may be hard to avoid coming in to rescue innocent sufferers of the government failure, and thus to function as an agent of restraint on the government.

An understanding of how the political process works is a crucial factor in the formulation of an effective donor-recipient relationship. Adam and O'Connell (1997) discuss this issue extensively. A problem as we have noted above has been the extensive executive discretion in Africa. When this is linked to uncertainly about the process of political succession, the absence of formal agencies of restraint minimizing such discretion raises uncertainly. Leaders with long horizons tend to internalize the collective interests in economic growth, while leaders with short horizons tend to sacrifice long term interests in order to maximize their own short-term rents. For example, the higher insecurity of the Moi regime in Kenya relative to the Kenyatta regime has tended to increase predatory behaviour under Moi (Bigsten and Moene, 1996). There is a conflict between executive discretion and contestability: "Thus policies of exchange rate unification, trade liberalization, financial liberalization, privatization and in particular the support for competitive elections, all undermine the scope for executive discretion, improving the capacity to commit to policy measures, but at the cost of making the political system more contestable, which may lead to only partial implementation and fail to reduce the uncertainly faced by the private sector" (Adam and O'Connell, 1997). There is thus a tension between the gains accruing from reforms which solves the government commitment problems and the costs of increased contestability on the other.

Adam and O'Connell conclude that for a developmental state unconditional transfers reduce distortions, thereby delivering benefits that are larger than those attached simply to a consumption transfer. But if the state is not fully representative, increased aid may also change the character of domestic taxation so that distortionary taxes are on the margin financing not only the public good but also transfer to the favoured group. Their conclusion thus supports the notion that aid tends to politicize life in developing countries, and this may in turn have detrimental effects on the private sector's ability to act as an agent of restraint.

Conditionality may first provide the recipient with a way of committing credibly to a course of action that is in the recipient's own interest, independently of the aid inflow. Second, it may support flows of resources in the face of a conflict of interest between the donor and the recipient, when the former is interested in the general welfare of the population and the latter mainly concerned with a certain section of the population. At least when the donor has a strong bargaining position, conditionality in the Adam and O'Connell model would lead to a reduction in distortionary taxation, with a simultaneous reduction in transfers to the governments support groups. Development outcomes would be better.

Here there is again a time inconsistency problem. Graduation from aid dependency is normally the long term aim of the donor, but to support such a graduation the donor would have to define policy choice over the policy process itself. This would imply conditionality concerning, for example, constitutional and judicial reforms and supporting developments in the civil society. These could include a freer press and independent trade unions as well as policies aimed at establishing interest groups outside of government control.

The dilemma with regard to conditionality is that it can, in the short term, function as an agent of restraint, but in the longer term it may instead crowd out the development of domestic agents of restraint on the actions of the recipient government. If aid is to be effective, donors must find ways to combine a move towards increasing self-reliance on the part of the recipients with the realization of the other goals for aid that the donor has, normally the improvement of welfare of the recipient population. This will only be possible if the social and political environment in the recipient country is such that predation tendencies of the recipient governments can be held in check. With the more open social climate in much of Africa, the chances for this are now much better than a decade ago. Democracy may thus make it easier to make aid efficient.

CONCLUDING REMARK

So far, aid has not been shown to have had a major positive impact on growth in Africa, although its impact via policy change may have been important. The conclusion of Burnside and Dollar is that if donors are concerned with growth and poverty reduction, then they should put high weight on the economic policies of the recipient countries. The recent shifts in policy in Africa have been in the "right" direction, which would suggest that the growth environment and thus the environment for efficient aid has improved. It is thus possible that there may be a stronger effect of aid on growth in the future. It will be particularly important if it can help crowd in private foreign and domestic private investment. Aid can only be a supplement to those resources. Once the growth environment is in place, donors may be able to cut back on aid and change the relationship to more normal commercial and political links. We are not there yet, but we seem to be in a position where there is a better chance than before that aid can bring about growth. That is not the time to withdraw support.

NOTES

[1] To capture donors' strategic interests Burnside and Dollar use dummies for Sub-Saharan Africa, the Franc zone, Egypt and Central America and a measure of arms imports lagged one period.

[2] This section draws on Adam et al. (1994a).

[3] For an analysis of Swedish aid to Zambia, see Adam et al. (1994b).

[4] "The justification for recurrent cost support in particular requires a careful evaluation of affordability and replicability of similar standards at the level of the sector as a whole. Donor supported islands of excellence in a sea of underfinancing are a poor use of resources, and ultimately unsustainable when donor fashions change. It is therefore desirable that proposals to support recurrent costs take a wider perspective, and it will normally be sensible to consider such proposals as part of a coordinated package for a whole sector or at least for an institution" . (ODA, 1994, pt 11)

[5] There is one caveat to the argument that there should be no conditions on disbursement of the ex post conditionality and that relates to the Dutch Disease problems. Suppose for example the attribute the donor is rewarding ex post is export diversification. In this case the winner will receive an aid "price" which by appreciating the real exchange rate may undermine the benefits gained in pursuit of the price. It may be necessary, therefore, to ensure that the implicit tax on exporters associated with the aid inflow is offset by some subsidy or compensation, wither by way of a subsidy on exported output, export production (possibly on the cost of credit) or on investment.

REFERENCES

Adam, C., Bigsten, A., Collier, P., Julin, E., O'Connell, S. (1994a), *Evaluation of Swedish Development Cooperation with Tanzania*, SASDA, Ds 1994:113, Foreign Office, Stockholm.

Adam, C., Andersson, P-Å., Bigsten, A., Collier, P., O'Connell, S. (1994b), *Evaluation of Swedish Development Cooperation with Zambia*, SASDA, Ds 1994:114, Foreign Office, Stockholm.

Adam, C., O'Connell, S. (1997), "Aid, Taxation and Development: Analytical Perspectives on Aid Effectiveness in Sub-Saharan Africa", Working Paper no 97-5, Centre for the Study of African Economies, Oxford University, Oxford.

Bigsten, A. (1993), "Regulations versus Price Reforms in Crisis Management. The Case of Kenya", in M. Blomström and M. Lundahl (eds.), *Economic Crisis in Africa: Perspectives on Policy Responses*, Routledge, London.

Bigsten, A., Moene, K-O. (1996), "Growth and Rent Dissipation: The Case of Kenya", *Journal of African Economies,* 5(2).

Bonnick, G.G. (1997), *Zambia Country Assistance Review. Turning an Economy Around*, OED, World Bank Operations Evaluation Study, World Bank, Washington DC.

Boone, P. (1994), "The Impact of Foreign Aid on Savings and Growth", London School of Economics, mimeo.

Boone, P. (1996), "Politics and the Effectiveness of Foreign Aid", *European Economic Review* 40(2).

Burnside, C., Dollar, D. (1997), "Aid, Policies and Growth", Policy Research Working Paper no 1777, World Bank, Washington DC.

Claessens, S. Naude, D. (1993), "Recent Estimates of Capital Flight", Policy Research Working Paper no 1186, World Bank, Washington DC.

Collier, P. Gunning, J.W. (1997), "Explaining African Economic Performance", Working Paper no 97-2, Centre for the Study of African Economies, Oxford University, Oxford.

Easterly, W., Levine, R. (1995), "Africa's Growth Tragedy: a Retrospective, 1960–89", Policy Research Working Paper no 1503, World Bank, Washington DC.

Easterly, W.R., Levine, R. (1996), "Africa's Growth Tragedy: Policies and Ethnic Divisions", World Bank, mimeo.

Mosley, P. (1987), *Overseas Aid: Its Defence and Reform*, Wheatsheaf Books, Brighton.

Mosley, P., Hudson, J., Horrel, S. (1987), "Aid, the Public Sector and the Market in Less Developed Countries", *Economic Journal* 97(2).

ODA (1994), "Aid, hidden transfers and conditionality", mimeo.

Paldam, M. (1997), "The Micro-Efficiency of Danish Development Aid", Working Paper No. 1997-13, Department of Economics, University of Aarhus, Aarhus.

Riddell, R. (1987), *Foreign Aid Reconsidered*, James Currey, London.

Rodrik, D. (1989), "Credibility of Trade Reform — a Policy Makers Guide", *The World Economy* 12.

Sachs, J.D., Warner, A. (1995), "Economic Reform and the Process of Economic Integration", *Brooking Paper on Economic Activity* 1.

White, H. (1992), "The Macroeconomic Impact of Development Aid: A Critical Survey", *Journal of Development Studies*, 28(2).

White, H. (ed.) (1998), *Aid and Macroeconomic Performance. Theory, Empirical Evidence and Four Country Cases*, Macmillan, London.

World Bank (1997), *World Development Report 1997*, Washington D.C.

CHAPTER 11

COST BENEFIT ANALYSIS OF FOREIGN AID FOR A HIGHLY DISTORTED ECONOMY:
The Case of Sudan

Kiyoun Han
and
Edward Tower

INTRODUCTION

How beneficial is foreign aid? This is a fairly simple question in an undistorted economy. In a distorted one this is a complex issue, and in a highly distorted one like the Sudan sorting out the interaction of foreign aid with the distortions is important. Foreign aid impacts both the balance of payments of the country and the balance of the fiscal authority; how the foreign aid ultimately affects economic welfare (the shadow price of foreign aid—"spfa") depends on what policies are used to obtain international and fiscal balance. Moreover, the granting of foreign aid is often conditional upon economic reform of various sorts; part of a foreign aid package may be in kind, taking the form of specific commodities like wheat or computers or foreign exchange that can be used only for the purchase of particular commodities. Evaluation of such a foreign aid package requires determination of the marginal social value, "msv," of the accompanying reforms as well as the shadow price of the foreign exchange and commodities, "spfx" and "spc" included in the foreign aid package. This paper develops a simple four sector linearized general equilibrium model of the Sudan in order to perform the requisite cost benefit analysis. It finds that the spfa depends strongly on how the fiscal authority adjusts to the foreign aid, the economic reforms required, and the form taken by the aid. We also use the model to calculate the income distributional effects and cost benefit ratios of the sorts of policy reform likely to be encouraged by donors. These ratios are useful supports for the policy dialogue.

Four issues are central to the policy reform debate in the Sudan in the 1980s, before Sudanese terrorism became an issue and USAID closed its Khartoum office. These are wheat policy, the desirability of exchange rate unification, protectionism, and the design of a sensible tax structure. The consumption, production and import of wheat in Sudan are subject to government imposed distortions of multiple prices, compulsory procurement policy, and import quotas. High trade taxes together with multiple exchange rates impose explicit and implicit export taxes on agricultural exports — while they give rise to heavy protection for the import-substituting industrial sector.

Heretofore, no applied general equilibrium model of the Sudanese economy has been built to assess the efficiency, revenue and equity effects of the country's trade, tax, and agricultural policy. Reforms in these areas have complicated effects on economic efficiency and income distribution in a highly distorted economy like the Sudan, and a partial equilibrium model is not sufficient to capture them. This chapter develops a simple four sector linearized general equilibrium model of the Sudan in order to calculate the associated tradeoffs.

The chapter is structured as follows. We describe the model and how we calibrated it. Then we measure the reasonableness of the model by presenting demand and supply elasticities. Next we assess the marginal welfare cost of taxation for incremental perturbations of the tax, wheat pricing and exchange rate structure. Then comes calculation of shadow prices and marginal social values under alternative tax closures. This is followed by calculations designed to support the policy dialogue which typically accompanies the negotiation of foreign aid: we analyze the income distributional affects of tax policy and calculate various cost/benefit ratios for wheat, trade and exchange-rate policies. All of these quantify the desirability of policy change. Now comes calculation of the shadow price of foreign aid of various forms with various policy reform scenarios attached. Finally, we draw implications for foreign aid and the policy debate.

Since the Sudan shares a number of characteristics with other less developed countries: subsidized food, taxed agricultural exports and industrial imports and multiple exchange rates, the analysis presented here can serve as a useful template for future research on other economies.[1]

THE MODEL

Production structure

We describe the Sudan as it was predicted by the World Bank (1985) to look in 1989/90.[2] We model the Sudan as comprising four sectors: wheat, all other agriculture (which for expositional convenience we refer to as exportable-ag. Think of this as cotton, one of the major exports), industry and services. The value added composite in each sector is produced according to a Cobb-Douglas production function of a sector specific factor (which we refer to as land in the two agricultural sectors and capital in the two urban sectors) and labor. Output of each good is assumed to be a first degree homogeneous function of the value added composite and an imported intermediate input, with an elasticity of substitution between the two factors of 0.4, which allowed some but limited substitution.

Factor supplies, factor mobility and tastes

Rural labor is fixed in supply and perfectly mobile between the two agricultural sectors. Urban labor is fixed in supply and perfectly mobile between the two urban sectors. There is no mobility of labor between the urban and rural sectors. This reflects educational and cultural differences between the two groups. Households obtain their earnings from all factor services described above (two types each of land, labor and capital). All households are assumed to face identical prices, do no saving and have identical Cobb-Douglas preferences for the four goods. The government is assumed to share these same preferences. Consequently, the government spends the revenue it collects from taxes and aid in the same proportions as the private sector does. Like the private sector it spends all of its income, except when we permit it to accumulate foreign exchange in order to assess the welfare impact of such accumulation.

Internal and external balance

The economy is competitive. Flexible wages and prices are assumed to maintain full employment. Foreign aid and agricultural exports pay for imports of intermediate inputs, wheat and the final industrial good. All intermediate inputs enter the country duty free. Agricultural exports are subject to an export tax. Wheat imports are provided by the government with the quantity of wheat imported subject to an exogenously determined quota. Services are not traded, and imports of industrial goods are subject to an import duty. The domestic consumption of services and industrial goods are subject to excise taxes. Both intermediate inputs for agriculture and agricultural outputs are transacted at the official exchange rate of 2.5 LS/$, where LS represents "Sudanese Pounds," and intermediate inputs for the two urban sectors are transacted at the free market exchange rate of 4.0 LS/$.[3] This constitutes a subsidy on industry relative to the other sectors. In effect, the government earns foreign exchange net from its agricultural transactions at the predetermined official exchange rate and then auctions the net supply off for non-agricultural uses.[4]

The wheat market

The government requires a proportion, (initially 60%), of all wheat produced domestically to be sold to the government at an exogenously determined procurement price, which is initially set equal to the world price at the official exchange rate. Farmers are permitted to sell the rest freely at a market determined price, (initially 35% above the procurement price). The government sells the wheat it procures from both domestic and foreign sources at an "administered price" (initially 30% below the procurement price), for use in baking bread, which is subject to price control (which is designed to grant a reasonable cost margin). We integrate the bakery sector with the household sector and assume that consumers view subsidized wheat for bread and free market wheat as perfect substitutes, and that they are permitted to buy a fixed quota of subsidized wheat and fulfill the rest of their demand for wheat on the free market. Tastes are homothetic, and we assume that each household has access to rationed bread in proportion to its initial income and hence initial expenditure. Consequently, at the margin households pay the free market price for wheat, and its marginal utility is the free market price times the marginal utility of income. Thus, we model the wedge between the free market wheat price and the administered price as a non-distorting subsidy, financed in part by the tax on wheat production represented by the wedge between the free market and procurement prices. We assume away all rent seeking behavior and inefficiency due to the rationing of bread. Consequently, we have underestimated the costs associated with government wheat pricing.[5]

Monetary closure

There is no bond market in Sudan, so any fiscal deficit must be matched by creation of money or destruction of foreign currency reserves.[6] The government pegs three prices: the official exchange rate, the free exchange rate and the wheat procurement price. It raises or lowers some tax depending on whether the government budget is in deficit or surplus. Private expenditure is proportional to the money stock. Therefore, when the money stock is high it will leak out of the economy as agents trade it for foreign exchange and then for goods. In equilibrium, taxes and the money supply adjust to create trade balance and a steady state money stock. Thus in our closure the exchange rates are exogenous and the money stock is endogenous.

The Sudanese government's policy was to inflate the money supply at a fairly constant rate. It would peg the official exchange rate for short periods of time, until cumulative inflation made it untenable, and it would adjust import restrictions to prevent the "free" rate from fluctuating too wildly. We had to decide whether to take the money stock as fixed with the free exchange rate flexible, or the money stock as flexible with the free exchange rate pegged. The comparative statics using the constant-money-stock closure is hard to understand and explain, because the price of the industrial good is endogenous. Therefore, we chose the closure which pegs the free exchange rate.

Had we chosen to close the model with an exogenously determined money stock and a flexible free rate we would have found that monetary expansion raises domestic factor prices. This squeezes exports and reduces foreign exchange earnings. So imports must shrink, and this is accompanied by depreciating the free pound. For more on how monetary expansion with a fixed exchange rate for exports squeezes imports, see Krueger (1978).

Implementation

The model consists of a set of 66 equations. These are linearized and solved using Lotus. We use matrix methods described in Gan and Tower (1987) and Tower (1984) to solve for the differential changes in the endogenous variables as functions of the differential changes in the exogenous equations. Conceptually, through substitution the model in effect simplifies to a set of 2 equations: These express the balance of payments surplus (B) and the growth of the money stock (G) as functions of the money stock, the free exchange rate, the level of lump sum taxes and a host of exogenous variables. We constrain B and G to equal zero. We let the money stock and one of the other right hand variables (say the proportional income tax) be endogenous. We perturb one of the exogenous variables. This uniquely determines the money stock, the level of the proportional income tax and all of the other endogenous variables. The equations and derivations of them are available from Tower in Han (1988).

Distortions

The distortions which characterize the Sudanese economy are described in Table 11.1. In that table the ERP refers to the effective rate of protection, which is the proportion by which value added at domestic producer prices exceeds value added at world prices — using the official exchange rate to convert prices.[7] The consumption distortion is the proportion by which consumer prices exceed producer prices (the amount by which the free market wheat price exceeds the average producer price in the case of wheat). The tariff is the proportion by which the (average) producer price exceeds the world price — at whatever exchange rate is used in the transaction (the negative figure for exportable-ag represents an export tax). Finally, the import margin is the proportion by which the (average) producer price exceeds the world price evaluated at the official exchange rate. Note that the high effective protection for import competing industry and negative effective protection for exportable-ag imply huge taxation of international trade, and leads to a presumption that significant costs are associated with trade policy.

Consistency checks

The only way to debug a complex model like this one is to be sure it behaves as it should in the special situations we understand (as well as checking for implausible results). Three tests we used are the following. A one percent increase in all factor supplies and the wheat import quota was found to increase all real variables by one percent, and leave all nominal variables unchanged, which is what one would expect with first degree homogeneity in production and utility functions. Also a one percent increase in the official exchange rate, the free exchange rate , the wheat procurement price and the administered wheat price was found to raise all nominal variables by one percent and leave all real variables unchanged. Finally, in the case where a non-distorting proportional income tax is used to balance the budget, a one percent in-

Table 11.1. Distortions (%).[8]

Sector	ERP	Cons'n Distortion	Tariff	Import Margin
Wheat	22.56	16.07	12.00[9]	12.00
Exportable-ag	–4.71	0.00	–4.39	–4.39
Industry	421.76	5.01	76.41	182.26
Services	–8.48	3.03	n.a.	n.a.

crease in both exchange rates and the wheat purchase price was found to raise all nominal variables by one percent and leave all real variables unchanged (rows 14, 15 and 20 of Table 11.4).

DEMAND AND SUPPLY ELASTICITIES

In order to give the reader some sense of how our version of the Sudanese economy behaves, so he can judge whether it is reasonable, we present general equilibrium demand and supply elasticities for the four sectors in Table 11.2, which were obtained from our simulations.[10] For wheat, we varied the procurement proportion. The elasticity in each case represents the proportional change in consumption or production per proportional change in consumer (free market for wheat) or (average for wheat) producer price. In each simulation presented in the paper, we assume that the government maintains constant real revenues collected from explicit taxes, implicit taxation (arising out of its multiple exchange rate regime) and foreign aid by varying a nondistorting proportional income tax, unless we explicitly note that an alternative model closure has been used.

All demand elasticities were negative and less than unity in absolute value, while all supply elasticities were positive and except for wheat, they were less than unity. The wheat sector is much smaller than the exportable-ag sector. Hence exportable-ag's supply elasticity is much smaller. The large import demand elasticity for industry reflects the assumption that domestically produced and imported industrial goods are perfect substitutes and the smallness of industrial imports relative to industrial output. We feel that these elasticities describe reasonable educated guesses for responses to changes in consumer and producer prices.[11]

THE MARGINAL WELFARE COST OF TAXATION

In order to assess the efficacy of alternative ways to raise revenues, we present in Table 11.3 the marginal welfare cost of taxation (MWCT) for various types of tax adjustments, ranked from worst to best. Each MWCT is expressed as the equivalent variation in income (welfare) per unit of additional real revenue collected due to the indicated adjustment in the particular tax, assuming that the increased revenues are

Table 11.2. Simulated General Equilibrium Elasticities.

	Demand	Supply	Import Demand	Export Supply
Wheat	–.97	1.02		
Exportable-ag	–.50	.03		.65
Industry	–.61	.59	–4.27	
Services	–.66	.35		

Table 11.3. Marginal Welfare Cost of Taxation.[12]

1. Depreciation of the Free Market Sudanese Pound	–3,459
2. Appreciation of the Official Sudanese Pound	–2,232
3. Increased Agricultural Export Tax	–538
4. Decreased Wheat Procurement Percentage	–214
5. Increased Industrial Excise Tax	–86
6. Increased Service Excise Tax	–9
7. Decreased Wheat Procurement Price	+44
8. Decreased Industrial Import Tariff	+96

returned as a non-distorting subsidy. A negative figure indicates that the change in welfare and real revenue have different signs, i.e. that there is a cost rather than a benefit associated with higher revenue collection.

Now we explore the logic behind Table 11.3.

(1) Depreciation of the free market Sudanese pound amounts to higher taxation of industrial imports. Since this tax is already quite high, the free exchange rate is close to its maximum revenue level, so further currency depreciation collects little real revenue. Also, because industry is implicitly subsidized, additional resources in industry have low social products and further subsidy in this fashion is inefficient. Consequently, this is a very inefficient method of collecting additional tax revenue.

(2) Appreciation of the official Sudanese pound raises the implicit tax on agricultural exports. This is also inefficient, since this sector is already highly taxed relative to industry.

(3) Increasing the agricultural export tax is less inefficient, than (2) appreciating the official pound, since the latter additionally subsidizes intermediate-input intensive wheat by making its intermediate inputs cheaper.[13] The latter also subsidizes intermediate inputs into exportable-ag. Consequently, with the former, per unit of revenue collected less labor shifts from taxed exportable-ag into less taxed wheat, and there is less reduction in agricultural prices, i.e. implicit subsidization of domestic agricultural consumption. Still, both MWCTs are exorbitant. The preference for the export tax is somewhat surprising, since if there had been no domestic consumption of agriculture, and if the wheat sector had been non-existent instead of small, a change in the official exchange rate would have been a non-distorting tax on the fixed composite factor: agricultural land and labor.

(4) A decrease in the procurement percentage saves real revenue because less wheat is procured. But it imposes an efficiency cost, because the increased average producer price of wheat draws more resources out of exportable-ag into relatively more subsidized wheat and also draws some consumption into wheat away from industry (where consumer prices are well above world prices).

(5) Increasing the industrial excise tax is also costly, because it shifts consumption from industry (where consumption is taxed) primarily to agriculture (where it is subsidized). But it is less costly, because resources are shifted out of the industrial sector with its high ERP into other less protected sectors.

(6) Raising the excise tax on services is even less costly than the above taxes. Nevertheless, it is still costly, because resources are shifted out of services into a relatively more protected industry.

(7) A decreased wheat procurement price raises both revenue and welfare because it drives resources from wheat into exportable-ag.

(8) Best of all, is lowering the import tariff on industry, since the tariff is apparently above the maximum revenue level, and a tariff reduction desirably increases consumption and reduces production of the industrial good. The reason that the industrial tariff lies above its maximum revenue level even though the free market exchange rate does not, is that depreciation of the free market pound is a more broadly-based implicit tax than is a hike in the import tariff, as the former, raises prices of inputs for both urban sectors whereas the latter does not.

SHADOW PRICES AND MARGINAL SOCIAL VALUES UNDER ALTERNATIVE CLOSURES

Table 11.4 presents shadow prices under alternative tax closure rules. We have arranged the taxes considered to be the adjustment mechanism for raising tax revenues from best to worst as one moves from left to right (drawing on Table 11.3). One particularly relevant closure rule is the non-distorting proportional income tax, because non-distorting taxes are available in the Sudan: for example land taxes and charging market clearing prices for wheat, services and import licenses.

A second important closure rule is adjustment of the free market exchange rate, as this requires no change in any official government price or tax. When the government needs additional resources, it simply charges a higher price for the free market exchange it sells, which increases the number of pounds it earns from such sales. Thus, higher government expenditure automatically leads to depreciation of the free market pound.

The concept of a shadow price and how to use them in policy reform and project evaluation is explained in Gan and Tower (1987) in a similar context and also in Tower (1991).[14] Thus we can be brief here. The shadow price of a good or factor is the contribution to welfare made by the government's selling a unit of a good or factor service to the private sector out of inventory or nonproductive government service, while simultaneously adjusting some tax in order to balance its budget, after all general equilibrium effects work themselves out. The shadow prices in rows 2–13 take a unit of measurement to be that quantity of the item which has a producer price of LS 1.

The marginal social values of the parameters indicated in rows 14–21 show the effects on welfare of a 1 % (rows 14,15 and 20) or 1 %age point (all other rows) increase in the parameter in question, where the welfare change is measured in LS millions. Thus, for example, assuming budget deficits are closed using a proportional income tax, switching land with rental value of LS 1 million from wheat cultivation to exportable-ag cultivation in government projects while simultaneously raising the agricultural export tax by .03% would shrink welfare by $-\{-.25+2.04-74.8*0.03\}=$ LS million .45, whereas exactly the same project using the free exchange rate to balance the government budget would swell welfare by $-8.8+66.7+406*0.03=$LS million 70.1.

Table 11.4. Shadow Prices and Marginal Social Values Under Alternative Closures.*

	Industrial Import Tariff	Proportionnal Income Tax	Excise on Services	Export Tax Rate	Official Exchange Rate	Free Exchange Rate
1.One Dollar	0.57	4.85	5.25	28.78	104.0	158.5
2.Free Market Wheat	–0.25	1.27	1.41	9.77	36.5	55.9
3.Administered Wheat[15]	–0.17	1.27	1.40	9.29	34.5	52.8
4.Exportable-ag	0.24	2.03	2.20	12.04	43.5	66.3
5.Industrial good	0.03	.69	.75	4.35	15.9	24.2
6.Services	–0.11	.95	1.05	6.87	25.5	38.9
7.Rural Labor	0.24	2.04	2.20	12.07	43.6	66.5
8.Urban Labor	–0.11	.82	.91	6.00	22.3	34.1
9.Wheat Land	0.01	.25	.27	1.58	5.8	8.8
10.Exportable-ag Land	0.24	2.04	2.21	12.10	43.7	66.7
11.Industrial Capital	0.11	.18	.19	.58	1.8	2.7
12.Service Capital	–0.17	.99	1.10	7.45	27.8	42.5
13.Government Wheat Imports	1.10	.47	–.52	–3.87	–14.6	–22.3
14. Official Exchange Rt(LS/$)	74.9	71.8	71.47	54.44	0	–39.4
15.Free Exchange Rate (LS/$)	–73.2	–71.2	–71.0	–60.12	–25.3	0
16.Agricultural Export Tax	–88.2	–74.8	–73.6	0	235.3	405.9
17.Industrial Tariff	–0.24	–54.4	–59.5	–358.5	–1390	–2000
18.Industrial Excise Tax	–112.	–54.9	–49.3	287.4	1364	2004
19.Services Excise Tax	–154.	–13.1	0	777.3	3262	5063
20.Wheat Procurement Price	0.65	–.540	–.650	–7.19	–28.1	–43.2
21.Wheat Procurement Fraction	0.65	.450	.430	–.680	–4.26	–6.85

*Entries in rows 1–13 indicate increase in Sudanese welfare, at consumer LS prices. Unit of measurement for rows 2–13 is the quantity of the item which has a producer price of LS 1. Entries in rows 14–21 indicate change in Sudanese welfare in LS millions at prices anticipated by the World Bank (1985) to prevail in 1989–90 per 1% (rows 14, 15 and 20) or 1 %age point (all other rows) increase in the parameter in question. The welfare changes are equivalent variations in income.

This example illustrates the importance of assumptions about tax policy in evaluating projects and policy reform. Of course, this same point can be seen by reading across rows in Table 4. It should be noted that the figures in each row are monotone increasing or decreasing, which is necessarily the case, as we have arranged the taxes in order of increasing marginal welfare cost of tax collection.

All shadow prices can be expressed in terms of dollar reserves gained by the government, holding welfare constant, by dividing the figures presented by the shadow price of foreign exchange, as Fane (1991) and Tower and Pursell (1987) among others note. Several points are worth noting.

(1) Except for one adjustment mechanism, the shadow price of a dollar exceeds both the free and official exchange rates, which is typically true in protected economies. However, this is not the case when the industrial import tariff is used as the adjustment mechanism. This is because when the extra dollar is auctioned of to the private sector, since the import tariff exceeds its maximum revenue level, the import tariff must be raised to keep the government's budget in balance.

(2) Shadow prices may change sign, depending on the adjustment mechanism postulated.

(3) Resources in the import competing sector have lower shadow prices than resources of equal market value to producers in the exportable sector. For example 1 LS of the fixed factor in the exportable-ag sector, which is really a composite of capital and land, is worth 2.04/0.18=11.3 times as much as the same value of the fixed factor in import competing industry. This dramatizes the importance of agricultural investment and the absurdity of investing in import competing industry.

(4) Unifying the exchange rates by either appreciating the free market pound or depreciating the official pound are beneficial regardless of what tax policy is used to balance the budget, but it is more beneficial the more sensible the tax is. However, devaluing the official pound will actually reduce welfare if no taxes are increased and wheat policy remains unchanged, so that the induced depreciation of the free market pound is the adjustment mechanism. This is because such a policy imposes a fiscal burden on the government by lowering the relative price of administered wheat, and with the marginal welfare cost of tax collection high enough, welfare falls. Moreover, if wheat prices were cut in proportion to the appreciation of the official pound, the free market pound would move by the same proportion, and welfare would be unchanged.[16] Thus in this scenario the official exchange rate is neutral as economic theory says it should be. The moral is that devaluation of the official pound should be accompanied by effective fiscal reform.[17]

(5) The shadow price of importing a pound's worth of wheat and selling it at the administered price (row 13) is positive, i.e. the activity is welfare improving, only for the two best tax closure rules.

(6) Assuming that the government budget is financed at the margin by adjustment of the free exchange rate, the shadow price of dollars in the hands of the government is an exchange rate of 158 LS/$ compared with an official rate of 2.5 LS/$. Moreover, the shadow prices of urban and rural labor are market values multiplied by 34 and 66 respectively! This means that in the absence of fiscal reform or adjustments in existing taxes, the government should scrutinize projects that use up these resources very carefully. Similarly high shadow prices emerge for other resources. Thus some shrinkage of existing government activities would be good.

TAX POLICY AND INCOME DISTRIBUTION

Policymakers in less developed countries are often reluctant to reform inefficient tax systems because of the income distributional consequences. Yet often tax reform is a requirement of a foreign aid package. However, if a tax is inefficient, the benefits to the gainers from replacing it by a better tax will dwarf the losses to the losers. This point can be illustrated using calculations from our model, and such illustrations should make the LDC policymakers more receptive to tax reform.

Table 11.5 shows the effects of changes in exchange rates and taxes on real government revenue, welfare, and disposable real incomes of the two types of labor, urban capital (employed in industry and services) and rural land (employed in the two agricultural sectors).

The percentage changes in after-tax real incomes denote equivalent variations in income expressed as a percentage of initial expenditure levels (after the perturbation in question including the proportional income tax closure. The percentage change in real government revenue is the percentage change in real government revenue arising out of all implicit and explicit taxation (except changes in the proportional income tax) plus foreign aid. Thus it measures the excess revenues which must be neutralized by a proportional income subsidy.

(1) A depreciation of the official pound shrinks the implicit agricultural export tax, shrinking revenue, raising welfare, and benefitting the rural sector significantly. Exports rise, increasing the foreign exchange available to buy industrial imports. This squeezes industrial capital, but even urban labor, some of which is able to escape into services whose prices rise (due in part to the increased real income) is enriched.

(2) A depreciation of the free pound has virtually opposite effects. Were the pound prices of wheat not pegged by policy, a one percent depreciation of the official pound would have exactly the same effect as a one percent appreciation of the free market pound, since only relative prices matter. However, a depreciation of the official pound (with the pound procurement price for wheat fixed) raises the price of

Table 11.5. Taxes and Income Distribution (% Changes In Real Incomes and Government Revenues With A Nondistorting Proportional Income Tax Closure Per 1% Change In Exchange Rates or 1%age Point Change in Taxes and Tariffs [%/%]).

			Real Disposable Income			
Exogenous Variable	Govnmt. Revenue	Real Welfare	Rural Labor	Land	Urban Labor	Capital
1. Offcl Exch Rate(LS/$)	–.038	.170	.617	.597	.025	–.172
2. Free Exch Rate(LS/$)	.024	–.169	–.618	–.612	–.021	.175
3. Agricultural Export Tax	.165	–.177	–.699	–.687	–.006	.211
4. Industrial Tariff	–.669	–.129	–.489	–.486	–.044	.181
5. Industrial Excise Tax	.753	–.130	–.273	–.269	–.021	–.124
6. Services Excise Tax	1.738	–.031	.300	.302	–.385	–.047
7. Intl Vals (LS Bln/yr)	8.443	42.173	8.373	3.635	10.763	10.958

exportable-ag relative to the procurement price of wheat. This is a desirable impact that is not generated by a change in the free pound. Thus, a 1 % depreciation of the official pound is better than a 1 % appreciation of the free pound.

(3) A hike in the agricultural export tax raises revenue while impoverishing all actors except for capital, particularly the rural sector.

(4) A hike in the industrial tariff shrinks revenue and impoverishes everyone except for capitalists, with the impoverishment of the rural sector being particularly severe.

(5) A hike in the industrial excise tax raises revenue but impoverishes everyone.

(6) An increase in the services excise tax raises revenue, but impoverishes the economy as it drives more resources into already subsidized industry. The rural sector gains at the expense of the now more highly taxed urban sector.

(7) We present initial values so that the reader can use the table to calculate cost/benefit ratios for these policy changes.

To conclude, trade taxes and even an excise on the industrial importable redistribute income away from the rural sector, which as Krueger (1983) has emphasized usually employs the poorest members of the economy, and all the methods of raising tax revenue we have considered lower welfare, except for reducing the industrial import tariff. This is not surprising since they are all distortionary and the industrial import tariff exceeds its maximum revenue level.

COST/BENEFIT ANALYSIS OF ALTERNATIVE WHEAT POLICIES

One of the benefits of granting foreign aid is the education of the policy makers that is part of the dialogue which accompanies the foreign aid agreement. One of the best forms this education can take is exploration of the tradeoffs inherent in the proposed policy reforms. In this and the following section, we explore some of these, using the same model which gives us the spfa. Sudanese wheat policy artificially encourages wheat consumption. What does this cost?

Table 11.6 measures the opportunity cost of increased wheat consumption as the welfare loss holding foreign exchange usage constant, assuming that the budget is balanced using non-distorting taxation. We see that the marginal welfare cost of increased wheat consumption is 82% or 54% of the increase (valued at consumer prices), depending on the instrument used for expanding wheat consumption.

We also see that it is more efficient for Sudan to import additional wheat than to grow it herself. The marginal welfare gain from switching from home grown to foreign wheat is 82.4% – 53.7% = 28.7%.

Table 11.6. Marginal Cost of Increased Wheat Consumption Measured in Welfare (at average producer prices).

1. Via n Increase in the Wheat Procurement Price or a Decrease in the Procurement Fraction	82.4%
2. Via an Increase in Imported Wheat	53.7%

COST/BENEFIT ANALYSIS OF TRADE AND EXCHANGE-RATE POLICIES

Another important lesson for policymakers is how international trade and the foreign exchange market operates to achieve or frustrate their goals of expanding exports, raising incomes of target groups; and raising employment and output in targeted sectors.

Table 11.7 shows the costs and benefits from using trade and exchange rate policy to accomplish various goals, again with the non-distorting tax closure. We see that export promotion through lower tariffs and exchange rate unification increases welfare by a multiple of between 1.85 and 3.46 of the increased exports stimulated. Using a higher import tariff, a depreciated free pound or an appreciated official pound to redistribute income to industrial capitalists imposes a deadweight loss of 169%, 268%, and 270% of the amount of real income transferred, respectively. Using tariff policy to increase industrial employment imposes a deadweight loss of 368% of the employment generated (valued at the initial wage). Moreover, depreciating the free pound or appreciating the official pound in order to accomplish the same goal are even worse with corresponding ratios of 554% and 553%. Finally, using an import tariff to increase industrial output imposes a deadweight loss of 136% of the output

Table 11.7. Cost/Benefit Analysis of Trade and Exchange-Rate Policies.

A. Marginal Welfare Gain From Increased Agricultural Exports (valued at producer prices)	
1. Via an Export Tariff Cut	185%
2. Via an Import Tariff Cut	346%
3. Via a Devaluation of the Official Pound	207%
4. Via an Appreciation of the Free Market Pound	205%
B. Welfare Cost of Increasing Real Income of Industrial Capitalists by LS 1	
1. Via an Import Tariff Increase	LS 1.69
2. Via Depreciating the Free Market Pound	LS 2.68
3. Via Appreciating the Official Pound	LS 2.70
C. Welfare Cost of Increasing Industrial Employment by LS 1	
1. Via an Import Tariff Increase	LS 3.68
2. Via Depreciating the Free Market Pound	LS 5.54
3. Via Appreciating the Official Pound	LS 5.53
D. Welfare Cost of Increasing Industrial Output by LS 1	
1. Via an Import Tariff Increase	LS 1.36
2. Via Depreciating the Free Market Pound	LS 3.46
3. Via Appreciating the Official Pound	LS 3.46

generated, with a corresponding figure of 346% when either exchange rate is used. All of these results expose the urgent need for freer trade and unified exchange rates.

THE SHADOW PRICE OF FOREIGN AID

Now let us explore the usefulness of foreign aid, using the calculations already presented.

Foreign aid and tax closure

Suppose the foreign aid takes the form of a grant of dollars with no strings attached. Then the spfa is given by the spfx in Table 4. We see that the shadow price of foreign aid exceeds the price of a dollar at either the official or free exchange rate (2.5 or 4.0 LS/$) even when a non-distorting proportional income subsidy is used to inject the purchasing power into the economy (4.85 LS/$). This is not surprising, since there are import tariffs.

However, the best way to introduce the foreign exchange is to include it with export earnings as part of the free exchange auctioned to the private sector. This multiplies the social value of the foreign aid by a factor of 33, boosting it to 158.5 LS/$. *Thus clearly the tax closure used is hugely important.*

Foreign aid in kind

Now suppose that the foreign aid consists of donating a dollar's worth of surplus wheat to the private sector (the proportional income tax closure). The spfa administered in this way is the value at producer prices of a dollar worth of wheat times the shadow price of a LS worth of wheat: 2.5*1.12*1.27=3.556 LS/$.[18] This is less valuable than straight aid. But when the wheat is given to the Sudanese government, which sells it off to the private sector at the free price thereby absorbing pounds and appreciating the free pound, the spfa multiplies by a factor of 44 to 2.5*1.12*55.9 = 157 LS/$.

Foreign aid and policy reform

If the foreign aid consists of a grant of one million dollars along with the requirement that the official Sudanese pound be depreciated by 1 percent, the change in welfare is (4.85 LS/$)(1 million $) + (1)(71.8) LS million = 76.65 LS million. In this case the benefit from reducing the distortion dwarfs the amount of foreign aid granted. Here the shadow price of foreign aid is 76.65 LS/$. This illustrates simply that *when foreign aid is levered by policy reform, the benefits can be staggering.*

Trade instead of aid

Another form that foreign aid could take is freer trade on the part of the would be donors who substitute the sacrifice that foreign aid entails for the donor with a win-

win policy of freer trade, which raise the world price of exportable-ag. This would increase Sudanese foreign exchange earnings, reduce the budget deficit of the Sudanese fiscal authority and move resources from artificially advantaged industry and services into disadvantaged exportable-ag. As Loo and Tower (1989) show, such trade in lieu of aid can generate substantial gains to economies like the Sudan. The gains can be determined by calculating the marginal social value of an increased world price of exportable-ag.

CONCLUSION

The agricultural sector is the mainstay of the Sudanese economy. It employs more than 80% of the country's labor force and agricultural exports are the economy's principal source of foreign exchange. However, Sudanese trade, tax and agricultural policy has severely taxed agricultural exports explicitly and implicitly, and restricted international trade flows. In this chapter we have attempted to quantify the benefits of foreign aid and freer trade. We conclude by emphasizing the following points.

First, tying foreign aid to policies and fiscal closures that encourage freer trade and more efficient taxation dramatically raises the welfare benefits per dollar of foreign aid, the shadow price of foreign aid.

Second, unifying the exchange rates, and cutting the export tax and import tariff are not only beneficial to the economy on efficiency grounds but also improve the income distribution by enhancing rural labor's real income. However, devaluing the official pound will actually reduce welfare if no taxes are increased and wheat policy remains unchanged. The moral is devaluation of the official pound should be accompanied by effective fiscal reform.

Third, the country's import tariff on final industrial goods (which contributes over half of the Sudan's indirect tax revenue) is above the maximum revenue rate. Thus, lowering it is consistent with higher government revenue in addition to improved efficiency and equity.

Fourth, replacement of these implicit and explicit trade taxes by a less distorting broadly-based domestic consumption tax would constitute a substantial spur to an improved standard of living or the ability of the Sudanese government to acquire foreign exchange to foster economic growth or repay debt.[19]

Fifth, any increase in Sudanese wheat production which comes at the expense of exportable agricultural production imposes a significant efficiency loss. In the 1980s, USAID tried to convince the Sudanese to privatize the wheat sector. Privatization of the Sudanese wheat is in effect a reduction of the official procurement percentage. Thus, USAID should be wary of this policy without accompanying it with its sister policy of a better exchange rate for agriculture.

Finally, our shadow prices together with our analysis of trade, tax, and agricultural policy reform consistently suggest that there is an unexploited scope for improving efficiency, equity, and revenue simultaneously for the Sudan through policies designed to facilitate export-oriented growth. Furthermore, unless the fiscal regime is improved, so that reliance on the free market exchange rate as a tax raising device is curtailed, the very high shadow prices which emerge imply that the government should shrink its role in activities which worsen its budget deficit.

NOTES

This paper is based on Han's (1988) PhD Thesis which was directed by Tower. Han is a consultant in Korea and Tower is a professor of economics at Duke University. Thanks go to Ohad Bauernfreund, Malcolm Gillis, Richard Hough, Kent Kimbrough, Anne Krueger, Tom Loo, Karim Nashashibi, Anne Pence, Hisanobu Shishido, and Jack Strauss for helpful discussions and comments on earlier drafts. Tower's interest in Sudan stemmed from consulting work he did there for USAID. He gratefully acknowledges a grant from the Walker Foundation of the Pittsburgh National Bank.

[1] For discussions of general equilibrium modeling for LDCs, see Tower (1984), Robinson (1986), and Tower and Loo (1989) in which we discuss the procedures used in this paper to debug the model.

[2] More detail is contained in Han (1988) and this paper's references to the Sudan.

[3] These exchange rates prevailed in 1985.

[4] Our macroeconomic model can be understood as follows. The private sector sells exportable-ag and buys agricultural intermediate inputs at a fixed price on the world market, earning D dollars, which it is required to surrender in exchange for P pounds at the official exchange rate. After paying taxes and buying goods and services from the government, it has P' pounds left. Since the private sector does not hoard pounds it seeks to spend P' pounds each period on dollars which it will then trade for imported industrial goods and intermediate inputs for industry and services. The government each period sells the D' dollars which it earned from agricultural transactions plus aid, in exchange for the P' pounds that the private sector wishes to sell at a market clearing rate called the free market rate. This free market rate will settle at P'/D' LS/$. Any increase in tax collections will decrease P' and automatically raise the value of the free market pound. Consequently, the government can peg the free market rate at a target level by adjusting its taxes.

[5] For more on Sudanese wheat see Awad (1983), Nashashibi (1980), Salih (1983), Salih and Afan (1986) and USAID (1985). In effect, we are pretending that the government gives ration tickets to households which entitles them to buy the bread from the bakeries. In fact, Tower found when he bought bread that Sudanese groceries and street vendors were meticulous about not overcharging for bread, but that they would run out at about 10AM. Thus, consumers, who in 1986 paid only $.06 (at the free market exchange rate) for a loaf of bread have an incentive to over purchase bread in anticipation of possible needs later in the day. Sometimes there was a queue at the bakery. The bread was cheap enough, so some Sudanese would eat only the crust. This means that in the real world, there are gains associated with raising the price of bread which we have not reckoned with. However, we cannot say how our failure to model this aspect of the wheat market affects our calculations of the desirability of additional wheat imports. Additional wheat supplies in the administered market will cause bakeries to run out later in the day and thereby cause less hoarding. Moreover, additional wheat will make bread available in rural areas where it was not available previously. On the other hand, the marginal utility of bread for those who actually get it is less than we have calculated it to be.

Rationing in the bread market is an important and interesting issue which awaits the efforts of someone with a better understanding of the Sudanese bakery sector than we can claim.

[6] Sudan is a classic case of a financially repressed economy. The government maintains a demand for its rapidly inflating currency by prohibiting the holding of foreign exchange and failing to foster the institutions and legal system which would enable a bond market to exist.

[7] For (non-traded) services the ERP is calculated defining the world output price equal to the domestic producer price. The negative ERP for services reflects the implicit import tariff on intermediate inputs into services due to the multiple exchange rate regime.

[8] The tariff on industrial goods is obtained by dividing import tariff revenue collected on these goods by the value of imports. We have ignored the additional distortions arising out of import licenses. Thus we underestimate the beneficial effects of liberalizing trade policy.

[9] The wheat tariff represents the proportion by which the average producer price exceeds the world price.

[10] For wheat, we varied the procurement proportion. For exportable-ag we varied the export tax. For industrial demand we varied the excise tax on industry. For industrial supply and industrial import demand we varied the industrial import tariff. For services we varied the excise tax on services.

[11] If reliable econometric evidence had been available on import demand and export supply elasticities, we would have made domestic and imported industrial and agricultural goods imperfect substitutes in domestic consumption and adjusted the elasticity of substitution until the model replicated the extraneously estimated import demand elasticity.

[12] Incremental deadweight loss as a % of increased real revenues.

[13] Recall that all intermediate inputs are imported.

[14] Also see Tower and Pursell (1986), Fane (1991) and Ghosh et *al.* (1997).

[15] The only difference between administered wheat and free market wheat in the table is that when the government sells a unit of the latter it receives a higher price and therefore balances its budget with a larger tax cut.

[16] Consequently, he welfare benefit of a 1 % increase in the administered wheat price is minus the sum of lines 14, 15 and 20. In the proportional income tax case it is zero, for by assumption its only impact is on tax revenue.

[17] Of course, in a monetary economy currency depreciation is a necessary element of inflationary finance if growth of the money stock is not to be accompanied by increasingly severe controls on international trade or reserve losses.

[18] The 1.12 arises from the 12% tariff discussed in Table 11.1.

[19] For further discussion see Due (1983).

REFERENCES

Awad, Mohamed H. "Why is the Breadbasket Empty?" Development Studies and Research Centre Seminar No. 40, University of Khartoum, 1983.

Due, John F. "The Budget Position and the Urgent Need for Tax Reform in the Sudan." Typescript, University of Illinois, 1983.

Fane, George. "The Social Opportunity Cost of Foreign Exchange: A Partial Defense of Harberger *et al.*" *The Economic Record*, December 1991, 68(203), pp. 307–316.

Gan, K.-P. and Tower, E. "A General Equilibrium Cost-Benefit Approach to Policy Reform and Project Evaluation in Malaysia." *Singapore Economic Review*. April 1987, 32(1), pp. 46–61.

Ghosh, Madanmohan, Hutton, Eric and Whalley, John. "Multiple Constraint Relaxation and the Shadow Price of Foreign Exchange." typescript, 1997.

Grossman, Gene M. "An Evaluation of Trade Policy in the Sudan," Paper prepared for USAID, 1985.

Han, Kiyoun. *Trade, Tax, and Agricultural Policy in a Highly Distorted Economy: The Case of Sudan*. PhD Dissertation, Duke University, 1988.

Krueger, A. O. *Foreign Trade Regimes and Economic Development: Liberalization Attempts and Consequences*, Ballinger Publishing Co. for the National Bureau of Economic Research, 1978.

Loo, Thomas and Tower, E. "Agricultural Protectionism and the Less Developed Countries: The Relationship Between Agricultural Prices, Debt Servicing Capacities and the Need for Development Aid." Chapter 2 of *Macroeconomic Consequences of Farm Support Policies*. A.B. Stoeckel, David Vincent and Sandy Cuthbertson (eds.). Durham: Duke University Press, 1989, pp. 64–93, summarized on p. 59 of *The Economist*, June 4, 1998.

Ministry of Agriculture and Natural Resources, Sudan. *Agricultural Situation & Outlook: Annual Report*, August 1985.

Nashashibi, Karim. "A Supply Framework for Exchange Reform in Developing Countries: The Experience of Sudan." *IMF Staff Papers*, March 1980, 27(1), pp. 24–79.

Robinson, Sherman. "Multisectoral Models of Developing Countries: A Survey." in H.G. Chenery and T. N. Srinivasan, eds., *Handbook of Development Economics*, Amsterdam: North Holland Publishing Company, 1986.

Salih, Siddig A. *The Impacts of the Government Agricultural Policies on Domestic Wheat Production in the Sudan*. PhD Dissertation, Duke University, 1983.

Salih, Siddig A. and Afan, Khalid. "Price System and the Strategy on Subsidizing Staple Commodities." Paper presented at the Conference of Macro-Economic Policies, Khartoum, 1986.

Tower, E. *Effective Protection, Domestic Resource Cost and Shadow Prices: A General Equilibrium Perspective*. World Bank Staff Working Paper, No. 664, 1984.

Tower, E. and Pursell, G. *On Shadow Pricing*. World Bank Staff Working Paper, No. 792, 1986.

Tower, E. and Pursell, G. "On Shadow Pricing Labor and Foreign Exchange," *Oxford Economic Papers*, June 1987), pp. 318–32.

Tower, E. and Loo, Thomas. "On Using Computable General Equilibrium Models to Facilitate Tax, Tariff, and Other Policy Reforms in Less Developed Countries." chapter 11 of Malcolm S. Gillis (ed.), *Tax Reform in Developing Countries*. Durham: Duke University Press, 1989, pp. 347–390.

Tower, E. "Cost Benefit Analysis and Project Appraisal," Chapter 30 of David Greenaway, Michael Bleaney and Ian M. T. Stewart (eds.), *Companion to Contemporary Economic Thought*. London and New York: Routledge, 1991, pp. 614–633.

USAID. *Food for Development: Program Activity Identification Document*. 1985.

World Bank. *Sudan: Investing for Economic Stabilization and Structural Change*. 1982.

World Bank. *Sudan Pricing Policies and Structural Balances*. 1983.

World Bank. *World Bank Country Study: Sudan Pricing Policies and Structural Balances*. 1985.

World Bank. *World Development Report*, various issues. 1983–87.

CHAPTER 12

FOREIGN ASSISTANCE AND DEVELOPMENT IN BANGLADESH

Anisul M. Islam

INTRODUCTION

With a large population (about 120 million) living in a small land area (55,000 sq. miles) and with a low annual per capita income (about U.S. $250), Bangladesh is classified as one of the poorest countries in the world. Because of its precarious economic condition, various donor countries and agencies have provided the country with substantial amounts of public foreign assistance. Since its independence in 1971 to the year 1992, Bangladesh has received a cumulative sum of 24 billion dollars in foreign aid (grants and loans) from all donor countries and agencies combined (ERD 1993). In 1992 alone, it received a sum of $1,611 million in foreign aid (ERD 1992) which constitutes about $14 per capita and about 7 percent of its 1992 GDP. More importantly, foreign aid constitutes an extremely high proportion (about 90 percent) of the country's development budget.

Bangladesh thus provides a test case for examining the role and effectiveness of foreign aid in promoting economic development in the context of a developing economy. The objectives of the paper are to study the following issues dealing with foreign aid to Bangladesh: (i) the need for foreign aid; (ii) trends in aid flows; (iii) types of aid flows; (iv) aid dependence; (v) sources of aid flows; (vi) costs and terms of aid; (vii) the debt burden; and (viii) the effectiveness and productivity of aid flows.

NEED FOR FOREIGN AID: THE TWO GAPS

Foreign aid has been used to overcome the following two critical gaps: (i) the domestic savings-investment gap; and (ii) the export-import gap (also known as the foreign exchange gap). The former is shown in Figure 12.1 as the difference between SY (domestic savings-GDP ratio) and IY (investment-GDP ratio). The graph shows that the gap has remained quite high over the years. In 1989, for example, the IY ratio was 11.7% whereas the SY ratio was less than 2%. Note that the SY ratio has remained quite low since independence. This fact indicates that the country has failed to generate adequate resources from domestic sources to finance it's development activities. The foreign exchange gap is shown in Figure 12.2 by the difference between TXY (export-GDP ratio) and TMY (import-GDP ratio). The import ratio remained consistently at a much higher level than the export ratio for all the years since 1972, and the gap reached a peak in 1982 (TMY of 21.8% minus TXY of 7.5% = trade gap of 14.3%). The gap declined somewhat after 1982 but it still remains at a high level (with TMY of 16.5% and TXY of 8.7%, the trade gap was 7.8% of GDP in 1990). Thus the extent of the two above mentioned gaps indicate the continuing need for foreign assistance to overcome these obstacles.

Figure 12.1. Savings and investment ratios (% of GDP).

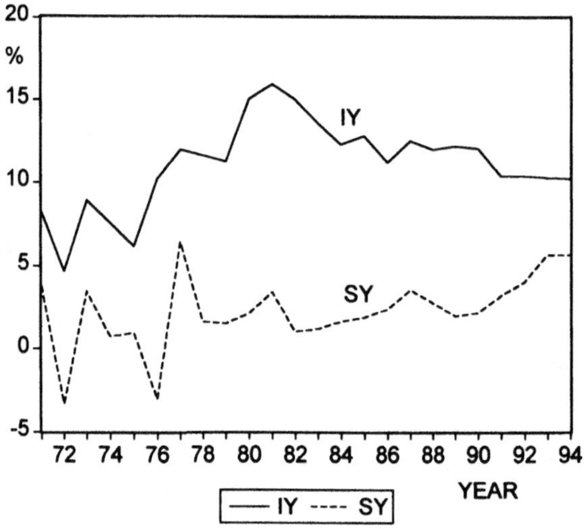

Figure 12.2. Export and import ratios (% of GDP).

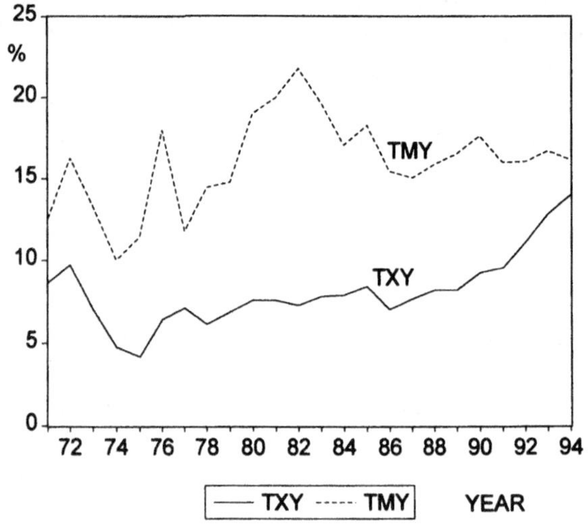

TRENDS IN VARIOUS TYPES OF AID FLOWS

Trend in Aggregate Aid Flows

As already mentioned earlier, Bangladesh has received a considerable amount of foreign aid over the years. From 1971 to 1992, it received a cumulative sum of 24 billion dollars in foreign aid from various bilateral and multilateral sources combined (ERD, 1993). In nominal dollars, the amount of aid flows has increased (with considerable fluctuations from year to year) from 270.8 million dollars in 1972 to 1,611 million dollars in 1992 (see TAIDN in Figure 12.3). Although the nominal flows have increased, the real (inflation adjusted) aid flows have declined in recent years. Deflating nominal flows by the import price index, the real dollar aid flows were calculated and are presented as TAIDR in Figure 12.3. The real dollar aid flows have also fluctuated considerably from 1972 to 1978, and then started to decline since the 1980s.

BILATERAL VERSUS MULTILATERAL AID FLOWS

Aid from both bilateral (such as aid from the U.S.) and multilateral (such as aid from the World Bank) sources have increased over the years. Bilateral aid has increased from \$232 million in 1972 to \$912 million in 1990 compared to multilateral aid which has increased from \$39 million to \$898 million over the same period. In terms of relative share, bilateral aid constituted 86% of aid flows in 1972 and only 14% was multilateral. However, in recent years, the share of both types of aid has changed to around 50% each (see STAIDB and STAIDM in Figure 12.4), thus indicating a trend towards growing importance of multilateral aid in financing development programs.

Figure 12.3. Aid flows in nominal and real dollars (m. US$).

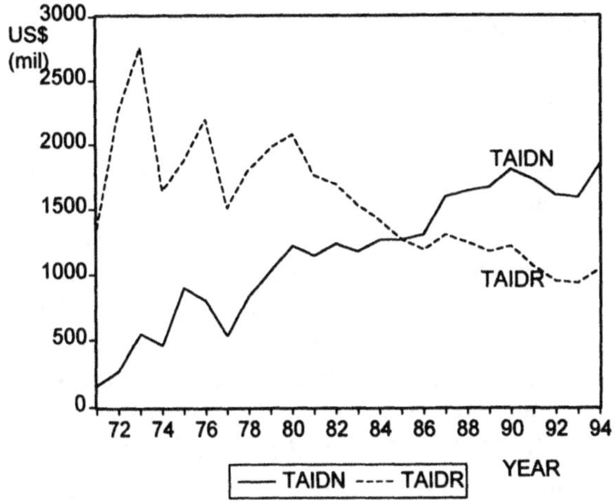

Figure 12.4. Share of bilateral and multilateral flows (% of aid).

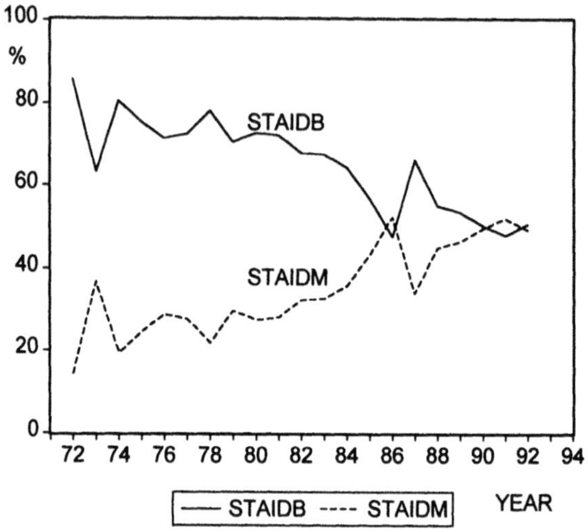

Aid Flows: Loans Versus Grants

Aggregate flows can also be classified into concessional loans and grants based on repayment requirements and concessionality of aid. The former is a type of assistance in which payment of interest and repayment of principal are required but with a lower than market rate of interest and/or longer maturity period. No repayment is required of the latter type (i.e. grants). During the early years, Bangladesh received a large proportion of aid in the form of grants (90% grants and 10% loans in 1972 (STAIDG and STAIDL in Figure 12.5). In recent years, the proportion of grants has significantly declined to about 58% in 1990, while the proportion of loans has correspondingly increased to 42% (see Figure 12.5).

SOURCES OF AID FLOWS

Aid Share By Major Donor Groups

During the initial years after independence, Bangladesh received foreign aid from only a handful of countries and international agencies. Later, it has successfully diversified its aid sources. In 1990, for example, Bangladesh received bilateral aid from thirteen DAC (Development Assistance Committee) countries, six international multilateral agencies, five oil producing countries (including the OPEC), and seven socialist block (such as the former USSR) and other countries (such as India and Pakistan). The share of total aid by four broad categories are shown in Figure 12.6. From 1972 to 1992, the DAC countries (see SADAC in Figure 12.6)) and the multilateral agencies (see STAIDM in Figure 12.6) were the two major donor groups providing aid to Bangladesh, distantly followed by the two other groups representing oil producing group (STAIDO in Figure 12.6) and the socialist block (see STAIDS in

Figure 12.5. Share of grants (STAIDG) and loans (STAIDL) (% of aid).

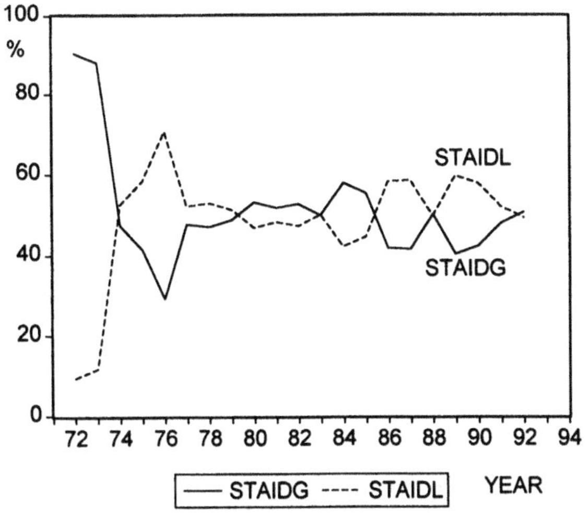

Figure 12.6. Aid share by major donor groups (% of aid by group).

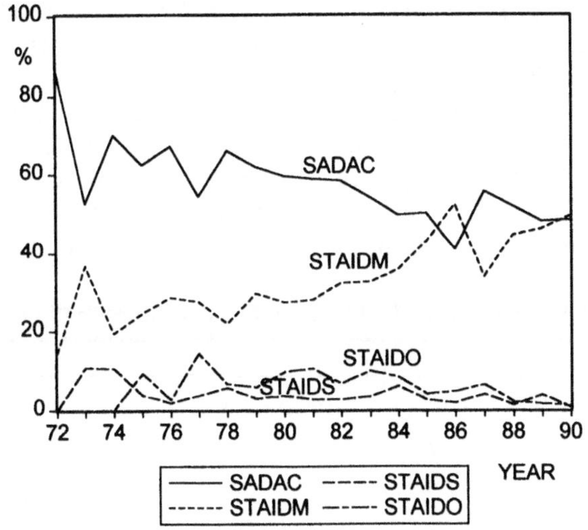

Figure 12.6). In 1990, for example, the aid share of the two former groups were 48% and 49% of total aid respectively while the combined share of the remaining two groups was less than 2% (oil producers including the OPEC: 1.02% and the Socialist block: 0.7%).

A few other interesting changes should be noted here. Firstly, the share of aid from DAC countries has significantly declined over the years from 86% in 1972 to about 48% in 1990. As a group, its ranking declined from the first to the second position. Secondly, the share of aid from multilateral sources has increased substantially over the same period from 14% in 1972 to about 50% in 1990, making it the largest donor group. Thirdly, the oil producing countries including the OPEC became the distant third largest aid group since 1975. Although remained third in ranking, the aid share from this group has continued to decline since 1983, dropping to a meagre 1% by 1990.

Finally, the socialist group became the distant fourth largest aid group since 1975 (STAIDS), the year which marked the end of Mujib regime in Bangladesh. The relative decline of the socialist block aid can partly be explained by the fact that the successive governments during the post-Mujib period have had a stronger preference for aid from the western donor countries and multilateral agencies over the socialist block countries (see Sobhan, 1982). The bureaucrats and politicians consequently acted to develop stronger aid relationships with those countries/agencies. However, it is also to be noted that the socialist countries in the seventies and eighties were not in a good financial position to offer much aid to Bangladesh. With the dismantling of communism in the USSR and other East European countries, the prospect of aid flowing from this group became bleak.

Aid Share of Individual DAC Countries

Focussing now on the aid share of individual DAC countries, it is obvious that Japan has replaced the U.S. as the largest aid donor country since 1986 (see SJAP in Figure 12.7). Japan's share in total aid (shown by SJAP) has increased from a meagre 2.7% in 1973 to 18.5% in 1990. On the other hand, the U.S. was the largest donor country up until 1979 (see SUSA in Figure 12.7). Reaching a peak in 1976 (35% of total aid), the U.S. share declined significantly to about 8.0 % in 1986, making it the second ranking donor country. Its share continued to decline further, and by 1989, with a share of 5.5%, her ranking declined to the third position after Canada. The aid share from Canada (SCAN in Figure 12.7) has increased from a low of 2.7% in 1972 to a recent high of 5.7% in 1990, slightly over the U.S. share for this year.

Figure 12.7. Aid share of individual DAC donor countries (% of aid).

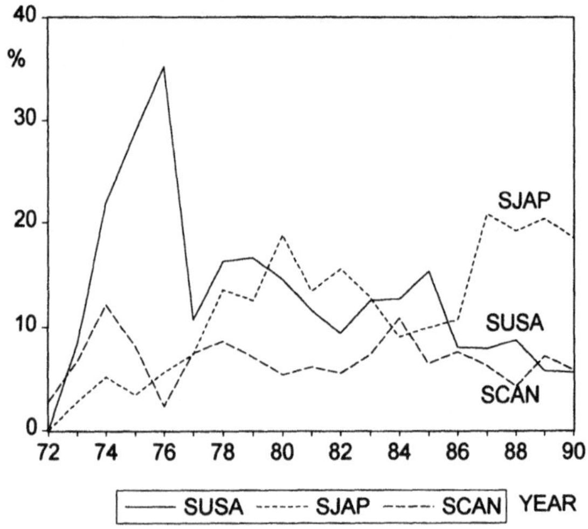

The share of aid from three other major DAC donors i.e., the United Kingdom (SUK), the Federal Republic of Germany (SFRG) and France (SFRA) from 1972 to 1990 are not shown to save space. This graph shows that the share of U.K. has declined over the years since 1977. Consequently, its ranking declined from the fourth to the fifth position (contributing 2.9% in 1990). The share of Germany fluctuated considerably over the years and currently it has become the fourth largest donor country since 1985. The share of France has also fluctuated considerably and, with its recent share of 2.03%, ranks 6th in aid giving.

Aid Share of Individual Multilateral Agencies

Within the multilateral aid agencies, the International Development Agency (IDA) of the World bank has emerged as the largest provider of aid (25.6% of total aid in 1990 (see SIDA in Figure 12.8) since 1974 and has maintained its first ranking until today. The share of the Asian Development Bank was small until 1984 (around 4%) but it has gradually emerged as the second largest donor agency since 1985, providing about 15% of total aid by 1990 (see SADB in Figure 12.8). The UN system was the largest supplier of aid until 1973, remaining in the second position from 1975 to 1984, and then dropping further to the third position since 1985, providing about 3.2% of aid in 1990 (see SUNS in Figure 12.8). Finally, the European Economic Community (EEC) appears to be the fourth largest provider of aid, supplying around 2.6% of aid in 1990 (see SEEC in Figure 12.8). The other multilateral agencies such as the UNICEF (1.3% in 1990), the OPEC (0.5% in 1990), the IDB (0.7% in 1990), and IFAD (0.4% in 1990) contributed only a small proportion of total aid flows.

Figure 12.8. Aid share of individual multilateral agencies (% of aid).

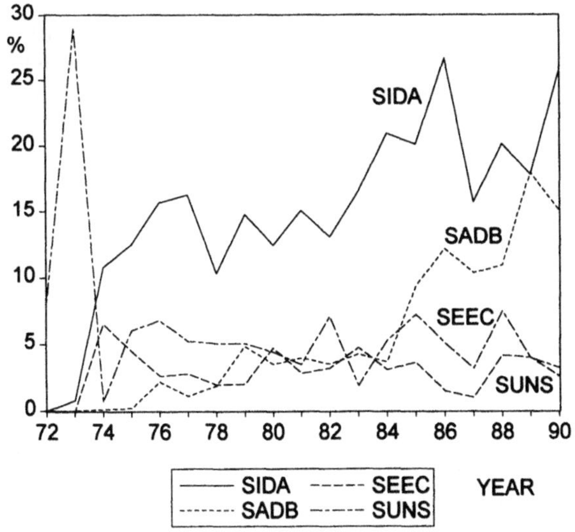

AID DEPENDENCE

As already mentioned, Bangladesh has relied heavily upon foreign capital since its independence. With the passage of time, the dependence on foreign capital has deepened. The following four indicators are used to show this trend: (i) aid-GDP ratio (AGDPR); (ii) aid-imports (of goods and services) ratio (AMGSR); (iii) aid-investment ratio (AIR); and (iv) aid-development budget ratio (ADBR).

Aid to GDP ratio (AGDPR in Figure 12.9) has remained consistently high for Bangladesh since 1971. The ratio reached its highest level in 1976 (11.4%). Although the ratio has declined somewhat in recent years, it still appears high (about 8% in 1990) compared to other countries such as India (around 2% (Sukhatme in Krueger et al. 1989, p. 206)), Pakistan (around 4% (Islam, 1972, p. 503)), and Korea (around 4% (Krueger and Ruttan in Krueger et al. 1989, p. 228)). Aid to imports (AMGSR in Fig. 12.9) ratio has also remained quite high over the years (48% in 1990) which indicates that about half of total imports were being financed by foreign aid.

The aid-investment ratio (AIR in Fig. 9) shows that foreign aid has financed about 70% of all investments in 1990 compared to India (5.3% for 1982 (Sukhatme in Krueger et al. 1989, p. 206)). More disturbing is the fact that aid has financed about 96% of the development budget of this country (ADBR in Fig. 12.9) compared to 17% for India (Sukhatme in Krueger et al. 1989, p. 206). Based on the above indicators and their trends, it is clear that these ratios have remained substantially high. They clearly indicate that Bangladesh has relied heavily on foreign capital in the past, and that it will continue to do so in the foreseeable future. One implication is that this heavy dependence may cause severe balance of payments difficulties in the future.

Figure 12.9. Aid as % of GDP, imports, investment and dev. budget

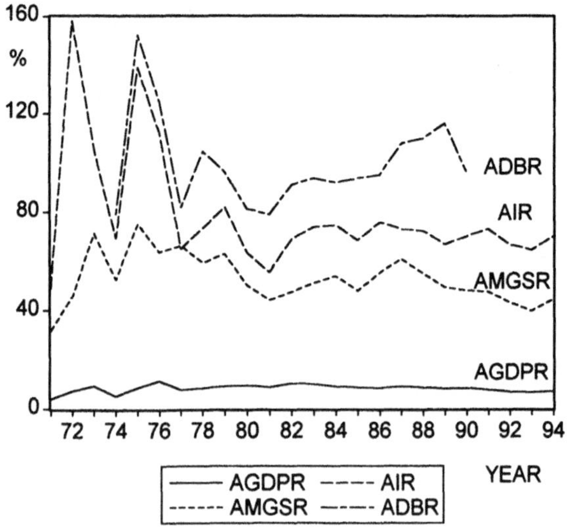

TERMS OF AID

The terms of aid can be analyzed by focussing on the average interest rate on loans, average age of loan maturity, average grace period, and average grant element in loans. The difference in the terms of aid between the official and private flows will also be discussed.

The average interest rate on official loans (OAI in Figure 12.10, left scale) remained below 2% while the average interest rate on private loans (PAI in Figure 12.10, left scale) was at a much higher level (7%). The average interest rate, however, underestimates the true cost of loans. The true cost is much higher because of aid tying of various kinds (e.g., project tying, source tying and reverse tying) practiced by most donor countries/agencies. The latter cost is presumably higher because a recipient country is given very little flexibility or freedom to purchase inputs (or supplies) from cheapest sources or to select the most appropriate technology or projects (see Sukhatme in Krueger et al. 1989, p. 211 and Bhagwati in Bhagwati and Eckaus 1970, pp. 235–293 for details). The information on the nature and extent of aid tying are not available for Bangladesh and, therefore, any estimate of the true cost of aid could not be provided.

The average age of loan maturity was around 37 years for official loans (OAM in Figure 12.10, right scale) and that of private loans was 11 years (PAM in Figure 12.10, right scale). The average grace period for official loans was around 9 years while that of private loans was 3.5 years (World Debt Table, 1994–95). Finally, the average percentage grant element in official loans was around 70% while that of private loans was only 15% (World Debt Tables, 1994–95).

It is thus clear that the terms of official flows in all respects were much favorable than those of private loans. Until recent years, Bangladesh was successful in obtaining a large proportion of aid in the form of official flows at very favorable terms. However, as the international aid climate deteriorates, and to the extent that the

Figure 12.10. Interest rate and aid maturity: Official vs. private.

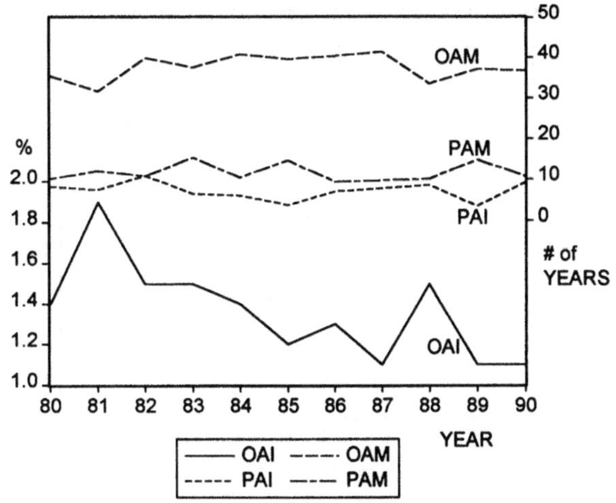

country borrows at a larger scale from private sources (e.g. supplier's credit), the terms of aid is bound to deteriorate in the future. It may put further pressure on the country's external balances and debt burden.

THE BURDEN OF FOREIGN DEBT

The total outstanding debt (TOD in Figure 12.11) and the total outstanding debt per capita (TODP in Figure 12.11) have dramatically increased over the years. The TOD in 1974 was only 501 million dollars (6.5 dollars per capita) which increased to 10,680 million dollars (97 dollars per capita) by 1990, an increase of about 2,031% over the 17 year period. This trend is expected to continue in the future.

Expressing TOD as a percentage of GDP, exports, and total foreign exchange receipts (measured as sum of exports of goods, services, and worker's remittances), the resulting TODY, TODX, and TODR ratios are shown in Figure 12.12. The TODY ratio has increased from 5.7% in 1974 to a high of 47% in 1990. For 1985, Sukhatme reports this ratio to be 15% for India, 2.6% for China, 32% for Pakistan, 49% for Sri Lanka, and 43% for South Korea (Krueger et al. 1989, p. 216). Thus, the ratio for Bangladesh appears to be higher than some developing countries in Asia. In addition, the TODX ratio has increased from 119% in 1974 to 542% in 1990, and the TODR ratio has increased from 114% in 1974 to 385% in 1990. The above analysis shows a high and rapidly rising trend in the debt burden of the country.

A related question is whether this rising debt burden will cause any serious problem in debt service payments (interest plus principal) in the future. The total debt service payments (TDS) as a percentage of GDP, exports, and foreign exchange receipts were calculated and are reported as TDSY, TDSX, and TDSR in Figure 12.13. Note that these ratios indicate a country's ability to service its debt. It appears that TDSY remained at a reasonably low level, increasing from 0.2% in 1974 to 2.5% in

Figure 12.11. Total and per capita foreign debt (TOD and TODP).

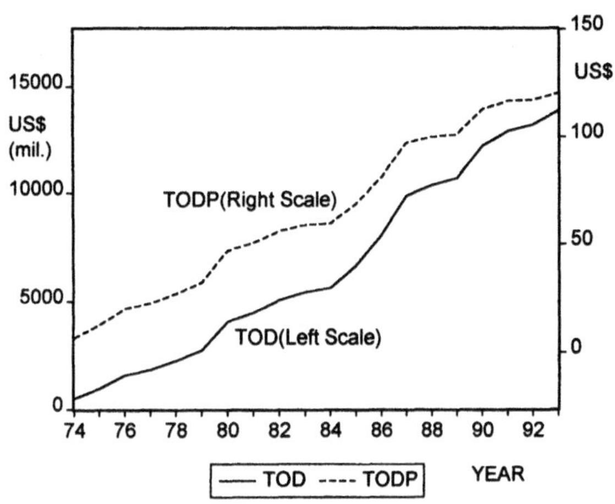

1990. However, TDSX increased from a low of 4% in 1974 to a peak of 46% in 1981 and then declined to about 28% in 1990. This ratio for Bangladesh is somewhat higher than some other Asian countries. For 1985, this ratio was reported by Sukhatme to be 13% for India, 7.8% for China, 30% for Pakistan, 15% for Srilanka and 22% for South Korea (Krueger et al. 1989, p. 216). It appears that interest payments has steadily increased over the years, while the repayments of principal has started to decline since 1985. The reason for this decline is not known. This trend may significantly add to the total debt burden of the country. Because of this decline in principal repayments, the debt service payments has slowed down in since 1987).

Figure 12.12. Foreign debt as % of GDP, exports, and receipts.

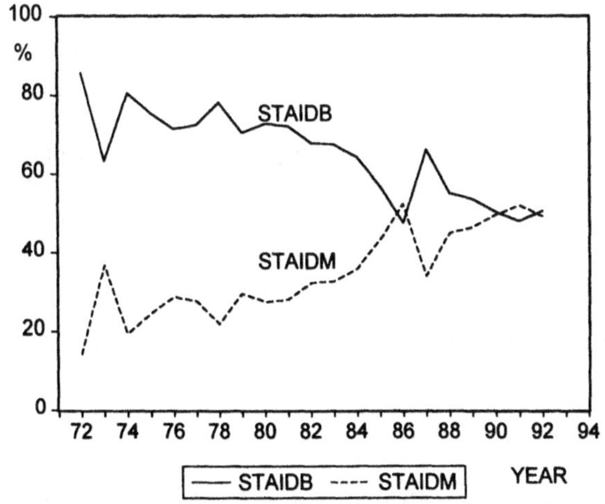

Figure 12.13. Debt service as % of GDP, exports, and receipts.

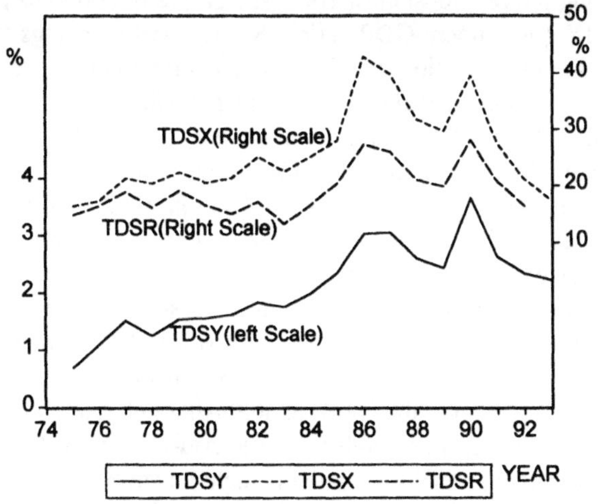

The interest payments as a percentage of GDP, exports, and foreign exchange receipts show the following: The interest payments as % of GDP has increased from 0.09% in 1974 to a peak of 0.65% in 1989 and then declined somewhat to 0.59% in 1990. The interest payments as % exports has increased from 2% in 1974 to a peak of 8.5% in 1988 and then declined to 6.8% in 1990. Finally, the interest payments as % total foreign exchange receipts has risen from 1.9% in 1974 to a peak of 5.6% in 1988 and then declined to 4.9% in 1990. Thus, the interest payment ratios have remained at reasonably low levels over the years and have even declined in recent years (in spite of a larger volume of interest payments). This was possible partly because of the fact that a large proportion of aid was contracted at very favorable interest rates, and partly because of a rapid rise in exports of goods, services and worker's remittances (the latter items, appearing in the denominator of the ratios, rose faster than the interest payments).

The principal repayments as percentage of GDP has increased from 0.1% in 1974 to a peak of 1.96% in 1983 and then declined to 0.96% in 1990. The same as % of exports also increased from 2% in 1974 to a peak of 24.2% in 1983 and then gradually declined to 11.16% in 1990. Finally, the principal repayments as % of total foreign receipts has increased from 2% in 1974 to a peak of 17.02% in 1985, then declined to 7.9% in 1990. Again these ratios appear to remain at reasonably low levels. However, the decline in recent years in these ratios is partly due to the decline in repayment of principals and partly due to the rapid growth of exports of goods, services, and worker's remittances.

AID EFFECTIVENESS

Aid, Saving, Investment, and Growth: Some Descriptive Indicators

Before providing the econometric results, this section provides some descriptive indicators showing the relationship of GR (growth rate of real GDP) with some key variables such IY (investment-GDP ratio), SY (domestic savings-GDP ratio) and AGDPR (foreign aid-GDP ratio), all of which may affect GR. Figure 12.14 presents these relationships. It appears that GR has fluctuated widely from a low of –13.9% in 1972 to a high of 12% in 1976, with an average growth rate of 3.5% over the period 1972 to 1989. Note that the fluctuation in GR occurred in spite of a relatively steady IY ratio, which has varied between a low of 4.7% in 1972 to a high of 15.96% in 1981, with an average of 11.3% over the entire period. This graph shows that the IY ratio is not strongly correlated with GR.

For further analysis, IY is decomposed into domestic resources (SY) and foreign resources (AGDPR) and their separate relationships with GR examined. The SY ratio remained quite small, varying from a low of –3.35% in 1972 to a high of 7% in 1977, with an average of 2.98% over the entire period. Although relatively small, this ratio appears to be strongly correlated with GR. The Aid-GDP ratio (AGDPR in Figure 12.14), on the other hand, remained relatively high; however, it has displayed considerable fluctuation from year to year from a low of 5.26% in 1974 to a high of 11.4% in 1976, with an average of 8.8% over the entire period. A look at this graph indi-

Figure 12.14. GDP growth (%) and aid, investment, and savings (% of GDP).

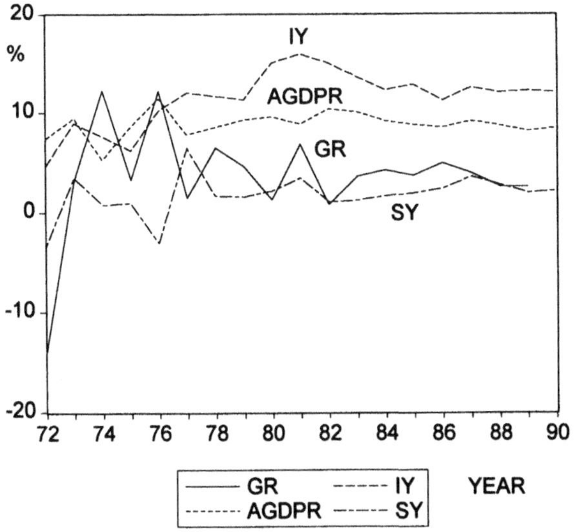

cates that the relationship between AGDPR and GR is not very strong, i.e. the GR ratio remained low and it fluctuated quite significantly in spite of a high and relatively stable AGDPR.

The Foreign Aid Controversy

The issue of foreign aid has always been a highly controversial subject. The debate on this issue dates back to the 1950s when the United States, then a capital surplus country, started an ambitious foreign assistance program to help the developing countries achieve rapid economic transformation. During the same time, many capital deficient developing countries adopted rapid economic growth as their most important national economic goal. These countries resorted to foreign capital as the primary means to achieve that goal. Unfortunately, the growth experience with foreign aid has not always been very satisfactory. The apparent failure of foreign aid to bring about significant prosperity led to a series of debates among economists and policy makers in both developed and developing countries on its effectiveness for promoting economic development.

A large body of literature exists on this subject covering different viewpoints, ideological orientation and theoretical and empirical results. A review of the existing literature indicates two easily identifiable views, i.e. the traditional pro-aid view and the radical (and conservative) anti-aid view. The pro-aid view contends that capital imports exert significant beneficial effects on the recipient countries. It is argued that foreign capital not only augments (complements) domestic resources, but also helps them mitigate severe foreign exchange constraints, provides access to modern technology, capital equipments, spare parts and managerial skills, and allows easier access to foreign markets, all positively contributing towards economic growth (Chenery 1960; Chenery and Adelman 1966; Chenery and Eckstein 1970; Chenery and Strout 1966; Clark 1957; Papanek 1972; 1973, Rosenstein-Rodan 1971, among others). In this context, it is also argued that capital flowing from the surplus countries with relatively low rates of return to the deficit countries with relatively high rates of return (in developing countries) would bring about an improved allocation of world resources.

However, the growth experience of many capital importing developing countries over the last four decades does not conform to the conventional wisdom. Some countries may have even witnessed a negative experience with foreign capital flows. This empirical phenomenon along with other adverse effects of aid led to the emergence of the anti-aid view on the subject. It is interesting to note that the anti-aid view is shared by both the radical and conservative views (based on different reasons, however). According to this view, foreign capital exerts significant negative effects on the recipient countries because it substitutes (rather than complements) domestic resources, helps import inappropriate technology, distorts domestic income distribution, and is biased towards a bigger, inefficient, and corrupt government in those countries (for the radical view, see Frank 1969; Griffin 1970; Griffin and Enos 1970; Rahman 1967; 1968, and Weisskoff 1972a; 1972b, among others, and for the conservative view, see Bauer 1971; Bauer and Yamey (1981); Bovard 1986; and Friedman in Bhagwati and Eckaus 1970, pp. 63–77, among others). On the issue of whether foreign capital acts as a substitute for domestic capital, the empirical results are mixed at best (Griffin 1970; Griffin and Enos 1970; Gupta 1970; Gupta-Islam (1983); Rahman 1968; Papanek 1973, among others). For Bangladesh also, the empirical results are mixed (Alamgir 1974 and Ahmad 1986).

From a pragmatic point of view, one can argue that the role of foreign capital should be evaluated based on a careful comparison of benefits and costs of such inflows. Obviously this objective approach emphasizes the quantification of the effects of foreign flows on the recipient economies. This study takes a pragmatic view on the subject and intends to examine the quantitative impact of foreign capital on economic growth using an improved theoretical and econometric framework and a unique data set on Bangladesh.

Effectiveness of Aid: The Theoretical Framework

The theoretical framework outlined below draws heavily from the author's previous work (Islam 1992; Gupta-Islam 1983). It is basically derived from the supply side of the economy. An explanation of the behavioural equations forming the model is in order. Equation (12.1) depicts the aggregate production function for a country involving capital stock (K) and the available labor supply (L) as two inputs, where Y stands for real Gross Domestic Product (GDP). The usual regularity conditions are specified in equation (12.2) to ensure that the production function is well-behaved. These conditions imply, among other things, positive but diminishing marginal productivities of factor inputs.

$$Y = f(K, L) \tag{12.1}$$

$$f_1 > 0;\ f_2 > 0;\ f_{12} < 0;\ f_{22} < 0; \tag{12.2}$$

Totally differentiating equation (12.1), dividing both sides by Y, rearranging terms, and assuming (dk/dt = I, where I stands for Investment, we obtain the following empirically estimable form (the mathematical derivation is not shown):

$$GR = a + b\,(IY) + c\,(GL) \tag{12.3}$$

where GR stands for the annual rate of growth of real GDP, "a" is the intercept term representing the effects of excluded variables (including technological change), IY stands for the investment-GDP ratio, and GL stands for the annual growth rate of the labor force. The coefficient of (IY) measures the marginal productivity of investment and the coefficient of GL reflects the share of labor in the GDP. Since data on GL was not available, following Gupta (1975), Gupta-Islam (1983) and Ram (1986), population growth rate was used as a proxy for it. Replacing GL by population growth (PG), and adding a stochastic error term (U1), one obtains:

$$GR = a + b\,(IY) + c\,(PG) + U1 \tag{12.4}$$

Equation (12.4) is the final equation which was subjected to econometric estimation. Several other versions of equation (12.4) were also estimated based on disaggregating the IY variable into its specific components such as investment arising from domestic sources and those arising from foreign sources. Investment from domestic sources was proxied by SY and that from foreign sources by AGDPR. Equation (12.5) represents this modification:

$$GR = d + e\,(SY) + f\,(AGDPR) + g\,(PG) + U2 \tag{12.5}$$

where U2 is the error term. Note that foreign direct investment was ignored because Bangladesh received a negligible amount of it since its independence.

AGDPR was decomposed further into grants as a proportion of GDP (GRNTDY) and loans as a proportion of GDP (LOANDY) in order to quantify their separate effects on GR. With this modification, the following equation was obtained:

$$GR = h + i\,(SY) + j\,(GRNTDY) + k\,(LOANDY) + l\,(PG) + U3 \tag{12.6}$$

Alternatively, AGDPR was decomposed into three components as food aid (FTDY), commodity aid (CTDY) and project aid (PTDY), all expressed as a proportion of GDP. The resulting form is given as:

$$GR = m + n\,(SY) + o\,(FTDY) + p\,(CTDY) + q\,(PTDY) + r\,(PG) + U4 \tag{12.7}$$

EFFECTIVENESS OF AID: EMPIRICAL RESULTS

Annual time-series data covering the period 1972 to 1990 were used in this study. Data construction was a major task in this project because of the non-availability of a consistent and easily comparable data set. Data were collected from a number sources such the publications of the Government of Bangladesh, The Bangladesh Bank, the World Bank, The I.M.F. and the U.N. Careful attention was given to check the consistency in the data.

Equations (12.4–12.7) provide the basis for econometric estimation. These equations were initially estimated by the Ordinary Least Squares (OLS) method. The residuals were then tested for the presence of autocorrelation by applying the Durbin-Watson test. This test does not indicate the presence of any serious autocorrelation in the residuals. Therefore, OLS estimates were used for the interpretation of the empirical results.

It is possible that the above equations suffer from simultaneous equations bias because some explanatory variables may not be truly exogenous. For example, the dependent variable GR may influence IY, SY, and AIDDY (including its various components) in addition to being influenced by them (Gupta 1975; and Gupta-Islam 1983). In order to minimize this problem, we have also estimated the above four equations after replacing the current values of the explanatory variables by their lagged values. These equations were again estimated by the OLS method and were tested for autocorrelation. The Durbin-Watson test does not reveal any significant autocorrelation in the residuals. Therefore, the OLS estimates were used for further analysis. Note that the lack of any good instruments prevented us from applying any simultaneous equations techniques (e.g. 2SLS method). Thus, each one of the above four equations have two regression estimates, one using current values of the explanatory variables and the other using their lagged values. A careful examination of all eight estimated equations (Table 1) indicates that the performance of some of the equations were not very satisfactory. This judgement was made on the basis of R^2 values, F values, and the sign and magnitude of the regression coefficients. The unsatisfactory results included equation (4.1) with the current and (4.2) with the lagged regressors, equation (5.1) with the current regressors, and equation (7.1) with the current regressors. Poor performance of equations (4.1) and (4.2) may be partly attributable to the presence of some collinearity between IY and PG (simple correlation coefficient (r) = –0.72).

Somewhat satisfactory results were obtained from the remaining estimates. These include equation (5.2) with lagged regressors (R^2 = .40 and F= 2.73), equation (6.1) with current regressors (R^2 = 0.55 ; F = 3.79) and equation (6.2) with lagged regressors (R^2 = .41 and F = 1.88) and equation (7.2) with lagged regressors (R^2 = .62 and F = 3.27). The F values indicate that overall regressions were statistically significant. The general conclusions that follow will therefore be based on these latter estimates. It is to be noted that the R^2 values were not very high but can be considered as reasonably acceptable. However, one needs to keep in mind that a substantial proportion of the variation in the dependent variable could not be explained by the regressors. It is possible that some important explanatory variables (e.g. technology and/or demand factors) were missing from the set of regressors and/or there exists serious measurement problems with the data. We now proceed to interpret the empirical results keeping these limitations in mind.

Focussing on the issue of the relative contribution of domestic *vis-a-vis* foreign resources in promoting economic growth, it appears that the domestic resources as proxied by SY performs better than foreign resources. In most regressions, the savings ratio came out with a positive and statistically significant (at 5% level) coefficients. Similar results were obtained in other studies as well (Ahmad 1983; Islam

Table 12.1. Regression results.

9.95 – 3.13 PG + 0.11 IY ; R^2 = 0.11 ; F = 0.90 ; D.W. = 1.71 ; N = 17	(4.1
(0.63) (–0.80) (0.16)	
–2.06 + 1.51 PG(–1) + 0.18 IY(–1) ; R^2 = 0.01 ; F = 0.07; D.W. = 1.60 ; N = 16	(4.2
(–0.13) (0.36) (0.27)	
10.74 – 3.29 PG + 0.07 SY + 0.07 AIDDY ; R^2=0.11 ; F=0.56; D.W.=1.77; N=17	(5.1
(0.52) (–0.78) (0.15) (0.06)	
–10.34 + 3.17 PG(–1) + 0.70^b SY(–1) + 0.68 AIDDY(–1) ; R^2 = 0.41 ; F = 2.73;	(5.2
(–0.97) (1.49) (2.79) (0.97) D.W. = 2.68 ; N = 16	
–10.79 + 2.82 PG + 1.03^b SY – 1.16 GRNTDY + 2.66^b LOANDY ;	(6.1
(–0.66) (0.80) (2.24) (–1.14) (2.20)	
R^2 = 0.56 ; F = 3.79 ; D.W. = 2.36 ; N = 17	
–10.47 + 3.21 PG(–1) + 0.71^b SY(–1) + 0.67 GRNTDY(–1) + 0.70 LOANDY(–1)	(6.2
(–0.89) (1.27) (2.16) (0.83) (0.80)	
R^2 = 0.41 ; F = 1.88 ; D.W. = 2.69 ; N = 16	
24.43 – 7.69 PG + 0.25^b SY + 2.82 FTDY – 2.21 CTDY – 0.43 PTDY;	(7.1
(1.01) (–1.36) (0.47) (1.18) (–1.02) (–0.25)	
R^2 = 0.26 ; F = 0.77 ; D.W. = 2.33 ; N = 17	
7.04 – 1.48 PG(–1) + 0.73^b SY(–1) +1.96 FTDY(–1)– 0.81 CTDY(–1) – 0.56 PTDY(–1);	(7.2
(0.52) (–0.50) (3.02) (1.69) (–0.85) (–0.48)	
R^2 = 0.62 ; F = 3.27 ; D.W. = 2.88 ; N = 16	

Notes: (1) Numbers in the parentheses below the regression coefficients are the t–values.
(2) “a” — significance at 1%, “b” — at 5% and “c” — at 10% levels; two–tailed tests.

1992; Gupta-Islam 1983; Weisskoff 1972a; 1972b; Griffin 1970; and Griffin and Enos 1970; Papanek 1973; among others).

With respect to the contribution of foreign capital, the results do not appear to be very consistent as judged by the sign and magnitude of their coefficients. The results also depend on the type of decomposition used. For example, the aggregate aid ratio (AGDPR) was not statistically significant. This insignificance may be caused by the aggregation of different kinds of foreign aid into one single category. However, its decomposition into grants (GRNTDY) and loans (LOANDY) improved the regression results significantly. The latter had a statistically significant (at 5% level) positive effect while the former did not. The poor performance of grants may be partly attributable to some degree of collinearity between the explanatory variables SY and GRNTDY r = 0.45). It may also be due to the fact that loans were more effectively utilized while grants were not (for theoretical arguments on this issue see Schmidt in Bhagwati and Eckaus 1970). Since grants were not to be repaid, it is possible that the public authorities allowed various administrative slacks and perhaps tolerated a greater degree of corruption in its utilization. It is also possible, however, that a greater proportion of grants were used to finance consumption oriented or non-income producing projects such that the effects of grants on GDP were not reflected.

Further decomposition of AIDDY into food (FTDY), commodity (CTDY) and project (PTDY) aid indicates that food aid made a marginally significant positive contribution to economic growth. It is somewhat surprising to find that the other two categories came out with negative signs although none were statistically significant. It is to be noted that the simple correlation coefficients (between GR and FTDY was 0.08, between GR and CTDY was 0.04 and between GR and PTDY was 0.16) were small but positive. One could have expected that the latter two would make stronger contributions towards economic growth. The poor performance of these variables is partly attributable to measurement problems and partly to collinearity problems (r = –0.70 between FTDY and PTDY). For project aid, it is also possible that the PTDY had distributed lag effects on GR which were not captured by the model.

SUMMARY AND CONCLUSIONS

The main findings of the study can be summarized as follows: (i) the magnitude of public foreign assistance has continued to increase in nominal dollars while its magnitude is declining in real terms; (ii) the amount of foreign private flows including foreign direct investment has remained almost negligible; (iii) the relative importance of bilateral aid has declined while that of multilateral aid has increased; (iv) the DAC countries and the multilateral agencies remain the major aid donors; (v) within the DAC countries, Japan emerged as the most important aid donor; (vi) within the multilateral agencies, the World Bank and the Asian Development Bank provided most of the resources; (vii) the oil producing and the socialist countries provided only a small share; their shares have significantly declined in recent years; (viii) within the oil producers, most aid came from Saudi Arabia followed by the OPEC; the share of these two also declined in recent years; (ix) the prospect of aid from the former socialist block countries and China appears to be bleak;

Further, (x) the proportion of grants in total aid, and the proportion of grants in commodity and project aid in particular, has decreased over the years thus raising the cost of aid; (xi) with respect to the terms of aid, official aid was received at much more favorable terms than the private flows (such as supplier's credit); (xii) the country's dependence on foreign aid has increased over the years; (xiii) various indicators suggest that the country's external debt burden remains at a high level; (xiv) the debt service ratios remain high but seems to remain within manageable limits; these ratios, in fact, have declined in recent years because of several factors: (a) a rapid rise in exports and worker's remittances in recent years; (b) a fall in the repayment of principals; and (c) the terms of aid continued to remain very favorable. In the future, this favorable situation may change in the opposite direction if foreign receipts (exports and remittances) fail to rise rapidly, the terms of aid deteriorate, or simply as more loans mature with the passage of time.

Finally, (xv) with respect to the effectiveness of foreign aid *vis-a-vis* domestic resources, the study found domestic resources to be more productive than foreign resources. However, foreign resources appear to make some positive contribution to economic growth, although not all of its categories were found to be equally significant. Loans and food aid appeared to exert a stronger influence on growth than grants or project and commodity aid.

POLICY RECOMMENDATIONS

The following policy recommendations can be made. Firstly, Bangladesh needs to put much greater emphasis on mobilizing domestic public and private resources. The public savings can be increased through various fiscal and monetary reforms and the reform of the bureaucracy and the public enterprises with the objective of generating a greater amount of public savings. Privatization of some inefficient public enterprises should be considered where feasible. This may significantly reduce public dissavings.

Secondly, foreign aid in general and, grants, project and commodity aid in particular, need to be more productively utilized. The productivity of these resources can be improved, among others, by the following: (a) the above mentioned domestic policy reforms; (b) continuation and further liberalization of the international trade and foreign exchange regimes; (c) strengthening the public accounting system to reduce fat and wastage in government; (d) strengthening the system of public accountability and the legal system to discourage the dissipation of funds through corruption and various other leakages; and (e) improving the process of aid utilization at various stages such as project approval, planning, implementation, maintenance and evaluation (see Sobhan 1982).

Thirdly, improve domestic financial and other institutions so as to provide incentives and a stable environment for greater domestic private savings and investment. In recent years, the multilateral agencies (notably the World Bank) and some western donor countries are pushing the government to channel a part of foreign funds to the private sector through the financial system. The success of this approach will depend partly on the dynamism of the private sector and partly on the efficiency of the governmental agencies and financial institutions in implementing and supervising the credit programs (e.g. loan utilization and loan recovery). To date, the loan recovery rate has been very dismal. To improve the latter, a system of accountability and a strong legal system to enforce it will be necessary.

Fourthly, provide incentives and a stable political and economic framework so as to attract foreign direct investment. Given the deteriorating international aid climate, the need for this investment may become greater as the supply of foreign public assistance dwindles. Fifthly, the government needs to develop a prudent debt management policy so as to avoid any serious balance of payments difficulties in the future. A prudent debt management policy may require a close monitoring of the debt burden and the various debt service ratios, and to arrange for the timely payment of interest and principal so as to minimize the risk of default (or rescheduling). Finally, the focus of government policy should shift from the current emphasis on foreign aid to export-led growth. This policy was successful in promoting growth in a number of Asian countries (Korea, Taiwan, Hong Kong, Singapore and Thailand). In Bangladesh, the rapid growth of the export garment industry in recent years also supports this conclusion.

NOTES

An Organized Research Grant from the University of Houston-Downtown is duly acknowledged.

REFERENCES

Alamgir, M. (1974), "Foreign Capital Inflow, Saving and Economic Growth: A Case Study of Bangladesh", *Bangladesh Development Studies*, 2, no. 2, pp. 577–598.

Ahmad, S (1983), "The Dominant Constraint on Growth in Bangladesh", *Bangladesh Development Studies*, 11, no. 4, Dec., pp. 77–86.

_____(1986), "Domestic Saving and Foreign Capital Inflow: The Case of Bangladesh", *Bangladesh Development Studies,* 14, no. 1, March, pp. 75–91.

Bauer, P.T. (1971), *Dissent On Development*, Weindenfeld and Nicholson, London.

_____and B. Yamey (1981), "The Political Economy of Foreign Aid", *Lloyds Bank Review*, Oct., pp. 1–14.

Bovard, J. (1986) "The Continuing Failure of U.S. Aid", *USA Today*, September, pp. 10–15.

Bhagwati, J. and R.S. Eckaus (1970), *Foreign Aid: Selected Readings*, Penguin Books, Middlesex, U.K.

Chenery, H.B. (1960), "Patterns of Industrial Growth", *American Economic Review*, 50, pp. 624–54.

_____and P. Eckstein (1970), "Development Alternatives for Latin America", *Journal of Political Economy*, 78, Aug. pp. 966–1006.

_____and A. Strout (1966), "Foreign Assistance and Economic Development", *American Economic Review*, 56, Sept., pp. 679–733.

Clark, C. (1957), *The Conditions of Economic Progress*, Macmillan, London.

Choudhury, K. (1990), *Foreign Aid, Government Sector and Bangladesh*, National Institute of Local Government, Dhaka, Bangladesh.

ERD (1993), *Flow of External Resources Into Bangladesh*, External Relations Division, Ministry of Finance, Dhaka, Bangladesh, various issues.

Faaland, J. (1981), *Aid And Influence: The Case of Bangladesh*, St. Martin's Press, New York.

Frank, A.G. (1969), *Capitalism and Underdevelopment in Latin America*, monthly review press.

Griffin, K.B. (1970), "Foreign Capital, Domestic Savings and Economic Development", *Oxford University Institute of Econ. and Stat.*, 32, pp. 99–112.

_____ and J.L. Enos (1970), "Foreign Assistance: Objectives and Consequences", *Economic Development and Cultural Change*, 18, pp. 313–27.

Gupta, K.L. (1970), "Foreign Capital and Domestic Savings: A Test of Haavelmo's Hypothesis With Cross-country Data. A Comment", *Review of Economics and Statistics*, 52, May, pp. 214–16.

_____ (1975), "Foreign Capital Inflows, Dependency Burden and Savings Rate in Developing Countries: A Simultaneous Equations Model", *kyklos*, 28, pp. 358–74.

_____ and Islam (1983), *Foreign Capital, Savings and Growth: An International Cross-section Study*, D. Reidel Publishing Co., Holland.

Islam, A.M. (1992), "Foreign Aid and Economic Growth: An Econometric Study of Bangladesh", *Applied Economics*, 24, May pp. 541–544.

Islam, N. (1972), "Foreign Assistance and Economic Development: The Case of Pakistan", *Economic Journal*, March, Suppl. pp. 502–530.

Krueger, A.O., C. Michalopoulos, and V. Ruttan (1989), *Aid and Development*, Johns Hopkins U. Press, Baltimore.

Maddala, G.S. (1977), *Econometrics*, McGraw Hill, New York.

Papanek, G.F. (1972), "The Effects of Aid and Other Resource Transfers on Savings and Growth in Less Dev. Countries" *Econ. Journal*, 82, pp. 934–50.

_____ (1973), "Aid, Foreign Private Investment, Savings and Growth in Less Developed Countries", *Journal of Political Economy*, 81, pp. 120–30.

Rahman, M.A. (1968), "Foreign Capital and Domestic Savings: A Test of Haavelmo's Hypothesis", *Review of Economic and Statistics,* Feb. 50, pp. 137–38.

_____ (1967), "The Welfare Economics of Foreign Aid", *Pakistan Development Review*, 7, no. 2, summer, pp. 141–159.

Rosenstein-Rodan, P.N. (1961), "International Aid For Underdeveloped Countries", *Review of Economics and Statistics*, 43, no. 2, May, pp. 107–38.

Ram, R. (1986), "Government Size and Economic Growth: A New Framework and Some Evidence", *American Economic Review*, 76, no. 1, March, pp. 191–203.

Sobhan, R. (1982), *The Crisis of External Dependence: The Political Economy of Foreign Aid To Bangladesh,* University Press Ltd., Dhaks, Bangladesh.

Stoneman, C. (1975), "Foreign Capital and Economic Growth", *World Development*, 3, pp. 11–26.

Weisskoff, T.E. (1972a), "An Econometric Test of Alternative Constraints on Economic Growth", *Review of Economics and Statistics*, 54, no.1, part 2, pp. 67–78.

_____ (1972b), "The Impact of Foreign Capital Inflow on Domestic Savings in Underdeveloped Countries", *Journal of International Economics,* 2, pp. 25–38.

World Bank, *World Tables*, Various Issues, Washington, D.C.

_____ World Debt Tables, Various Issues, Washington, D.C.

CHAPTER 13

MAIN PHASES AND SALIENT FEATURES OF TURKISH FOREIGN AID EXPERIENCE

Fikret Senses

INTRODUCTION

The interaction and complementarity between foreign aid and the "major strategic themes" of development economics like industrialization, rapid capital accumulation, mobilization of underemployed manpower, and planning and an economically active state[1] have been so strong that one is tempted to view it as an integral part of the package of strategic themes.

Despite this close interaction, the fact that the evolution of foreign aid was characterized all along by a strong sense of economic and political self-interest on the part of donors has threatened the inner consistency and harmony of the package. In other words, while foreign aid was an integral part of the structuralist development approach, it has in practice proved to be its most volatile and least reliable component.

The decline of foreign aid has coincided so closely with the decline of other themes that one can talk of the rise and fall of these themes as a package. It has been more than a decade since Singh (1984) has written about the "interrupted industrial revolution of the Third World" while the demise of planning has been echoed by concepts like rent-seeking and government failure in theory and extensive privatization throughout the Third World in practice. Likewise, the decline of aid has been so rapid that in 1996 it accounted for only 0.27% of the combined GNPs of developed countries representing its lowest level since 1950 (Burnside and Dollar, 1997:7).

Turkey's foreign aid experience has exhibited a close parallelism with global trends. In the global context, the single most important factor in the evolution of aid has been the rivalry between socialism and capitalism. As a result, countries in the "communist block's periphery" such as Turkey have been among the main beneficiaries of international aid flows, especially those originating from the United States.[2] The degree of donors' attention to these countries has varied directly with the extent of conflict between the two rival blocks, reaching its zenith at the height of the Cold War and its nadir in periods of cooling off of tensions.

The post-war evolution of foreign aid has been earmarked by several major developments. As opposed to bilateral international aid flows in the 1950s as dominated by the United States, the 1960s were characterized by the emergence of other OECD countries as major donors and increased coordination among them. The advent of the world economic crisis in the first half of the 1970s has signalled the beginning of a secular decline in official sources of aid and the rise of private lending as the major source of external finance for developing countries.

The end of the 1970s has witnessed the adoption of a common lending policy by the IMF and the World Bank based on a free market position and reflecting a broader view of the adjustment process in developing countries. As Structural Adjustment Loans (SALs) by the World Bank and IMF stabilization programs together emerged as their main source of external finance, LDCs have been subject to the strict conditionality of these two institutions for policy reform.

In this new era popularly characterized by "disenchantment with aid" and "aid fatigue", the prospects for foreign aid except for the poorest countries look rather dim (see Ruttan, 1991:10). In this process, countries like Turkey have been adversely affected by factors like the end of the Cold War, the diversion of Western attention to the reform process in Eastern Europe, and their middle income status requiring "graduation" from the process.

Turkey provides an ideal setting in tracing the evolution of foreign aid against this general background. Not only has it been one of the major recipients of foreign aid since the early postwar years, it was also one of the first to abandon its traditional industrialization strategy based on import substitution in favor of export orientation. The fact that this transformation began with the introduction of a stabilization and structural adjustment program (SSAP) in January 1980 in the midst of a deep foreign exchange crisis merits a detailed examination of this experience not least because it has involved a substantial inflow of external resources and policy interference by international donors, most notably the World Bank.

The main objective of this chapter is to trace the evolution of Turkey's foreign aid experience and identify its main phases and salient features. Taking a long-term view of this process, we also hope to come to grips with the full complexity of the debate on foreign aid and capture the main economic and non-economic factors guiding donor attitudes with respect to the timing, magnitude and type of aid.

The plan of the chapter is as follows. In the second section we present an overview of the Turkish experience with foreign aid from the beginning of this process in the immediate postwar years to the mid-1980s which by and large signalled the end of this process.[3] The third section is devoted to an examination of the differences between the Turkish and donors' perceptions of foreign aid. In section four we identify the salient features of this experience with relevance for other developing countries. Finally, in section five we present the main conclusions.

MAIN PHASES OF TURKEY'S EXPERIENCE WITH FOREIGN AID

The emergence of Turkey as a modern nation state in the early 1920s was accompanied with the adoption of industrialization as the main objective of economic policy. Although the industrial trade strategy in its evolution until 1980 had several distinct phases, it remained heavily biased towards import-substituting industrialization (ISI) under strong direction and active participation by the state. One major shift in the implementation of this strategy was the transition from self-reliance until the end of the Second World War to an aid-dependent and external-debt propelled variant thereafter.

The emphasis on self-reliance during 1923–46 was so strong that foreign aid was confined to only several loans received during 1933–39. With much emphasis given to the repayment of Ottoman debt, the decrease in long-term debt was more than twice as large as the rise in short-term liabilities during this period.[4] As Turkey had a long history of external indebtedness extending back to the Ottoman period (reaching crisis proportions in the second half of the 19th century), the 1923–46 period can be viewed very much as an interregnum.

Against this general background, Turkey's post-war experience with foreign aid until 1985 can be examined under five distinct phases: a) 1946–62 b) 1963–70 c) 1970–77 d) 1977–79 and e) 1980–85.

a) 1946–62: This phase began with Turkey abandoning its self-reliant pattern of development and instead seeking special relations with the West, most notably the United States, in the immediate aftermath of the Second World War. In terms of aid flows, the first sign in this direction was the US military aid of 100 million dollars as early as 1947 (Hershlag, 1968: 150). The landmark in this direction, however, was the inflow of substantial US resources under the European Recovery Program which was supplemented subsequently by the provision of considerable technical assistance under Point Four and surplus agricultural commodities under PL 480, and loans by a number of international organizations such as the World Bank.[5]

As shown in Table 13.1, the United States was by far the most important source of aid to Turkey during this period. Out of a total of 1,582 million dollars provided by the United States during this period nearly two thirds (62.9%) consisted of grants. This was not, however, a uniform pattern with loans being the more important category both at the beginning of the period until 1951 and again at the end, during 1961–62.

Although the significance of these aid flows for the Turkish economy cannot be assessed with precision, indications are that they played an important role in facilitating an increase in imports and new investment and made a significant contribution to the balance of payments. In the late 1940s and early 1950s, for example, they accounted for one half of the increase in imports and for approximately 40 percent of the increase in investment.[6] Their contribution to the balance of payments, while fluctuating sharply during the period was even more significant, accounting for one half of the current account deficit in 1950, a third in 1954, and two thirds in the late 1950s (Hershlag, 1968: 151).

US aid during this period was directed primarily to the development of agriculture and infrastructure. The importation of around 40,000 tractors during 1948–52 was instrumental in the rapid increase in agricultural production mainly through the expansion of the area under cultivation. This was supplemented by efforts focussed on training and technical assistance at the field level by US aid agents. More significantly, the inflow of aid was used for increasing agricultural and infrastructural investment involving the construction of harbors, ports, silos, but most notably the construction of a nationwide road network (Krueger and Ruttan, 1989: 254)

The World Bank was an active participant in this process until at least 1956, contributing a total of 50.9 million dollars in loans during 1950–56. Apart from financ-

Table 13.1. Foreign Aid to Turkey, 1946–1962 (million dollars, in current prices).

Year	United States	Other Sources	Total	Loans Grants
1946–48	45.4	—	45.4	5.0
1949	33.8	—	33.8	—
1950	40.0	31.9	71.9	80.4
1951	—	49.8	49.8	—
1952	11.2	58.4	69.6	35.2
1953	—	58.6	58.6	20.0
1954	—	78.7	78.7	3.8
1955	25.5	83.8	109.3	—
1956	25.0	104.3	129.3	—
1957	25.1	62.3	87.4	13.5
1958	23.2	90.4	113.6	125.5
1959	97.2	107.0	204.2	—
1960	26.5	99.0	125.5	37.0
1961	131.0	89.8	220.0	161.7
1962	102.5	81.6	184.2	15.0
Total	**586.4**	**995.6**	**1582.0**	**497.1**

Source: Kepenek and Yentürk (1994: 93).

ing projects in agriculture and infrastructure, these were used for industrial projects sponsored by the Industrial Development Bank (Hershlag, 1968: 152) , which itself was established in 1950 with World Bank assistance.

After trying for at least two years to cope with the growing imbalances in the economy as manifested by severe balance of payments difficulties and accelerating inflation (through such measures as import compression and extensive price controls), the government finally accepted a stabilization program in August 1958 (see Krueger, 1974: for details). This was a standard IMF package involving devaluation, import liberalization and price decontrol in both the private and public sectors. These measures were accompanied by a sizable consolidation of external debt at rates of interest below international rates to the value of 422 million dollars, accounting for about one half of total Turkish external debt and arrears. In addition, there was a substantial inflow of fresh facilities amounting to 359 million dollars. Apart from the 75 million provided by the OEEC and 25 million by the IMF (Krueger 1974: 76–77), the bulk of this was provided by the US.

ii) 1963–70 The distinctive feature of this period was the adoption of the programming approach to development assistance with strong implications for both recipients and donors. On the Turkish side, the introduction of central planning in the early 1960s was instrumental in the closer integration of aid with domestic economic policies.[7] For donors, this meant emphasis on better coordination of aid policies of different donors.

The OECD consortium for aid to Turkey established in 1962 comprising most W.European countries, the US and, subsequently in 1965 the World Bank, was established primarily with this objective in mind but was also motivated by US desire to shift the aid burden on to the European countries, mostly W. Germany. An additional factor may have been the growing Turkish-European relations during this period as stimulated by substantial Turkish labor migration to Europe and Turkey's associate membership to EEC.

In sharp contrast with the earlier period, the 1963–70 period was characterized by relative macroeconomic stability. The major devaluation in August 1970 as part of an IMF-supported stabilization program was motivated by the desire to give a major boost to Turkish exports and was again accompanied by import liberalization and an inflow of project and consortium credits.

Gross and net aid flows during this period are given in Table 13.2 which shows them increasing towards the end of the decade. This was in large part due to the increase in project credits in the late 1960s, partly reflecting increased World Bank finance for this purpose.[8]

Data on consortium credits during this period given by Uras (1979) indicate that they have amounted to 1404.5 million dollars (766.8 million dollars of which in loans and 637.7 million dollars in grants). Although the data on total inflow of aid from these two sources do not match, they confirm the broad trends in terms of the rise in the relative share of project credits towards the end of the decade.

By all accounts the inflow of aid does not seem large during this period. Krueger (1974: 134) argues that it was only in the exceptional years of 1963 and 1970 that net aid flows exceeded 2 percent of GNP. In a similar vein, Celasun (1991:5) has stated

Table 13.2. Gross and Net Aid Flows to Turkey, 1963–70 (millions of U.S. dollars).

Year	Consortium Credits	Project Credits	Commodity Imports	Debt Service	Net Aid
1963	169	97	94	145	215
1964	145	36	32	141	72
1965	169	57	29	191	64
1966	175	56	17	148	112
1967	161	60	—	133	88
1968	145	127	—	106	166
1969	106	174	41	152	169
1970	217	179	83	205	274

Source: Krueger (1974: 134)

that concessional capital inflows did not exceed "cross-country norms for external resources in relation to GDP".

A closer examination of Turkey's aid experience during this period reflects two other major trends. The first is the decline in total aid from the United States which fell sharply from a total of 832.2 million dollars during the First Five Year Plan period (1963–67) to only 412.0 million dollars during the Second Five Year Plan period (1968–72). Furthermore, in sharp contrast to the earlier period, more than 80 percent of total US aid during this period consisted of loans, representing a sharp reduction in the grant element in total aid.[9] These broad trends in US aid during this period should, however, be seen in the light of increased activity of US aid agencies in Turkey, most notably the USAID, in spheres like agriculture (land and water development, economic and technical assistance for large-scale demonstration of high-yielding varieties of wheat and fertilizer use), education (development of technical education and mass literacy programs, educational planning), and health (family planning and nutrition improvements), see Krueger and Ruttan (1989).

The second major trend of Turkey's aid experience during this period is related to the big discrepancy between targeted and actual aid flows which was largely due to the "slow operation, endless formalities and overcautiousness" that characterized consortium aid. During 1963–67 for example, the actual flow from this source (827 million dollars) was just over one half of the estimated flow (1573 million dollars).[10] This no doubt was a major source of uncertainty for Turkish planners, all the more so because consortium aid pledges were made on an annual basis as opposed to the medium-term targets of five-year plans.

iii) 1970–77: This phase covers the period from the devaluation in August 1970 to the emergence of a full scale payments crisis early in 1977. The sharp increase in exports, workers' remittances and foreign exchange reserves during 1970–73 in response to the large devaluation in 1970 created a great deal of exuberance in Turkey and led many to conclude, as it turned out prematurely, that the foreign exchange constraint had simply disappeared. Although consortium credits kept their momentum and reached an average annual level of 130.8 million dollars during 1971–73 (58.4 million dollars for program and 72.4 million dollars for project credits), this was followed by a very sharp drop in program credits, averaging only 5.5 million dollars during 1974–77. This left project credits (averaging 77.5 million dollars) as the only major source of official finance during this period.[11]

The set of factors behind the Turkish economic crisis in the late 1970s are well known. On the domestic front, large and increasing public deficits partly due to the public investment boom to sustain and deepen the industrialization drive was the most prominent factor. This in turn was due to a succession of coalition governments competing for political support on the basis of an economic agenda of a mixture of rapid growth and populist polices. Furthermore, this was taking place against the background of sizable external shocks contributing to a sharp deterioration in the current account, turning from a surplus of 2.4 % of GNP in 1973 to a deficit of 5.1% in 1975 and 7.1% in 1977 (Celasun and Rodrik, 1989: 634).

As a result, resorting to borrowing from international banks emerged as the only option available for Turkey to realize the ambitious industrialization targets of the Third Five Year Plan (1973–77). The form of borrowing was based on the government subsidizing private sector foreign borrowing by providing blanket protection against foreign exchange risk.[12] As a result, there was a substantial increase in short-term debt in a very short period of time, rising from only 223 million dollars in 1974 to 6.1 billion dollars in 1977 with the share of short-term debt in total external debt rising from 10.2 percent to 56.3 percent[13] and the debt/GNP ratio rising from 10.0% to 22.3% during the same period (Öniş, 1989: 78).

d) 1977–79: Periods of rapid growth being punctuated by crisis, the so-called boom and bust cycles, were nothing new in the post-war Turkish economic history (see Öniş and Riedel, 1993). In fact, there were two such episodes in 1958 and 1970, each leading to a sizeable devaluation, the introduction of liberalization policies, and a large inflow of foreign aid.

The main significance of Turkey's economic crisis in the late 1970s for our purposes is less for its causes than its extent and impact on the economy. When the short-term borrowing came to a rather abrupt end in early 1977, Turkey was faced with a severe foreign exchange crisis which resulted in the indefinite suspension of all foreign transfers by the Central Bank. The foreign exchange crisis was so severe that foreign exchange reserves could finance only two days' of imports and salaries of Turkish missions abroad could not be paid.[14] Turkey's international creditworthiness rating was only 1.48 (out of ten) which placed it within the group of five countries with lowest level of international creditworthiness among a group of 93 countries (Kepenek and Yentürk, 1994:243–44).

As expected, a foreign exchange crisis of this magnitude resulted in severe import shortages with a devastating impact on both domestic production and investment and led to a sharp acceleration in inflation.[15] Given its heavy dependence on imports, manufacturing was the sector most affected from the crisis.

The central issue in the emergence and deepening of economic crisis was the shortage of foreign exchange, unifying the internal and external factors. As the crisis deepened, the need for foreign exchange became chronic, requiring an international rescue operation and elevating foreign aid to the top of the economic agenda.

The G-7 Summit in Guadeloupe in January 1979 entrusted the OECD consortium with the task of raising as much aid as possible for Turkey from OECD member countries and coordinate with the IMF and the World Bank. Soon afterwards at the OECD conference in May 1979, the OECD pledged 1 billion dollars of fast-disbursing emergency loans at low rates of interest and with long repayment periods which, however, was made conditional on a new IMF stand-by agreement.

Turkey's foreign aid experience from the onset of the crisis in early 1977 to the introduction of SAP in early 1980 was characterized by the incompatible positions of Turkey and potential donors which in turn was shaped by a lack of realism on both sides. Donors' lack of realism was manifested by the fact that they were trying to force their conditionality onto a new government which was deeply committed to growth and industrialization and was more than critical of policy intervention by donors.

As the donors saw foreign aid to serve their strategic interests and as a leverage for economic policy reform, the Turkish side viewed it as a means of serving its plan objectives.

This "business as usual" attitude reflected a basic failure to understand the changing attitude of donors and overoptimism, if not shear unrealism of Turkish planners and policy-makers on the availability of foreign external resources.

The international environment was not, however, at all conducive to the realization of this objective especially for a country in deep economic crisis. As it turned out, efforts to raise bridging funds for the realization of the objectives of the Fourth Five Year Plan from official sources, the demand of an eight billion dollar subsidy from the EEC in support of this, and the expectation that international banks would soon recommence their lending proved to be totally unrealistic. Another sign of unrealism in this respect was the strong resistance to IMF demands for stabilization, most notably for exchange rate realignment in the face of accelerating inflation.

All this should not be taken to mean that there was no relaxation by donors and Turkey of their respective positions. While the IMF showed some flexibility by relaxing its performance criteria of the 1978 stabilization program the Turkish side showed some resilience for adjustment. With much of the period dominated by stubbornness not to devalue, much of this had to rely on import compression. Although this, together with some attempts at export promotion were responsible for the reduction in the current account deficit from 3.4 billion dollars in 1977 to 1.6 and 1.2 billion dollars in 1978 and 1979, respectively, it also exacerbated import shortages and inflationary pressures.

In the face of the deep-seated conflict between the government and the IMF, the only course of action that was acceptable to both sides was the rescheduling of the massive Turkish debt. There were two major debt rescheduling agreements under the auspices of the OECD consortium in May 1978 and July 1979.[16]

The long negotiations for debt rescheduling as well as OECD pledging conferences involved a rather cumbersome process, creating a lot of uncertainty in Turkey. With the official donors dragging their feet and commercial banks unwilling to take part in negotiations in earnest until the 1979 devaluation, the amount of resources that Turkey could draw on was largely confined to the aid element in debt rescheduling. Fresh funds from official sources, on the other hand, did not reach significant levels and were confined to aid from the US and Germany, mostly in the second half of 1979. As Wolff (1987: 69) has observed, "neither the instruments used by donors nor Turkey's adjustment policy were ... commensurate with the scale of the crisis".

e) 1980–85: The introduction of SSAP in January 1980 opened a new era of special and close relations with virtually all the donors which seemed to be guided primarily by the objective of relieving Turkey of its debt-servicing obligations during the difficult initial years of adjustment, especially during 1980–83. Long-term (gross) capital flows during 1980–85 were sizable, amounting to 11 billion dollars, 9 billion dollars of which from official sources (Aricanli, 1990: 248).

A certain division of labor between international organizations was in evidence in the post-1980 period. The OECD was active mostly during 1980–82 and was concerned primarily with the immediate "rescue" aspects of the crisis, leaving policy reform aspects to the Bretton Woods institutions (BWI). Aid from the OECD in 1980 amounted to 1 billion dollars, half of which provided by the US and Germany alone, with the other half coming from a total of 12 different countries. The major contribution by the OECD, however, involved a massive debt-rescheduling operation in 1980, amounting to 2800 million dollars. This covered the Turkish debt falling due until 1983, including the debt already rescheduled in 1978 and 1979 (see, Wolff, 1987: 88–90).

Through successive stand-by agreements, (the three-year stand-by covering the 1980–83 period followed by a further one-year stand-by), the cumulative net transfer from the IMF during 1980–83 reached 2 billion dollars. Net transfers by the World Bank through project loans and SALs reached 1486.2 million dollars.

The massive inflow of external resources starting in 1980 was accompanied by the radical transformation of economic policies under SSAP which involved a variety of reforms involving substantial liberalization in key spheres like foreign trade, foreign investment as well as financial markets. The Bretton Woods institutions, in particular the World Bank through SALs were the main mentors behind these reforms.

DONORS' AND TURKISH PERSPECTIVES ON AID

Perspectives on aid have been dominated by a strong sense of self-interest on the donors' side[17] and a deep commitment on growth and industrialization on the Turkish side.

Donors' perspectives: Self-interest is not an easy concept to define not least because it has shown a great deal of dynamism, guided by a variety of motives and taking different forms over time. It is possible, however, to identify three closely interrelated motives that may fall under this heading. a) strategic and political interests b) economic interests and c) the desire to influence recipients' economic policies.

a) There is general agreement that security concerns were the primary motive for aid, with the US aid program aptly described as "probably the single most anti-communist program".[18] Turkey has been the "object of important US strategic and political interests" since the Second World War and has "one of the longest history of any nation as an US aid recipient". This has been due to Turkey's special geopolitical situation in a particularly sensitive area. Following its membership of NATO in 1952 Turkey was entrusted with the task of guarding NATO's southern flank. Furthermore, Turkey's efforts to maintain a secular and democratic form of government in a conflict-ridden region were expected to enhance its significance in Western eyes. As can be expected, the intensity of strategic interests has not been uniform over time. US aid in the 1950s, emphasizing transport infrastructure, while also stimulating agricultural and regional development may have been prompted by strategic NATO interests. Events like the coup in Iraq in 1958, leading to Iraqi withdrawal from CENTO, may have revived US willingness to provide aid to Turkey, after a lull during the preceding two years.

At the other extreme, there were several cases of deep conflict between the two sides. US anger over the use of US-supplied arms by Turkey in the Cyprus conflict was one such case which may explain the lack of enthusiasm by US to provide aid to Turkey during the 1960s. Likewise, US pressure on Turkey to ban opium production has resulted in the reduction of the number of opium-producing provinces from 20 to 4 in 1970, followed by a total ban in 1971. While such deference by the Turkish government led to an improvement in US-Turkish relations, the lifting of the ban by the government coming into office in 1974 as well as the Turkish armed intervention in Cyprus in the same year opened a new period of conflict. This led to the imposition of an US arms embargo on Turkey in 1975.

After a lull in the 1970s under detente, there was a revival of potential donors' strategic and political interests on Turkey, the first sign of which was the lifting of the US arms embargo on Turkey towards the end of 1978. There were, however, several other factors at work in this revival of interest. The first was the severity of the Turkish economic crisis, which posed a big threat to Western interests in a particularly sensitive area. This was reflected by increased concern of all major parties such as NATO, OECD, and EEC, but most notably the United States and Germany which were convinced of the need for an international rescue operation. Germany's concern was, apart from strong trade relations with Turkey, primarily related to the presence of 1.5 million Turks (migrant workers and their dependents) in that country. Germany, far from being ready to accommodate a new inflow was becoming increasingly inclined to encourage the voluntary repatriation of existing migrants (see Wolff, 1987: 67).

Secondly and more importantly, there was a chain of major events directly related to Western strategic and political interests in the region. The most important of these was the Iranian Revolution in 1979 which elevated Turkey's strategic importance to new heights. Turkey was now seen as the "only pro-western state between the USSR and the Middle East", as a model secular state, and an "example of democracy in Middle East" (see Celasun and Rodrik, 1989: 757) and Aricanli (1990: 243).

The escalation of the US-Iran conflict after 1979, the Soviet invasion of Afghanistan in the last week of 1979 and the outbreak of war between Iran and Iraq in September 1980 were among other major events that were instrumental in further increasing the strategic importance of Turkey in the region.[19] The close link between these events and US aid flows into Turkey provides some proof that strategic factors can cut both ways. It also confirms that even in the case of a country with considerable strategic and political significance, the slightest deviation from the donors' political stance could well prompt strong retribution from the donor in question with an adverse impact on aid flows.

b) Economic Interests

Unlike some other developing countries, especially those in Latin America, donors' direct economic interests in Turkey do not seem to have played a major role in aid flows. Even in the heyday of official aid flows during 1954–74, for example, direct foreign investment in Turkey on a cumulative basis remained at very low levels amounting to only 189.6 million dollars (Öniş, 1989: 85). Similarly, Turkish imports both as a share of its GDP and in absolute terms have remained at very low levels. Neither can one, on the basis of the low level of Turkish exports, establish the existence of any strong interest in Turkish raw materials. Imports and exports as a share of GNP in 1978, for example, were only 8.9% and 4.3 %, respectively. As Wolff (1987: 65) has observed, economic interests of western industrialized countries in Turkey were of "minor importance".

This may, however, be a simplistic conclusion for two closely interrelated reasons. First, the fact that the emergence of Western Europe as the main source of aid to Turkey in the 1960s was accompanied by an increase in the share of this region in

Turkey's foreign trade as well as in DFI inflows raises the possibility of complementarity between these and aid flows. Secondly, such a conclusion, by emphasizing the importance of interests at a certain point in time may be discarding the *potential* economic interests.

The US advice and aid in the early postwar years emphasizing agricultural growth in Turkey through the utilization of untapped labor and land resources may be seen in the light of US desire to assist European reconstruction through the provision of adequate supplies of agricultural raw materials.[20] As confirmed by more recent developments, large and buoyant domestic markets as propelled by rapid growth and large and rapidly increasing population in Turkey have attracted much attention from industrialized countries.

c) Donors' Desire to Influence Policy Choices in Turkey: Turkey's foreign aid experience has clearly indicated that donors have been consistent with regards to their policy preferences throughout the period under consideration and have done their best to bring Turkish economic policies in line with these preferences.

Donors' policy choices right from the onset of aid flows in the immediate postwar years were based on an open economy as driven by domestic and foreign private initiative with the state playing a minimal role in economic activity. Another major pillar of their policy choice has been a preference for the development of infrastructural facilities and specialization in agriculture with industry relegated very much to the background.[21] Furthermore, Turkey's major donors like the US, OEEC (subsequently OECD), IMF, and the World Bank have shown a striking unanimity in their advocacy of these policies.

The US aid missions visiting Turkey in the context of the Marshall Program have, for example, left no doubt on these policy choices, strongly emphasizing the need for investment in infrastructure, especially in transport facilities and in increasing agriculture's production capacity with only lip service being paid to industrialization. The IBRD report published in 1951, for example, explicitly stated: "We do not suggest that Turkey should abandon its goal of industrialization, we suggest rather that the quickest path to the goal is through emphasis on agricultural development".[22] The downsizing of the public enterprise sector, a strong opposition to heavy industry, and a clear preference instead for light industries like the processing of agricultural raw materials, leather, and wood, constituted other components of this policy advice.

The debate on aid in US Congress provides some clues for this opposition to industrialization with a number of congressmen proposing to restrict US foreign aid on grounds that industrial progress in the Third World constitutes a threat to US interests. In the 1958 congressional debate, for example, one congressman complained that the aid program was setting up competition against American business, another warned that "these programs will wreck the economy of our country" while yet another went as far as moving to "prohibit funds for the establishment of any kind of plant that might compete with U.S. industries".[23] Although these proposals were not accepted, they were indicative of the deep concern of US industrial interests on this issue.[24]

Turkish Perspectives: Even a cursory examination of postwar Turkish economic history indicates a strong link between foreign aid and development objectives based on ISI. An early sign of this link was the development plan that was prepared by a group of Turkish specialists in 1947 which left no doubt about the central role of foreign aid in the emerging pattern of development. Although the plan was not implemented, it nevertheless was indicative of donors' preferences and the spirit of times not least because 40 percent of the investments envisaged under the plan were to be financed by foreign aid. The dependence on foreign aid became more or less formalized with the adoption of central planning in the early 1960s which while envisaging the end of the dependence on foreign aid by the end of the first three five-year plans in 1977, counted on an inflow of foreign resources to close the gap between the amount of resources compatible with the target rate of growth and investment and the available domestic resources.[25]

This presented a potential source of conflict right from the outset with aid being viewed by Turkey as a crucial instrument of its industrialization strategy while guided by a strong sense of self-interest on the part of donors. Under such a setting it was natural that the harmony of donor-recipient relations depended on how closely their respective motives overlapped. As our discussion of the main phases of Turkey's experience with foreign aid has shown, periods of strong strategic interest on the part of donors have been accompanied by a large inflow of aid with periods of waning interest reflected in the reduction and increased volatility of aid flows.

SALIENT FEATURES OF TURKEY'S FOREIGN AID EXPERIENCE

Against the background of the above discussion the salient features of Turkey's foreign aid experience can be classified under eight main headings.

a) The Link Between Investment and Foreign Aid: In sharp contrast to the pattern of aid in the global context,[26] the bulk of aid in Turkey was used to finance investment rather than consumption. In the 1950s, foreign aid was largely used to finance agricultural mechanization early in the decade, infrastructural investment mostly in transport, and private investment in manufacturing financed through the Industrial Development Bank. Even the Columbia School of Law report (published in 1962) which was otherwise highly critical of the Turkish aid experience in the 1950s conceded that aid was "a *crucial* factor in making possible the investments of the past decade".[27]

As noted before, the link between foreign aid and investment became more formal and explicit after the introduction of central planning in the early 1960s. This link was so close that the reason for imports of investment goods falling behind their plan targets during the First Five Year Plan period (1963–67) was adduced to the shortfall in project credits expected to finance these imports (Krueger, 1974: 154–57).

Turkey's heavy resort to short-term borrowing during the 1970s was again a reflection of its commitment to rapid growth and industrialization and was largely prompted by the objective of increasing public investment in manufacturing and infrastructure. This process was so rapid that public investment during 1974–76 reached four times its level during 1970–73 with the investment/GNP ratio rising sharply from 18.1 percent in 1973 to a massive 25.0 percent in 1977. Public investment accounted for the bulk of this increase rising from 7.0 percent of GNP to 13.1 percent during the same period. Of the rise in the external borrowing ratio by 9.1

percentage points during this period, 6.9 percentage points was due to a rise in investment and only 2.3 percentage points to consumption (see Celasun and Rodrik, 1989: 635, 637).

b) Aid and the Culture of Indebtedness: Another important aspect of Turkey's foreign aid experience has been the entrenched expectation in Turkey that should a deep payments crisis arise, international donors will eventually come to the rescue. Although such rescue operations have invariably led to policy interference by donors, domestic policy-makers were confident that this would last only a short while as they found it not too difficult to evade the short-term conditionality of stabilization programs. As the pace of industrialization was pushed beyond available resources and became increasingly dependent on foreign exchange, external indebtedness became endemic. This led over time to the emergence of what we may describe as a culture of indebtedness.[28]

The following events present clear manifestations of this attitude. Turkey was the first country to overdraw its IMF quota in the early 1950s and the first to ask for an extension when its obligations were due. In April 1978 Turkey became the first country to take advantage of the possibility of exceeding its quota under the Supplementary Financing Facility of the IMF (Wolff, 1987: 70). Turkish demands for rescheduling in 1979 were described as the "biggest rescheduling of a country's private external debt ever proposed".[29] Shortly after having a major portion of its debt rescheduled in 1978–79, Turkey successfully reached a new rescheduling agreement in 1980.

c) Confronted with donor pressure for policy change, the Turkish policy-makers have developed a number of coping strategies. First, Turkish governments have adopted a strategy of playing one group of donors' with the other. With the bulk of aid coming from the West, this strategy has often involved efforts to establish closer ties with the socialist countries. The success of this strategy depended largely on the strategic importance of Turkey as strongly influenced by the state of relations between the two blocks.

Second, Turkish governments have often resisted donor pressure for policy change until economic problems deepened and reached crisis proportions. In the 1950s, for example, the 1958 stabilization program was accepted only after strong resistance to US calls for austerity which began as early as 1953 (Maxfield and Nolt, 1995: 642–45). What prompted Turkey to finally accept the stabilization program was more than anything else the foreign exchange crisis which was so severe that because of shortages of oil exports could not be taken to port . Similarly, the devaluation decision in 1970 was related to the growing overvaluation of the lira in the late 1960s and more importantly increased difficulties faced by Turkey in meeting her debt servicing obligations, requiring as early as 1965 another major debt consolidation.

Third, even after an agreement with the donors was reached Turkish governments had a tendency not to stick to their commitments beyond the initial several years. Soon after the 1958 stabilization program, for example, involving substantial inflow of aid, the Turkish government resumed expansionary policies.

d) Learning by Donors: Direct experience with successive Turkish governments over a long period of time has been an important source of learning by the donors. This served donors particularly well during the 1978–79 crisis when major western governments, international financial organizations, and commercial banks took a common stand in their approach to the crisis. This broad coalition of donors used aid leverage successfully to first break the resistance of the social democratic government in office and then prepare the ground for more comprehensive reforms after January 1980.

Aid from both the official and private sources was made conditional on the "green light" of the IMF, which thus had substantial leverage over Turkish course of action through both the timing and magnitude of aid. Such leverage concentrated in the hands of one single organization was skillfully used to deepen the crisis and increased the desperation for aid. It also made the government believe that aid would not be forthcoming until and unless it reached an agreement with the IMF. Given the extent of the crisis and the size of external resources required to get out of it, such coordinated action by the donors left the government with little room for manoeuvre. With official donors less than enthusiastic to provide aid and commercial banks confining their efforts to rescheduling of existing debt rather than the provision of fresh funds even after the agreement with the IMF, the non-availability of aid had a highly negative and disruptive impact on the economy.

Industrial activity felt the full brunt of the lack of foreign exchange which had a severe adverse impact on production as well as new investment. The sharp drop in capacity utilization exacerbated shortages and inflationary pressures in the economy. These difficulties were instrumental in eroding the political support of the social democratic government, discrediting ISI as a whole, and creating an atmosphere of gloom in the midst of which neoliberal reform was presented as having no viable alternative.

e) The massive inflow of external resources into the Turkish economy after 1980 can be explained by the fact that it was this phase more than any other that fully incorporated the set of factors representing the donors' main motives for aid. Although previous phases were characterized by the dominance of one or the other motive, it was their presence all at once which was instrumental in generating such a big magnitude of aid.

The all-embracing factor behind this was the extent of the 1977–80 crisis which was not only much deeper than the previous crises, but was also accompanied by a severe political crisis, with domestic unrest bordering on civil war.

Donors' concern which was rather half-hearted at the beginning of the crisis increased directly with the increase in Turkey's strategic importance towards the end of the decade. The broad coalition of donors was determined to use the funds collected in this manner for two main purposes, that is to kill two birds with one stone. i) get the Turkish economy out of the immediate crisis i.e as part of their rescue operation and ii) as a means of policy reform.

It was the simultaneous occurrence of these events together which led to the inflow of substantial aid to Turkey during this period. It is highly unlikely that such an inflow would have taken place in the absence of any one of the set of motives for aid. Increased concern by donors for the economic and political crisis, for example, was far from being translated into actual aid flows. Likewise, without the strategic interests, the introduction of SSAP would not have been enough for donors to provide aid.

It was therefore not a coincidence that in line with donors' traditional policy preferences, World Bank conditionality under SALs was most strict in the sphere of public investment and trade policy. The revision of the public sector investment program in 1981 involved the removal of a large number of public investment projects in the manufacturing sector.[30] Trade policy reform, on the other hand, involved substantial import liberalization together with the provision of sizable export incentives with a view of moving to a neutral policy regime. As foreign aid facilitated a large inflow of imports to remove the domestic production bottlenecks, the rapid increase in exports, which was hailed as the most successful aspect of SSAP, enhanced Turkey's ability to service its external debt on a regular basis.

f) Although the strategic case for aid to Turkey was in part based on it being the "only democracy in the Middle East", donors seem to have set aside any concern with democratic decision-making when it came to policy reform. The clearest manifestation of this was seen in the attitude of donors towards the military takeover only nine months after the introduction of the SSAP in January 1980. Although it was the minority government that introduced the neoliberal program only several weeks after coming to power, the military government's immediate endorsement of SSAP gave the program a major boost, silencing virtually all sources of opposition to it.

The military leaders were aware that domestic political stability depended on economic stability which required good relations with donors, particularly those in Washington D.C. It is clear that authoritarianism and SSAP and the large inflow of external resources to support it represented mutually reinforcing processes especially in the crucial early years of the program.

In addition to its crucial role in the initiation of the reform process, foreign aid played an even more important role in its implementation and sustainability. In contrast to its negative role by way of deepening the crisis through its non-availability, foreign aid played a "positive" role after 1980 with the substantial inflow of resources instrumental in deepening the reform process largely through stabilization programs with the IMF and SALs with the World Bank.

g) Apart from strategic and political issues, the attitude of successive Turkish governments vis-a-vis donors was another strong influence over aid. One can distinguish several episodes in Turkey's relations with donors over economic policy. The brief period of harmonious relations in the early 1950s was followed by deep conflict until the introduction of the stabilization program in 1958. As donors became increasingly critical of Turkish economic policy, Turkish government's sensitivity on the issue of policy interference by donors became more intense. In 1953, the government refused permission of entry to the country by a US aid mission headed by H.B. Chenery and terminated the World Bank mission in Turkey in the following year (Maxfield and Nolt, 1995: 643)

Donors' increased tolerance of Turkish economic policies in the 1960s opened a new episode of harmonious relations. By all accounts, it was the amicable relations between the government and aid agencies that facilitated the behind-the-scenes agreement on a major devaluation in 1970. After a period of deep conflict between the social democratic government and the IMF during 1978–79, the minority government that introduced the SSAP was by far the most sympathetic of all Turkish governments to the neoliberal policy agenda of the donors.[31] It is in this sense that the military government's adoption of a similar attitude to BWI was of crucial importance for the sustainability of aid flows, and indeed of SSAP itself.

h) Another factor behind the massive inflow of aid to Turkey in the 1980s was BWI's desire to create a showcase of their new approach. Turkey was the first country to reach a three-year stand-by agreement with the IMF in 1980, shortly after the introduction of SSAP. The loan involved in the agreement was the largest ever allocated by the IMF until that time. Likewise, the fact that Turkey was the first country (along with Kenya) to receive SALs, the first to complete the full course of five successive SALs, and to implement them with the lowest "slippage" was also indicative of Turkey's special relations with the BWI as well as the extent of the inflow of external resources involved.

It was mainly on the basis of rapid export growth early in the reform process that Turkey has regained its creditworthiness in the eyes of the international financial community and was elevated to the status of a "model" country. This was the donors' side of the coin with the Turkish side presenting a more gloomy picture.

Shortly after introducing a major structural adjustment program in response to a severe debt crisis, Turkey was faced with an increasing debt burden. This was due to the end in 1984 of the OECD debt relief for short term debt rescheduled during the 1978–80 period. Another factor was the servicing of debt to the IMF which was characterized by "high repayment obligations and short lives", leading to a net outflow as early as 1984 (see Wolff, 1987: 81).

As Wolff (1987: 95) has noted, Turkey's debt servicing requirements during 1983–85 was 9000 million dollars as opposed to an inflow of only 6000 million dollars. This meant that Turkey, to prevent a net outflow, had to resort as early as 1983 to short-term borrowing on a large scale. This was the beginning of a new process of growing indebtedness for the Turkish economy which in 1992 was cited among the top ten of international debtors and among countries with the highest debt-servicing obligations.[32]

CONCLUSION

Turkey's long experience with foreign aid has indicated a strong parallelism with the international experience in terms of its main characteristics and phases and has incorporated the key aspects of the debate on the subject. From this rich history of donor-recipient relations in the Turkish case one can draw a number of important conclusions with relevance for other developing countries.

The long history of relations has involved substantial learning and was characterized by a great deal of pragmatism on both sides. The "culture of indebtedness" extending back to at least the second half of the nineteenth century has often subjected the Turkish economy to the economic policy conditionality of its creditors. Having aimed at the start of its planned development in 1963 at ending its dependence on foreign aid by 1977, Turkey has paradoxically found itself facing the deepest of its foreign exchange crises and eventually facing a policy framework diametrically opposed to the one previously envisaged.

Given the difficulties of coping with a crisis of this magnitude without massive external support, foreign aid was elevated to the top of the agenda as the only way out of the crisis. This has increased the aid leverage of donors for economic policy reform. The donors were guided throughout this long process by a strong sense of self-interest. When they were forced, basically for political and strategic reasons, to rescue the Turkish economy facing by far the most severe of its many boom and bust cycles they took this opportunity to shift the course of Turkish economic policies on to the course they have preferred all along. The main instrument employed in this process was the conditionality of BWI, in particular the SALs provided by the World Bank.

The Turkish experience with foreign aid provides an ideal setting for testing some of the most common hypothesis pertaining to the factors responsible for policy reform (see Rodrik, 1996). There were a number of internal factors accounting for the crisis and the ensuing economic policy shift. It was, however, external factors as dominated by the aid leverage of donors which largely accounted for both the initiation of the neoliberal reform program and its sustainability, thanks to a substantial inflow of resources. This experience also corroborates the importance of crisis as being the main "instigator of reform" and indicates the importance of foreign aid in this process. Likewise, it lends support to the hypothesis that new governments are in a better position to introduce reforms and that authoritarian regimes are better placed in sustaining them. It also shows the tendency of international agencies to set aside any scruples that they might have for democratic decision-making when it comes to committing substantial resources to initiating preferred reforms and create a model of "successful" adjustment in the process.

It is pertinent to ask at this stage what would have happened to Turkish industrialization if the substantial resources that were made available to Turkey after 1980 were made available *before* the crisis, during 1973–77. Could Turkey have replicated the experiences of successful industrializers in East and South East Asia? While not even attempting to absolve ISI as implemented in Turkey before 1980 of all its many shortcomings, one should recall that it was responsible for rapid industrial growth in Turkey averaging 9% per annum during 1963–78. Furthermore, given the fact that there was a broad consensus for industrialization in Turkey at the time and that Turkey ranked fifth in terms of its industrialization level among the developing countries, such a possibility should not immediately be ruled out. But herein lay the main dilemma confronting development practitioners in Turkey. At the heart of this dilemma were the different perceptions of aid by donors and Turkey with the former guided by self-interest and the latter by the industrialization objective.

As it turned out the leverage in the hands of donors over the timing and magnitude of aid led to the worst form of adjustment. Although aimed initially at getting Turkey out of its debt crisis and in fact prompted by it, the reform process has witnessed a substantial increase in Turkey's external debt.

The whole agenda of economic policy-making has shifted to the short term with development objectives with medium and long-term connotations relegated very much to the background. In this environment, the chief victim has been industrialization with the expected boom in private investment in manufacturing failing to materialize. Moreover, in the new global environment the major traditional tools of industrialization are no longer accessible to developing countries like Turkey.

Under such a setting, it would indeed be optimistic to talk about the interrupted industrial revolution as it would be more apt to talk about its demise. Donors' role in the transition to the neoliberal policy framework makes one wonder whether the real target was industrialization itself and not industrialization strategy. The performance of manufacturing investment after reform reflect a pattern closely in line with donors' traditional preferences and causes alarm with respect to the future of industrialization in Turkey. It is in this sense that foreign aid which was perceived as a chief component of the process of industrialization in counties like Turkey and in fact contributed significantly to it before 1980 has been at the center of a process which brought its eventual downfall.

NOTES

*Research assistance by Alper Duman and Safa Saraçoğlu is gratefully acknowledged.

**Department of Economics Middle East Technical University Ankara 06531 TURKEY

[1] See Sen (1983: 746) for details.

[2] Turkey was one of the "strategically-located countries" (along with Greece, Israel, Egypt, India, Pakistan, Taiwan, and Korea) which were the main recipients of US aid during the Cold War (1946–88). See Levitt (1990: 408).

[3] Although Turkey received external resources during and in the immediate aftermath of the Gulf crisis in early 1990s, these are beyond the scope of the present chapter as they were aimed at compensating Turkey for its actual losses and did not represent a continuous process.

[4] For more details see Günçe (1967: 16–17).

[5] See Krueger (1974: 68–71) and Hershlag (1968: 149–52) for details.

[6] According to Hershlag (1968: 151), the contribution to investment declined to 12% towards the end of the 1950s. Foreign aid financed around 80 percent of foreign trade deficit during 1951–55 (Kepenek and Yentürk, 1994: 125).

[7] See Tinbergen (1967) for details.

[8] The high levels of aid for 1963 and 1970 reflect the aid received in relation to the construction of Turkey's second steel mill and the inflow associated with the August 1970 devaluation, respectively (Krueger, 1974:134).

[9] Kepenek and Yentürk (1994: 243). Weiker (1981: 213) gives total US aid during 1949–73 as 2.7 billion dollars (958 million dollars in grants, 1041 million dollars in loans and 586 million dollars in shipments of agricultural commodities). Figures given in Uras (1979) covering a longer period show that total US aid during 1946–77 amounted to 2704.4 million dollars, 1445.3 million dollars of which were in loans and 1259.1 million dollars in grants.

[10] See Krueger, 1974:124–5. The discrepancy was even bigger when net, rather than gross inflows are taken into consideration. In 1964, for example, actual net inflow was only 46 million dollars as opposed to a planned net inflow of 308 million dollars (Krueger 1974: 131).

[11] Figures are based on data given in Uras (1979).

[12] Turkey's exposure to short-term borrowing during this period was so big that even the international banks themselves, let alone the IMF and the World Bank, were unaware of the total amounts involved. For a detailed exposition of the process of short term borrowing during this period see Celasun and Rodrik (1989), Öniş (1989), and Wolff (1987).

[13] This was accompanied by a substantial increase in the debt service ratio from 42 percent in 1975 to a massive 97% in 1976, and 231 % in 1977. See (Wolff, 1987:60).

[14] See Barkey (1990) on the extent of the crisis.

[15] Investment/GNP ratio declined from 25.0% in 1977 to 18.3% in 1979 which was accompanied by a sharp fall in the public investment/GNP ratio. The rate of inflation increased from 10.1% percent in 1975 to 52.6% in 1978 and 63.9% in 1979.

[16] The amount of debt that was rescheduled in 1979, for example represented 20.6% of Turkey's total debt and 59.7% of total debt rescheduled on a global scale in that year. See Öniş (1989:79–80).

[17] A draft report of the U.S. House Foreign Affairs Committee issued on 23 December 1956 concluded that "foreign aid appears to be the most useful nonmilitary device available to the United States for influencing other nations." In a similar vein, the beginning statement of the Foreign Aid bill discussed in the US Congress in 1961 succinctly stated that the bill is to "promote the foreign policy, security, and general welfare of the U.S. {by} assisting peoples of the world." Both statements quoted in Hagen and Ruttan (1988: 7 and 16).

[18] U.S. Senate Foreign Relations Committee Chairman on 28 July 1954, quoted in Hagen and Ruttan (1988: 5).

[19] General Alexander Haig's remarks at the US Senate's Committee on Armed services on 22 February 1979 that "Turkey is absolutely irreplaceable" is rather telling in this respect. Drawing attention to the strategic importance of Turkey in the region US Deputy Secretary of State remarked that "...the importance of a stable, democratic and pro-Western Turkey has never been clearer" Proposing a generous rescue operation for Turkey, P. Findley at the US House of Representatives on 20 March 1979 stated, "...our overall losses in the Iranian debacle are sure to run many times the amount Turkey now needs". These three statements quoted in Aricanli, 1990:243) reflect the strategic importance of Turkey during this period.

[20] See Kepenek and Yentürk (1994:84) for this view.

[21] Kìray (1990) draws attention to the close similarity between the stabilization program of the British mission in 1860 in the context of the Ottoman debt and the more recent pronouncements by the proponents of neoliberal reform. In this sense donors' policy choices based on "the allocative mechanism of free markets and a curtailed role for the state" have a longer history than usually allowed for.

[22] IBRD, The Economy of Turkey, Washington D.C. 1951 as quoted in Wolff (1987: 46).

[23] See Hagen and Ruttan (1988: 14).

[24] It seems that such concern was not confined to the early post-war years. Amsden (1997: 477), referring to the 1980s has argued that "there is much to suggest that the competitiveness problems of US industry were a major factor behind Washington's insistence that emerging economies open their markets".

[25] Jan Tinbergen, the chief advisor to the State Planning Organization at the time wrote: "With the aid of a simple Domar-Harrod model, an investment volume of 18 per cent of national income was found to be necessary. With foreign aid at about 4 per cent of national income, this meant that the country's own savings should be brought up to 14 per cent from the initial level of about 11 per cent [to achieve a target rate of growth of 7 per cent per annum]". Tinbergen (1967:72).

[26] A major study by P. Boone covering overall aid flows to 96 countries between 1971 and 1990 has found that "in almost all cases aid is spent entirely on consumption". See *The Economist* December 10th, 1994 and Nixson (1996), for details.

[27] Quoted in Krueger (1974: 69).

[28] "Debt is a stimulant to a brave man" is a popular saying in Turkey.

[29] *The Economist*, 28 October 1978, as quoted in Wolff (1987: 68).

[30] See Türel (1981) for details.

[31] It was not perhaps coincidental that the 1970 devaluation decision was taken during the reign of the same political party that introduced the SSAP.

[32] See Nixson (1996: 87). Ceyhun (1992:36) confirms this and draws attention to the fact that during the 1980–90 period, the growth in Turkey's debt and debt service payments (by 157% and 342%, respectively) compared unfavorably with the corresponding indicators of major groups of debtors.

REFERENCES

Amsden, Alice (1997), Editorial: Bringing Production Back in—Understanding Government's Economic Role in Late Industrialization. *World Development* 25, (4), 469–480.

Aricanli, Tosun (1990), The Political Economy of Turkey's External Debt: The Bearing of Exogenous Factors, in Aricanli and Rodrik (eds.) (1990), 230–53.

Barkey, Henri J. (1990). *The State and the Industrialization Crisis in Turkey*. Boulder: Westview Press.

Burnside, C. and David Dollar (1997). Aid Spurs Growth—in a Sound Policy Environment. *Finance and Development*. December, 4–7.

Celasun, Merih (1991), Trade and Industrialization in Turkey: Initial Conditions, Policy and Performance in the 1980s. Mimeo. paper presented at the UNU/WIDER Conference within the Project on "Trade and Industrialization reconsidered" held in Paris, 31 August–3 September 1991.

Celasun Merih and Dani Rodrik (1989). "Debt, Adjustment, and Growth: Turkey" In *Developing Country Debt and Economic Performance* edited by Jeffrey D.Sachs and Susan M.Collins. Chicago and London: The University of Chicago Press. 617–808.

Ceyhun, Fikret (1992). "Turkey's Debt Crises in Historical Perspectives: A Critical Analysis" *METU Studies in Development*. 19 (1), 9–49.

Günçe, İlkin (1967), Early Planning Experiences in Turkey, in S. İlkin and E. İnanç (eds.) *Planning in Turkey*, Ankara: Middle East Technical University.

Hagen James M. and Vernon W. Ruttan (1988), Development Policy under Eisenhower and Kennedy, *The Journal of Developing Areas* 23, October, 1–30.

Hershlag, Zvi, Y. (1968), *Turkey The Challenge of Economic Growth* Leiden: E.J. Brill.

İlkin, S. and E. İnanç (1967), *Planning and Turkey,* Ankara: Middle East Technical University, Faculty of Administration and Administrative Sciences, Publication No. 9.

Kepenek, Yakup and Nurhan Yentürk (1994) Türkiye Ekonomisi, Remzi Kitabevi: İstanbul.

Kìray, Emine (1990). "Turkish Debt and Conditionality in Historical Perspective: A Comparison of the 1980s with the 1860s" In *The Political Economy of Turkey Debt, Adjustment and Sustainability* edited by Tosun Arìcanlì and Dani Rodrik. London: MacMillan Press. 254–68.

Krueger, Anne O. (1974). *Foreign Trade Regimes and Economic Development: Turkey*. New York: National Bureau of Economic Research: Columbia University Press.

Krueger, Anne, O. and Vernon W. Ruttan (1989). "Assistance to Turkey", Anne O. Krueger, C. Michalopoulos, and Vernon W. Ruttan (1989)(eds.), *Aid and Development*. Baltimore and London: The Johns Hopkins University Press, Chapter 14, 250–68.

Levitt Kari, Debt, Adjustment and Development: Looking to the 1990s, Lecture delivered at the 8th. Dr.Eric Williams Memorial Lecture at the Central Bank, Port-of-Spain, 5 May, 1990.

Maxfield, Sylvia and James H. Nolt (1990) in Stephan Haggard (ed.) (1995). *The International Political Economy and the Developing Countries* Vol. 1. The Library of International Political Economy. An Elgar Reference Collection.

Nixson, Frederick I. (1996), *Development Economics*. London: Heinemann.

Öniş, Ziya (1989), *Türkiye'de Dìş Ticaret Politikalarì ve Dìş Borç Sorunu.* İstanbul: İstanbul Ticaret Odasì.

Öniş, Ziya and James Riedel (1993). *Economic Crises and Long-Term Growth in Turkey* Comparative Macroeconomic Studies, World Bank: Washington, D.C.

Rodrik, Dani (1996), Understanding Economic Policy reform, *Journal of Economic Literature* XXXIV, March, 9–41.

Ruttan, Vernon W. (1991), The Future of U.S. Foreign Economic Assistance (1991), Economic Development Center University of Minnesota Bulletin No. 91–2

Sen, Amartya (1983), Development : Which Way Now? *The Economic Journal,* 93, December, 745–752.

Şenses, Fikret (ed.)(1994), The Stabilization and Structural adjustment Program and the Process of Turkish Industrializaytion: Main Policies and Their Impact in F. Şenses (ed.) *Recent Industrialization Experience of Turkey in a Global Context,* Westport; Conn: Greenwood Press. 51–74.

Singh, Ajit (1984), The Interrupted Industrial Revolution of the Third World: Prospects and Policies for Resumption, *Industry and Development*, No.12, 43–68.

Tinbergen, Jan (1967), Methodological Background of the Plan, in İlkin and İnanç (1967). 71–77.

Türel Oktar (1981), Planning and International Organizations: The Case of Turkey's Relations with the World Bank (in Turkish), *METU Studies in Development*, 1981 Special Issue, 635–54.

Uras, Güngör (1979), Aid and Some Facts (in Turkish) *Hürriyet* 5–6 February.

Weiker, Walter F. (1981), *The Modernization of Turkey—From Ataturk to Present Day.* New York: Holmes & Meier.

Wolff, Peter (1987). *Stabilization Policy and Structural Adjustment in Turkey, 1980–1985* The Role of the IMF and World Bank in an Externally Supported Adjustment Process. Berlin: German Development Institute.

CHAPTER 14

THE MACROECONOMICS OF FOREIGN AID IN SUB-SAHARAN AFRICA:
Dutch Disease Effects Reconsidered

Jørn Rattsø
and
Ragnar Torvik*

INTRODUCTION

The economic development in Sub-Saharan Africa since independence has been disappointing (World Bank, 1993, Helleiner, 1990). Since large amounts of foreign aid have been channeled to the region during this period, it is no wonder that some observers have raised the question that foreign aid has held back growth. In this article we concentrate on only one of the arguments concerning a possible negative growth effect of foreign aid - the Dutch disease.

Foreign aid can have negative macroeconomic effects on external competitiveness and economic growth. Michaely (1981), Corden and Neary (1982) and Van Wijnbergen (1986) clarify the Dutch disease mechanism, whereby foreign aid is associated with real exchange rate appreciation. The demand effect of aid strengthens the internal competitiveness of non-traded production against traded production, while the external competitiveness of the traded sector is worsened. The deterioration of trade performance can have negative long run effects when the traded sector is of strategic importance for productivity growth.

Van Wijnbergen (1985) documents that these mechanisms are of some relevance for Sub-Saharan Africa. He finds empirical evidence that aid flows have led to real exchange rate appreciation in an econometric analysis of 6 countries in the region. This aid effect may contribute to an explanation of the stagnating export performance. Van Wijnbergen concludes that 'policy makers must introduce measures designed explicitly to reduce the conflict between export promotion and aid'. We agree that this is a serious concern.

To understand the adjustments to aid in Sub-Saharan Africa, we suggest two modifications to the standard dependent economy model applied to analyze the Dutch disease. First, the model must be modified to represent the structural characteristics of the region. Second, the trade policy regime has included import rationing, and this has influenced the effects of aid.

A dependent economy model relevant for Sub-Saharan Africa is developed in section 2, emphasizing unemployment/ underemployment and import dependence. Foreign aid is shown to give real appreciation consistent with the conventional Dutch disease story in this benchmark model. The dependent economy model is extended to take into account import rationing in section 3, and foreign aid is investigated under two alternative assumptions about import priorities. A CGE-model of Zimbabwe is applied to investigate the quantitative importance of the theoretical results. The CGE-model is presented in section 4, and three policy experiments of higher foreign aid are discussed in section 5. Concluding remarks are offered in section 6.

FOREIGN AID AND DUTCH DISEASE IN A SUB-SAHARAN AFRICA VERSION OF THE DEPENDENT ECONOMY MODEL

A separation between traded and non-traded goods, the dependent economy model, has been the favorite framework to investigate structural and macroeconomic effects of aid. The standard model formulation must be modified to take into account the structural characteristics of Sub-Saharan Africa. The traded sector is export oriented and typically dominated by commercial farming and mining, while the non-traded sector includes protected industry dependent on imported intermediates.

We do not think that movements along a transformation curve between traded and non-traded sectors offer a realistic description of the structural adjustment problems of the region. Most observers agree that shortage of labor has not been an important growth constraint in a situation of rural underemployment and open urban unemployment. Excess supply of labor here is assumed to be the result of real wage rigidity. The unemployment assumption is included in disequilibrium versions of the dependent-economy model, e.g. Kouri (1979), where short run nominal wage rigidity and long run real wage rigidity cause unemployment. To capture the import dependency in production, imported intermediates are added. The formulation of the production technology is similar to that of Katseli-Papaefstratiou (1990). Rattsø and Torvik (1998a) develop a related model to investigate the effects of shocks given the structural characteristics of Sub-Saharan Africa.

The sectoral balances are formulated as in Rattsø (1994a): the traded sector delivers its output X_T to consumption C_T and exports E. The non-traded sector output X_N is applied to consumption C_N and investment. Construction and capital goods production take place in the non-traded sector, and the formulation takes advantage of the stylized fact (Ndulu, 1991) that the import share of investment is stable. A fixed share α of the investment J is produced domestically. The sectoral balances are:

$$X_T = C_T + E \tag{14.1}$$

$$X_N = C_N + \alpha J \tag{14.2}$$

The traded sector produces its output X_T with capital and labor according to a neoclassical production function. The capital stock and the world market price are given. Profit maximization, taking into account the real wage rigidity, generates a compact form supply function $X_T = f(p)$, where p is the price of non-traded relative to traded goods, i.e. the real exchange rate. A higher p represents a real exchange rate appreciation. The derivative f_1 with respect to p is negative, implying that a real exchange rate appreciation decreases output supply of the traded goods sector. It should be noticed that the real appreciation effect does not reflect a movement along the transformation curve, but follows from the assumption of real wage rigidity. When the price of non-traded goods increases for a given world market price of traded goods, nominal wages are pushed up, and the real product wage in the traded sector increases. In this way, a real exchange rate appreciation implies a higher real product wage in the traded sector, and a lower real product wage in the non-traded sector.

The non-traded sector applies imported intermediates in addition to capital and labor. The short run supply function depends on the real product prices of labor and imported intermediates. For simplicity, one world market price is assumed for all foreign goods. Given the rigidities assumed, both the real product price of labor and imported intermediates can be represented by the real exchange rate p. The reduced form supply function is $X_N = g(p)$, with $g_1>0$. The demand for imported intermediates depends on the real exchange rate as well, which in reduced form is $B = B(p)$, with $B_1>0$.

To simplify the handling of import rationing, fixed consumption shares of the three consumer goods are assumed in the benchmark version, including imported consumer goods C_I. The formulation is consistent with a Cobb-Douglas utility function. Total consumer spending D is defined as the national income less domestic savings, which are a constant fraction of income. To emphasize the foreign exchange channel, we keep the savings rate constant here. Income consists of the production in the two sectors, minus the outlays for imported intermediates, plus the amount of foreign aid A. With no public sector, foreign aid is allocated to private income. The analysis concentrates on the demand effects of aid, and policy uses of the aid are outside the scope of the paper. The formulation assumes that aid works as tranfers to the private sector. All variables are measured in traded sector goods units, and the demand side is defined by:

$$D = (1-s)[f(p) + pg(p) - B(p) + A] \qquad (14.3)$$

$$C_I = c_i D \qquad (14.4)$$

$$C_T = c_t D \qquad (14.5)$$

$$pC_N = (1 - c_i - c_t)D \qquad (14.6)$$

The model is solved by developing the excess demand functions for the traded and non-traded markets:

$$-[1-c_t(1-s)]f(p) + c_t(1-s)[pg(p) - B(p) + A] + E = 0 \qquad (14.7)$$

$$\begin{aligned} &-[1-(c_i - c_t)(1-s)]pg(p) \\ &+ (1-c_i-c_t)(1-s)[f(p) - B(p) + A] + p\alpha J = 0 \end{aligned} \qquad (14.8)$$

The compact form of the model shows how exports and the real exchange rate clear the two markets. Figure 14.1 presents the unemployment version of the Salter-Swan diagram. Only the logic of the model is explained here, and full differentiation of the market balances is shown in the appendix. Excess demand of traded goods rises with p for two reasons. First, a real exchange rate appreciation increases production in the non-traded sector, and demand based on non-traded income thus goes up. Second, a real exchange rate appreciation reduces supply of traded goods. To drive the excess demand for traded goods to zero, exports E have to decline, allowing more supply on the domestic market to satisfy the increased demand. The equilibrium locus T of the traded goods sector hence slopes downward. The equilibrium locus N of non-traded goods is horizontal in conventional dependent-economy models. The exports are a residual and they do not affect the market for non-traded goods. The non-traded market balance determines a unique value of the real exchange rate consistent with equilibrium. Excess demand for non-traded goods is eliminated by a real appreciation, implying reduced demand and increased supply. The savings-investment equilibrium point is denoted m in Figure 14.1.

The macroeconomic responses from increased foreign aid are shown by the dotted lines in Figure 14.1. When A increases, the traded sector equilibrium locus shifts to the left. More foreign aid increases the demand for traded goods, and less is left for exports. Increased foreign aid shifts the non-traded sector equilibrium locus up. Excess demand from the foreign aid appreciates the real exchange rate, and the market for non-traded goods is brought back to balance by a combination of increased supply and decreased demand.

In Figure 14.1, the equilibrium moves from point m to point n. Two symptoms of the Dutch disease effects of foreign aid come clear in the figure: The real exchange rate appreciates and exports fall. The real exchange rate appreciation increases production of non-traded goods and decreases the production of traded goods. Exports fall because of the combined reduction of traded goods production and increased

Figure 14.1.

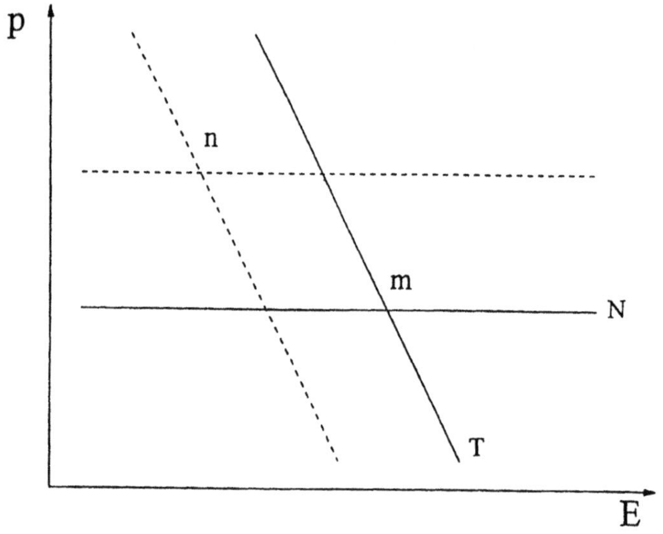

domestic demand for traded goods. The introduction of unemployment and intermediate imports does not eliminate these Dutch disease effects of aid.

FOREIGN AID IN THE REGULATED SUB-SAHARAN AFRICA POLICY REGIME

Most countries of the Sub-Saharan Africa region have combined tariffs with quantitative trade restrictions. The World Bank (1993) has documented these import controls and their gradual elimination when some countries embarked upon trade liberalization programs. The import rationing systems in place must be taken into account in order to understand macroeconomic effects of foreign aid. Our formulation describes the general characteristics of the import rationing systems, as presented by Davies (1991) for Zimbabwe and Ndulu (1986) for Tanzania: consumer and intermediate imports have been compressed, while investment imports have had priority. The rationing of consumer and intermediate goods is dependent on import capacity, a system which Bevan et al. (1990) call endogenous trade policy. Endogenous rationing is the policy response to shortages of foreign exchange. Fix-price rationing (import quotas), as compared to flex-price rationing (the exchange rate), is used to allocate scarce foreign exchange.

The rationing rule produces a new relationship between the traded and the non-traded sectors through the supply side: the export of traded goods influences the capacity to import intermediates to the import-dependent, non-traded sector. This inter-sectoral linkage was proposed by Gibson (1985) in a model of Nicaragua. A similar formulation of the rationing system is applied by Rattsø (1994a,b) and Torvik (1997a) in theoretical studies of the dynamics of sectoral balances and macroeconomic policy effects. Consequences of alternative rationing rules are analyzed by Torvik (1994).

Foreign exchange scarcity is represented by an exogenous trade balance, set equal to zero to save notation. The scarcity can be the direct result of government interventions or rationing in international credit markets, or both. The import capacity determined by exports and foreign aid is used to import investment goods (1-α)J, and minimum levels of imported intermediates and consumption goods, denoted B^* and C_I^* respectively. The allocation of the residual import capacity between consumer and intermediate goods is determined by fixed policy-determined shares. The two import rationing functions are:

$$B = B^* + \beta[E - (1-\alpha)J + A - B^* - C_I^*] \tag{14.9}$$

$$C_I = C_I + (1-\beta)[E - (1-\alpha)J + A - B^* - C_I^*] \tag{14.10}$$

Rationing influences both the demand and supply sides of the economy. Even if the production technology is the same as in the benchmark model, the rationing of imported intermediates implies a modified reduced form supply function for the non-traded sector, $X_N = h(p,B)$. Since imported intermediates are rationed to firms, they are forced to apply an inefficient mix of labor and intermediates. The supply is lower for each p compared to the non-rationed case. Improved access to imported intermediates increases the supply of non-traded goods, $h_2>0$.

We will assume that foreign exchange rationing also influences the demand side. When consumer imports are rationed, frustrated consumers respond by shifting the composition of demand and savings. Torvik (1997b) shows how increased saving is the optimal consumer response to rationing in the expectation of future liberalization. The change of savings behavior influences the determination of consumer spending in (14.11). The larger the gap between desired (C_I^d) and actual non-competitive consumer imports, the smaller is consumer demand. The size of γ determines the strength of the savings response. The old debate about aid effects has focused on the crowding out of private savings. We identify a negative effect of aid on private savings through the import rationing system.

Since the underlying utility functions are the same as in the benchmark model, desired non-competitive consumer imports C_I^d are determined by equation (14.4), given D as defined by (14.11). As shown by Neary and Roberts (1980), the demand functions for the unrationed goods, when one good is rationed, are given by equations (14.12) and (14.13). The logic is straightforward. First, as much as possible of the rationed good is purchased. The rest of the demand (D - C_I) is directed towards the unrationed goods. Hence, the marginal propensities to consume these goods are scaled up by a factor of $1/(1-c_i)$. The consumer demand system is equivalent to the benchmark model when $C_I = C_I^d$:

$$D = (1-s)[f(p) + ph(p,B) - B + A] - \gamma(C_I^d - C_I) \tag{14.11}$$

$$C_T = \frac{c_t}{1-c_i}(D - C_I) \tag{14.12}$$

$$pC_N = \frac{1-c_i-c_t}{1-c_i}(D - C_I) \tag{14.13}$$

The market equilibrium conditions for traded and non-traded goods are revised under rationing:

$$\begin{aligned}
&-[1-\frac{c_t(1-s)}{(1-c_i)(1+\gamma c_i)}]f(p) + [1-\frac{c_t[1-\beta s-\gamma(1-c_i)(1-\beta)]}{(1-c_i)(1+\gamma c_i)}]E \\
&+\frac{c_t(1-s)}{(1-c_i)(1+\gamma c_i)}ph(p, B^* + \beta[E-(1-\alpha)J + A - B^* - C_I^*]) \\
&+\frac{c_t[1-\beta s-\gamma(1-c_i)(1-\beta)]}{(1-c_i)(1+\gamma c_i)}[(1-\alpha)J - A + B^* + C_I^*] \\
&-\frac{c_t(1-s)}{(1-c_i)(1+\gamma c_i)}(B^* - A) - \frac{c_t(1-\gamma(1-c_i))}{(1-c_i)(1+\gamma c_i)}C_I^* = 0
\end{aligned} \tag{14.14}$$

$$
\begin{aligned}
&-[1-\frac{(1-c_i-c_t)(1-s)}{(1-c_i)(1+\gamma c_i)}]ph(p,B^*+\beta[E-(1-\alpha)J+A-B^*-C_I^*]) \\
&+p\alpha J+\frac{(1-c_i-c_t)(1-s)}{(1-c_i)(1+\gamma c_i)}f(p) \\
&-\frac{(1-c_i-c_t)[1-\beta s-\gamma(1-c_i)(1-\beta)]}{(1-c_i)(1+\gamma c_i)}[E-(1-\alpha)J+A-B^*-C_I^*] \\
&-\frac{(1-c_i-c_t)(1-s)}{(1-c_i)(1+\gamma c_i)}(B^*-A)-\frac{(1-c_i-c_t)(1-\gamma(1-c_i))}{(1-c_i)(1+\gamma c_i)}C_I^*=0
\end{aligned}
\tag{14.15}
$$

The new interactions of exports and the real exchange rate are shown in Figure 14.2. The equilibrium curve in the traded goods market T slopes downwards, but the equilibrating mechanisms are changed. Real exchange rate appreciation, an increase in p, creates excess demand for traded goods by both reducing supply and increasing demand based on higher income in the non-traded sector. To restore equilibrium, exports must go down, involving feed-backs through the import-rationing system. The reduced import capacity results in tighter rationing of intermediate imports in the non-traded sector, and demand for traded goods based on non-traded production income is reduced. The demand for traded goods is also reduced because savings go up. The two effects are assumed to dominate the forced substitution towards traded goods resulting from tighter rationing of non-competitive consumer goods.

Figure 14.2.

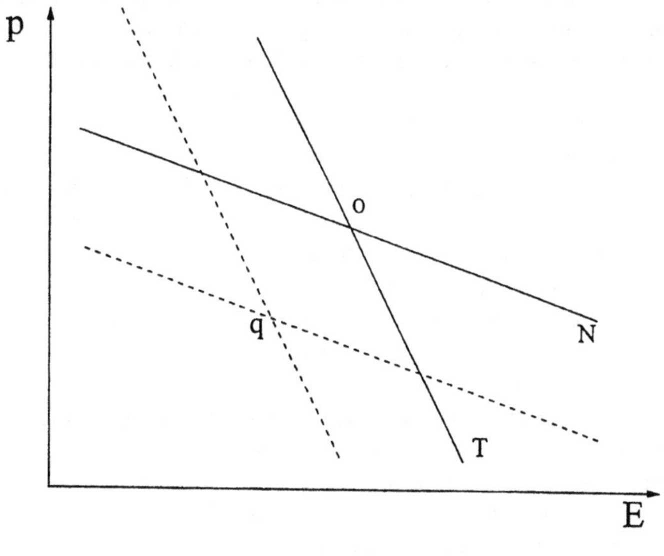

Endogenous import rationing explains why the equilibrium locus in the market for non-traded goods N is no longer horizontal. Increased exports are associated with excess supply in the non-traded goods market. The higher export revenues allow for more imports of intermediates to the non-traded sector, generating higher supply. At the same time, increased exports create room for more imports of non-competitive consumer goods and demand switches away from non-traded goods. Only a dramatic reduction of savings can turn the excess supply to excess demand. If this does not occur, both the supply and demand sides contribute to excess supply of non-traded goods with increased exports. In order to drive excess supply to zero, the real exchange rate has to depreciate. Macroeconomic equilibrium is established at point o in Figure 14.2. For the model to be stable, the equilibrium locus of the traded sector must be steeper than the non-traded.

In this foreign exchange constrained economy, foreign aid allows for a relaxation of the import rationing. When the rationing is determined according to political priorities, the government will have a strong influence on the effects of aid. In the context of our model, the main choice is between allowing for more imports of consumer goods and more imports of intermediates. As will be seen, this priority has dramatic effects for the macroeconomic effects of foreign aid.

Foreign aid is used to import intermediates

The first option is to use the extra foreign exchange available to import more intermediates to the rationed non-traded sector. In terms of the model, $dB^* = dA$. Increased access to imported intermediates allows for higher production, and excess supply is created at the non-traded goods market. To bring the non-traded market back to balance, the real exchange rate has to depreciate. The locus N for equilibrium in the non-traded market thus shifts down in Figure 14.2. The market balance curve T for the traded sector shifts inward when increased foreign aid is used to import intermediates. The reason is that the intermediates increase supply in the non-traded sector and thereby raise demand for traded goods based on non-traded income. To satisfy the increased demand, exports have to go down, and the locus for equilibrium in the traded sector shifts as depicted in Figure 14.2.

If indirect effects do not dominate, the outcome is as illustrated by point q. Foreign aid allocated to imports of intermediates depreciates the real exchange rate and decreases exports. In contrast to the conventional Dutch disease story, the expansion in the non-traded sector is supply driven, fueled by the increased imports of intermediates. This is the reason the real exchange rate response is the opposite from the benchmark model discussed in Section 2. The real exchange rate depreciation in turn increases production in the traded sector. In Figure 14.2 the increased production in the traded sector is not sufficient to increase exports, since domestic demand for tradeables also increases.

We note that the effects of foreign aid in this case are clearly expansionary. The supply driven expansion in the non-traded sector pushes the price level down, increases competitiveness, and pulls the traded sector along. Production in both sectors increases, an outcome not possible in the full employment version of the dependent economy model. In that model, by definition, when production in the non-traded sector increases, production in the traded sector has to fall. When the economic structure and the policy regime of Sub-Saharan Africa are taken into consideration, the aid pessimism generated by the Dutch disease models can be turned around.

Foreign aid is used to import consumption goods

The import allocation of aid is under full government control with rationing, and an alternative is to allocate the aid to imports of consumption goods. To clarify the mechanisms involved, we assume the special case of $dC_I^* = dA$.

The new consumer goods imports affect the demand side of the economy. The first effect is an old issue in the development aid debate, the crowding out of private savings. The savings adjustment reflects the import rationing. Most observers think that tight import rationing has helped keep up private savings. Consumption is postponed in the expectation of access to imported consumer goods later. A relaxation of the consumer imports rationing then will increase consumption demand. Second, for a given level of consumer expenditure, less of the demand is directed towards domestically produced goods. The aid induced inflow of foreign exchange allows consumers to substitute domestically produced consumer goods for imported consumer goods, and demand for traded and non-traded goods falls. Both an expansion and a contraction of demand may result depending on the size of the parameters for the country under investigation. If $s < \gamma(1-c_i)$, the increased consumer expenditure effect dominates, and the increased consumer imports financed by foreign aid stimulates demand for traded and non-traded goods. If $s > \gamma(1-c_i)$, the substitution effect dominates, and demand for traded and non-traded goods falls as foreign aid allows for more consumer imports. We discuss these cases in turn.

Figure 14.3 shows the case when foreign aid increases consumer expenditure, $s < \gamma(1-c_i)$. With a strong drop in savings, the increased consumer import is associated with increased demand for traded and non-traded goods, and the shifts in the curves are shown in Figure 14.3. Excess demand is created at both markets. The equilibrium locus T for the traded sector shifts to the left, since less traded goods are available for exports. The equilibrium locus N for the non-traded sector shifts up, since excess demand in the market for non-tradeables pushes the price up, and thus appreciates the real exchange rate. The new equilibrium point is denoted u. Foreign aid is associated with real exchange rate appreciation and reduced exports. This case is the most similar to the Dutch disease story discussed in section 2, but the disease might be more dramatic since production in both sectors may go down.

The demand expansion and the following real exchange rate appreciation increase production of non-traded goods. But reduced imports of intermediates because of reduced exports pull in the opposite direction. The shift in the non-traded sector supply curve may dominate the price induced movement along the curve. This is the worst case scenario of macroeconomic effects of foreign aid. The initial increased demand for both traded and non-traded goods ends up as output contraction in both sectors. In this case, the existing aid-pessimism based on standard models of the Dutch disease may in fact be too optimistic.

Figure 14.3.

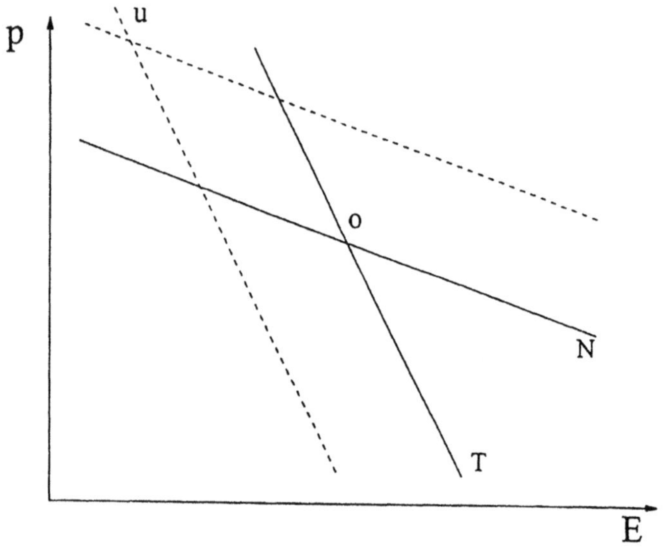

When the substitution effect dominates, $s > \gamma(1-c_i)$, and consumer expenditure goes down, the shifts of the curves are opposite from Figure 14.3. The aid induced inflow of imported consumer goods moves demand away from traded and non-traded goods, since the fall in savings is not sufficient to outweigh the substitution effect away from domestically produced goods. The real exchange rate depreciates and exports increase. Also in this case, production in the traded sector is stimulated by foreign aid. Foreign aid to import consumer goods reduces the demand for non-traded goods. As a consequence, the real exchange rate depreciates and the traded sector expands.

Note that even if the real exchange rate depreciates, production in the non-traded sector might increase. The increased exports mean that the amount of foreign exchange increases more than the amount of foreign aid channeled into the economy. A fraction β of these extra foreign exchange earnings is used to import intermediates to the non-traded sector. Hence, if this effect of reduced rationing outweighs the effect of a depreciated real exchange rate, production increases also in the non-traded sector.

It might seem surprising that what started out as reduced demand for both domestically produced goods, can end up increasing production in both sectors. Again, the intuition for the result is to be found in import rationing regime assumed. Reduced demand means increased production in the traded sector because of lower costs when the sector is a price taker at the world market. The increased foreign exchange earnings that follow, reduce the rationing of intermediate imports, and shift the non-traded sector supply curve out. If this shift in the supply curve dominates the movement along the supply curve from the real exchange rate depreciation, production in the non-traded sector increases. Also in this case the effects of foreign aid associated with the Dutch disease are turned around, but for different reasons than in the imported intermediates case. Whereas the priority of imported intermediates generates a direct supply effect, in this case the aid response works through reduced demand. In a foreign exchange constrained economy, reduced demand might work expansionary.

To sum up the theoretical analysis, we have seen that Dutch disease results are influenced by the policy handling of the foreign exchange market. The results derived are based on a model with structural characteristics and policy regimes assumed to give a stylized representation of the region after independence. The consequences of aid to a specific country depend on policy and behavior. The policy choice concerns the import priority of intermediates versus consumption goods. The key behavioral parameters are the strength of the substitution effect versus the reduced savings effect from increased consumer imports. If foreign aid is used for imports of intermediates, aid-pessimism on macroeconomic grounds is misplaced for Sub-Saharan Africa. The same is the case if aid used for consumer imports decreases demand for domestically produced goods because of substitution. However, if the foreign aid is used for imports of consumer goods, and the demand for domestically produced goods is stimulated, the picture is different. In this case the outcome may be less favorable that the standard model of the Dutch disease predicts. In the worst case scenario, foreign aid causes an economy wide contraction with lower production in both the traded and non-traded sector.

A CGE MODEL OF ZIMBABWE

The construction of a CGE model of Zimbabwe permits a quantification of the effects involved and a richer analysis of the macroeconomic effects of foreign aid. Conflicting effects in the theoretical model can be sorted out. In order to compare the effects of foreign aid with and without import rationing, the model is set up with two closures. One version is formulated and calibrated to reproduce the import regulations of the base year, 1985. Davies et al. (1994) apply the model to counterfactual analysis of the sources of growth fluctuation under the control regime of the 1980's. The other version assumes the elimination of protection and rationing, and simulates the liberalized regime of the post-structural adjustment program of the 1990's. Davies et al. (1998) establish a counterfactual 1985 with liberalization in order to discuss the short run adjustment problems of removing controls. The main features important for the transmission of external shocks are explained here, while full documentation is given in Davies et al. (1998). Rattsø and Torvik (1998b) have analyzed the Zimbabwean trade liberalization ex post using the model.

The CGE model is an extention of the Sub-Saharan Africa version of the dependent-economy model in section 2, which distinguishes between traded and non-traded sectors. In the Zimbabwe context, the traded sector is called exportables and includes mining, large scale agriculture and part of manufacturing. The non-traded sector, 'importables' here, includes the protected and import dependent part of manufacturing. The main interaction is between these two sectors, but they do not give a full description of the economy. Three additional sectors are specified in the model, food agriculture, non-traded consumer goods ("services"), and non-tradable capital goods ("construction"). The separate treatment of food agriculture links the model to the dual flexprice-fixprice approach of Taylor (1983), distinguishing between agriculture and the rest of the economy. Our formulation is different from Taylor since both food agriculture and non-agriculture outputs are supply driven. The service sector is characterized by mark-up pricing and demand determined output.

The supply side is important for understanding price and output responses in the two alternative closures. The production technology of construction, importables, and exportables is nested CES functions in skilled labor, unskilled labor, domestic intermediates, imported intermediates, and fixed sectoral capital stocks. Skilled labor is in short supply, and the wage rate adjusts to achieve equilibrium. Excess supply prevails in the market for unskilled labor, and the nominal wage is set exogenously. In the trade liberalization closure, similar to the theory model of section 2, the demand functions for imported intermediates are allowed to operate without rationing. The sectors have rising supply curves because of fixed sectoral capital stocks. As in the traded sector in the theory model, exportables is a price taker in the world markets, and the residual output, taking into account domestic demand, is exported.

The importables sector behaves as the non-traded sector in theory because of imperfect substitution between domestic and imported importables goods. A combination of imports and domestic production equilibrate supply and demand for the composite good. With imperfect substitution there is room for endogenous determination of the domestic price.

Under the import rationing closure, similar to the theoretical model in section 3, the supply-side mechanisms are somewhat different. Several assumptions are made about the import rationing system. First, available foreign exchange is allocated to satisfy priority needs (investment goods, intermediates for the exportables sector, and food). Second, the importables sector is protected, and only a limited volume of importables is allowed to be imported. Third, any remaining foreign exchange is allocated as policy-determined shares to meet requirements of construction and importables for imported intermediates, and to non-competitive consumer imports. Since the inputs to export production have priority, the supply side of the export sector is the same as under trade liberalization. The import compression of manufacturing and construction supply is endogenously determined, and dependent on the existing capacity to import. The formulation is consistent with the empirical description of Davies (1991) and the econometric results of Mehlum and Rattsø (1996).

When imported intermediates are rationed in the construction and importables sectors, these sectors are forced to substitute towards domestic goods, resulting in an inefficient mix of inputs. The availability of imported intermediates influences the supply curves. Implicit rents are created because the prices in these sectors are higher under import rationing than under trade liberalization. The import-rationing system also includes protection of domestic final-goods markets. Here, the import compression almost eliminates both importables and non-competitive consumer-goods imports. In addition, a domestic market for the imports allowed in is nearly absent in Zimbabwe. This is surprising, given the rents potentially associated with the overvalued exchange rate, but it motivates our assumption of the fixed price rationing of final goods. In the model, the government receives the rents.

Two effects of this protection are captured on the demand side, similar to those that the theoretical model outlines in section 3. First, demand switches to domestic goods when foreign goods are not available. The linear expenditure formulation under rationing is modified as suggested by Neary and Roberts (1980). Since consumer imports are rationed, the ratio of imported- to domestically-produced consumption is lower than desired at the prevailing prices. The notional price of consumer imports is higher than the actual. Second, when demand for imports is not satisfied, part of the income can be set aside as savings - in the expectation of less severe rationing in the future. Empirical evidence is identified by Chhibber et al. (1989) and Morande and Schmidt-Hebbel (1991). In the model this stylized fact is taken care of by linking private savings rates to the rationing of non-competitive consumer imports.

Investment imports are assumed to have priority in the rationing system. The investment level is fixed exogenously, and the import share responds to relative prices. The formulation reflects the problem of identifying a well-defined investment function (see Mehlum and Rattsø, 1996, and Chhibber et al., 1989), and the understanding that investment demand is restricted by political and business uncertainty (see Dailami and Walton, 1992). Our formulation, which assumes a given total investment, is consistent with the alternative understanding that investment has been restricted by import rationing. In comparing the two regimes, the investment level is held constant.

THE CONSEQUENCES OF FOREIGN AID IN ZIMBABWE

We suggest in the introduction that possible Dutch disease effects of foreign aid depend on the policy handling of the foreign exchange market. Three policy alternatives are investigated with the CGE model, corresponding to the three theoretical cases studied in sections 2 and 3. The first experiment studies the macroeconomic responses to the aid inflow with no import rationing. The second and third experiments analyze the responses with import rationing, when the aid is used for intermediate and consumer imports, respectively. In all the experiments foreign aid is assumed to increases by 1% of GDP, and feeds directly into private incomes. The results of the model simulations are reported in Table 14.1.

As seen from Table 14.1, foreign aid works expansionary with respect to the GDP in all three alternatives, given our parameterization of the Zimbabwe model. Foreign aid does not lead to contraction. However, the size of the expansion depends on the policy regime. In the case of no import rationing, the elasticity of of GDP with respect to foreign aid is 0,4. Import rationing can increase or decrease the expansion of GDP dependent on import priority. If foreign aid is used to import intermediates, the elasticity is raised to 1,6. If the aid is used to import consumer goods, the elasticity is reduced to 0,2.

When imports are not restricted by rationing, foreign aid leads to a general demand-driven expansion of the economy. All sectors except exportables benefit from the increased demand. The demand sensitive service sector, together with the importables sector, gives the main contribution to increased GDP. Demand expansion favors the importables sector since imperfect substitution between importables produced domestically and abroad is assumed. The demand for construction is basically determined by the fixed investment level, and construction output is hardly af-

Table 14.1. Model simulations. Effects of foreign aid equal to 1% of GDP. Percentage deviation from benchmark.

	No Import Rationing	Import Rationing and Aid Allocated to Intermediates	Import Rationing and Aid Allocated to Consumer Imports
GDP	+0,4	+1,6	+0,2
GDP Services	+0,8	+1,4	+1,1
GDP Construction	+0,1	+1,2	–0,5
GDP Exportables	–0,2	+0,4	–0,9
GDP Importables	+0,8	+5,1	–0,6
Private consumption	+1,8	+4,4	+2,1
Consumer Price Index	+0,4	–1,3	+3,0
Exports	–0,8	+0,7	–1,3
Imports	+1,1	+4,4	+2,3

fected. The combined effect of economic expansion and foreign aid increase private consumption by 1,8%, or about 1,1 percentage points of GDP.

The adjustments in the real exchange rate and exports are similar to Figure 14.1. The Consumer Price Index (CPI) is influenced by cost push factors. With fixed capital stocks, supply curves are upward sloping, and increased prices are necessary to expand production. Since skilled labor is in short supply, increased labor demand push the wage level, and thus the costs of production, up. The model suggests a rise in the general price level by about 0,4%. Some of the goods in the CPI are traded goods with their prices given from the world market. Since these prices are unchanged with foreign aid, the prices of the goods produced at home increase more than what is represented in the CPI. For this reason, the real exchange rate appreciation is also higher than the increase in the CPI. Higher prices and wages hurt the competitive position of the exportables sector, and exportables GDP declines. In addition, the expansion of demand means that more of the export goods are consumed domestically. The combined result is a decrease in exports of 0,8%, or about 0,3 percentage points of GDP.

The higher level of economic activity increases the imports of intermediates and consumption goods. Higher prices in domestic production sectors reduce the relative price of imports. More import intensive production, consumption, and investment result. The falling exports and rising imports worsen the trade balance, but the current account position improves because of the increased foreign aid.

In the case of no import rationing, the conventional Dutch disease effects of real appreciation and reduced exports result from foreign aid, consistent with the theory results in section 2. The production structure is shifted from exportables to importables and services. The results are similar to the recent CGE analysis of aid to Pakistan by Vos (1998). The African dilemma presented by van Wijnbergen (1985) is relevant. But for most of the post-independence period, Zimbabwe has not allowed free imports.

When imports are rationed, the priorities of the foreign exchange allocation committee strongly influence the effects of aid. When imported inputs are given priority, the expansionary effect of foreign aid will be much stronger than under no rationing. Foreign aid in this case expands the economy from the side of supply. The first round effect of increased imports of intermediates relax supply constraints in the construction and importables sectors. Lower prices and higher activity result. Through intermediate deliveries the price impulse spreads to the rest of the economy. The more favorable cost position stimulates the export sector, and brings in more foreign exchange. The new export revenues add to the foreign aid in improving the import capacity. The combined effect of more foreign aid and a higher export volume is to increase the import capacity by about 4,4%. An economy wide expansion with higher production in all sectors follow.

As discussed in the theoretical section 3 and shown in Figure 14.2, the supply driven expansion results in a real exchange rate depreciation, contrary to standard Dutch disease analysis of foreign aid. The effect is recognized in Table 14.1 by the fall in the consumer price index of 1,3%. As discussed above, some traded goods with unchanged prices is contained in the index, and as a consequence the real exchange rate depreciation is higher than revealed by the drop in the CPI.

The economic expansion brings with it a much higher increase in private consumption than without import rationing. Of course the stronger expansion in itself explains part of this increase, but it is not the only reason. The increased amount of foreign exchange means more imports of non-competitive consumer goods. As a result, private savings rates drop, so that more of a given income is consumed. In addition, income-distribution effects are more important under import rationing. The CGE model assumes that the savings rate out of profits is higher than the savings rate out of labor income. Increased imports of intermediates reduce the profits in the importables sector, and the income shift to labor adds to increased consumption demand. In contrast to models with a representative consumer, such as the theoretical model presented above, the income distribution effects of rents do indeed matter.

We see that, as in the theoretical model, the Dutch disease effects of foreign aid are turned around to a supply driven economy wide expansion with higher exports and real exchange rate depreciation. When foreign aid is used to import intermediates in a foreign exchange constrained economy with rationing, foreign aid crowd in rather than crowd out production also in traded sectors. In this situation there is no conflict between foreign exchange earnings from aid and own production. One of the effects of foreign aid is to stimulate foreign exchange earnings by the country itself.

If the foreign aid is used for consumer imports, the story is quite different. The economic expansion is dampened, even compared to a situation with no import rationing, and the Dutch disease effects of foreign aid are more serious. The elasticity of GDP with respect to foreign aid is reduced to 0,2, and remains positive only thanks to increased demand which stimulate service production. The increased consumer expenditure effect thus dominates the substitution effect discussed in the theoretical analysis, and the adjustments are consistent with Figure 14.3. But the increased demand only succeeds in raising service production, while output in the other sectors drop. The reason is that increased demand involves contractionary effects in a foreign exchange constrained economy.

When increased consumer imports stimulate demand for domestically produced goods, the first effect is to move the economy upward rising supply curves. As a result, the domestic price level increase, and through intermediate deliveries the export sector becomes less competitive. In addition the increased domestic prices switch demand towards exportables. Exports decrease, and imports follow along. The decreased imports mean stricter rationing of intermediates to the rationed construction and importables sectors, and supply curves shift in. The reduced production and increased prices kick off another round with lower exports and stricter rationing. As a result, only the demand driven service sector increases output when consumer expenditure increases. Output in the other sectors contract.

The real appreciation is stronger than in the case of no import rationing, as shown by the higher increase in the CPI. It explained by the negative shift in supply curves in the foreign exchange constrained sectors. When decreased foreign exchange earnings mean less imports of intermediates, Dutch disease effects of foreign aid become much more damaging and the real exchange rate appreciation stronger despite less expansion in output.

Even if the aid induced economic expansion is smaller than without import rationing, private consumption increases more. Again the reason is to be found in the rationing system. The increased consumer imports push saving rates down because of better access to rationed goods. Therefore, private consumption increases more even if incomes increase less than in a situation without rationing. The effect of lower savings rates with foreign aid can be strong in a foreign exchange constrained economy when foreign aid is used to satisfy demand for consumer imports.

CONCLUDING REMARKS

Foreign aid can lead to real exchange rate appreciation, reduced external competitiveness and lower exports. These are the key ingredients of the Dutch disease, which have been shown in various versions of the dependent economy model. We have shown that Dutch disease effects of foreign aid also can be important in models representing structural characteristics of the Sub-Saharan Africa countries, notably unemployment/ underemployment and import dependence. However, the macroeconomic consequences of aid are dependent on the handling of the foreign exchange market.

Since independence, most countries of the region have introduced quantitative controls on imports. In the case of import rationing, we have shown how the consequences of aid depend on the import priorities of the government. When foreign aid is allocated to rationed imported intermediates, the economy experiences a supply induced boom with real depreciation and higher exports. Dutch disease is not a necessary result of aid given the import policy regimes of the region. If foreign aid is allocated to consumer imports, Dutch disease is possible, depending on the strength of the substitution effect versus the savings effect in consumption. When the negative savings effect dominates, real appreciation and reduced exports are expected.

The consequences of aid are quantified using a CGE model set up and calibrated to reproduce the Zimbabwean economy. Foreign aid always is expansionary in the CGE model, and Dutch disease results in the case of no import rationing. With import rationing, foreign aid allocated to imported intermediates is shown to expand exports and depreciate the real exchange rate. Even when all production sectors expand, the foreign aid implies a relative weakening of exportables production.

NOTES

*We are grateful to Rob Davies for CGE model collaboration. The project has been funded by the Ministry of Foreign Affairs in Norway.

REFERENCES

Bevan, D., P. Collier and J.W. Gunning, 1990, *Controlled open economies: A neoclassical approach to structuralism* (Clarendon Press: Oxford).

Chhibber, A., J. Cottani, R. Firuzabani and M. Walton, 1989, Inflation, price controls, and fiscal adjustment in Zimbabwe (Working Paper 192, Country Economics Department, The World Bank).

Corden, W.M. and J.P. Neary, 1982, Booming sector and de-industrialisation in a small open economy, *Economic Journal* 92, 825–848.

Dailami, M. and M. Walton, 1992, Private investment, government policy, and foreign capital in Zimbabwe, in: A, Chhibber et al., eds., *Reviving private investment in Developing countries* (North-Holland, Amsterdam).

Davies, R., 1991, Trade, trade management and development in Zimbabwe, in: J. Frimpong-Ansah, S.M. Ravi Kanbur and P. Svedberg, eds., *Trade and development in Sub-Saharan Africa* (Manchester University Press, Manchester).

Davies, R., J. Rattsø and R. Torvik, 1994, The macroeconomics of Zimbabwe in the 1980s: A CGE-model analysis, *Journal of African Economies* 3, 153–198.

Davies, R., J. Rattsø and R. Torvik, 1998, Short-run consequences of trade liberalization: A CGE-model of Zimbabwe, *Journal of Policy Modeling* 20, 305–333.

Gibson, B., 1985, A structuralist macromodel for post-revolutionary Nicaragua, Cambridge *Journal of Economics* 9, 347–369.

Helleiner, G., 1990, Structural adjustment and long-term development in Sub-Saharan Africa (Working Paper 18, Centro Studi Luca D'Agliano — Queen Elizabeth House).

Katselli-Papaefstratiou, L., 1990, Transmission of external price disturbances and the composition of trade, *Journal of International Economics* 10, 357–375.

Kouri, P., 1979, Profitability and growth in a small open economy, in: A. Lindbeck, ed., *Inflation and employment in open economies* (North-Holland, Amsterdam).

Mehlum H. and J. Rattsø, 1996, Import compression and growth constraints in Zimbabwe (Mimeo, Department of Economics, University of Trondheim).

Michaely, M., 1981, Foreign aid, economic structure and dependence, *Journal of Development Economics* 9, 313–330.

Morande F. and K. Schmidt-Hebbel, 1991, Macroeconomics of public sector deficits: The case of Zimbabwe (Working Paper 688, Country Economics Department, The World Bank).

Ndulu, B., 1986, Investment, output growth and capacity utilization in an African economy: The case of the manufacturing sector in Tanzania, *East Africa Economic Review* 2, 14–30.

Ndulu, B., 1991, Growth and adjustment in Sub-Saharan Africa, in: A. Chhibber and S. Fischer, eds., *Economic reform in Sub-Saharan Africa* (World Bank, Washington).

Neary J.P. and K.W.S. Roberts, 1980, The theory of household behavior under rationing, European Economic Review 13, 25–42.

Rattsø, J., 1994a, Medium run adjustment under import compression: Macroeconomic analysis relevant for Sub-Saharan Africa, *Journal of Development Economics* 45, 35–54.

Rattsø, J., 1994b, Devaluation and monetary policy with import compression, *Open Economics Review* 5, 159–175.

Rattsø, J. and R. Torvik, 1998a, Economic openness, trade restrictions and external shocks: Modelling short run effects in Sub-Saharan Africa, *Economic Modelling* 15, 257–286.

Rattsø, J. and R. Torvik, 1998b, The Zimbabwean trade liberalisation: Ex post evaluation, *Cambridge Journal of Economics* 22, 3, 325–346.

Taylor, L., 1983, *Structuralist macroeconomics* (Basic Books, New York).

Torvik, R., 1994, Trade policy under a binding foreign exchange constraint, *Journal of International Trade and Economic Development* 3, 15–31.

Torvik, R., 1997a, Agricultural supply-led industrialization: a macromodel with Sub-Saharan African characteristics, ***Structural Change and Economic Dynamics*** 8, 351–370.

Torvik, R., 1997b, Real exchange rate dynamics and trade liberalization: The case of multiple tariffs and unemployment, *Journal of International Trade and Economic Development* 6, 329–344.

Van Wijnbergen, S., 1985, Aid, export promotion and the real exchange rate: An African dilemma?, CEPR Discussion Paper No. 88.

Van Wijnbergen, S., 1986, Macroeconomic aspects of the effectiveness of foreign aid: On the two-gap model, home goods disequilibrium and real exchange rate misalignment, *Journal of International Economics* 21, 123–136.

Vos, R., 1998, Aid flows and 'Dutch disease' in a general equilibrium model of Pakistan, *Journal of Policy Modeling* 20, 77–109.

World Bank, 1993, Adjustment in Sub-Saharan Africa: Progress, Payoffs, and Challenges (Policy Research Report No 2, Washington).

APPENDIX 1: DOCUMENTATION OF THE THEORY MODELS.

In this appendix we show the differentiation of the market balances with respect to the two endogenous variables E and p, and the variables affected by foreign aid. We start out with the benchmark model with no import rationing. Differentiating the two market balances (14.7) and (14.8) yields:

$$a_1 dE + a_2 dp = a_3 dA$$

$$b_1 dE + b_2 dp = b_3 dA$$

where

$$a_1 = 1 \qquad (>0)$$

$$(>0)$$

$$a_3 = -c_t(1-s) \qquad (<0)$$

$$b_1 = 0$$

$$b_2 = -[1-(1-c_i-c_t)(1-s)]g(p)(1-\epsilon_N) + (1-c_i-c_t)(1-s)(f'-\beta') + \alpha J \qquad (>0)$$

$$b_3 = -(1-c_i-c_t)(1-s) \qquad (<0)$$

Here, ϵ_j denotes the supply elasticity with respect to the price for sectors j=T,N. B' is the derivative of B with respect to P_N. The sign of a_2 follows from the first order condition for profit maximization. The sign of a_3 results from the traded market balance and the condition that the value of production must be larger then the value of imported intermediates. The sign of b_3, which ensures stability of the model, holds if J is not too large. The stability condition implies that a_1 must be positive (increased E creates excess at the traded goods market), b_2 must be negative (increased price of non-traded good creates excess supply at the nontraded goods market), and that the determinant $a_1b_2-a_2b_1$ is negative (the cross effects do not dominate). The stability condition implies that the equilibrium locus of the traded sector in Figure 14.1 is steeper than that of the non-traded sector. Since the cross effects disappear under this closure (b_1=0), it can be verified that the model is stable.

We next turn to the model version with import rationing. Differentiating the market equilibrium conditions (14.14) and (14.15) yields:

$$d_1 dE + d_2 dp = d_3 dB^*_{|dB^*=dA} + d_4 dC^*_{I|dC^*_I=dA}$$

$$e_1 dE + e_2 dp = e_3 dB^*_{|dB^*=dA} + e_4 dC^*_{I|dC^*_I=dA}$$

where

$$d_1 = \left[1 - \frac{c_t[1-\beta s-\gamma(1-c_i)(1-\beta)]}{(1-c_i)(1+\gamma c_i)}\right] + \frac{c_t(1-s)}{(1-c_i)(1+\gamma c_i)}\beta p h_2' \qquad (>0)$$

$$d_2 = \frac{c_t(1-s)}{(1-c_i)(1+\gamma c_i)} X_N(1+\epsilon_N) - \left[1 - \frac{c_t(1-s)}{(1-c_i)(1+\gamma c_i)}\right] f' \qquad (>0)$$

$$d_3 = -\frac{c_t(1-s)}{(1-c_i)(1+\gamma c_i)} ph_2 \qquad (<0)$$

$$d_4 = \frac{c_t[s-\gamma(1-c_i)]}{(1-c_i)(1+\gamma c_i)} \qquad (?)$$

$$e_1 = -\frac{(1-c_i-c_t)[1-\beta s-\gamma(1-c_i)(1-\beta)]}{(1-c_i)(1+\gamma c_i)}$$

$$-\left[1 - \frac{(1-c_i-c_t)(1-s)}{(1-c_i)(1+\gamma c_i)}\right] \beta ph_2 \qquad (<0)$$

$$e_2 = -\left[1 - \frac{(1-c_i-c_t)(1-s)}{(1-c_i)(1+\gamma c_i)}\right] X_N(1+\epsilon_N) + \alpha J +$$

$$\frac{(1-c_i-c_t)(1-s)}{(1-c_i)(1+\gamma c_i)} f' \qquad (<0)$$

$$e_3 = -\left[1 - \frac{(1-c_i-c_t)(1-s)}{(1-c_i)(1+\gamma c_i)}\right] ph_2 \qquad (>0)$$

$$e_4 = \frac{(1-c_i-c_t)[s-\gamma(1-c_i)]}{(1-c_i)(1+\gamma c_i)} \qquad (?)$$

η_N is the supply price elasticity of nontraded goods, and h_2 denotes the derivative of the supply function with respect to the imported intermediates. We assume that the first parenthesis on the right hand side of the expression for d_1 is positive, the indirect effects are not sufficiently strong to have increased exports lead to excess supply at the traded goods market. As discussed in section 4, we also assume that the indirect effects do not dominate the sign for d_3. Stability requires that the determinant $d_1e_2-d_2e_1$ is negative, that is the equilibrium locus of the traded sector is steeper than that of the non-traded sector, as drawn in Figures 14.2 and 14.3.

INDEX